MW01618430

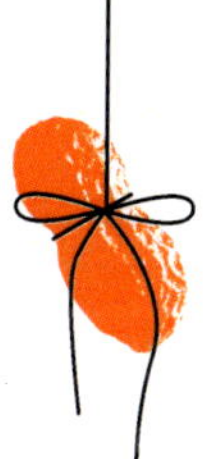

Fishing for Elephants
Insights and exercises to inspire authentic creativity

Written by Larry Moore, edited by Michael Ludden

Cover design: Jeff Matz, Lure Design Co. ©Lure Design 2018
Interior design: Victor Bokas

Unless otherwise credited, all art herein
was created by Larry Moore.

ISBN# 978-0692100387

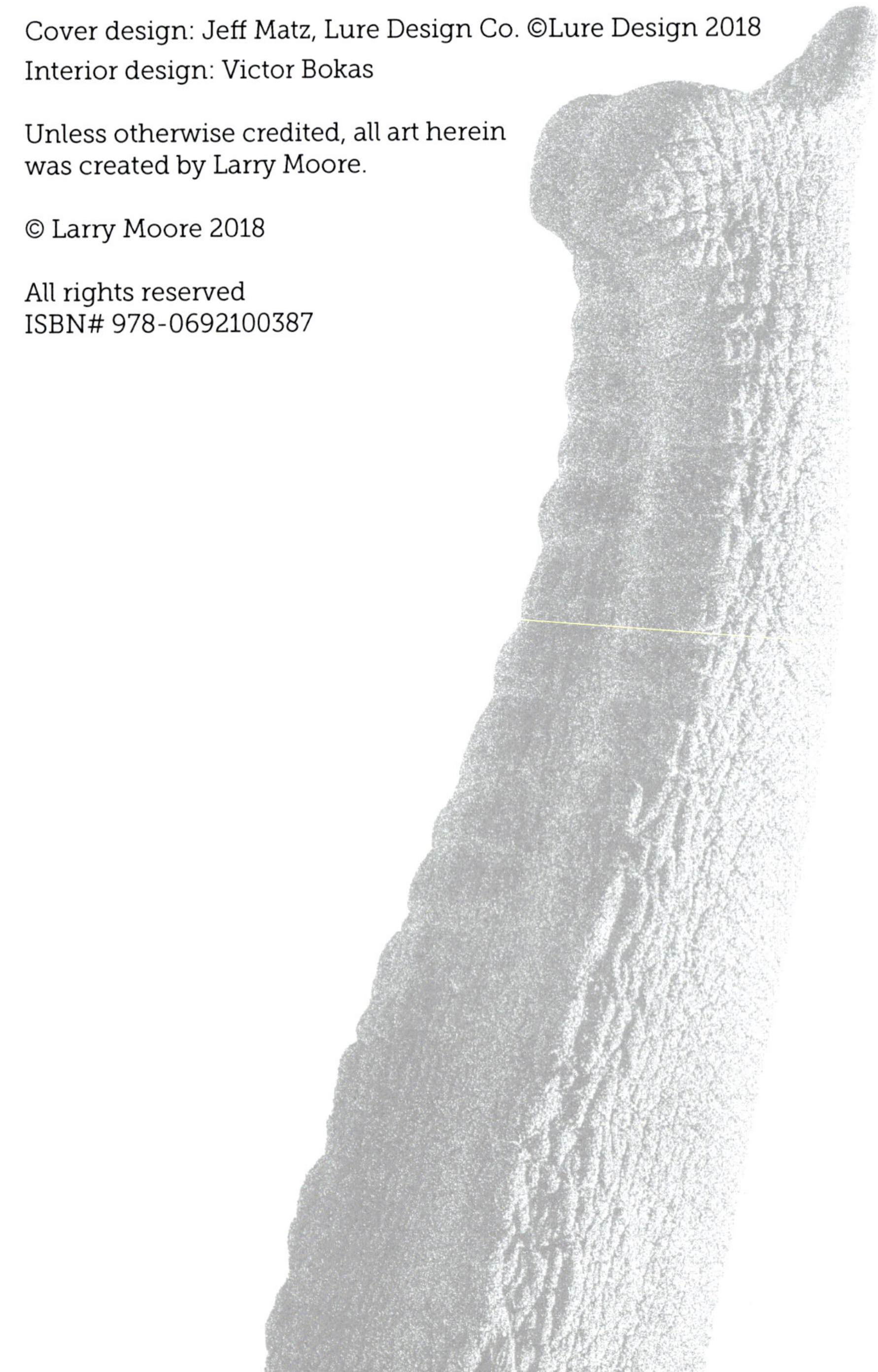

Foreword

I can give you 100 reasons why Larry Moore cannot be profiled. He is a man of complex mind, impregnated with hard-earned wisdom and remarkable wit. Without pretense or deceptive cloak, he is a divergent thinker who is generous and compassionate.

One can never expect what he will say next, although you can be certain it will always be new. Practiced and skillful in his approach, he is a qualified practitioner of his pursuits.

And he's a great artist.

He's also an implausibly faithful friend and my greatest critic, although I seldom get a simple answer. Instead, he guides me with probing questions to help bring my real intent to the surface. You might find yourself, as I have, learning to sit with being uncomfortable, which is both daunting and exciting. To be an artist means to learn this trait precisely.

Typical how-to-paint books are instantly out of date. They all contain the same ideas, worded differently. In *Fishing for Elephants*, Larry brings a remarkable understanding of the creative process.

And he's somehow found a way to communicate that to others.

Some of what he says will often carry hidden meaning, perhaps more easily understood in person, because of peculiar clues and facial quirks that urge us to "figure that out." But this work will guide you to that understanding.

Fishing for Elephants is not a simple how-to-paint book, not at all in the same caravan of vagabondage that crushes the artistic responses we all aspire to pursue.

This will be a voyage of uncharted seas. Let these thoughts be acquaintances. Recognize them, at the very least. Keep these ideas as an impression to revisit. Make a petition with yourself to be sure that there is not some validity in what is provided.

I believe Larry's words will be cherished beyond your work in the art studio, as they pertain to everyday life. *Fishing for Elephants* will be one of the most sacred works on the art of divergent thinking, helping rewire the brain -- as to not crush the inner spirit.

Scott Christensen

World renown landscape artist, Scott L. Christensen, lives outside Jackson Hole, Wyoming. His oil paintings are found exclusively at Christensen Studio in Teton Valley, Idaho. His work has been exhibited at the National Cowboy and Western Heritage Museum, Oklahoma City; the Gilcrease Museum, Tulsa; the National Museum of Wildlife Art, Jackson Hole, Wyoming; Denver Art Museum; Kimball Museum, Park City, Utah; Salmagundi Club, NY; and the Autry Museum in Los Angeles. His many honors include "Most Distinguished Alumni" at Chadron State in 1997, and in 2000 he earned the distinguished Prix de West award.

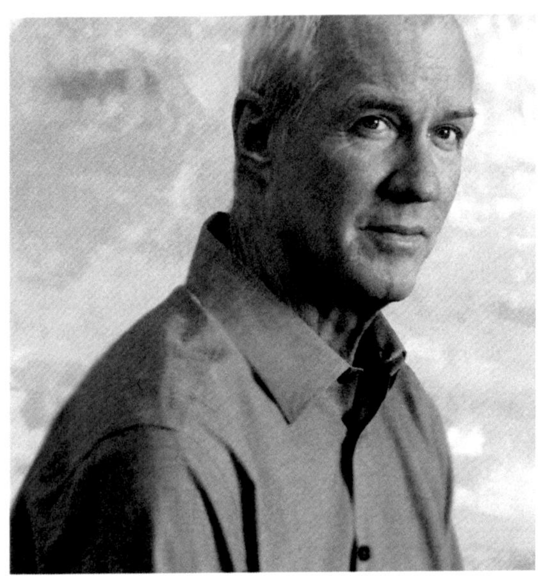

Larry Moore
Photo: Mark Horton

The methods presented in this book are the same ones Larry has used over decades of success in advertising, graphic design, illustration and fine art. He's been a college and workshop instructor for nearly 30 years. From winning a Gold Medal at the Society of Illustrators in New York, to winning Best of Show in national plein air invitationals, inclusion in Society of Illustrators annuals, and Communication Arts design and illustration annuals, he's developed and refined the essential creative process you'll read about in this book.

This is not his first time at the rodeo. Larry has relationships with multiple galleries around the country, has been published by 15 of the country's largest publishers, articles in five major art magazines, has produced 7 public art projects, and his work has been exhibited in over 20 museums nationwide.

You can find out more about Larry at **www.larrymoorestudios.com**

1. Introduction

Why does it seem that some people are more creative than others, and some less?

Don't believe it. I'm convinced that we all carry the potential to create marvelous things. I see it every time I teach a class. It doesn't take a whole lot to unlock the door -- a few simple steps, some understanding of what this magic thing really is, permission to play and explore, a bit of fearlessness -- and off the students go, galloping through the pastures of imagination.

The key to fulfilling this creative potential is in the doing... and doing so with a thoughtful process.

Tucked away in the hidden vaults of those who dig deep are uncharted maps to the limitless powers of mind, spirit, inspiration. And all the treasures are there for the taking.

The students and professionals I've taught and advised over the years have progressed the fastest when they are open enough to push into new and sometimes uncomfortable territory, even if they have no idea where they're headed.

When they do, something good always shows up. Some little grain of an idea or a new direction will fuel that next spark of inspiration. Each time it happens, the artist, the musician, the poet discovers another piece of who they are.

We are a little like Sir Ernest Shackleton, intrepid sojourners in search of our authentic self -- without all that nasty frostbite. Lately, I'm seeing a quiet undercurrent of change in the air, a yearning for growth beyond the usual fundamentals of creating, as if the Mother Muse were whispering to everyone at once. In some, it shows up as a willingness to do something different, to step away from what they believe is the "correct" way to do things.

"The destination reveals itself as you go forward."

It can come as a series of questions or doubts about one's work, a feeling of faltering complacence or just good old curiosity for whatever else may be out there. It comes even to the most accomplished professionals who find they've hit a plateau along the way. This is when the inner voice, the creative spirit, decides it's time to speak up.

You don't have to know where you are going before you start. The destination reveals itself as you go forward. All you need to know is that you are right where you are supposed to be, and that you can get to wherever it is you'd like to go.

This book is designed to help you discover those new directions and open the neural pathways to creative problem-solving. It's presented in two halves. The first contains everything you need to know about the process of creativity; what keeps you from it, what it is, how to use it and how to get unstuck.

Flipping all your light switches on kind of stuff.

The second half, **VoiceFinding**, is the first half put into action for artists who want to get to their core authentic self, or just want to push out a little.

There are more than 150 examples and unconventional exercises designed to break this process into bite-sized chunks so your genius skill set will expand exponentially. Your confidence will grow. You might even feel a little taller.

I know some of you will go immediately to the contents, and then browse through sections that sound the most appealing. For that reason, some concepts are reiterated, first as ideas and then in action, to make sure that you hear certain messages. But the book is designed to build gradually on fundamental principles. So, the rewards will be there for those who read from the beginning. At the tail end of the book are case studies of prominent artists that present many of these ideas in their work.

One of the greatest benefits of this way of life is a richness of experience that comes from being open to creativity, and in fellowship with it. To have it, to be it and to live it takes courage, faith, commitment and a bit of soul-searching.

I'm not here to challenge your purpose, your priorities, your journey or what you believe. These things constitute who you are. I only want to encourage you to be open to what is all around, and to move in your direction, or any direction, inquisitively with intent and desire.

You won't be required to become a long-suffering recluse, wear brightly colored clothing or jump ship from your existing tribe... you can do all this growing in the comfort of your own sandbox. It may be that the greatest gift of creativity is simply understanding who you are and attaining your greatest potential.

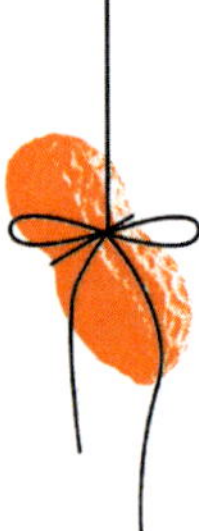

The sheer joy of creating something authentic and unique is just the icing on the cake.

2. Table of contents

Why isn't everyone creative?

Truth is, anyone can use this process. To understand what each chapter holds, here's a brief description.

3. The creativity molecule

The thought molecule shown here gives a quick overview of the relationships within the creative process. Often, looking at a problem from a different perspective allows for a much greater understanding. The same way walking completely around a foreign contraption helps to better grasp its purpose.

This molecule works, for the most part, from the outside in... the components of play, connectivity, and intent are vital but how do you get to them?

Even though this is written by an artist for artists, the basic nuts and bolts of this can be utilized by anyone -- architects, Anthropologie window dressers, interior designers, musicians, cake makers, advertising people, writers.

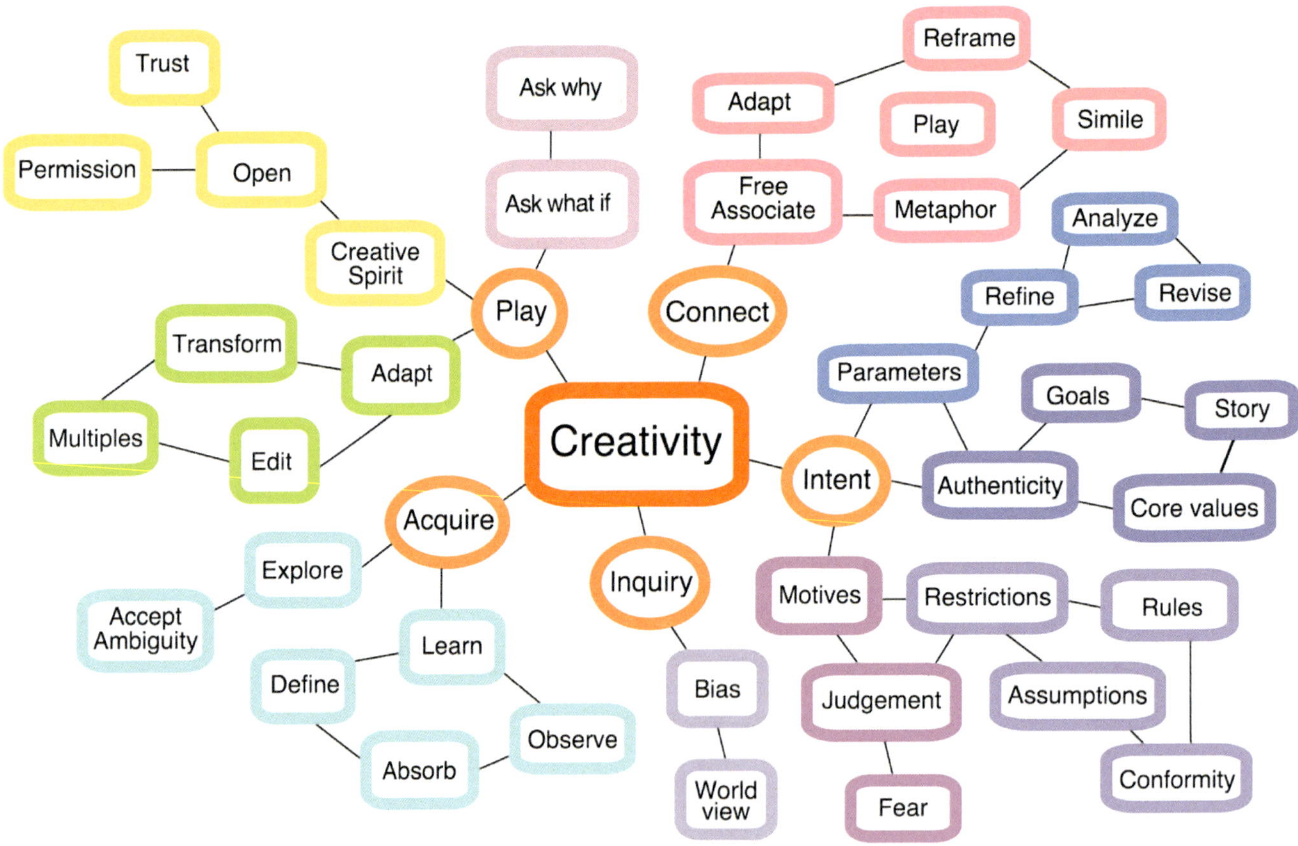

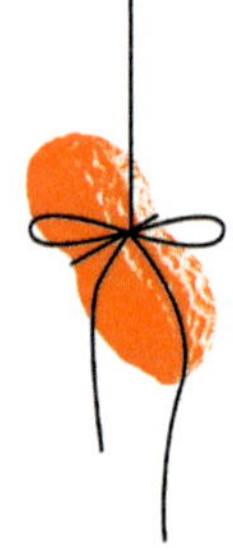

4. Resistance:
ATTACK OF THE BRAIN THING

If we are going on a voyage to the heart of creativity -- and, ultimately, authenticity -- then there is no better place to start than with what keeps us from it. We make our own speed bumps along the way and manufacture entire herds of roadblocks and detours on our journey toward authenticity. Why? No one is holding us back. We aren't living in a locked prison cell.

It seems that we just become restrained somehow by a set of rules that we impose on ourselves. Our Cranium Cops like to over-think and push us toward conformity and away from creativity. Knowing what roadblocks are waiting for you in that American Ninja Warrior course in your head is a big step toward giving yourself freedom -- a gift that you have, in fact, always had.

Here's what we are going to be discovering:

- **Creativity conquers resistance**
- **Know what makes you tick**
- **Understand what holds you back**
- **Know your motive**
- **Open has its rewards**

The presumption of creativity

There is a misperception that all artists are creative, but there's a big difference between skill and creativity.

Being able to paint a thing to look like a thing is certainly a high-craft, right-brained, hard-won skill. But some artists may be reluctant to push outside of their comfort zone and step beyond the familiar to find a different solution. Or to take risks and be open to different ways of creating, other than what they know.

This is not necessarily a bad thing *unless* there is a lack of authenticity in the work. The truth is, mastering the fundamentals of any creative effort is only phase one. It's what is done with those rudiments that defines the artist.

There is an ongoing debate about this, which is true in any creative genre. Does being a great technician mean that one is the definition of an artist? I lean toward free-thinking and problem-solving, so I would contend that one can be a great artist without being a great technician (think Rauschenberg... Pollock... Cezanne).

One can certainly be held in high esteem as an artist equipped with the skill set of a master hand, perfected over time. But the combination of the two, ability and thought, is unbeatable. As in any art form, the subjective point of view abounds and your opinion of what is good or constitutes art may differ from mine. But it's my book.

"Mastering the fundamentals of any creative effort is only phase one."

The human condition comes with just a few little quirks, such as the subjective frame of reference, or bias, which shows up in a variety of ways and informs how we see the world and how we view others' points of view. And biases can mean resistance to new ideas. We all know people who quickly dismiss the notion that there is a different but equally acceptable way to do something or to view something.

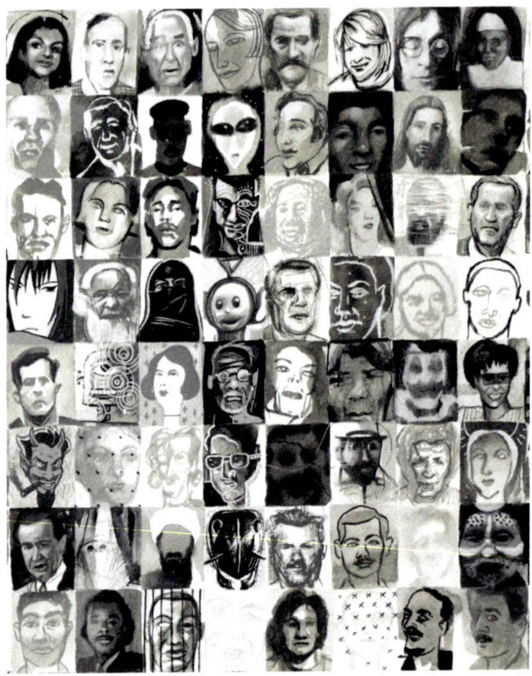

Even artists can pass judgment on alternative forms of visual expression, believing, for example, that only true representational work (paintings that accurately represent an object or person) should be considered "art."

All forms of expression should be sacrosanct, but this is not always the case.

Art is art. Because one has mastered one form of expression doesn't mean that other forms aren't acceptable or relevant. While the subjective opinion is certainly an inalienable right, this kind of judgment is one of the impediments to true creativity. Being *open* means being open to the unfamiliar and the unknown. One doesn't always have to like something for it to be significant, creative, meaningful.

My point is this, authentic creativity is a gift from everyone to everyone. It is open-source thinking that we can all tap into.

Creativity and authenticity are two words that will show up a lot in this book, because there aren't better ways to express these qualities.

Imagination? That's a good word, and boy howdy, is it important... it is thought without borders where anything is possible. It is a component of both creativity and authenticity. But for the purposes of this effort, let's just say that creativity is the application of imagination to a specific problem -- and then actually doing something about it.

Another term you will encounter here is *open*, or the state of being open, when your mind accepts new things and is receptive to anything that sparks an idea. It is a place of constant connectivity.

Individuality is a piece of authenticity, but one can be an individual and still not be true to oneself. Wearing a giant rainbow wig and carrying a baby coatimundi might make you an individual, but it won't mean a true connection to authentic self. It just means that someone (and I'm not saying who) doesn't care what other people, or coatimundis for that matter, think.

Authenticity is pretty much what Shakespeare meant with, "To thine own self be true", which is great if you know what that means for you. This authentic-self thing is a work in progress, an act of self-discovery.

Even if you have a fair idea about who you are or what you wish to be or what your "bliss" is, it evolves as you go. It's not uncommon to start on one path and then fork to the left to follow another less-worn route. Being open to authenticity is a willingness to see other paths that might be off your radar until they start pinging.

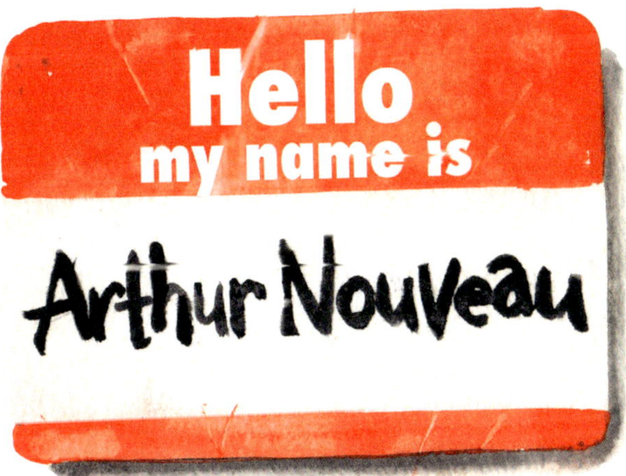

The domain of creative expression isn't comprised of separate king-doms. There's a lot of overlap. It helps to view art as a very wide spectrum that goes from photo realism on one end to 4,000 pigmented cubes stacked on a floor of a forest on the other. As searchers, it's important that we first seek our place in the spectrum and then gain inspiration from other forms across the span.

Putting a label on your direction is a way to identify with your tribe, if you have one. Sort of like having a name tag that says: Hello, my name is Story teller, or Hi, I am Mr. Neo Classicist. You may already be pretty clear on this or you may not.

So, let's look at some ways to break down the functions of art:

Purposes of art

Decorative:
wallpaper, clothing, furniture, ornamentation

Inform/Influence:
propaganda, advertising, airplane pamphlets

Confront/challenge:
question current trends, confront status quo

Entertainment:
video games, animation, bar bands, comic books

Narrative/document:
present the human condition, historical, graphic novels

Utility:
industrial design, packaging, furniture, tea pots, cars

Emote/express:
pure personal aesthetic and subjective point of view

Take a minute to write down a brief description of where you fit and what you do.

Creativity spectrum

Grasping the purpose behind what we do is a good start. Our mechanical and creative abilities are equally important to consider as well. For now, let's look at the stages of creative growth and the levels of self-perception that come with it. Each is linked with a state of mind and a stage of learning. The stage we are in affects how we view our capabilities:

Self-perception within stages of growth.

Beginner: Rudimentary skill level / not yet aware
Intermediate: Developing skills / expanding creativity
Advanced: Concept generator / active seeker
Master: Idea guru / confident, aware, open

From feeling like you're not creative at all to being an idea guru... we're talking about states -- and stages -- of acquired skill. All reflect a process of improvement, just like playing the piano. But it's also a process that is very much affected by self-perception, temperament and personality type.

If you've never taken a Myers-Briggs personality test, I highly recommend you do so before you really get into the meat of this book. We're all made up of a combination of the characteristics: Extrovert, Introvert, Sensing, Intuition, Thinking, Feeling, Judging, and Perceiving. The amounts of each vary from person to person. If you are the Introvert, Intuition, Thinking, Judging type (INTJ), you are going to handle creative problem-solving in a completely different way from someone who is more the Extrovert, Sensing, Feeling, Judging type.

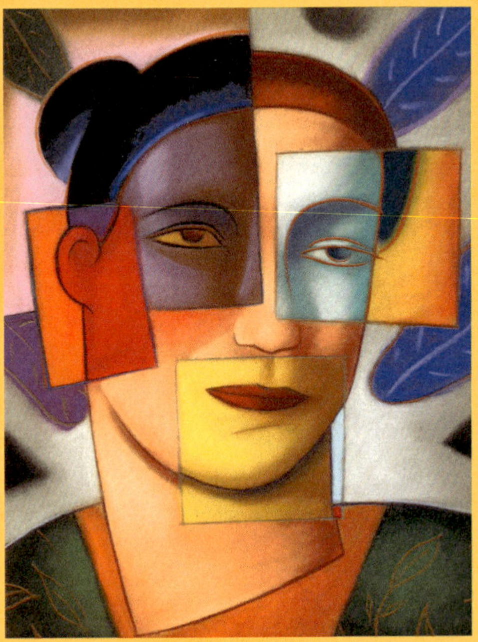

If you are curious about understanding yourself better, you can go to MyersBriggs.org and take the test. Knowing your temperament is just one part of knowing yourself, but it can tell you a lot about how you operate in problem-solving, at work and in relationships (and life in general).

Regardless of your personality type, the search to know more is everything. Vital to the search is *knowing* you want to move beyond where you are, having an idea of where you want to end up and figuring out what's holding you back. That's when you get to who and where you really want to be, your authentic self, unrestricted.

If you're happy where you are, then that's good. Perhaps you haven't gotten to the next passage of curiosity. But if you aren't content, (and perhaps that's why you are reading this), you may be on the hunt. This search, by the way, is self-actualization in action, whether you play a guitar, work in acrylic, write stuff, make cakes, whatever it is you are into. It is a physical manifestation of self-discovery, the realization of one's greatest potential. And the more enlightenment you receive from discovering who you are, the more you want. And the more you want, the deeper you dig.

If your "me" time is filled with making dough ornaments for family or profit, and that makes you happy, what better way to spend that time? It's a win-win.

But if you had the urge to branch out, really stretch it on the dough ornament idea and you could come up with something unique, why wouldn't you? You could reenact the battle of Gettysburg with little dough people and dough cannons, or build the Emerald City in self-rising flour, depending on the other thought components that make you tick.

Sounds crazy, right? What would people think? Who would do such a thing?

Someone has. The point is, if the desire is in you, it can be manifested and if it has been manifested it can be perfected.

An act of passion

What is passion? It seems to be one of the very few characteristics that separate us from the rest of the animal kingdom. Creativity? Lots of that going on with monkeys and dolphins. Problem-solving? Same. Play? Love? Most mammals do that. Communication? Ditto. But passion for something that is not directly related to survival, that's pretty much a human thing. We seem to have it in spades for the most unusual things -- football teams, chess, civil war collectibles, our favorite ism, cooking, etc.

Somehow it has been baked into our DNA to want to do something really, profoundly well, to achieve our greatest potential. Which leads to a common question: "Are we born with talent?"

I think we are born with the desire to be good at something and a lucky few come out of the chute with a high level of unique aptitude, or intelligence, for music, language, visual and spatial. We are given a blank-slate passion to be filled in at the appropriate time... and sometimes never.

For a lot of folks, the attribute of creativity was seemingly left out when God gave out the gift basket of fun characteristics. But that doesn't mean we can't acquire some of the abilities. Having the big zeal for something is the great motivator.

The passion for creating is not confined to brush and canvas, or even to the musical instrument or written word. Is there any less creativity in making a Rube Goldberg city out of toothpicks or knitting brightly colored sweaters for trees? It comes in every configuration, more than all the stars in Hollywood and all the candles at Tuesday Morning. Landing on it is the trick. Finding the one that lights you up, that makes it almost impossible not to do, that is the one you want. If you don't have it in your sights by now, then it has not yet walked across your path. Grandma Moses started painting in her 70's.

So many late bloomers to all facets of the imaginarium... the message to us is simply, stay open. Strive to actively put yourself into creative situations. That's how you find it. I love painting, I've been doing it in one form or another since 1970 and will always do so because there is a desire to come to my purest authenticity. But my real passion, my purpose, is to encourage creativity, a discovery that came from putting myself on the instructor's path.

If you have a passion to do something but have been holding back, an idea that has been needling you for a long time, but you haven't taken action, there's usually a reason.

Fear. The great inhibitor.

There is no greater destroyer of good ideas and personal growth than fear. It's the oppressive despot ruling over the bouncy castle of your mind, the trickster fox, placing barriers where they don't exist, creating doubt, worry, concerns of failure and the judgment of others. It ain't right.

It shows up as performance anxiety or Captain Downer at places where one should be learning, excelling, collaborating, exploring and celebrating the joy of accomplishment. Fear can present itself as a tendency to follow rather than lead, or worse, not do anything at all. It just messes up the place and is the big buzz-killer of fun. Fun is the opposite of fear. Which would you rather have?

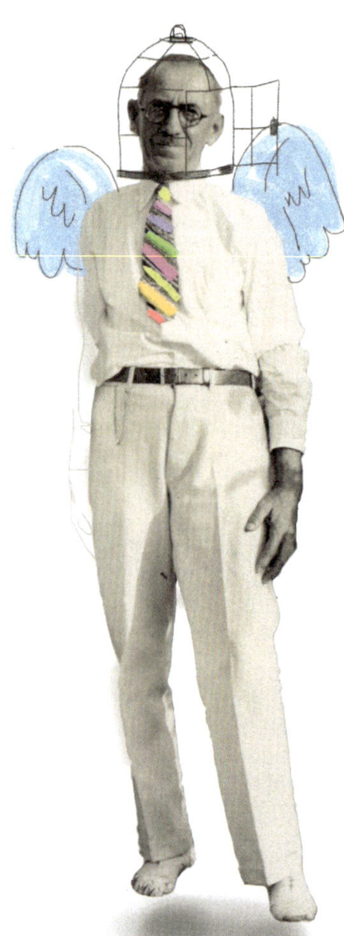

"We live our lives in chains and we never even know we have the key." The Eagles

Worry is a fear-based app that, for many, constantly runs in the background. And what is worry? It's prognosticating trouble; living, not in the moment but in a potentially problematic future. Of course, there are many things that are reasonable to have concern over. But wallowing in stress and agonizing over a future outcome that may or may not happen does not help anyone.

A more positive solution is to invest that nervous energy in proactive change, running toward the monster, rather than hoping it doesn't come your way. When we worry about something that may or may not happen, we are not living in the present.

All that thinking / feeling takes up vital space that could be spent on: A) Appreciating the moment and, equally important, B) Problem-solving, not problem-worrying. The state of being open applies to the future as well. Staying in a positive frame allows for more and better solutions to tackle impending storms. Worry interferes with the very creative process that could come up with ways to solve the worrisome thing.

Sometimes a chronic worrier needs to take charge and Do Nothing, try a daily meditation regimen to clear the mind to make room for more positive thoughts and kick out the repetitive doomsday stuff. Yoga is designed for this very task and nearly 73% of everyone looks good in yoga pants.

Judgment is another form of fear that quashes all sorts of potentially brilliant wonderfulness. I'm referring to the subjective kind of conclusion-making, as opposed to the judgment we associate with *being objective in establishing an educated response*.

The subjective response is usually the one that comes from personal feelings, tastes or perceptions. Valid, of course, but one big trick to creativity is not letting a subjective judgment come in too soon and kill a potential idea. Understanding the difference between the two and using both at the right time during the creative process makes for better solutions..

The subjective vs objective

There's a need for both. True authenticity comes from within, born from one's own feelings and intellect. The subjective and objective frames comprise the platform that defines you as you. The subjective drives passion, though it is also the stuff that makes social media sites so annoying.

This is where objectivity comes in. A little logic can go a long way to balance out the affective. It's the reality check for all those raging emotions and opinions. It can be used to assess a subjective response by adopting an inquiry method of fact-checking. Are your assumptions or perceptions correct? Is what you are feeling or doing effective? Is the information that you have based your assumptions on valid and factual? Is your intent thoughtfully informed?

Creativity isn't just for you to give, it's for others to receive, so others need to catch what you are throwing. You don't play baseball with a bowling ball because someone is going to be on the other end of that thing with a catcher's mitt.

Stepping outside of one's personal frame is critical. It's like stepping back to analyze the whole painting or the quilt when you are three-fourths of the way through, getting distance from a work in progress, or playing a song for an audience that isn't comprised of your mother, brother, kids and the slightly buzzed uncle. Get an outside opinion. Ask others if what you are doing is working.

In visual communication, communication is the operative term. The message needs to be constantly evaluated for clarity. The creative's intent may be clear to the creator, but can it be decoded by the intended audience?

Story time: I was invited to submit ideas for an information station design that needed to represent our local art museum, a Shakespeare theater and Children's Repertory theatre. It needed to act as an icon for the group and offer show dates and general info for each arts group to passersby on the main road.

I fed the parameters of the problem into my brain: info board, simple non-arts-specific presentation, sculptural, weather proof, timeless, budgetary constraints, etc. My solution was a 20-foot, copper-sheathed, monolithic structure that housed the message board and was topped with three very large geometric forms in bright primary colors; a big blue square, one large red ball and a bright yellow cone. A simple primary building-blocks concept.

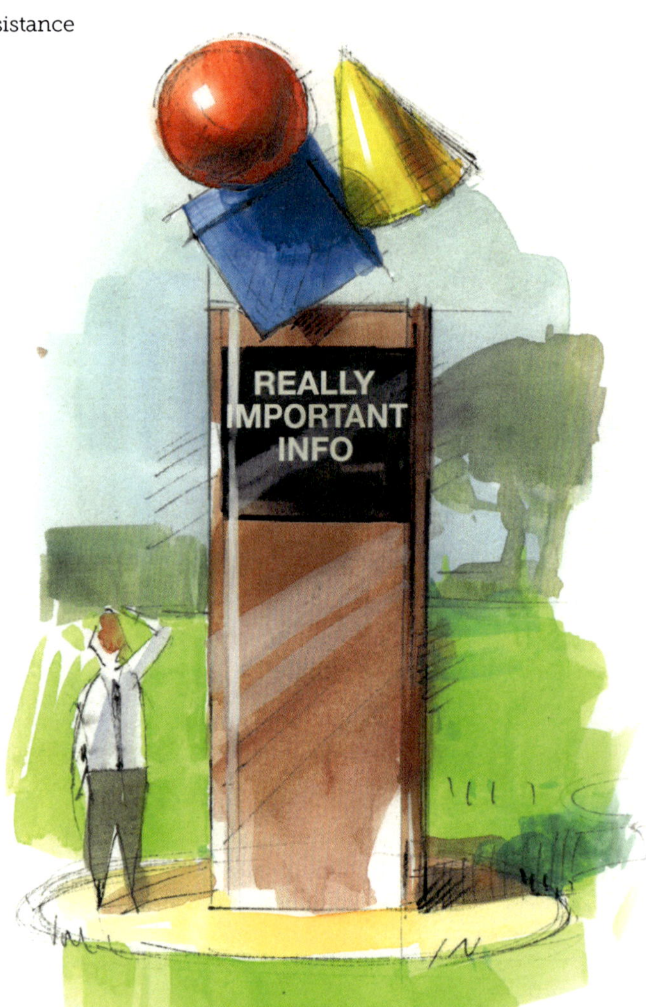

I even enlisted a gifted designer friend of mine to do a 3-D animation that showed how it would look and work from the road, because I knew that many people can't visualize an idea in a practical application. Some serious effort was put forth on this bad boy. It was a lock.

And now it's presentation-thirty time. I'm standing before a panel of 12 people. The jury thing was not lost on me as I rolled through my well-rehearsed, concise and brilliant solution, which surely would land me on the cover of Message Board Monthly. Done, I waited for the response.

Praise flowed like honey as they went around the table... two opposable thumbs-up from most of the panel. And then we got to juror number 6, who said very succinctly, "I don't like yellow."

My mind was racing.... *You don't like yellow? I don't like cotton candy, but am I commenting on your hair? What does that have to do with anything?* It was a powerfully subjective response that just sucked the air right out of the room.

I stood for what seemed like two hours and twirled, sure they could read the thought bubbles that exploded like popcorn out of my head. The closed-mindedness of that one comment threw me off-kilter.

If I had really been on my toes, I would have calmly said, "Thank you so much for your input, but your aversion to happy color has nothing to do with whether or not this is a good solution."

I didn't get the gig, but I did get a star example of a subjective response for this book. "I don't like yellow" will show itself in your life many times over. It will come from others and it will come from you. When it presents itself in class critiques, I bring in the inquiry squad and start asking questions to nudge a subjective viewpoint into the objective realm, something I should have done with Judge Yellow.

No one gets away with the "I don't like it" response in my classes. And it goes a little something like this:

Does anyone have any comments about this student's painting?

Yes. I don't like it.

What don't you like about it? Can you tell me more?

It's too busy.

In what way?

Too many notes! All over. Too many and I don't like that blue.

Do you have a solution to offer?

Maybe if she quieted down that area on the bottom a little, to give it a place of rest for the eyes.

That's a good solution, anything else?

And maybe the blue doesn't work because it seems out of place with the rest of the painting, perhaps warming the blue up will make it more harmonious with the other colors.

(Well, that's way better than 'I don't like it'... don't you think?)

This inquiry method helps to get to the real meat of the problem. You can't always help people who aren't able to think objectively, but you can help yourself and your work. We'll get more into developing this kind of thinking in the **Discernment** section.

Roadblocks

Please don't herd me.

External pressures to act or think a certain way are greater than the pressures at the bottom of the ocean. I blame Carl Jung, the guy who invented the collective unconscious. The truth is, we are hard wired from millions of years of surviving to conform to invisible mores and laws. It's a kind of societal imprinting in which we are stuck because we are, for the most part, pack animals.

I don't mean you, of course. You are a unique individual and beyond influence -- but everyone else is.

This follower instinct is a throwback to the hunter-gatherer days. It's the thing that holds societies and cultures together. These group pressures are there for a reason, but they can keep us from pushing out in even the littlest ways. That invisible electric fence is all around you all the time.

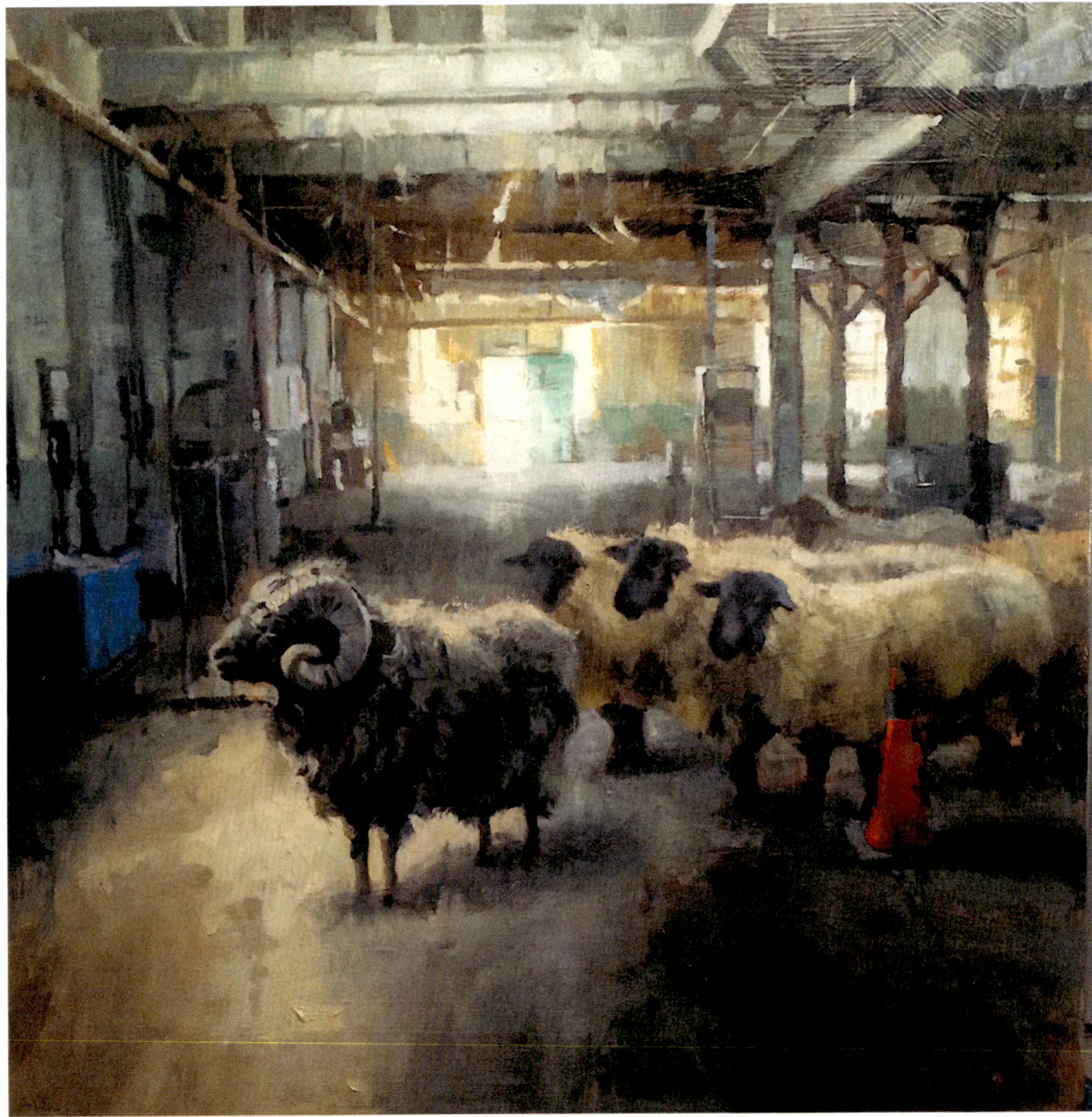

Black sheep. 30" x 30" oil on wood

Identifying your hidden constraints, the good and the bad, will help you gain a clearer picture of who you are and where you come from, why you think the way you do and what things keep you from your authentic self, or that thing you are resistant to changing, and why. To be clear, these forces and influencers are certainly not all negative. They can be the stuff that informs a lifetime of work. In fact, as often as not, those strong forces have been the impetus for some enormously creative efforts. Beliefs, relationship, loss, abuse, struggles and strife are powerful vehicles for authentic creative response and change.

Example list of external influencers:

Parents/Upbringing

The family norm

Past teachers/mentors

Race

Culture-subculture norms

Birth order

Personality type (Myers Briggs --- do the test if you have not already)

Relationship

Belief system and/or related tribe

Trauma, loss, heartache

Income bracket

Urban/suburban/rural

Proximity to water

Aversion to yellow things.

Circle the ones that apply to you or list a few of your own influencers.

All these sociological structures exert gravitational force on who you are and how you think. These influences create an internal bias that can profoundly affect one's perceptions. At the very least, being aware of these personal biases can lead to a more open awareness of what they can mean to you. Your beliefs are yours to keep or to discard. But it is valuable for you to know why you think what you think.

As they say in art, you must first learn the rules before you can know how to break them. This applies to art and it applies to you. Know thyself.

Here come da judge

Story time: Years back, I was invited to be a part of a brain trust for Darden restaurants, the creators of Red Lobster and Olive Garden, to concept a new food chain. What's a brain trust? It's a think tank with people from all professional walks; writers, designers, art directors, management, money people, etc. I had already done a great deal of design and illustration work for various restaurants that were up and running and had worked on concepts for restaurants that never saw the light of day, so I was familiar with what they were about.

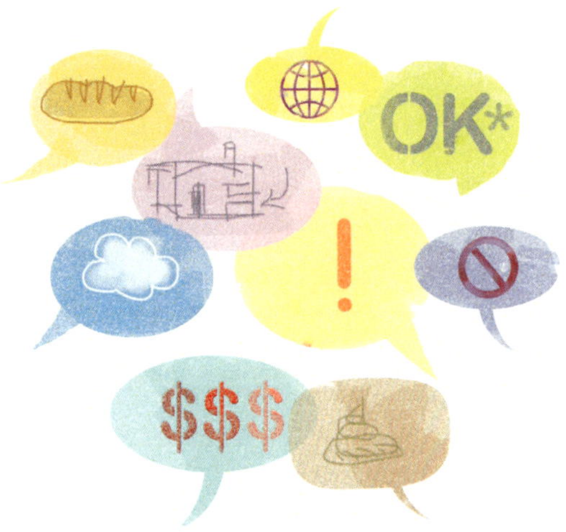

We split into three groups and were given the assignment of producing a fast-food restaurant that centered around bread and artisan bread and sandwiches made of bread and other stuff with bread in it. It was a no-holds-barred think tank concept party and I brought my experiences as an art director, my drawing skills and my thinking out of the container tool kit. And everyone else brought their stuff to the table as well. If brains were buildings, we were New York City.

Our group was comprised of myself, another graphic designer, a writer and two corporate representatives, one an account manager and the other was an accountant (or similar). As creatives, we were well versed in the concepting process. We called it blue-skying, because nothing was off limits and everything was doable, no restrictions... We know this part is important because that's where ideas come from. No limitations mean bigger ideas.

But the restaurant people didn't really grasp our intent and every time one of us threw out an idea, it would be met with the sound of gunfire. BOOM! Shot down. After a while it started to sound like a duck hunt. What we were hearing was the sound of judgment born of fear. "No that won't work because blah, blah blah." It was killing the process.

So, what was happening? The restaurant people were asserting their paradigm into the program. "I know what a restaurant is and that's not a restaurant." "That can't possibly work because of the expenses involved in setting up the snow machines" or whatever. The two company guys were thinking like, well, company guys.

At the core of their responses was the I-don't-want-to-lose-my-job-aphobia. They were self-appointed referees in a game where there were no rules. A big part of the creative process is to be open to the initial, even crazy ideas, because they may lead to something new and more practical. Their fears were tethering our explorer balloon.

Once we explained to the suits that these initial concepts were just the beginning part of the formative process, and that they would not get fired for having an idea -- even a bad one -- they calmed down and started to have fun. They joined in and the ideas flowed like honey. We shaped up three or four restaurant ideas, got them on paper and presented them, along with the other participants, at the end of the weekend. Eventually the brain trust's efforts turned into a restaurant and we all got free sandwiches and a thousand bucks.

Point is, allay those fears, matey. Save them for your next flight to Kabul. Many ideas mean more chances for success. The more you have, even the crazy ones, the more you have to work with. First solutions are rarely the best. Be aware of premature judgmentalism. It can squelch the seeds of something better that may evolve out of a crazy notion. I'll cover the right time to consider the pros and cons of a solution in the **Discernment** section.

Rules and regs

Constraints also show up in the form of preexisting models, processes, the "approved" methods for doing things, social and cultural constructs, what the authorities may have to say about your groundbreaking efforts, all of which can keep us quietly in line.

Identifying and analyzing these imprinted assumptions can help to assess which ones are real and reasonable, which work for you and which do not.

How do you spotlight these barriers? Which file cabinets in your brain contain the roadblocks? How do you identify which beliefs are helpful and which are not? Surely there must be an app for this. Oh wait, there is, and it's comes with your current software. It's a surprisingly low-tech method of discernment that involves sitting down with paper and pen.

I like pen over pencil because there's no eraser and it's more of a commitment for list-making, jotting notes and sketching. We'll get more deeply into this in the Intent section, but a quick exercise for the barrier search is to write down any influencers, the good, the bad and the ugly. The goal is to evaluate each in pro or con style. Some influencers can have both positive and negative impact. A spouse, for example, may be supportive in one way but not in another. Write those down too, i.e.:

Current art instructor: Gets me on the easel (plus); Is too conservative (minus); Smells like cooking sherry (minus)

Church: spiritual growth (plus); bagpipe ministry (plus); not approving of my interpretive belly dancing (minus)

Pottery group: glazing is fun (plus); facilitator is a control freak (minus); not learning anything (minus); drinking too much wine (plus)

Take an honest look at the things that define your life. Sometimes just identifying the roadblocks is enough to facilitate movement. And you can't fix a problem if you don't know what it is.

List a few of your own, pro and con style.

____

____

____

____

____

____

____

____

Assumptions: The ego and the idiot.

Many of us have read how Abraham Maslow described the early stages of learning, identifying four stages of comprehension. From the first stage, unconscious incompetency, to the last, unconscious competency.

And the first is: We don't know what that we don't know -- the "I'm pretty good" phase. The second stage is realizing there is much to learn and the third is knowingly committing to learning and becoming proficient. The last stage is being so adept at a process that the mechanics no longer interfere with the process of creating. The beginning level is a kind of 'ignorance is bliss' stage, a certain joy that comes from the act of doing. Feels good, so all's good.

But, in the beginner to intermediate stages, awareness rises from practice and thoughtful observation. Many creatives become conscious of their true state of learning, usually from being face to face with a true master, or at least someone who is perceived to be so.

A humanities trip to Europe during my college years to experience all the originals I had studied in art history brought this moment to me. I got smacked in the head by a Botticelli painting, immediately followed by a conscious reframing of my true current ability, or lack thereof. You may have had a similar moment or you wouldn't be on the search for more information.

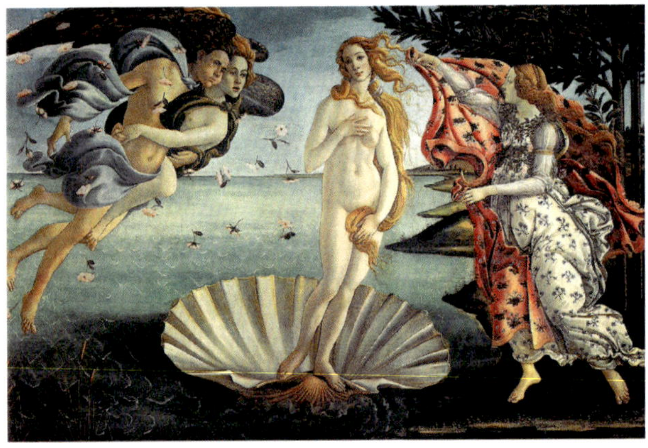

Sandro Botticelli, Birth of Venus, c. 1486, 67.9 x 109.6 in. tempera on canvas. Uffizi Gallery

Reframing. It's a pattern of learning and adjusting that repeats over and over in our lives. You remember elementary school, right? 6th grade. You did it. Top of the world. Next year the move to 7th grade sends you to the bottom of the pond again. Graduating senior with honors or maybe superlatives, king of the world and then, first day of college, military or job, back to grunt level again.

Learning is a lifelong event of constant readjustment. In the beginning, we strive for that next level, moving up only to find there is a lot more that we don't know. It is a marathon commitment, an honorable pursuit. Each time the true creative explorer gets knocked back there is an adjustment, a recalibration to get back on track with even more focus. It is the desire to learn that fosters greatness, not the ego.

Being open means checking your ego at the door. I've noticed that the better the artists are, the more they become focused on learning. People who could very easily rest on their laurels are nose to the grindstone in a constant state of improvement. The individuals who have attained *Unconscious Competency* are still looking for new ideas and inspiration from any source. If you are going to compare yourself to another, look to the known masters (across the creative spectrum), not to the hot person du jour.

Find only the Grade A certified best to stand up against and assess where you are. Stay objective. Don't accept the kind and supportive words of friends and relatives as fact. That's what nice people do. Ask a pro for an opinion. Be in the state of learning always.

"The individuals who have attained Unconscious Competency are still looking for new ideas and inspiration from any source."

Most of the attendees in my classes are women by a ratio of 20 to one over men. I wondered the why of this for some time but, since there were rarely any males present, there was no one to poll. My assumption is that guys (I am one and therefore certified to opine) either don't like being told what to do, have the belief that they can figure it out for themselves or don't want anyone to see that they don't know it all yet. It's ego showing up and limiting access to new information.

This is not exclusively a gender trait, of course. Ego shows up in response to critique with statements like, "Well, I studied with so and so and I was taught that this is the only way to do it." There are hundreds of ways to solve any one problem and, while a specific solution or process may be right for one individual, it's not always perfect for another. You can never have too much information, especially about things that you believe you already know, even if it feels counter to your current sensibilities.

An ego defined as a sense of self-esteem and strong personal identity gives you the gumption to get through the tough spots, like a mental shot of tequila. It motivates individuals to dance to a different drumbeat even when those around them aren't even listening. Pay attention to when the good ego is working and keeping you on your path and when the bad ego is holding you back.

Hey brother, can you paradigm?

Or, "Geez, If I only had two paradigms to rub together..." As it turns out, two models of thought are better than one because you are at least considering other templates and modes. Assumptions based on just one point of view can be limiting. If you ever start to question why you believe a certain "truth," it may be time to go paradigm shopping.

Because I'm writing as an artist of the general realist order, I'll use a few examples from this point of view. If you are of another persuasion... musician, apparel designer, clock maker, or any kind of Ism follower, then just insert your model here.

Story time: While teaching a workshop in south Florida, one of the attendees, a follower of the Cape Cod school of painting, said that he made the trek down from Cape Cod because he believed that there might be a different way to go about a painting than what he had been taught. The Cape Cod movement is comprised of followers of Henry Hensche, a renowned colorist, who adhere to his principles of high key, saturated, vibrating color over, say, the Hudson River School, which has more neutral and naturalistic leanings.

Many artists from schools with this type of specific focus aren't terribly accepting that there are different ways to go about a painting. Or they simply choose that way because it suits them at the time. My workshop-taking friend said he thought he felt stuck in this system, and believed it was time for a shift.

Although his bread and butter was primarily colorist in nature, the desire to experience a new way meant he was open to take a chance. More importantly, he wanted something different. He questioned his bias. He thought for himself.

Once he was able to get outside of his own assumption bubble he was free to explore new ideas, step into new territory to see how it felt, then apply what he learned to what he already knew. His work grew more in 4 days than it had in several years.

For the record, I'm not saying there's a thing wrong with any system. If it works for you, great. However, accumulating new info will only add to your arsenal, encouraging you to evolve.

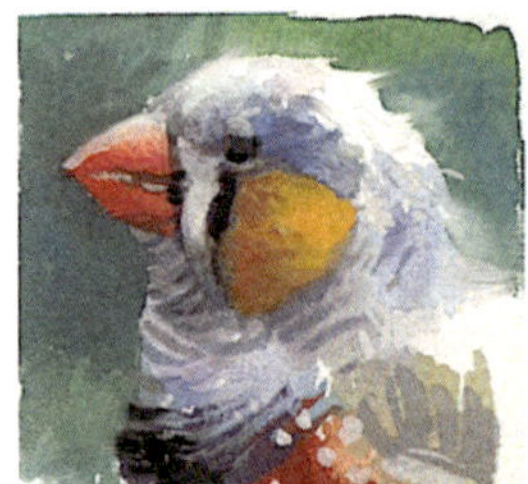
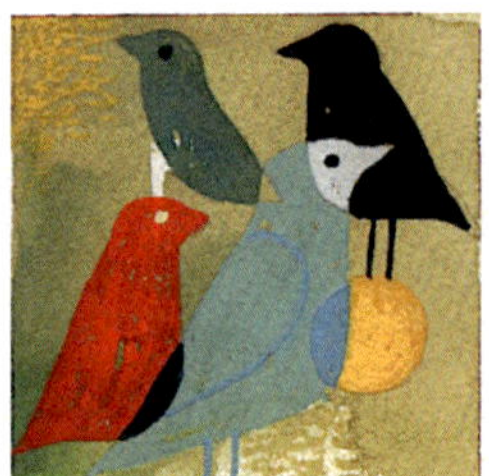
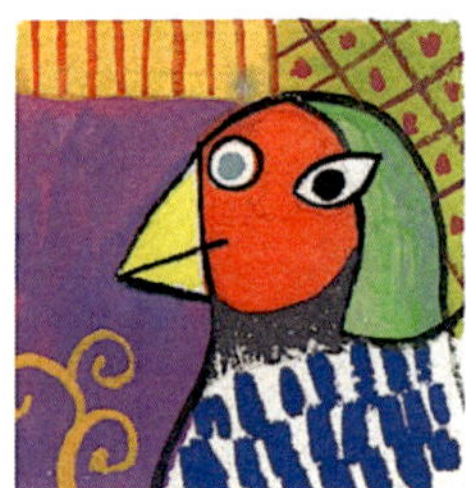
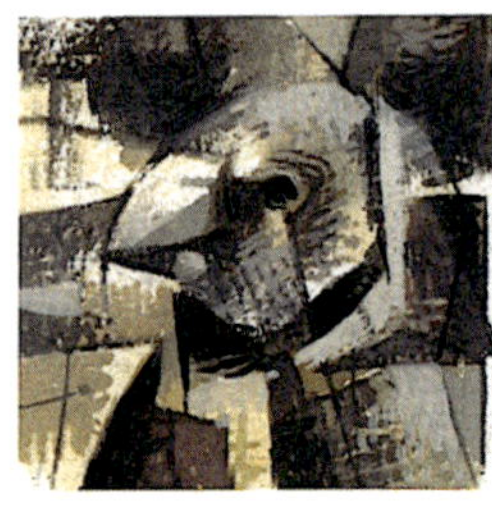
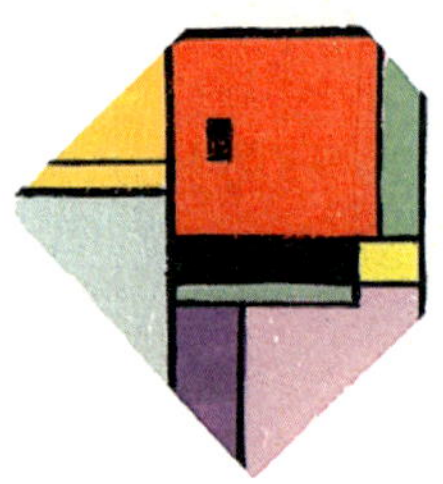

One could look at all methodologies of nature paintings, as an example, and compare them to the finches of the Galapagos Islands. They all share common features, like the application of colored pigments with bristle brushes on flat rectangular grounds such as linen or canvas. But because of environmental and regionalized influences, they evolved differently. Is one better than the next?

Can I get a Hell NO?

Like the evolution of all living creatures, an artist's evolution takes time, and it requires the willingness to receive new influences and ideas to adapt.

Story time: An example of resistance and awareness came during one of my *Abstraction and Intention* classes. It's designed to throw people out of their comfort zones and force them to solve something in a new way... critical thinking mixed with paint. And it is unlike a class on painting stuff to look like stuff, which relies heavily on drawing and technique.

This one is all about discovery. The class focuses on the components of painting that are important to each artist individually and on filtering out the less important to focus on what's vital to the voice of the artist. The ultimate purpose is to develop a personal intent and direction.

The exercises are more open-ended, rather than telling the students what to do specifically. The control is on the back end, rather than up front, as in most workshops. The first few days can be difficult because many feel they are walking a tightrope without a net, but, by the end, there is a room full of wide-eyed converts.

At the end of Day Two during of this five-day class, a woman told me that, until mid-day she had been feeling a lot of resistance to this new way of approaching the process, because it didn't match what she knew to be "truth."

Despite her discomfort, she had made a conscious decision to work through the unknown in the hopes that she might make new discoveries. It's a familiar place to us all, learning something new is always uncomfortable. But once she made the decision to be open, she freed herself up to play and effortlessly move her hands across the canvas. She began to feel the paint respond and to develop a dialogue with the new stuff that showed up. She went on to create a cartload of wonderful, fresh new works by week's end.

Identifying what you are fighting is the beginning of your personal freedom. This is the state of being *open* in action. Throw open the windows and let that fresh air in.

Comparative thinking

Being open also means checking your judgments at the door. Think about paradigms as a line graph, with openness on one end and fundamentalist adherence to anything on the other.

Take an honest look at where you fit in. Figuring out where you are on the spectrum is a healthy thing to do. If your opinions don't negate the views of others, blow people up or require living in the tail of a comet, it's all good. The narrower the beliefs become, the more closed off from new or different ideas. Judgment is putting yourself above another's way, comparison is putting yourself beneath the same. Neither is helpful.

Blog posts are great for this, where the informed and the uninformed go to vent because they can. Not long ago, on a popular art blog, there was a showcase and discussion about an artist who may have been a tad on the fundamentalist side of realism. One writer posted a relatively decent wildlife painting, a tiger in the bushes, and stated categorically that this style of painting was it. No others were real art.

So... we should only paint tigers realistically from here on out? What about all that other art that hangs in every museum in the world. Did no one inform the museum curators of this? I guess we'd just need one museum of tiger art per city, like the NYMOTA, New York Museum of Tiger Art.

This may sound like an extreme example, but it's very common. My tribe is the only tribe that should exist. Where have I heard that before?

The other side of this comparative coin is judging one's work against another's to such a degree it becomes artificially positive or dangerously negative. In the right framework, the comparison of one's own work to a master's can create a benchmark to aim for. But the opposite response can be frustrating and debilitating, slowing or even halting progress until any movement seems impossible. Keep in mind when viewing a wondrous finished work that you are only seeing the final results of countless struggles. Doing great work requires great effort. It's not easy for anyone, even if it looks that way.

Progress in any mode is like developing six-pack abs you can crack abalones on. It takes a little effort each day to get there. But if you stop, it gets harder and harder until movement stops altogether. The positive goal of mastery of craft or washboard stomach will keep you in the game.

And this has what to do with creativity? Our inherent tendency is to move toward conformity, other folks are doing it a certain way; therefore, so should I. History is filled with examples of discoveries and shifts that moved *against* the norm, sometimes with historic or tragic consequences, but ultimately (though not always) for the greater good.

It was because one individual questioned the status quo. What if there were another way? It's always the ones who zag while the herd is zigging. Where would we be without all the zaggernauts? We'd be painting Byzantine Icons or realistic tigers, that's where.

Know your motive

People have a variety of motives for wanting to paint or make quilts or cakes or play the guitar. Any motive that gets you moving is okay by me. But knowing that motive, being clear on why you are doing what you are doing helps define and hone the path.

Not knowing can really hang you up down the line. For some, the motivation is to make money, for others it's self-expression. Some just want to make all their Christmas presents because bracelets and ties are out, or they want a group coffee-mug painting experience while they drink wine. It's all good.

If it's the coffee mug thing, go, enjoy and bring a decent bottle of pinot noir. If it's a living you are after, be clear on how important it is to be authentic, compared with making the bucks. You can make a decent income by producing dough ornaments and painted light switches or S.O.S.'s, (what we used to call Shit on a Stick at the art festivals), but there's not much self-expression there.

Being unique as a creative individual is not easy because: A) It's all been done (almost), making a new niche is now more a matter of nuance than developing a whole new thing; and B) Your buying demographic just got very narrow. Marry rich, get a job, find a bag of money or get used to liking baloney and cheese (it's better when it's grilled).

"Judgment is putting yourself above another's way, comparison is putting yourself beneath the same. Neither is helpful."

Finally, C) Finding a venue is a lot harder when you aren't creating for the buying masses, unless you live in New York where being different is the norm. If you understand your motivation, that becomes your beacon in the storm, the thing to focus on while you are doing the hard work.

Economic concerns can be a huge inhibitor of authenticity. Our paths can become skewed once the sell-ability of the work gets factored in. Once commerce is introduced to the creative process it can become compromised.

I've experienced this force in the form of pressure from galleries (and also the mortgage company). Some wonderful galleries just want good paintings. Some will be very specific about what they want, and don't want. Putting income in the mix means you are open to this kind of influence.

Example: Gallery, "I really like your scary Gotham city work, but I can't sell it. I sell happy, bright, clean colors and no black frames!"

Artist, "Ummmm, okay, sunsets and unicorns it is. You want fries with that?"

Is this wrong? No, that's the gallery's prerogative. They know their buyers and their market and it's the artist's choice to capitulate or not.

From my point of view, If I go along with it, my authenticity may be dented. If I don't, I may go hungry. The answer to that conundrum lies in the motive of the creator. David Bowie once said that we should never be influenced by external pressures, but then, he was David Bowie. His identity and his evolution came from within.

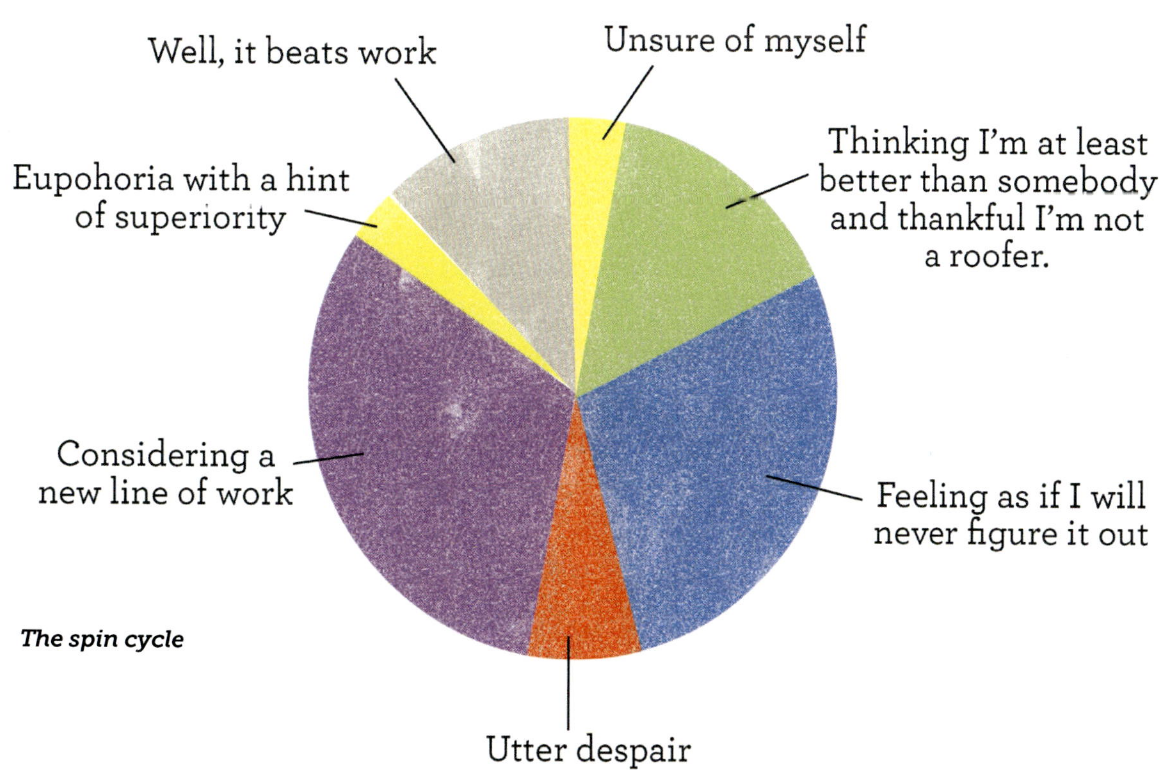

The spin cycle

Hanging your stuff on a wall is a set-up for judgment from a chunk of the viewing public. Get used to it. If your motive isn't clear or your message isn't nailed down or if you are hanging in the wrong venue, the disapproval ratings may increase.

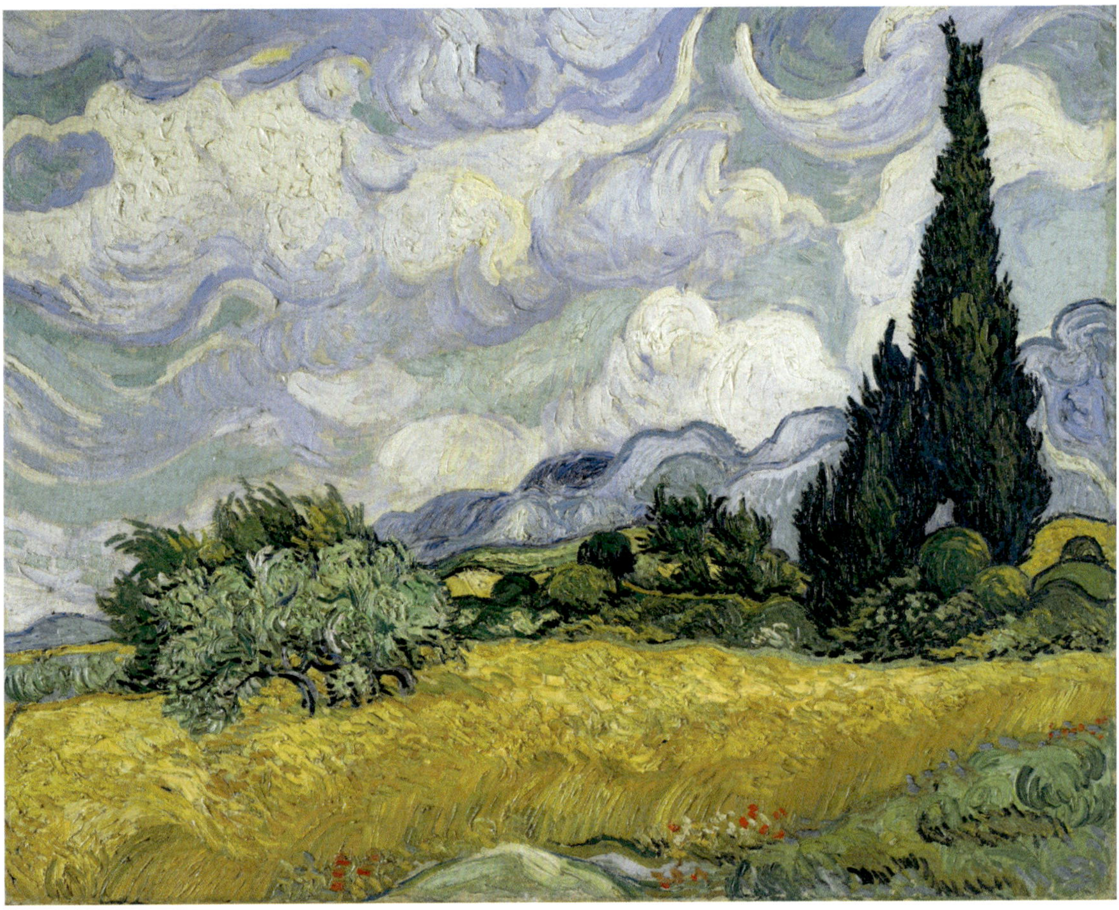

Wheat field with Cypresses Vincent Van Gogh, 1889 28 7/8 x 36 3/4 in. oc Image courtesy of The Metropolitan Museum of Art.

If you have any kind of thin skin, you'd better layer on the body armor. Unless, of course, you can learn to not give a rat's butt about what people think, which is central to being authentic. That faith in yourself, that trust in the creative spirit, is what can pull you through the lean years.

Look at Vincent Van Gogh fercryinoutloud. He never sold a single painting. Not one. Did he care? Probably. But, that did not deter him. I rest my case.

Unless you are of the Van Gogh ilk, having your work not sell or not be recognized means there's no external reward and that can put a big fat question mark square in the middle of your path. And you'll have to climb up and over it every time if you don't have your motivation firmly set in place.

Your motivation can be money, joy, recognition, a sense of accomplishment, self-expression or any combination. Being clear helps you stay on track and assists you in defining workable goals, paths and venues for your work. Know your motive, know your why. In the **Intent** section, there are worksheets to help you nail this down.

Some artists want to be different, but are afraid to try. Resistance in all caps!!!!!!!! That's not just fear of judgment. It's fear of financial loss, which we view as the same.

But what if you reframed this thought?

Numero uno in the reframing department is this:

Change does not occur overnight. If it is to be authentic, it's usually a gradual progression. You don't have to reveal the new you to anyone until you are ready. You don't have to reveal anything to anyone. You don't have to hang it up, play it for family or post it on social media. In fact, I would advise against it.

This process is about long-term growth, exploration, applying the things you like and leaving the rest, not suddenly getting a gallery show in New York with your chocolate pudding installations. But then, who doesn't like pudding?

Technology, the brain snatcher

We are living in the best 100 years in history for individual freedom. We all have a shot at the opportunity to do what we want and take the chance at being a self-sustaining creative. Even in the desolate recesses of the earth, smart and creative can rise to the top when it's met with the right circumstances, the incidence of opportunity, when these three forces cross paths.

Now, we have so many ways to be creative. Too many. They come in the form of apps, software, smart phones, how-to classes, cameras, the internet and more. The problem with entertainment technology is that it does the thinking for us, solves a little problem, gives us an answer and we feel near genius. My really smart phone has so many amazing apps for creating interesting images to show on social media or for creating music. Yay! But where am I in all of this? Sad face emoji.

"... our technology will serve as a buffer between us and nature, a block between us and the deeper dimensions of our own experience."

- Rollo May, The Courage to Create

A lifelong artist, I was lucky enough to grow up in the time before the Tyrannosaurus Techs dominated the earth. Rather than have painting apps on an iPad, I had to learn everything on my own. I studied graphic design, not fine art. Art history yes, drawing yes, design, color theory and concept, yes. But zero painting.

From a young age, I was figuring out what paint could do: fabric paints, airbrush, watercolor, pen and ink, acrylic, pastel, gouache, you name it. Ideas were produced in sketch and word form, roughs, comps and studies. No buttons were pushed in the making of this idea.

As you will see, the sketch / word methodology is integral to creative connectivity.

My self-guided exploration up the Artizon River resulted in a set of manual and intellectual tools that became infused into my professional creative and everyday life, my vestigial tail of experience always wagging happily in whatever I set my mind to.

Mid-career, during various exploits in visual communication, I wound up on many different paths. Now I know that all paths have led me here. It's the accumulation of experiences and knowledge acquired the old-fashioned way, with hands and mind, that informs my work, the daily creative decisions, the writing of this book, how I think and what I teach. This life experience has provided something unique to bring to the table, as yours does for you.

Story time: As a college art instructor, I incorporated the thought systems presented here into each syllabus, because teaching students how to think for themselves was sorely lacking in the curriculum.

It bothered me that we did not teach critical thinking. We taught kids how to perform functions, how to make a Photoshop image, how to create a brochure in the current software. But nowhere in the curriculum did we focus on how to think.

The department head and I set about to create a class for which there was no book, the perfect start for a class on critical thinking. At that time, the number of brain sucking techno-gizmos numbered only in the hundreds. Now it's an epidemic. Why bother to think? I know that some of this techno-stuff helps us, but it limits our individual thinking ability potential.

Even something as seemingly inert as the use of photography in painting can filter out the voice of the artist. For many realist painters, the use of photos as reference is de rigueur. There is nothing wrong with this if you just want to render. But the result is only technique.

There is little insertion of the artist. Separating yourself from the herd takes thought. Historically, the most favored artists were the ones whose paintings transcended the subject, whose voice was as much a part of the work as the message.

Edward Hopper, a great example of individuality, would frequently go out and do pencil drawings of his lonely buildings and figures, making notes of what the colors were on the sketches. This allowed him to interpret and push into the next level in the studio, to make the final painting his own and not a rendering from a photo. Working in this manner brought Hopper that much closer to his authentic self.

I am not saying the use of technology is wrong. Use whatever is available to you in your work to inform ideas, then figure out how to infuse those ideas in your own way or figure out how to adapt the contraption to fit your intent. "The idea is king", that pretty much covers it.

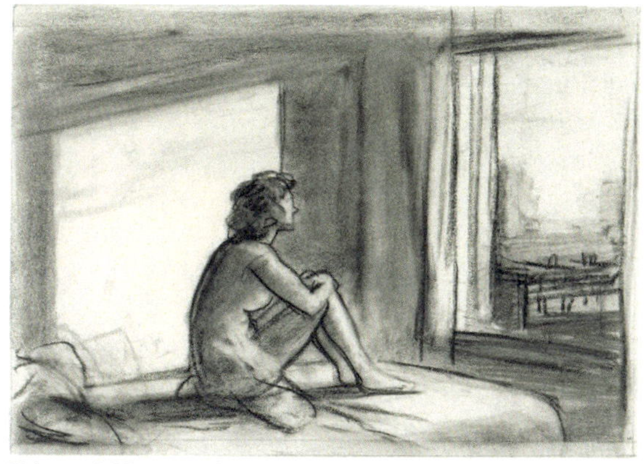

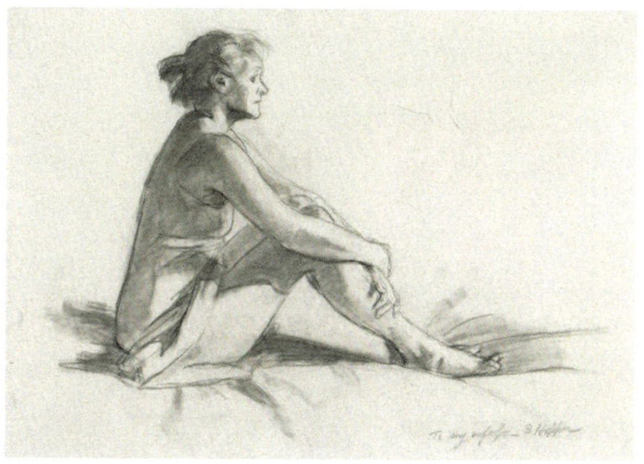

Edward Hopper (1882-1967)
Study for Morning Sun, (1952). Fabricated chalk on paper, Sheet: 12 x 19in.
Study for Morning Sun, (1952). Chalk on paper, Sheet: 11 15/16 x 18 15/16in.
Study for Morning Sun, (1952). Chalk and graphite pencil on paper, Sheet: 12 1/16 x 18 15/16in
Whitney Museum of American Art, New York © Heirs of Josephine N. Hopper, licensed by Whitney Museum, N.Y.
Photograph Sheldan C. Collins

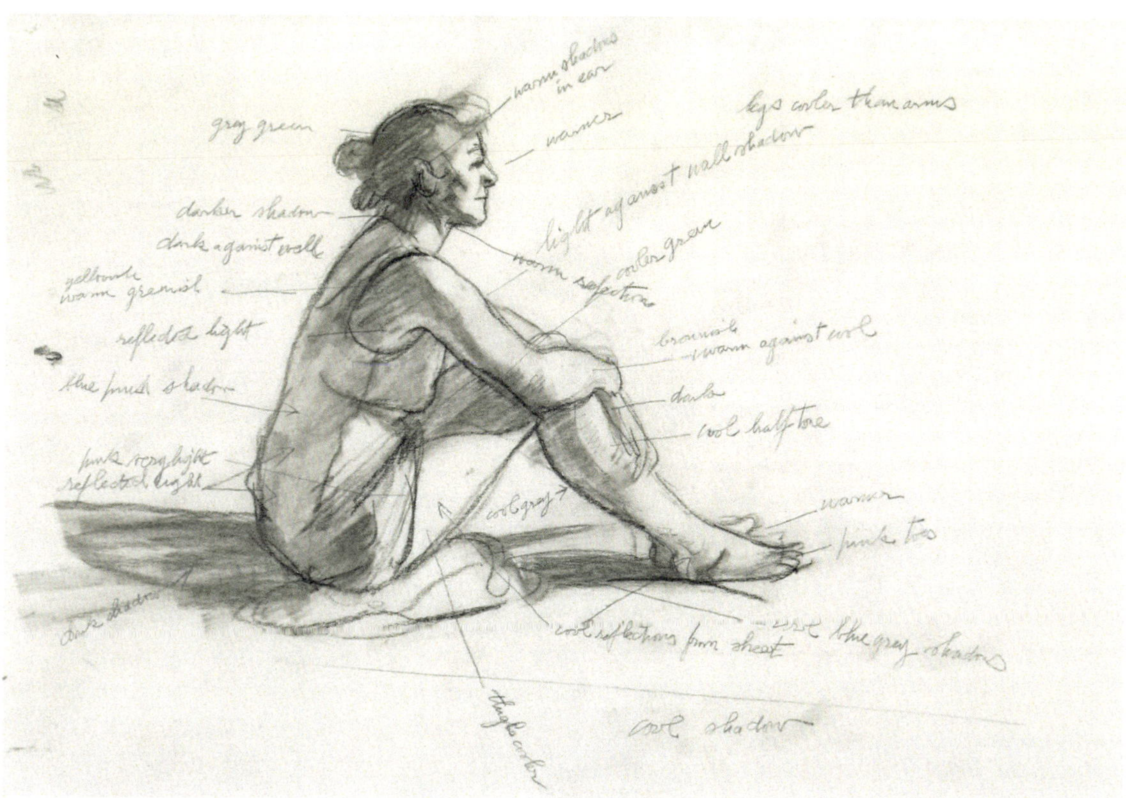

Hopper's drawings

The insertion of the artist is essential to authenticity. American artist Edward Hopper would make sketches for his paintings to not only "get the drawing" but to annotate the color. Working directly from a photo or an app filter minimizes the voice of the creator.

Your own worst enemy

That wicked person in your head is your worst enemy. The internal voice is the yammering spouse from whom there is no possibility of divorce, (though it tries to be helpful).

"Where did I leave my keys? Jeez, I always do this to myself... am I getting old? Is this Alzheimer's setting in? Great. I'll be broke and living in an old folks' home. What if I get Rheumatoid arthritis? I won't be able to play guitar anymore... once I learn how. I love the guitar in that song from that band, what was the name? Can't remember. Oh, here are my keys."

Often, that voice will talk you out of trying something new. It gets all up in your business and fuddles with clear and informed thinking. Talk about boundary issues.

Though it can be annoying, the voice has a purpose. It lets us bounce ideas, consider alternatives, weigh pros and cons. But you need to stay focused on your game and be aware of the tendency of this inner voice to sometimes run amuck. Think back to that night when a child or a spouse didn't call on time and you were ready to dial 911.

Try keeping your goals in writing, or snap a rubber band on your wrist to stay in the moment (it works). Get a dry erase board, the best interactive software money can buy, and think it out in erasable marker.

Inner child spanks inner adult

Your inner child wants to play, but your inner Dad wants to mow the yard. Who is going to win that battle? Play is central to creativity. You need to intervene with your idiot parental voice and say, "not now."

The act of creative play is essential to our mental and emotional well-being. It is fundamental to problem-solving, and it works for MacGyver. Most public schools took art and music out of the curriculum because they were perceived to be a waste of time and money. All linear thinking and zero creativity, big mistake.

An education that includes the arts and critical thinking gives kids greater ability to solve problems creatively, rather than looking for standardized solutions.

Plug play into your schedule just like yoga or bowling. Give yourself this gift of fun time. There are plenty of brain-honing apps, but I'm going to recommend you sit down with a pen and paper and work on some of the exercises in this book.... the old-fashioned way.

Take the idea of the process for the assignments here and make your own to solve one of your specific issues. Wear a stupid hat or water wings, put Sesame Street on, dance like an idiot. To thine own elf be true. Give yourself permission... it's just good parenting.

I'm not creative

What is creative anyway? Writing, music, painting? Creativity is not confined to advertising agencies or galleries or music halls. It shows up in the wall colors you choose, those crazy golf pants, scrapping a small bench together from the stuff in your garage, even making refrigerator stew out of whatever you can find and making it yummy.

We make hundreds of creative decisions in a week. Many times, the choice you make because of personal taste is just inches away from being a really creative decision. All you need do is make one little connection.

Imagine shopping for something to go over your couch. You're flipping through the bins of pre-framed posters. Then your creative angel voice says, "Hmmm, that old door from Granpa's barn is so good looking, and it reminds me of my childhood, maybe I'll just hang that up instead." Going just one step further can put you on the idea trail.

Imagination. Don't tell me you've never caught yourself mentally wandering off toward Bora Bora in a sailboat with Brad Pitt when mermaids suddenly sneak aboard and steal your mac and cheese.

Everyone daydreams, or at least they should allow themselves that moment once in a while. Something like half of our day is taken up with mental vacationing.

Why so much? It turns out a large percentage of our thoughts reflect or relate directly to a personal goal, even little goals, like remembering to pick up eggs at the store, or larger ones, like sailing off to Bora Bora in your retirement.

It is also a way to work through current problems, and, you guessed it, it's a fundamental part of creativity.

Daydreaming is easier than sitting down and purposefully conjuring up an imaginary realm because it's involuntary and there are no constraints. It can all start with a thought, a sketch and an imaginative idea that isn't dismissed by your inner adult. Giving yourself permission to play and to dream can lead to worlds and places no one has been before.

Dreams are the way we deal with -- and dump -- stimuli from the day, the way we work things through, a miracle of imagination unrestricted by the laws of should and can't. And you can learn to tap into them, more on this topic in **Connectivity**.

Why bother? Because deep inside of your cortex are uncharted universes to conquer and flying unicorns to ride.

The potholes on Bliss Valley Road.

The hallmark of any great artist is a unique voice and continual growth. And you can't have one without the other. Both require risk and risk is daunting.

So many artists, people whom you would assume have it all dialed in, can be found sitting in their Barcalounger with a stack of books and a Scotch, wondering what the hell to do next. One of the reasons we get stuck in this pothole is that change goes against our basic need for certainty. And certainty equals comfort, but it's as boring as tofu.

Solving the same problem every day the same way starts to feel stale. Boredom sets in, which can compel the creator to find a different way. The hard part is figuring out what comes next.

Uncertainty is where all the growth lies. For an artist or musician, it's easy to get stuck in a style because consistency is where the money is, and it's a tough pigeonhole to climb out of.

Reframing again. Think of it more as an artist-goes-into-home-gym-and-works-out story. The growth you seek is for you. The best excuses to stay on the bench -- fear of failure, loss, wasted time, the unknown, are the best ways to stay stuck.

The creative geniuses of the world share a common trait in cognitive fluidity, the ability to step into the unknown. But this key characteristic can be developed just like any other skill, in small steps.

Work on your acceptance of uncertainty, what is known as the *tolerance of ambiguity*, in little bits. Try something you would not normally do, like going up in a biplane or skydiving (with a pro, of course), paddling out on a surfboard or adopting a 23' python. Okay, maybe not that last one. Build up your acceptance of the unknown and whittle away at your fear factor... you might end up enjoying it.

Here are a few more potholes and how to get around them:

Pagina en blanco

No ideas. The blank page syndrome. Nothing.... crap, what am I gonna do now? You are going to turn to the **Connectivity** section and make some inspiration, but only after you've finished this section.

A) Do something that will lead to something else. Do the mind and method exercises. Keep doing them, even when you're not stuck.

B) Do something completely different after studying the problem for a while and allow your subconscious mind to work on it. It works.

Problem solved through problem-solving.

Time challenged

Seriously, who has time for this? Like staying physically active, challenging the brain with a side of self-actualization is important to a rich, full, sustainable life. Working on your CQ (Creativity Quotient) makes you a better problem solver and a happier you. Don't make me put it on your calendar for you, I'm too busy.

Failure to launch

As artists, we sometimes have to trick the mind to stave off performance anxiety. Here are a couple of tips to get you over that hump:

1) Work small, think big. Do small sketches, write small stories. Don't jump straight into the epic painting of Moses crossing the Red Sea.
2) Draw what is right in front of you in black and white. Take the fear out of screwing up a nice white canvas with all that color. Keep it simple. 4 per page.
3) Practice the rudiments, one at a time.
4) Divide a canvas into quarters with tape and do small color studies. Turn off the part of your brain that puts the pressure in making a successful painting.
5) Nothing inspires like a deadline. Give yourself 2 hours to solve it.
6) Play with a different medium or instrument just to wake your creative spirit up.
7) Use your hands to do anything other than manipulate a piece of technology.
8) Memory sketches. Draw anything that comes to mind. Don't judge, just do.
9) Collage. Glue stick, scissors, art board and anything you can cut up and glue down. Go.
10) Don't do it at all. The world won't stop turning and your life will be just fine.

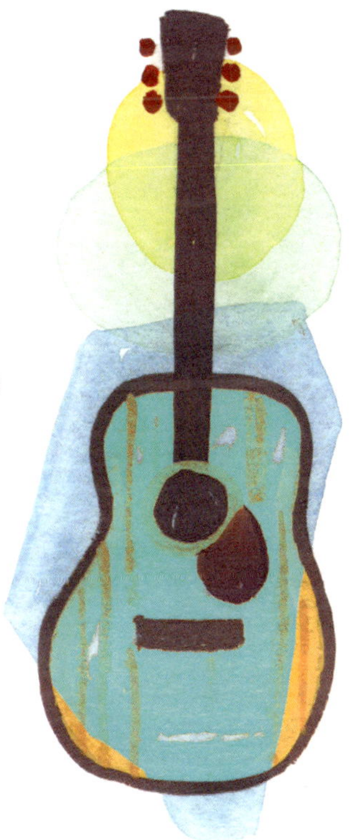

It ain't gonna play itself.

In the absence of information comes... not much

Do your homework, you can't work in a vacuum. Read the **Acquisition** section.

The path of most resistance

We've already covered a bunch of personal growth inhibitors, but here are the inertia makers that I see most often as an instructor and a creative coach:

I'll never be as good as the pros.

The pros weren't good at some point either. Step by step and one day at a time. Start small. The words "I can never do that" should never enter your mind. Mastering anything takes time, commitment and dedication.

Anyone who has mastered a skill set will tell you that getting to that level of ability is just the beginning. The more you learn, the more you discover how much there is still to be learned. Create goals and break your giant task into digestible chunks.

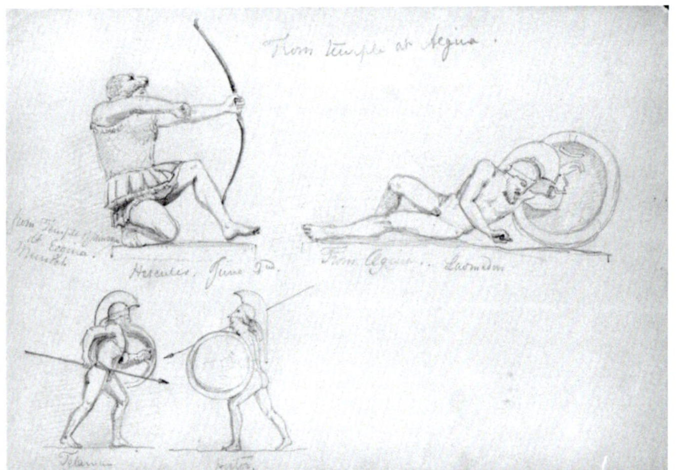

A Sargent sketch at 14 years of age.

Giudecca watercolor on paper, 13 1/16 x 20 15/16 in.
Image courtesy of Metropolitan Museum of Art.

Before and after.

John Singer Sargent was arguably one of the greatest realist painters of the 19th and 20th centuries. Was he born with talent? The drawing on the left was created at age 14 and the effortless watercolor on the right at age 57.

What will people think?

A) Spend your time practicing, playing, exploring, experimenting in private.
If your secret dream is to become an avant-garde cake maker, don't post your first efforts on social media. Show no one what you are doing until you feel you are ready, if at all. Andrew Wyeth spent 15 years painting the Helga series before he showed anyone. And that went okay for him.

B) Here's a secret that will set you free, what others think has no bearing on you, the days of stoning someone are over. Some people may feel uncomfortable and maybe a little envious, but you will always have the support of like-minded people.

I put it out to the universe but so far nothing.

Okay, bear in mind this is coming from an extremely pragmatic mind, but the universe is way too busy expanding and forming new galaxies and keeping us confused to worry about your desires. Yes, putting out positivity and placing wishes in a bottle can have impact on your life but only because you are living in a positive frame of mind, positive thoughts enable positive action. The universe favors the bold.

Expectations, the little green adversary

Number one cause of disappointment? Unrealistic expectations. Going into any endeavor with high hopes is positive. Anticipation of success is a powerful motivator. But unrealistic expectations are a recipe for disappointment. "I'm going to open my art stand right in the middle of the Chihuahuan desert. No competitors!"

Set achievable goals and quantifiable definitions for successes, based on ability and time.

In a classroom setting it helps to set aside firm expectations in the beginning. Go with an open mind. Try not to anticipate an outcome. Don't worry about what everyone in the class might think. They're all worried about their own stuff.

The epic fail

We learn from failing not from successes. If the latter were true I would be a rock star artist from my first amazing painting on. It don't work that way. The most important thing to know is that even a bad idea or ineffective effort can evolve into a great one.

What if I don't know where to start?

How do you follow your bliss if you don't know what it is? If you are just starting out on this creative journey of self-discovery, try the sampler platter. Start with what interests or inspires you, or even something that you have no opinion about. It will connect you to something new:

Write, journal, then write some more.

Collect old magazines and books to tear up and collage.

Buy a children's set of watercolors, some cheap watercolor paper and move color around without expectation.

Expecting to be good will keep you from even starting, expect to be bad, that way you will never be disappointed.

Play-Doh. No kidding. It's cheap and it's fun. Your brain will feel like a kid again and play like one. Think about how many ways you can use it; sculpture, rolled flat and cut shapes, as a thick paint.

Take accordion lessons or a class in anything that blips on your radar.

Cooking classes. You get to eat what you create! You can't do that with clay.

Make assignments for yourself: like a travel poster or something inspirational for your church, fashion birds from the magazine pages you've saved, take old paint cans from the garage and slop paint on big sheets of cardboard or canvas.

Travel to an exotic port -- India, Italy, Bali or even the demolition derby in Bithlo, Florida -- that will generate profound and unforgettable creative energy. Document everything you see and experience. Note the stuff that really resonates with you. It takes a while sometimes to discern why an experience is valuable or inspiring. If it's not recorded, the true nature of the event will be lost and you will only have the distorted memory that loses focus over time... but at least you did it.

Inertia makers for the established creative

Feeling stuck can be harder for an established creative because there seems more to risk, more invisible barriers to overcome and more to unlearn. Turn to the **Connectivity** and **VoiceFinding** section and do the exercises (and then tell me you got nuthin'. I won't believe you).

I'm already pretty good, thanks.

You may be in the place of not knowing what you don't know. But you will eventually realize you can always improve. Pretend that you could stand to learn something new right now. You might also be in the third stage of learning, conscious competency, where you are already hot on the trail of getting good, assimilation and refinement, still a great place to push out. Growth takes a lifetime.

A little success can stop you from growing and improving. Don't let ego get in the way of true transcendent growth. Feeling a little too good about yourself stops growth dead in its tracks. There is nothing more dangerous than success to turn someone into an egomaniac. Strive for humility. There is always some-one better.

I am raisin toast. The burn-out phase.

You aren't a vending machine. It takes balance and regular refills to stay juiced. Take a break. Go to the gym. Walk around the lake. Take a trip. Be with fellow creatives. Read a lot of good books that have nothing to do with what you do. Join Habitat for Humanity. Learn something new. Employ all your senses. Get a massage. Take a science class. Go on a road trip. Take a workshop and trust the instructor.

Being successful doesn't mean making crap-tons of money. It means enjoying the now, being in love with the process and a life well-lived. Trust me when I say this -- a full life informs your work in ways you would never have imagine. Even the smallest things can recharge your passion and reestablish delight in the doing, I have seen it countless times.

My brain gets in my way

This could be Number One on the list, I hear it so much. We beleaguered creative souls can find a gaggle of ways to self-sabotage. No shortage of side emotional distractions, ADD distractions, family distractions, thinking too much, not enough, procrastination.

There are countless reasons for not following through, and they might feel valid because you're sitting in a big puddle of self-induced distraction called avoidance.

And, like anything else, you either make time to do it and power through your roadblocks or nothing happens. Time goes right on by and the only loss is your own. One solution is to create your own space to work in, as discussed in **Connectivity** and let the closing of the door be the trigger for you to work. And shut out the rest of the world.

Here are a few other ways we make our process harder, and what can be done to minimize these impediments.

1) ADD. Make a list or a contract of what you want to accomplish. Write it down on a sticky note. Put it in front of you and work in short, intense spurts.

2) Overworking. For beginner to intermediate painters, too much of a good thing is too much. Too many notes, too much detail. Stay on the bigger idea, step back, work in stages, put the small tools away, do small studies first. Put a time limit on it.

3) Procrastination. Put your studio time on the calendar, mornings or nights, but be consistent. Set a reminder on your phone or computer. Start with short spans of time, 30 minutes to an hour. Just do something.

4) Clutter. Plan time to just organize and clean your space so the next time you come in, the clutter won't distract you.

5) Canvas fright. Plan simple exercises rather than going for the main event. Just move paint.

6) Commit. Get an accountability partner to create with to keep you in it.

7) I shouldn't even have to say this. Stay off your technology for one hour each day.

8) Delegate. Get others to do the stuff that interferes with your *you* time. It will pay for itself.

9) Take a workshop or painting trip *out of your area* for concentrated study time.

10) Get cheap materials so you aren't afraid to waste, put the expensive stuff on top.

11) Stop doing it the way you've always done it and do something different.

12) Sequester yourself. Apply for an artist in residence or get an RV and go to Moab... but not the one with the 1-800 number on the side, that's embarrassing.

13) Can't get no satisfaction. Your aesthetic exceeds your ability. You can't change that, nor should you. It is the thing that drives you forward. Get used to it.

My teacher said I was A) no good or B) that I'm supposed to only do it his/her way.

I've heard versions of this a lot, your teacher was A) an idiot or B) an egotistical idiot. I've taught hundreds of people, I know that anyone can learn anything and that there are almost an infinite number of ways to solve any problem (I've counted). Stop replaying that old tape.

Museums bank on the fact that there are many ways to solve a creative problem, that's why they have so many wings. But most adopted truths are fostered simply because someone didn't think for themselves, or trusted that someone else was right.

"My teacher said we had to do it this way." "An artist must always suffer for his art." "You are never supposed to put something dead center in a painting."

It's an assumption bubble. Here's one thing that is true: Learning the foundational components of any creative act is critical. Only then can you choose which components and lessons to keep and which to bend to your will, or toss.

My biker gang would shun me if they knew I wanted to be a florist.

Ah, the tribal influence. Maybe you should start your own Floral Fantasy Outlaw gang. This is how change happens. (But be wary of rival FFO groups. I've heard they can be very bitchy). If something is getting in your way, move away from the obstacle and drive around it. Take another route.

3 kids and a job... seriously, who has time for this?

1) I can't tell you how many times someone has said, "My (insert parental figure) was an artist" and how much that meant to them. Think of the legacy you will leave, the most important thing you can teach a child is to be an innovative problem solver.

2) Creative exercises can be done anywhere and don't require massive time or money. They can, but they don't always have to.

3) This time is like meditation or yoga. It clears your head, lowers your blood pressure and makes you a more centered, happier individual. It may feel like a luxury, but it pays off in so many ways. Your family will thank me.

4) The thing about creative play/problem-solving is that it can be adapted to anything in your life and can provide you with new ways to look at and solve most problems.

Maybe when I retire I can get some me/play time in.

Why wait? Life is short. DIN (Do it now) should be your credo on all things important.

My family thinks I'm good enough already.

Some families have a hard time with change and frankly they are a little biased. If you have a dream and you follow your dream, everyone benefits: you, family, the world, in that order.

It's just silly.

A 10-year-old came up with the idea of making rubber bands in the shape of animals and made a killing financially. Ideas aren't silly.

Doing and being what is true to you despite what others may be doing or thinking requires courage and trust in one's own vision. True authenticity overcomes all resistance, meets every battle and advances, despite any barriers, real or imagined. It shows itself in time-tested commitment to practice, immunity to failure and to success. It is the singular voice in a crowded room of voices. It is heralded in the great writers, artists, warriors, visionaries and inventors, from cowboys to captains and musicians to missionaries.

If you want it bad enough, then do it.

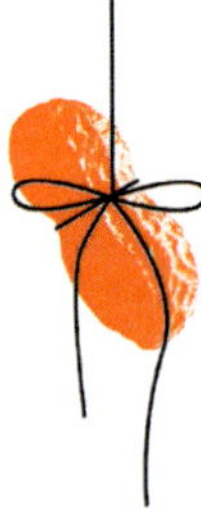

5. Acquisition:
FILLING YOUR LIBRARY

Unprepared. Perhaps you have had this dream or one similar. You sit restlessly in a packed and unfamiliar college classroom. A vague feeling of unease surrounds you as the final exam is plunked in your lap. Then comes the sickening realization that you've not attended a single class or done a lick of the reading. You have done zero homework, no study and, of course, you really need this class to graduate.

Sound familiar? What a horrible feeling that is. Worse, you realize that you are clad only in your underwear (but that may be for another book). This dreamscape comes with a very real sensation of anxiety, dread and a hazy feeling of inadequacy because you realized that you've neglected to fill your brain with the necessary information to complete the task. You were caught flat-footed. It's a little tough to write an essay on the leadership of General Dunncare during the battle of Perspicacityville if you haven't properly and fully prepared yourself.

Creating anything, from new ideas to paintings to Shaker furniture requires a wealth of knowledge, gained experience and experiences, a veritable Alexander the Great library of information, inspiration and training. It's a tad tough to connect the dots if you haven't gone by the DotMart to get some.

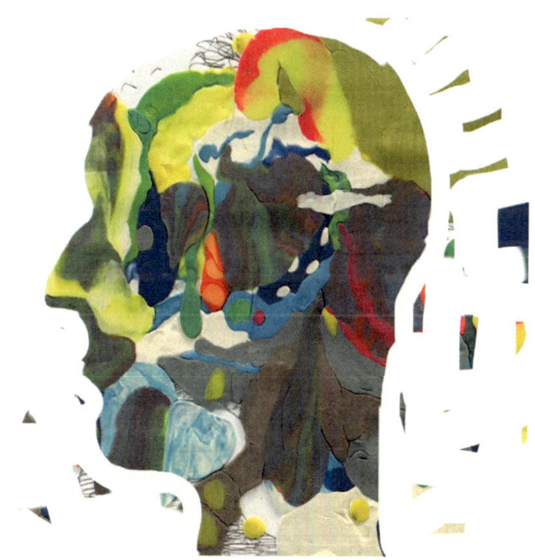

... and by library, I mean brain.

Knowledge is everything. Each little piece is important and, like inspiration, it comes in many forms. Essential to the acquisition phase of the process is assimilating anything and everything from facts to feelings because the most obscure notion or item can be just the trigger you need to build the perfect mousetrap. So how does one go about building such a library?

Here's what we are going to be discovering:

- **Creativity requires knowledge**
- **Be open 24/7**
- **Observe, collect, absorb**
- **Cross-pollinate**

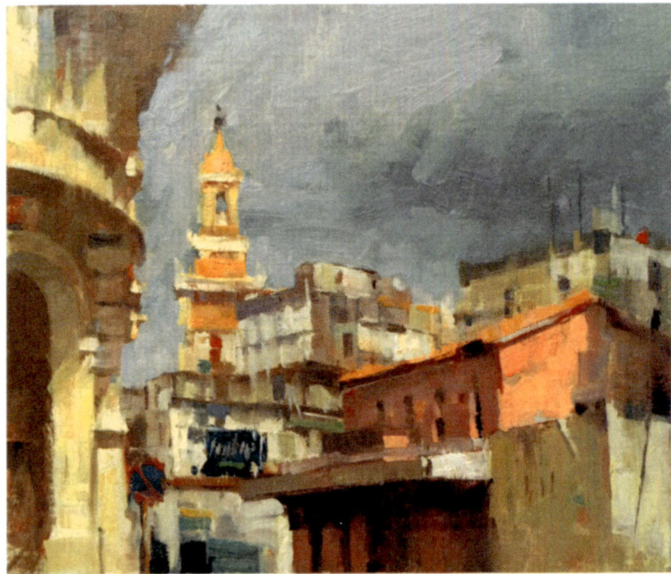

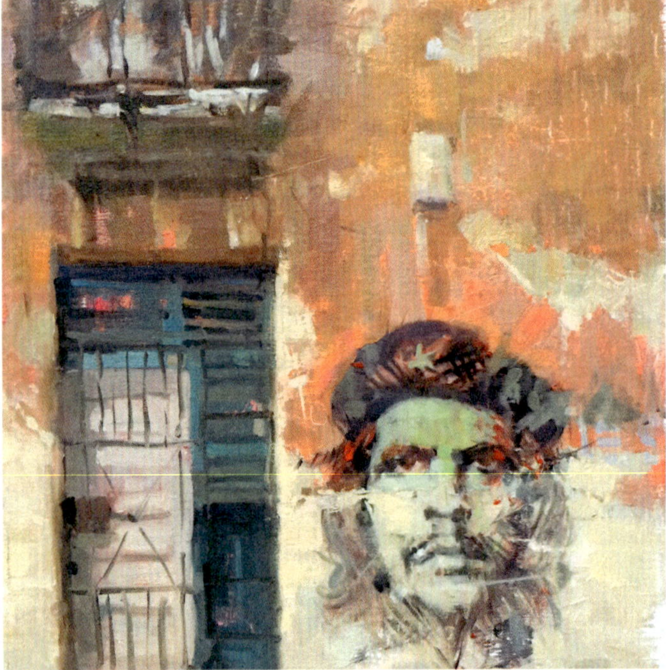

2 small on location paintings from a trip Cuba.
La Floradita, oil on canvas 10 x 12 in., *Chez Che* 12 x 12 in. Oil on canvas

Survey. A trip to Italy can put an entire rack of both real and metaphorical books in your personal library to be filed under Rise and Fall or Ancient Civilizations, Architecture, olive oil, St. Peters Basilica, Romance for that beautiful person whose eyes met yours and inspired that fiery scenario, authentic handmade pasta and so on. In lieu of that, visit some ethnic shops; Mexican, Italian, Chinese in Anywhere USA and you will find endless stacks of ideas, stories, textures, things that do things, kitsch, bad art and period whatevers. All fertile soil from which new ideas grow.

During the writing of this book, I took advantage of a year of travel to Hawaii, Cuba, Italy, Maine, New Mexico and Idaho to paint, spent time with respected artist friends, discuss, ask questions and put the things I learned into my classes. As I was also in the state of acquisition for this effort, I became acutely aware of the importance of each experience, every conversation and event, pulling from the experiences more and more pieces to fit into the puzzle. Not only did I return with a satchel of paintings, I came back with notes, observations and small epiphanies about the creative process. It wasn't so much planned this way, but I was open to everything that crossed my path.

Study. It shouldn't need to be said -- to be good at anything one needs to practice, absorb and apply over and over, mastering the fundamentals of whatever modality in which one wishes to excel. Each of the facets of creating are essential. The filling of the library is for inspiring the design of your Gaudi castle, which is built on top of the foundational slab of fundamentals that you've toiled so hard to acquire.

Experience. Four years of art history in college, AKA Sleep Study class, where reams of art data flew at me only to fall in futility on the desk beside my head. That is until my third year when I signed up for the magical inspiration tour of lifetime, a six-week humanities survey of Italy, Greece, England, France, Switzerland, and Germany. Through this class I experienced first-hand almost every art form and architectural landmark that I had slept through. Learning in a college slide presentation about Michelangelo carving the Pieta out of cold marble at 21 is somewhat better than doing math problems. But seeing this moving work of perfection in the St. Peters Basilica is the Rolling Stones live in concert.

It sparked an entirely new point of view of every art form that had been summarily dismissed by somnambular detachment, because it was experienced and not just learned. I then committed to reabsorbing what I had worked so hard to not learn in the first place. The words in the humanities books became real. Experience becomes knowledge, which transforms into comprehension, then assimilation.

Being a creative individual means being open to everything, whether it's in your wheelhouse, a different point of view or something the Creative Spirit drops in your lap. Being exposed to new information expands your view to make bigger, brighter, newer mental constellations to guide you down your path.

I have an unrequited love of physics. By this, I mean that I love it, I'm fascinated by it, but it doesn't love me. However, I don't have to fully understand it, to add to my library the general concepts of how the universe operates and the many ways scientists have tried to explain the nearly unexplainable. The atom works in a way that is similar to a solar system, as does a galaxy and a thought molecule. I can see a connection between a science-based belief system and a faith-based one.

Both believe in the seemingly unbelievable, both have fantastic stories of the unseen, alternate universes, powers that are felt, but not visible, and both have various sects and systems that don't agree with the opposing points of view. One thing can inform another completely unrelated thing, as when two elements are combined to form something new. It doesn't take a genius to realize the bigger the brainhouse, the bigger the ideas.

All this gathering of experiences and knowledge and existing notions, movements, concepts, processes and experiential doing is not just preparation for the game. It's adding a thousand plays to your playbook. Practice makes more perfect, sure, but it also makes you just like all the others who are practicing the same stuff. Perform at your best level with the highest degree of practice, acquired knowledge, experience and resources.

Stay Open

Get yourself out there. Immerse yourself in the new to further expand and refine your objective and subjective points of view. The curious mind is ever-vigilant for the unfamiliar, adding new insights, expanding world views. Watching the news or a television documentary might teach you a little. But immersing yourself physically in an issue will teach you a lot. Trips to Honduras for Habitat for Humanity and Cuba on a painting expedition were well-fillers for me.

Again, my paradigm pants got altered. Viewing third-world life from a first-world chair doesn't offer much beyond a small case of the uncomfortables. But standing in it, experiencing it with all the senses, digging up the dirt and lifting out the stones with few tools and witnessing powerfully poor yet happy children gives much.

Notebooks, sketches and paintings of experiences brought home to be placed in the real or metaphorical library were the impetus for several new series of paintings. Key to this kind of experience, beyond being intrepid enough to go, is being in a state of acceptance of everything around you, more than a series of events, a series of ideas.

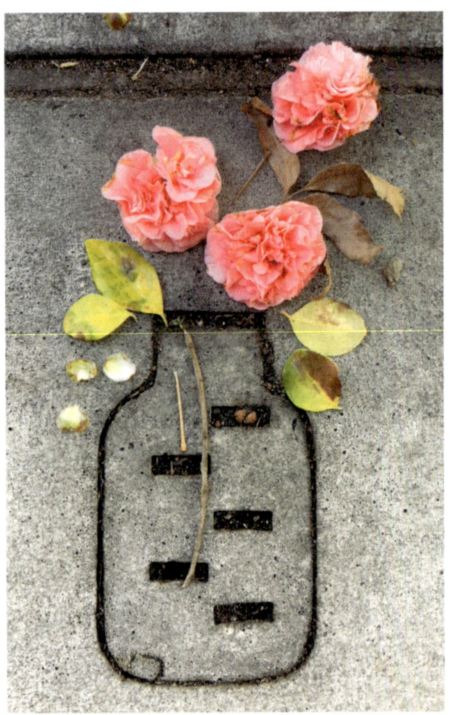

One of the greatest lessons one can receive from painting on location is that the process allows for so much more absorption of stimuli. Standing for hours in one spot while painting the Grand Canyon expands the sensory perceptions. It's no longer just a big hole in the ground. It becomes a living, breathing organism, an ever-moving monument to the power of time.

Anything that you can do that is unfamiliar or uncomfortable can provide new insights that can be applied to solution-finding. How many stories have we heard of some Eureka moment that came when the inspired experienced something outside his or her area of expertise? The moment comes when the inspired is in the state of being open, either consciously or subconsciously. An idea bridge is built when the seeker does the hard work and study, fills the library and places themselves in a position of connect-ability.

Open is...

Open is looking for the things you haven't seen, making a connection on the fly, having your radar set on everything, never hesitating to ask "What if?" While on a spring walk, I noticed two things in my path, a sidewalk access "key" that resembled a ball jar and some fallen flowers. Putting these two things together altered the meaning of each.

When visiting a favorite spot, look with fresh eyes. Look for what you haven't seen. In a museum, rather than going straight for desert, seek out new inspiration for your shelves, look not just for the favored art forms but the ones yet undiscovered to you. One may have a passion for realism or impressionism, but seeing the familiar for the 10th time does little to add to the inspiratoreum.

Pore over abstracts, absorb the installations, take in the African ritual masks, find the narratives, the experimental, Pre-Columbian, armor, Chinese propaganda art, and the in-your-face WTF art that may just hold a jewel of an idea that can be taken home and applied to fashion a new connection. The inquisitive mind views all things through the WHY and WHY NOT filters.

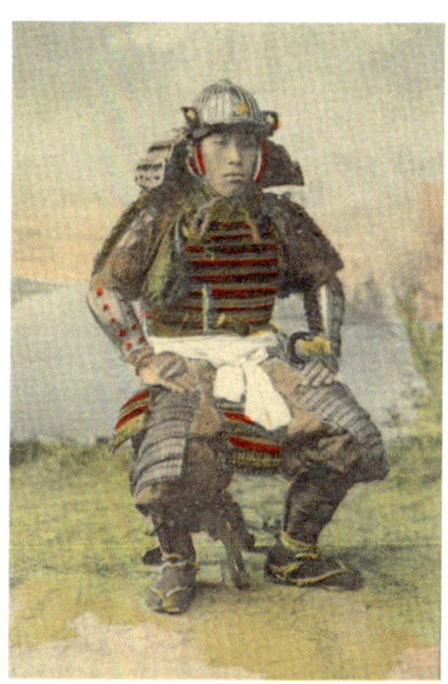

The last of the samurai. I'd kill for that suit. Image courtesy of The New York Public Library.

Why was this made? What was the purpose of this thing? What am I to receive from it? What can I do with this information? Why not another way? It's easy to let inspiration slip past when focusing on the next item on the to-do list, but, whenever possible, practice turning on these receptors. Ask why. Make note of the answers and write them down to etch them into your brain.

Acquiring in this open state means being both left- and right-brained, intellectual and emotional, a problem-solver and a problem-finder all at once. How is this possible? There are countless ways to solve any problem but the solutions based on a very specific set of parameters related to the problem are the ones that usually work best. Collecting solutions from one set of parameters (like why a Samurai suit is designed the way it is) and applying it to a different set (like how to make a comfortable bear-defense suit) can give you an instant synergetic AHA!!

Divining test

4 glyphs found painted on the floor of a cave. No way to know which way is up. The cave location is unknown. What story is being told? How we interpret these symbols depends on our background and knowledge base. Is that a cloud or waterfall or snake triplets. Sun or roundtable meeting?

Your story depends on your story.

Being in touch with both the intellectual responses and the feelings of an experience will bring expanded understanding to what you already know. Gaining access to the minds and motives of others, and seeking as much understanding as possible, enlarges your world view to the epic. To make this point, consider this problem:

***Record and absorb.* Why create in a vacuum? There's no air in there. Go and experience.**

Example: What if you aspire to paint the atmospheric effects on distant mountains, to capture the way light is filtered and refracted by all those little particulates of dust and water? You could make it up based on a few hazy memories or perhaps work from photos of foggy landscape OR you can go, observe, study and absorb it on location. Experience it in the round. Feeling it is as much a part of understanding as seeing it. Use all the senses, you have them for a reason. Write about it, sketch it out, make color notes, feeling notes, what the sounds and textures were, create on-location analogies... *the air in thick veils filters the trees across the soft distance reforming them into hazy deckle-edged paper shapes.* Think metaphorically. You can "see" fog or you can add its multiple inspirations and uses to your understanding of it.

Once the foggy event is recorded and etched into your mind, deeper connections can be formed and new associations can be made from that experience. When the sensory aspects are fully experienced, the intellectual understanding, the physics of it, follows. Then the metaphorical connections (i.e. the fog was like a sheet of frosted mylar between me and the mountain) can be made and the conceptual applications, whether literal or figurative, follow. Merely witnessing an occurrence or event, even the seemingly unforgettable, only places that moment in temporary storage. But participating in it, by recording in words or in paint that moment in time, ingrains the stimuli into the library for good, so that relationships can be forged from the events and applied in future situations.

These collections of recorded experiences captured intellectually, in the affective and the visual, as well as physical items and totems acquired along the way, can be the materials to construct new thought bridges.

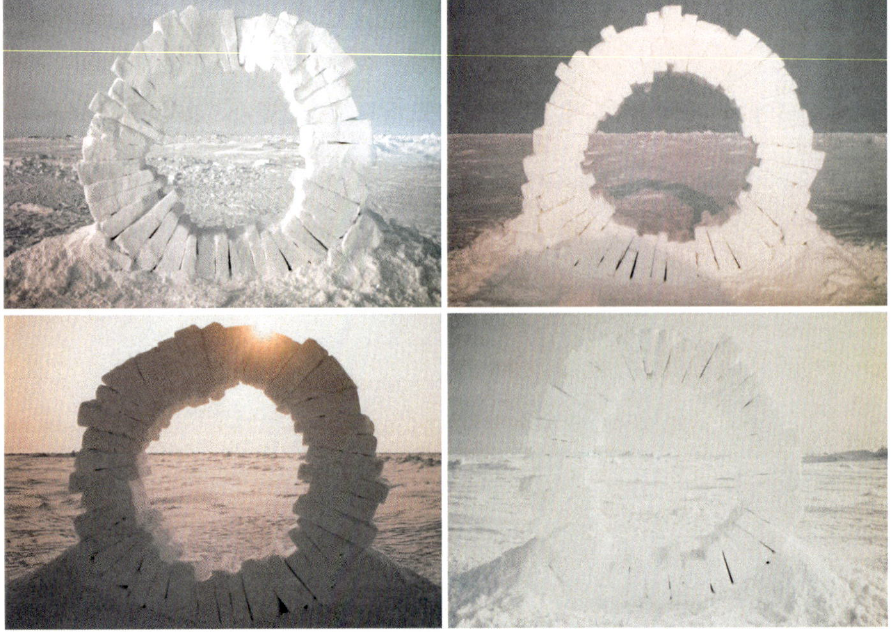

Andy Goldsworthy
Touching North, North Pole, 22, 23, 24 April 1989
Suite of 5 color photographs, 45" x 57 ¼" each.
Edition of 10

These 4 massive snow rings were constructed using the traditional snow cutting and packing techniques of the indigenous Inuit. The center of this construction marked the location of the North Pole, so that to look through any two rings was to look due South. As with most of Mr. Goldsworthy's works, these sculptures were designed to return from whence they came. The only record being his photography of the work.

The artist Andy Goldsworthy is one of those rare creatives who takes the everyday wonder of environment, the accessible and taken for granted nature of nature, and twists it in a way that challenges the perception of an environment. What he does with concepts that are born from snow, water, fog, ice, rock, and the juxtaposition of the organic natural and geometric forms, changes the way the viewer sees the relationship between nature and art.

His unique creations are visual metaphors built from the familiar. After seeing his work, I have new ways to file experiences in my library, new references for rain, for example. I can see it as a physics event, an idea diffuser, ribbons of water, a digital grayscale filter of the largest order, particulate wall, mind clouds, constellations of water droplets, ruiner of picnics and on and on.

Collect-Observe-Absorb

Visiting other artist's studios, I am often impressed by their library of art books, prints and paintings that are lined up, stacked and strewn about as a physical testament to the quest for knowledge and inspiration. But there's more to understanding art than looking at paintings and more to inspiration than looking at like-minded material. From an illustrator's standpoint, just studying other artists (or if you are a musician, other musicians in your genre) gives you only the point of view that you already have. It's preaching to the choir.

In other words, I know how I see the world, I want to find out how others might see it differently. Being open to the diversity of visual communication methods will springboard you more quickly to new ways of seeing.

For example, a book on the Quilters of Gee's Bend is a great addition to any painting archive. This band of women, without formal training, created quilts in isolation from the rest of the world. They didn't follow the rules of quilting, so they had no concern for breaking them. They had no real awareness of abstract art and yet they created some of the most wonderfully complex and inventive abstracts an art lover could see. Moreover, each quilt held a story because the fabrics were only what they had at the time, a collection of worn jeans from a deceased or unfaithful husband, sheets, dresses and curtains, etc.

Being aware of the purity and authenticity of these things adds to the impact. And it's a fascinating response. An untrained artist can get lucky once in a while. But, somehow, each of these works is as strong as the next.

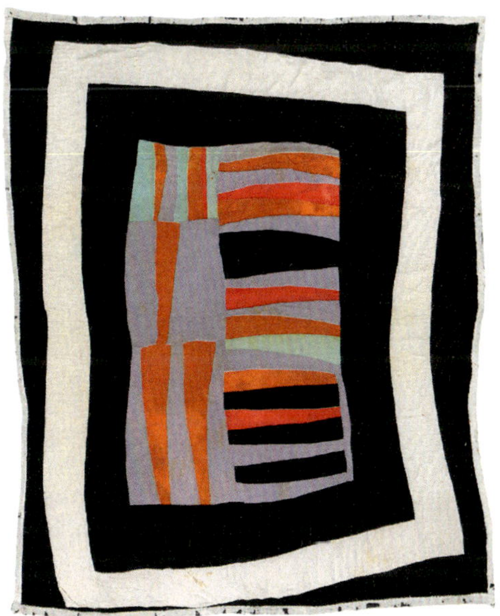

Loretta Pettway (b. 1942)
Medallion, c. 1960.
Synthetic knit and cotton stacking material. 80 x 70 in.
Photo Credit: Pitkin Studio / Art Resource, NY

A matriarch of the quilters of Gee's bend, Ms. Pettway's work is a mix of improvisational and traditional methods handed down through generations. The quilters often created "my way" quilts which were more exploratory and expressive. Her quilts (and those of other G.B. artists) are included in the permanent collection of the Museum of Modern Art, NY.

The Visionary artists are unique individuals who are compelled to make their art, not as an exercise in commerce or self-expression for the masses. It's pure compulsive, unfiltered, untethered, crazy art. It's raw and primitive. They speak to no one in their own private language. These works are not for everyone and you may wonder why you should bother to investigate. The Visionary artist has no external why and no rules. This is art that has no influence, no constraints, no training and is purely authentic. That's why.

One of the biggest things to take from viewing a variety of styles and varying methodologies in art, music and the written word is that intent differs from artist to artist and piece to piece, and the intent drives the nature of the work. A period travel poster is a lesson in simple graphic communication with the purpose of inspiring wanderlust at a time where the only other modes of communication were books and word of mouth.

A book on wallpaper design brings boundless adaptable ideas for color and pattern and period styles where the sole intent of each sample is simply to decorate a wall. Italian mid-20th century design and Streamline design give worship to the curve with clean, aerodynamic shapes in architecture, transportation, power tools and appliances, though, for the life of me, I don't know why an iron would ever need to be aerodynamic.

A collection of African masks gives insight into tribal ritual and can inspire new ways to represent form and fashion, to wit, one Mr. P. Picasso, whose work was changed by exposure to these art forms.

There are countless examples of artists pulling from not just other styles and intents, but completely different sources to inspire a concept, a body and even an oeuvre. Both Pablo Picasso and Paul Simon were greatly influenced by African art and artists. They used it as a point of departure and transformed the context to come up with new visual and auditory languages. Japanese wood-block prints became a source of inspiration for many European Post-Impressionist painters who added the flat interpretations of shape and pattern into their own vocabulary. Influence and adaptation from outside sources is a launching pad for growth.

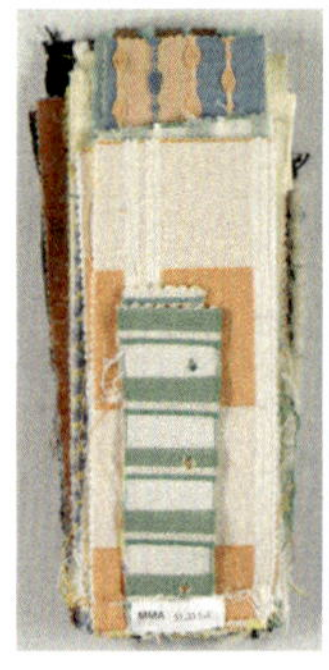
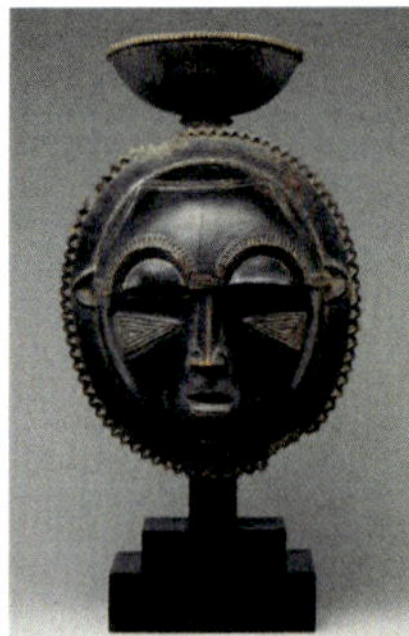
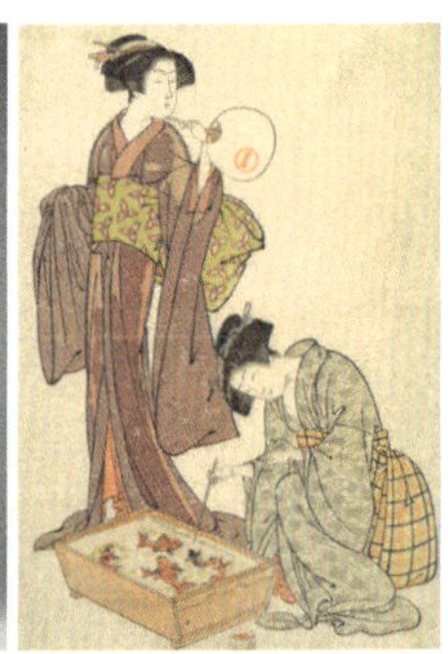

From the archives of the Metropolitan Museum of art, a swatch book of Bauhaus fabrics, an African Moon mask, and a Japanese wood block print by Kitao Shigemasa, one can find boundless inspiration.

I'm sure you have tastes that go beyond your genre or scope. But, the point is, diversity is key. Look beyond your usual sources. Go to a flea market, not to peruse the junk or ogle anything that fits your area of interest, but to find the heavily patinaed things with outmoded purposes, stuff that was designed, crafted and produced to fill a utilitarian need in the prevailing style of the day. Look for beauty in something in which you have no interest, objects to which new meanings can be assigned.

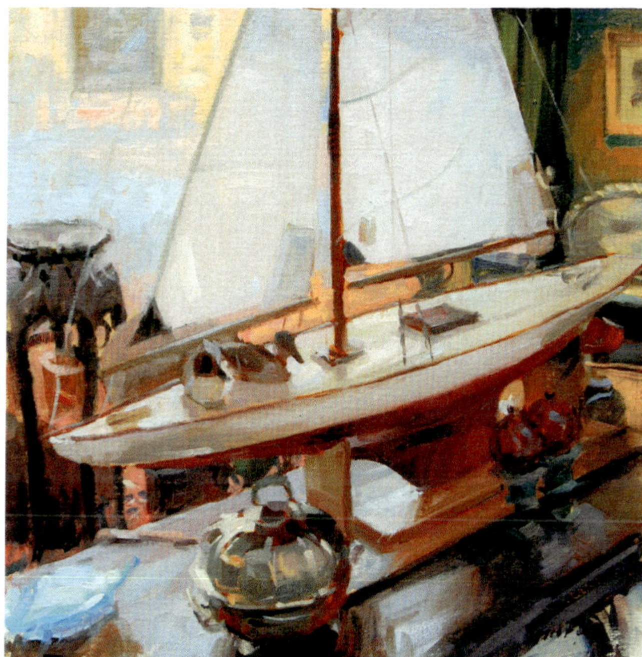

The long journey 20 x20 in. oil on canvas

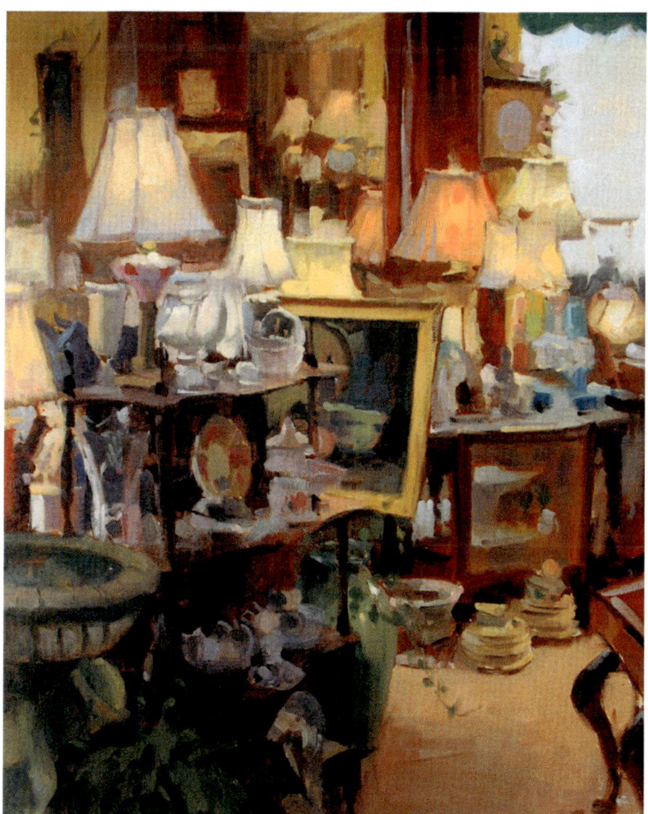

Hardy's lights 16 x20 in. oil on canvas

A mid-1940's electric drill could inspire the design of an office building or an awesome spaceship. When one is open, places of this nature can be viewed in a myriad of ways -- by its parts, by its groupings, culling compositional ideas or stories and prompts that may come from unusual random pairings of things. One could write novels.

Got a blank page to fill? Go on assignment. Visit one of these conceptual playgrounds. Pick two or three items that are unrelated and connect them with a story. Write it, sketch it, graphic novel it, don't judge it just let it run. See where it takes you.

One of my favorite sources of inspiration is to gain access to this kind of visual treasury, whether a store or a personal collection, to create compositions out of the clutter. It is a challenge to make order out of chaos and create visual essays from the items. It's an example, in and of itself, of being open.

Having spent a lifetime, as we all have, in stores and shops, focused only on what was on the to-do list to pick up, I paid no attention to my surroundings in any other way than where I might find the pickles or the #4 Gangley-Sprocket wrench. While wondering around on a rainy day, I ducked into a vintage book store during a heavy downpour, one of those dusty old antiques and retired book marts with a cat. My little muse whispered, "You should paint this." By being open to the different, an idea was born, followed by an ongoing body of work.

Stay Open

Look closer to see a sidewalk or the top of a tattered school desk for what seems like the first time and receive inspiration from the patterns and textures. The brain is a miracle of connections, both literally and figuratively. When your mind is receptive, as in not focused on your taxes or the leaking pipe that awaits you when you get home, it's free to peruse the smorgasbord of stimuli and piece things together like a jigsaw puzzle to create new associations and links.

When on visual walkabouts, two very handy tools to have on board at all times are the notebook and the camera. In case you don't want to bring that Ming-ish Dynasty vase home, take a pic and file it under All things Ming. Not up to buying that string-art ship creation? A few quick notes and sketches about compositional ideas to take the intent home and bend it to your own. And sketching and writing allows for freer interpretation and adaptation than videos or photos. Just sayin.'

As a plein air (outdoor) artist, I've had the good fortune to go to all sorts of new places and really soak in the regional experiences and revelations. Often the paintings that come home with me are picked up later for ideas. These Polaroids in paint produce visceral memories that a smart phone photo can't; sensations, temperature, wind, smells, meeting an elk family in Yosemite, etc. The paintings themselves become portals to life experiences, a kind of a postcard with smell-o-vision. Holding any of these studies in my hands can spark plenty of connections and inspiration for a painting or a story.

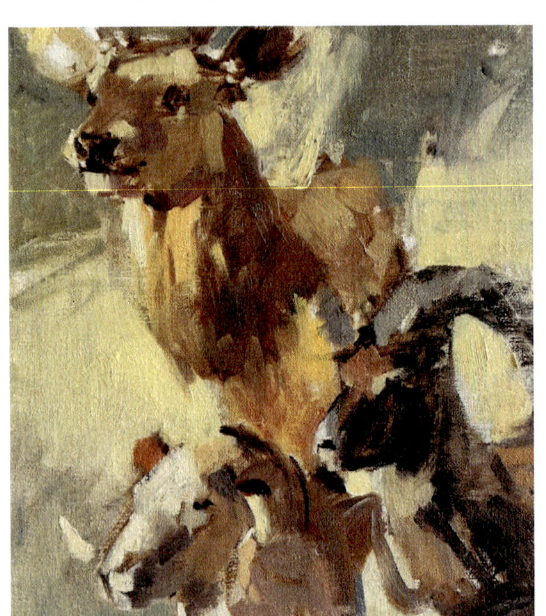

Trophies 11x14 in. oil on canvas

Story time: While painting in Sedona, Arizona, I wandered into a local medicine man store. They don't have those where I'm from (Normal town), and the CVS was out of sage sticks. It was unfamiliar, so surely it had to be explored. In this richly textured and visually fecund store were rabbit foot pendants, jade beads, sage smudge sticks, incense, snake skins, herbs for potions, (more than likely, eye of newt and warthog hair) and, of course, a pile of cow skulls (yes, I painted them).

It was like Spellmart. On the wall was every kind of taxidermy animal head (painted those too), along with a whole herd of unusual critter skulls.

I stood there, taking in a large, alien-looking oxen head, with horns many times the size of the head, and zero room for brain cavity. A lovely, patchouli-scented, bead-adorned woman with cascading hair walked up to join me in appreciation of this behemoth and said: "It's an Ankole-Watusi from Africa. I have one over my bed. I'm a fertility goddess and it brings good juju to me and all of my lovers." To which I evasively responded, "No kidding, do you have a card?"

I took home a few artifacts, an entire line of painting ideas and the business card of a fertility goddess to file in my library, all from one 35-minute side trail to a MagiMart. Open has its rewards.

Cross-pollinate

Allow new stimulus to exist without judgment and hone the ability to accept it as is, and harvest it. If you are an opera fan, with the music and the drama and the people dying for love, and it is your favorite thing to do, then go and do something that is not that. Go to a monster truck rally and experience that subculture. Challenge your bias.

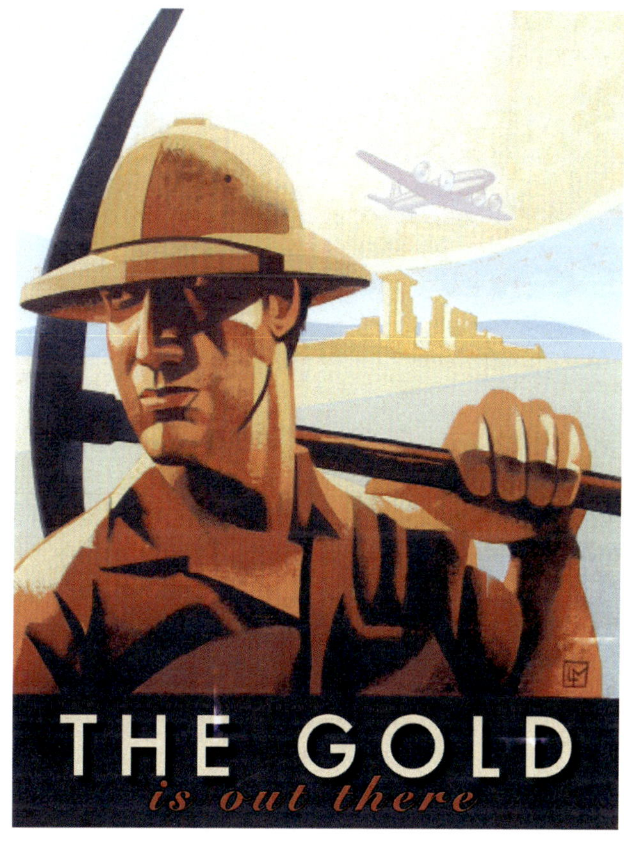

Not your thing? Perfect! Sailing into unfamiliar territory, especially ones marked with dragons on the map, means you are exhibiting one of the hallmarks of the creative mind -- tolerance of ambiguity. You are unafraid of placing yourself in new situations and experiences. It is the allaying of fear for greater gain.

Look for the story. A biker bar (just an example), can get you in touch with a subculture unlike your own, unless, of course, you are already a confirmed biker. You can frame it as a sociological observation, watching people who wish to be different but still feel the need to belong, so they end up all being the same. Penguins in leather. But if you are open, you might find the possibilities in it, an operetta in leather and chrome.

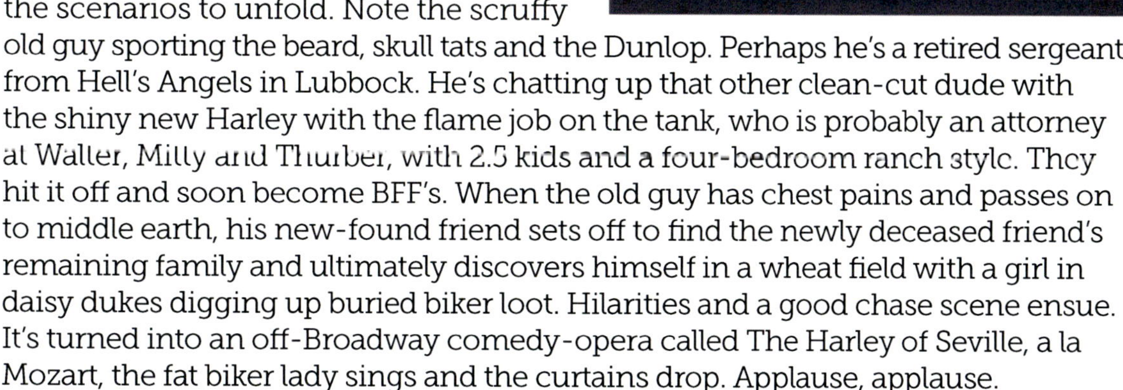

Find the story opportunities and allow the scenarios to unfold. Note the scruffy old guy sporting the beard, skull tats and the Dunlop. Perhaps he's a retired sergeant from Hell's Angels in Lubbock. He's chatting up that other clean-cut dude with the shiny new Harley with the flame job on the tank, who is probably an attorney at Waller, Milly and Thurber, with 2.5 kids and a four-bedroom ranch style. They hit it off and soon become BFF's. When the old guy has chest pains and passes on to middle earth, his new-found friend sets off to find the newly deceased friend's remaining family and ultimately discovers himself in a wheat field with a girl in daisy dukes digging up buried biker loot. Hilarities and a good chase scene ensue. It's turned into an off-Broadway comedy-opera called The Harley of Seville, a la Mozart, the fat biker lady sings and the curtains drop. Applause, applause.

What would your inner adult say about such foolishness? "Quit your daydreaming and dawdling, it's just wasteful flibbertigibbet." This no longer applies to you. You can take that inner adult voice and store it under "S" for Shut the hell up. Paying attention, collecting, accepting, absorbing and adapting is the mother-in-law of invention.

You might even end up with a cool collection of African masks, exotic oxen skulls and snow globes from India, starting a new art movement or writing a libretto involving bikers.... perhaps even the next Wizards of Oz.

Define-Filter

So, now you have an in-progress collection. Hopefully, it's not all stored in your head, because sooner or later you may forget where you put it, overwritten by some other memory or immediate need. You may already have a lot of objects and collectibles and you don't need any more. But some things just need to get got, like a clay pot with the surface that you want to get in your work because it is tactile and doesn't translate to a photo or note pad. If it applies as inspiration, it will pay for itself in the long run. It's probably even a write-off.

Usually, sketch books, notebooks, book books and digital files can suffice, but the acquisition phase is not just for intellectual fodder. It's for the sensory experiences of sight, sound, touch, taste, smell and the associative aspects. While some people cherish more the experiences that money can buy, and not the things, the objects themselves (raku pots, vintage medicine jar, blue willow vases, etc.) can trigger the magic and the results can pay for your next library expansion experience.

Collect observations, weird old tools and artifacts. Journal, save old magazines, buttons, vintage photos, catalogs of travel posters, textures, unusual materials and surfaces, period toys, cropped photos of old wall patinas and torn handbills, anything that can lend you some of its one-of-a-kind juju. I'm not suggesting becoming a hoarder, the old-school illustrators had what was called a morgue file, drawers filled with tear sheets and photos, closets of costumes and shields, a repository for ideas yet unborn.

Yes, we have the internet search engines to track down things when we need them. But it's not the same as finding a unique item that can be held and turned and the history felt with the fingers, the surfaces analyzed in different light.

This assortment of things and events is for now and later use. Trust what this stuff can at some point be used for. Your library is just like those other libraries, (except homeless people don't use your bathroom). It's the erector set for your future MindCraft city. I can't tell you how many times an old sketch, collectible, notion or old photo album has come to good use.

Now, to be honest, I have purged most my morgue files from days' past, at least the things whose inspirational radiation has been spent. As collecting is essential, purging is cathartic. Loads and loads of old sketches and paintings have been burned or painted over, unless they have some unique quality that is yet to be harvested. It is a rite of passage to let go of the dead, release the weary into the universe. I use this as a transitional passage to the next body of work, the next chapter.

The connections. Items, notes, sketches, notions, compositional motifs, one-line jokes and favorite photos are pinned and taped to the wall in my studio, Beautiful Mind style, while the more tactile things and experiments are filed on various shelves and tables to be touched, considered and connected.

Photos are stored in my computer and phone, but nothing replaces the tactile feeing that comes from the vintage. Having all these things visible at a glance makes it easier to form the connections, much like having two word lists side by side, I can circle one item and draw a line to a completely different item, join the experiences or underlying concepts, and see what synergy shows up.

Acquisition is not confined to home or library additions. You can be in acquisition mode all of the time; inspiration is 24 / 7. Being open is both a right- and left-brain event, observational and intellectual in form and function, while also being cognizant of emotional responses. Being open means being aware, like walking into a crowded room and scanning for ninjas. Inspiration can come from anywhere at any time. You may see something that leads to a connection with another element or idea, and that resulting connection generates new thought. No matter how seemingly superfluous, make note of it.

Recently, while driving on the long straight, unchanging stretch of highway that goes from where I lived in Florida to pretty much anywhere else in Florida, I began to pay attention to the billboards. At first I noted the variety of designs of the billboards, almost all bad, and wondered if the person who created the designs had ever driven a car on a highway before. Then I noticed the set of messages, white type on a black board that were purportedly from God that said, "I'm still here... God" and "I'm not mad... God".

And I thought, I wonder if God really did have his own billboards, what would they say?

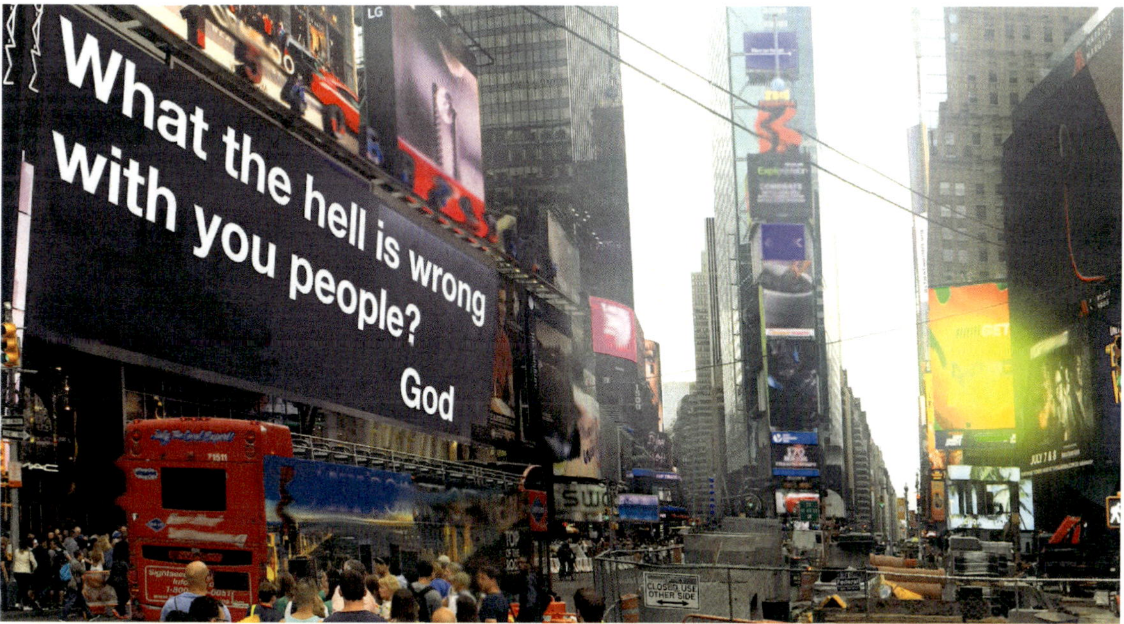

What if God really did have his own billboards?

This is a creative connection on the fly. The idea truck is rollin.' Seemingly unimportant connections can show up when you need them and sometimes when you don't. Learn to trust and allow them to happen and write them down. Every five seconds a great idea gets forgotten. Trust in it when it comes and have the foresight to record it. The subconscious mind is a terrible thing to waste.

The trick to all of this collecting/observing stuff is having the presence of mind to view each thing as something else. Visual simile. I liken thee to a summer's day. Bikers in a bar are like penguins in leather. An old topography map could be a map of a face or a fabulous background for mixed-media assemblages. Vintage black and white photos are a past-moment story yet to be written. The ceramic bulldog from the 60's and the penny and the 1950's alphabet block combined are an odd narrative waiting to be portrayed.

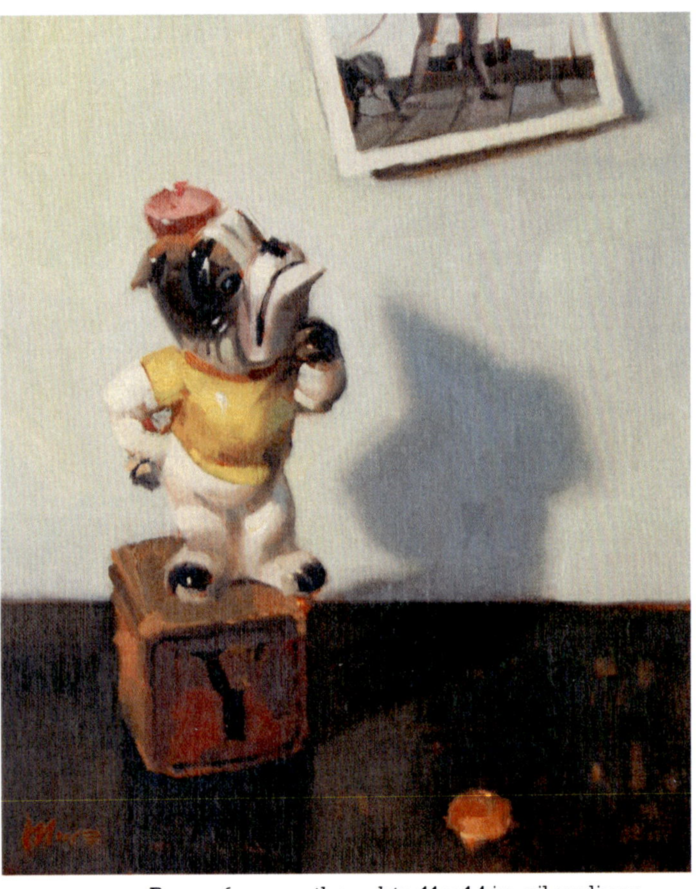

Penny for your thoughts, 11 x 14 in. oil on linen

By the way, if you choose to add real stuff to your library and come home with a lot of oddities, you should have some pretty darn good rationales at the ready:

That other person in your life: Excuse me, and what's with the Yak skin?

You: Well, if we should ever move to the north after the Armageddon, we'll have something comfy to wear and we can blend in better with our natural surroundings.

Yaks don't live on this continent.

Well, if we were to be in a tribal-based cult and live in a commune, we will have something to trade for food.

But we go to a Catholic church.

Well, did you know the smell of a Yak skin can ward off termites?

Really?

Yes, and also, I like it, that's why. I may design an entire line of towels called DRYAK and sell it to Ikea.

Oh. Okay then. Put it in the garage next to the Iditarod sleds.

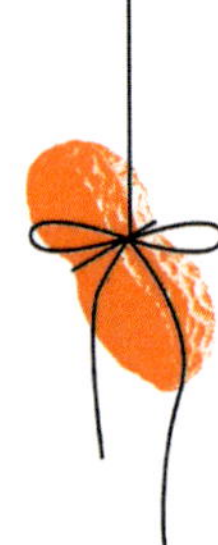

6. Connectivity:
CREATIVE ALCHEMY

It seems some people assume that those who are creative are just naturally that way, able to produce an idea, a painting or song without much effort. While it's generally understood that there are some who are gifted with high intelligence quotients in the areas of language, visual/spatial skills and music, the lion's share of us come by it the old-fashioned way.

Gradual refinement, employing a multi-leveled thought and implementation process combined with years and years of practice. Furniture designers, science fiction writers, painters, fashion designers, the Beatles... all polish their craft through experience and thought.

The epicenter of the creative mind is connectivity, which is the pairing of two or more things in order to make a brand-new thing, a kind of intellectual alchemy. It is Shakespeare's use of metaphor to convey a thought, a lyric in a song describing a sky as bone-colored rather than gray. It is the unlikely marriage of African rhythms and American folk music, a sculpture of a two-story garden shovel in a corporate park or a highly interpretive landscape painting. And it can also be found in a really good joke.

Getting to the state of being open to this kind of thinking takes a bit of process, a pinch of logic, a good deal of unrestricted exploration, a heaping mound of concentrated effort and a whole lot of trust. And, like anything else, it gets easier and better the more you do it.

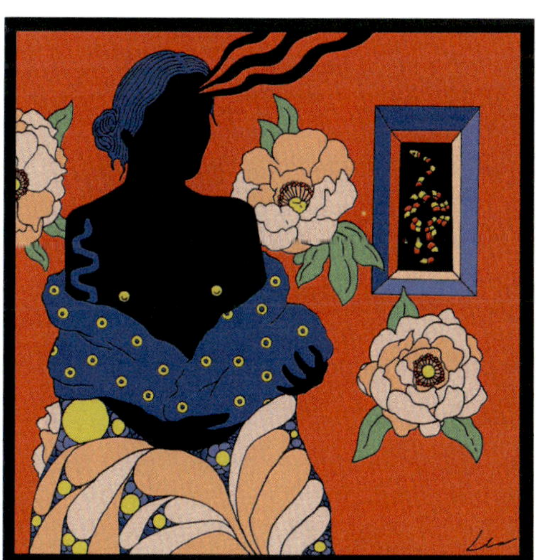

Leo Cagan Horton, ink and digital
While other kids his age are taking selfies with bunny-ear filters, this 16 year old is busy creating his own unique art.

Here's what you'll need:

- **The right frame of mind and permission**
- **Know your stuckness**
- **An environment for creative alchemy**
- **All-points resistance and assumption check**
- **Learn the tools of free-range thinking**
- **Define the parameters of the problem**
- **Define intent and what you bring to the table**
- **Assess your solutions**
- **The problem is a problem**

Permission, play and building sand empires

"How much fun is this?" The thought flits through your mind as you make a drip-sand castle on the beach for the first time in 35 years. You did it as a kid at the lake or on summer vacay. But now as an adult, there you sit, ass-deep in sand, dripping your way to a Gaudi-like thighscraper. As you build this baby with your child or a loved one, your mind brims with stories that fill the small scale granular village, the reigning sand oligarchy, the sand minions, the great location on the beach with the unfortunate eight-hour flood zone, which, as you and the wise sandcastle leaders know, will take this structure and its rich brief history and wash it back to the sand age.

Then you look up in that child-like state of mind and scan the clouds, picking out the creatures, monsters and dinosaur-shaped vessels that are always there, but unnoticed until now. And it occurs to you, "How come I don't do this more often?" Play is fun.

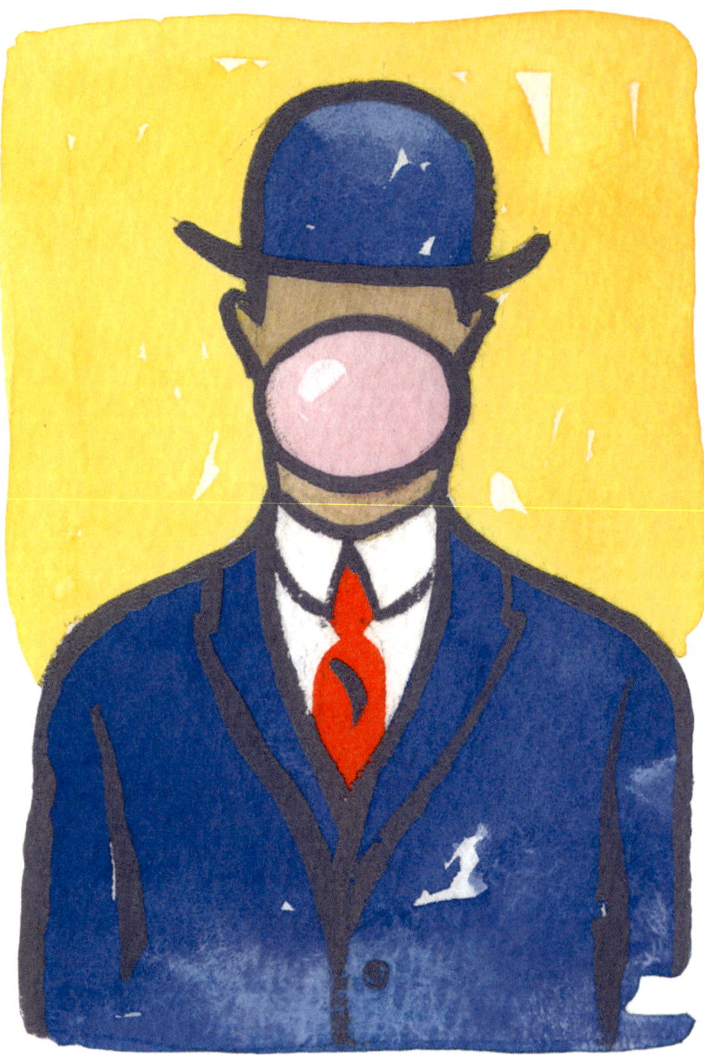

You've probably experienced something similar. If not directly, then perhaps as you've visited the beach you've witnessed it. A child at play. But how often do you see an adult just sitting there alone playing like a child for no reason? Play time, daydreams, imagination... all require permission, as in, "Hey Mom, can I go play sand castles with Big Freddie, Mikey and Gidget?"

Only now it's an internal dialog, one where you give yourself a pass to do the things that might seem silly or a waste of time, even counter-intuitive. This part of the process requires trust, faith and courage and filing the old book of rules under N for "Not today." You are no longer an adult, you are now a big wrinkly kid who does not require permission from anyone to enter the hallowed grounds of imagination and wonder. The last words you should hear from your inner adult should be, "This will be fun, dammit, or you will get a rockin' time-out that you will not soon forget."

If you are a newcomer to the act of play and the path of the curious mind, this pardon from adulthood might be a challenge. You will be moving into uncertainty and that can be uncomfortable, because why, otherwise, have you not done so before? The act of play is now done for us. The current world of creative apps has made us all a bit complacent. They do all the work and make you look good. But where are you in that?

A Martha Stewart recipe on how to make cool birthday unicorn-glitter sprinkle cakes that are gluten free doesn't count either. While satisfying, except for the gluten-free part, it is guided construction. Yes, you make something. But it's handed over to you on a little bamboo tray wrapped in raffia. What I am talking about is more like finding your authentic self in a multi-colored case of Play-Doh. It will take trust in the process and a Magellan-like sense of exploration.

If you are the experienced creative looking for the next in your long line of nexts, this guided play time will help to open the doors, move you out of neutral and quickly get you to a lot of new unexplored territory.

If you are quite happy where you are -- and there is nothing wrong with that -- it could be because you just haven't gotten to that next place. You could be in the process of flesh-ing out whatever you are working on, and not ready for the new growth phase. That's a plateau, the space between growth cycles, which doesn't necessarily mean stuck. A plateau is a stage of assimilation, refinement of intent and process. Being a creative person can mean having more stages than the Rolling Stones.

Usually this growth / plateau cycle repeats in the life of a creative in-dividual. The span of time between the stages of exploration, discovery, inspiration and refinement can run from a few months to a decade or the entire life of the artist. Even if you are comfortable where you are, it's exponentially beneficial to continue to search beyond existing bound-aries to seek new ground and new inspiration, if for no other reason than to give your existing process a little push. Giving yourself this gift of explorative play is like opening all the doors and windows on a beautiful fall day. It's a refresh button for your brain and extra cylinders in your engine.

"It's not what you look at that matters, it's what you see."
- Henry David Thoreau

Imagination: Creativity without boundaries

Permission is to play as imagination is to creativity. You can't have one without the other. Imagination -- creativeness, vision, inspiration, inventiveness, resourcefulness, ingenuity; originality, innovativeness -- we want all these tools in our utility belt. Developing these skills means empowering yourself to go from what is to what if, allowing the mind to break free of the laws of physics and the shackles of the general rules of the day to explore a universe where anything is possible.

The biggest inhibitor to imagination is the self-conscious mind. We place constraints on new ideas or thoughts as being unacceptable, impractical or unrealistic, while, conversely, the unconscious mind, unfettered, in a dream state, can create fantastic scenarios without limitations. What strange irony that the same mind has two vastly different states, confined and free. Developing conscious imagination means, in simple terms, to lose the practicality filters *long enough* to explore any possibility.

In the creative process of problem solving, the first stages of play are just the imagination running free without the judgment of the practical mind. That judgment is saved for later stages to gain access to a broader range of concepts without limitation.

You must commit to freeing your mind and tearing up your logic contract, the one you made long ago with your inner adult. Close your eyes and create a mental picture of you ripping up the Agreement of Practicality as dictated by said Inner Adult, heretofore referred to as you, so that you can be unrestrained to explore the unknown. If you can create that image in your mind, you are using your imagination and you're on your way. While you are at it, make it automatically renewable with a 30-day notification clause.

The difference between imagination and creativity, at least for the purposes of this process, is that imagination is uninhibited inventiveness and creativity is inventiveness, as in, imagination with a purpose, with intent. Intent means solving a specific problem, not just coming up with cool *what if* stuff.

Assignment-based imagination requires more than one idea. It requires a lot of them. I'm going to show you some exercises that are designed to help you with this process of idea development. One thing to be aware of -- your first idea for most things may seem good enough at the time, but first ideas are rarely ideal.

Greatness demands extensive digging, like panning for gold. It's not going to land in the pan on your stove. Look in unfamiliar places and push way past what is reasonable to find what works best. First, develop a lot of concepts; then filter them; then distill the ones that have merit.

But first, a little about how to set ourselves up for brilliance.

Emotional states

A proper emotional state can be a cracker-jack assistant to your mental frame during any creative undertaking. Feelings like joy, happiness, contentment, and ecstasy are pretty darn conducive to free-thinking and allowing your mind to run down the beach naked, while states like stress, distraction, sadness or anger are not.

There are some exceptions to the list of negative states that aren't helpful, and one is dismay, the feeling that you are just flat done with whatever you are doing. When you don't really give a damn about the outcome, you can do surprisingly wonderful things because, well, you don't give a flying donut. And when you don't care you take more chances.

Another powerful driver is emotional distress, like that borne of trauma, loss, grief or heartbreak. Industrial-strength creations need the same level of intense motivation. It is one of the more unfortunate ways to get unstuck. The contemporary soul pop singer Adele made her career on a breakup album. Alphonse Mucha, the Czech Art Nouveau decorative painter, abandoned his popular Art Nouveau style to portray the massive Slav Epic that depicts the history, strife and mythology of his people.

Creators of scores of songs, poems, movies, sculptures and paintings use this intense pathos as an inspirational muse. Art can be a great healer of personal loss as well as the impetus for discovering new ways of interpreting experience.

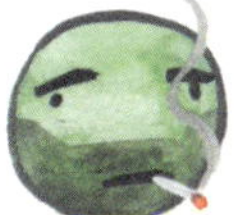 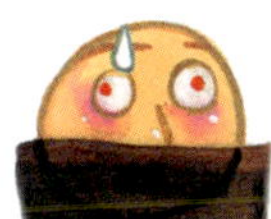 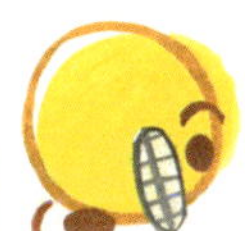  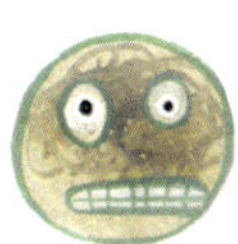 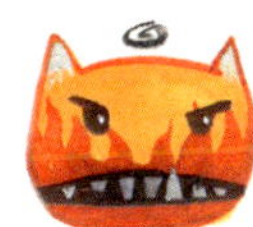 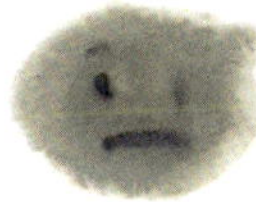 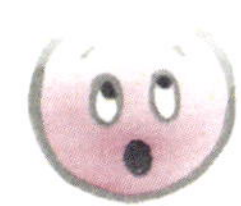

Malaise, tar pit, train wreck, altschmerz, deadlined, pissed, doubt, blank

Stuckness, while not found in the National Emotions Registry, is a state of mind. A two-ton dinosaur with a four-ounce brain in a tar pit is stuck. Facing a blank page or canvas and not knowing what to do is fear and, as any good life coach will tell you, you must face your fears to move forward.

If, for example, you are reticent to make a move in a new direction because you think you are going to suck, get used to it. The feeling that you aren't good or will never be fully proficient at something can be reframed as a positive, because that notion can drive you forward. It can be a compelling force to master a thing. All the very best artists I know share one common trait; they all think they are nowhere near where they want to be.

A true master knows that there is no such thing as a true master. Somewhere in the learning schema comes the realization that perfection, though always the goal, is never attained. This state of mind is the engine of growth that moves the courageous forward. The best, brightest, most talented creatives are the ones who did not give up. They push through the internal negative dialog and external negative forces from associates or peers to overcome whatever barriers they face. Reframe that emotion and see it for what it is. Among all the beautiful muses you might end up with, it's the ugly, short, nagging muse that moves you constantly forward. It ain't pretty, but it works.

Keep in mind always, returning to the **Resistance** part of this book, that there are so many ways we sabotage our own efforts. Fear being number one. Doubt is the right-hand inhibitor that works in conjunction with fear.

You think you are in a rough spot because you are facing a blank page? Think about the pioneer explorers who sailed for months and months knowing that there were giant sea monsters in the dark waters, only hoping there would be a place to land at some point, preferably not at the ends of the earth. They sailed forward anyway. Sure, most of them drowned or were eaten by dragons, but the point is they had courage.

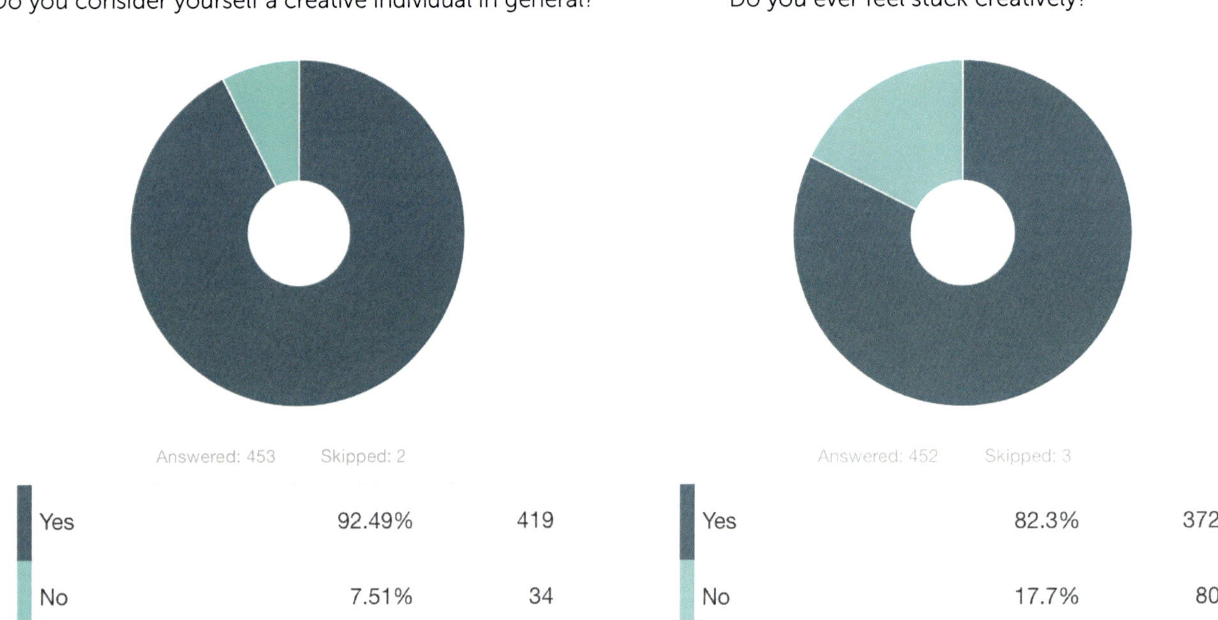

Know your form of stuck

Stuck comes in all flavors and shapes. The first form of stuck is knowing that you want to do something creative, but you just don't know what that is.

You've pondered, but haven't found which direction your passion compass is pointing. For some, finding it can sometimes take a while, usually because they have spent most of their lives on the responsible things, not orbiting in the creative realm. Some have no need to look because they are content where they are. Some have their passion firmly rooted in family or helping others or following a favored sport.

For others still, the joy, the passion of the arts and crafts, is simply enjoying it as a viewer or a listener. And we love them. We need them to exist. After all, if an artist creates a painting in the woods, is it art?

But, whatever the reason, if you are reading this, you may be searching for something new.

If this is you, the not-sure-yet type, you are in a good place. You are free to look around the buffet line and try different things, see what feels right and tastes good. If you've never really had a compelling desire to carve wood, fashion a quilt, make a pan flute, write a book or create a renaissance style painting of one of the saints doing sainterly things, then here's the best place for you to start your search -- with your hands.

Try a little of everything. Go from one to the next until you feel it click. Stop there for long enough to get a feel for whether it's your thing. Take a class in, say, mixed media or collage and, while learning, pay attention to what others are doing in their lives, because these are like-minded people, searchers just like you.

You'll make friends while you are shaping your first copy of Michelangelo's David in paper-clay. I always suggest starting with a sculptural medium like clay, Sculpey or Play-Doh. It's cheap, fun and rewarding and can lead you in all sorts of different directions. If you can apply a little imagination, you can use it in ways that were never intended, which is the point.

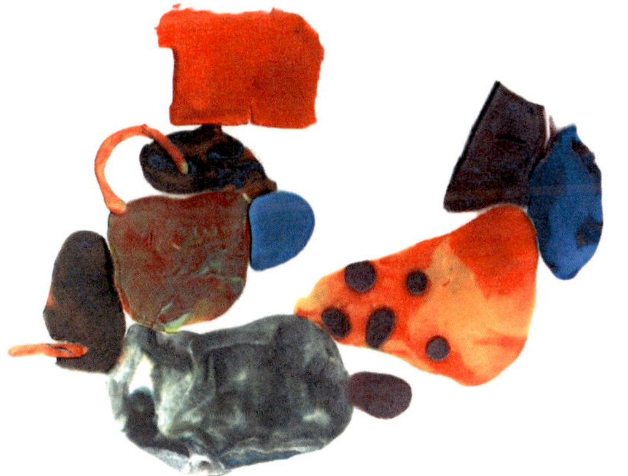
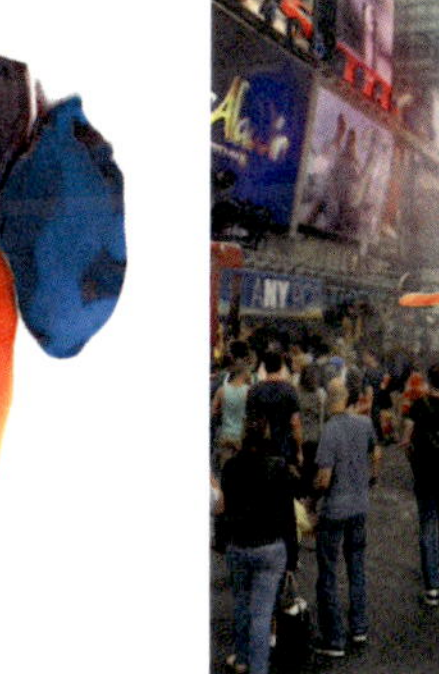

Cost of Play-Doh, $3.00

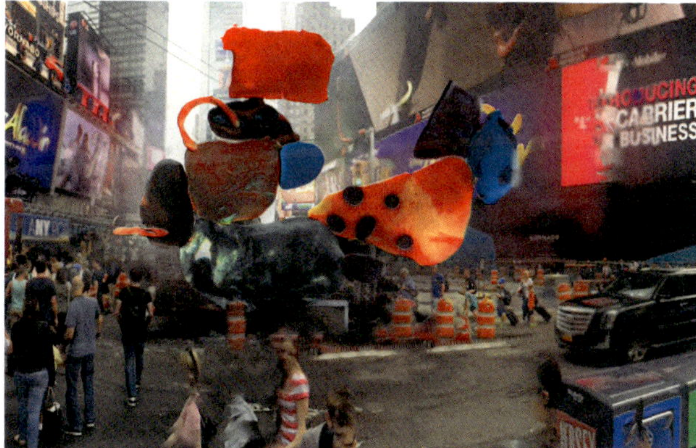

$4,500,000 for a Pop art sculpture in Times Square... priceless.

The most important thing is just do. Don't wait for that pixie-dust fairy moment. If you don't have an idea by now, it probably won't get discovered without a small search party. Try anything and everything that time and money will allow. Take the initiative, throw a create-a-thon party where everyone brings something to work on.

Set up a workshop with an instructor in whatever your heart desires. Online classes are as abundant as mice in a grain silo. They're affordable and you can do them on your own time. There is but one caveat to this do-it-on-your-own kind of learning. You actually have to do the work. The knowledge doesn't absorb through your skin. *Doing is your best instructor.* Try and do and keep trying until you find something you really like, that thing could be THE thing or, more importantly, it could lead you to THE thing. Stay open.

Note: In study, repetition is great for learning but always strive to add something new into your routine.

The second form of stuckitude is knowing what you want to do creatively, but just not quite being able to get around to it. This isn't so much a creative problem as it is a resistance problem. There are a lot of quality excuses used to avoid something you really want to do. Identifying what's behind it can help. Usually it's some form of fear. If you skipped the front end of the book, take a look. There you'll find the type of resistance that fits you like a glove and what to do about it. It has been said that, when you know what you want to do with all your heart, there will be no resistance.

Another branch on the stuck tree is knowing your passion, but being so deep in your existing process that you can't get beyond where you are. You are mired in what you've done for so long that the next move feels unknowable. After many explorative conversations with accomplished artists, I am convinced that this is the beginning of the next growth cycle.

The hardest step is the first one. That's where the exercises in this section and in ***Intent*** will help you to play, push, absorb, take risks, do multiples and assess. Sometimes the anticipation of a negative response to change keeps an artist stuck.

But one can experiment in the closet, so to speak. It takes the pressure of failure out of the equation. Practice on your own or with a trusted peer or coach until you are comfortable. Creative growth should be authentic. It should be slow and methodical, so take your time before you throw the new stuff into public view. Unless you just want to rock it like Bowie.

The fourth destroyer in the stuck fleet is hearing the muse but being afraid to follow it. This, again, goes back to the major forms of resistance, like fear of judgment, being different, feeling uncomfortable, or taking a financial risk and, not just on your behalf, but anyone who depends on you. If you happen to have a supportive spouse or partner, then your reluctance can be nailed down to an anticipated judgment or perceived failure. If you try and fail, you've already done 100% more than those who don't try. Taking these kinds of risks requires an enormous amount of faith and long-haul stick-to-itivity. Perseverance is the steam that drives the talent engine, rarely the other way around.

The fifth genus of the stuckasaurus family is the empty mind and the solution that just hides out there in the tall grass. It's a more temporary form of stuck, but it takes a bit of reframing. Realize that your next steps, your next book or painting series, is just a work in progress. It's okay to take a path and realize that it may lead nowhere. This happens to every kind of talent. Even nowhere paths can give you a glimpse of blue sky. So, just start walkin.'

One way to break out of this is to go back to what you know and add a twist. Change one small thing in your process. If you make quilts, make a kimono. If you paint, change your color palette or painting tools. Paint on cardboard or create a portrait with non-traditional materials. If you play guitar, borrow a sitar and give it a whack. Little changes will lead to bigger changes.

And medium changes lead to large changes. If you are feeling adventurous, try some of the creative challenges and exercises here, no matter what your preferred -ism is. Or try some peyote, I hear that works pretty well, or -- and probably the smarter thing to do -- experience the completely unfamiliar.

If you paint, plink around on a piano, take a shag class, read a book about quantum physics. Have an opposite day, doing the same thing every day and expecting different results is just crazy. Look for the subtle connections that can bring new inspiration to your existing way. The act of entering unknown territory requires two important characteristics of the creative mind -- permission and courage. Give yourself a hall pass to encounter something that you've never tried before and then go in without fear.

Not knowing the outcome of any act should never hold you back, except maybe in ice climbing. This adds to your acquisition library and flexes your explorer muscles.

The ideal sandbox for your brain

Story time: I went in for my 50,000-mile checkup and rear chassis probing at the urologist office. Nothing quells the inner child like thinking about your prostate while surrounded by the scent of cleaning fluid and books on Bible trivia. But, as my little Peter Pan self is always in action, when I was left to my own devices while waiting for two hours to drop trou in the little room, I started looking around to see what I could have fun with.

Under the sterile metal table of rear-chassis-checking supplies was a box of finger condoms. And what do finger condoms resemble? Balloons!!!!! Balloons for me and Peter Pan to play with. I started blowing them up, to fill the boring room with their wondrous latex roundness and make the doctor's day. Then I remembered that you can rub them on your shirt to build a static charge and proceeded to stick them to the wall. I made an art installation out of finger condoms. Nowhere in this process did my inner parent say, "No, no, no and hell no! You put that down right now!" I just did it. It was mostly harmless fun.

There I sat on the cold paper-covered table and waited for the good doctor to open the door and reveal the big surprise that makes his day a happy doctor day. He opened the door, looked around at the walls, then at me as if I were an orangutan in his office, said rather sternly, "bend over." Nothing. Oh well, best laid plans. I guarantee he at least told his wife about it.

Who can be creative in a doctor's office? Your place to create should not smell like cleaning fluid, nor be sterile. It should not be all left-brained. It should be filled with inspiration of all sorts, even if it's just a corner in your living room. Make your studio your own little chunk of Pixar. Use trigger devices to your childhood memories, pics of your dog, snow globes, tear-sheets of favorite creative work that inspires, unusual found stuff that could be inspiration for something else. Surround yourself as if you were 12 again and worshipping the Beatles. This is the altar to your inner child.

Fixing up a good space in which to work and think is vital to premium mental acuity. If you already have a studio, you rock and you are golden. But if you want to come up with new stuff, it helps to switch your regular surroundings up. It's difficult to make your brain operate differently when you are in your everyday operating room surrounded by your usual stuff.

Take a quiet corner of any space and tack up a wide variety of visual stimulation, the more variety the better: old toys, tear sheets of Italian furniture, fabric swatches, period French travel posters, African masks, paint-by-number paintings, toy dinosaurs, torn-out pages from old civil-engineering books, anything that can spark a thought or a line of thought will do.

Surround yourself with stuff you like, it doesn't have to relate to the other stuff, more opportunity for connections to be made. If you've ever seen a documentary on Pixar studios, arguably the greatest digital animation think tank ever, their work spaces look like a giant kindergarten playground with huge amounts of encouragement from the management, because a happy, playful team makes happy, playful geniousness.

If having your own play room is out of the question, borrow one. Got any artist friends with their own space? Ask if you can spread out there for a day or two. Nothing inspires like another artist's space, especially when you aren't responsible for cleaning it. Wander in to an antique mall, one of my favorite places to think. Find something to sit on that isn't for sale and pull out your blank paper with your creative problem on hand. Wander into an over the top hotel lobby, a bowling alley, get a ticket to Disney World or a picnic table in your favorite park. Put yourself in any space that can precipitate new thoughts.

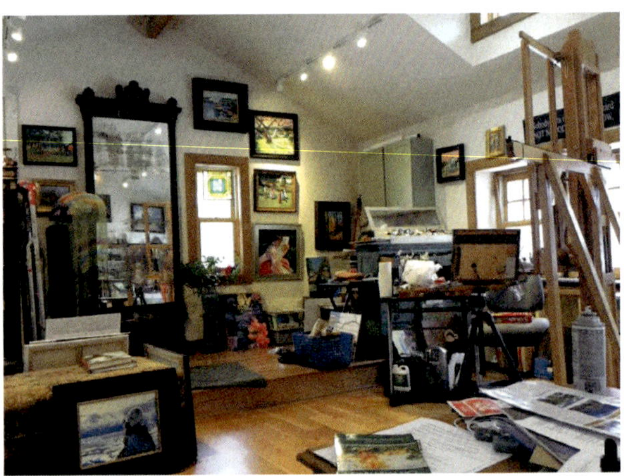

A Stone's Throw Studio, ***A labor of love that gives artist Lori Wallis Feldpausch all she needs; north light and 3500K full-spectrum lighting, plenty of creative inspiration, room to move and do yoga, and a mirror to check her work in reverse.***

What you want is a place that facilitates openness and free thinking, a place that is unlike your usual is more likely to allow you to trigger new viewpoints when you consider a problem that needs solving. For some individuals and for some projects, a big open, blank walled space is optimal. Depending on the project, a conceptually sterile environment is one without any influence, so you start clean and from ground zero. This works best with think-tank environments. If we are blue-skying this idea, and that's the whole point, a room that has at least two walls lined with dry erase boards or giant post-it pads (they actually have those) can allow for amazing linear progressions of thoughts and visuals. You can literally see your thoughts and edit them as you go.

Story time: During the G. H. Bush administration and his 1,000 points of light campaign, our fair city sought out a collective of free thinkers and business folks to form several brain trust groups for creative solutioning our way out of everyday city problems. The rooms they provided were made of dry erase board material, top to bottom and all the way around. A large table in the center was covered with sketch books and crayons and various other materials to inspire free thought.

"First, develop a lot of concepts; then filter them; then distill the ones that have merit."

It was a marvelous weekend of no-holds-barred thinking. The room itself was like a new brain waiting to be filled with great ideas. I used my skills as a thinker and as an artist and became the town scribe for such events, jotting bullet points and drawing ideas in icon form and making connections.

Stark, pristine white walls and a room of blank pages waiting to be filled that just begs for ideas to be poured out onto it makes for a lot of good ideas. We are going to employ some of these same techniques in a smaller format.

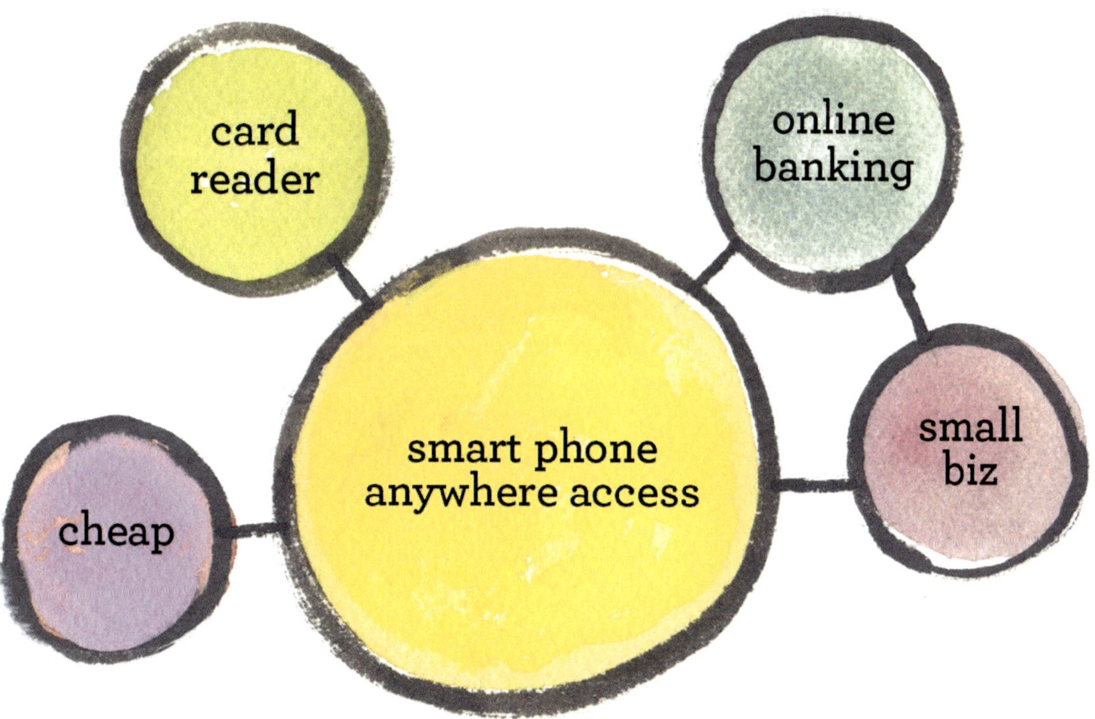

A think tank-full of ideas

One can imagine Jack Dorsey and Jim McKelvey, founders of Square, an ingenious yet simple mobile payment product, sitting in a room of smart people with a wall of connect-the-dot thoughts. Might have looked something like this. Compound ideas are created though connectivity.

Sequestration. Many of the greats and pretty greats arrive at a stage in their journey when the need to remove themselves from all outside influence becomes paramount.

Though it may seem like a luxury, making the effort to confine oneself and shut out the outside world for a time is the best way to focus on new directions, percolate concepts, and redefine in general. One month may seem like a big commitment, but it can provide years' worth of advancement and growth in short order.

Artist in residence programs, usually lasting a month or more, a friend's cabin on the lake, a religious retreat, a tent and a state park would suffice to give the necessary space to produce without interruption or influence, with sometimes career and life-changing consequences.

Music. We like it right? Great music is the perfect accompaniment to a fine idea soup. The obvious thing here is to say to you, throw on some Bach or some Mahler or maybe some Zep or whatever currently floats your boat. But I'm saying the opposite. Try something that is new to you and make it something you don't have to think about too much that won't take you to the old familiar places.

Brian Eno, Aboriginal music, African, Soundscape stuff, Phillip Glass, French pop, anything that will shift you into a different gear. If you don't love it, turn it down, but keep it going. Making new connections is at the heart of creativity and anything that will provide that spark is good. The familiar doesn't do that, it may give comfort and feel good, but it's not going to put you into that brave new world of thought and openness.

Beautiful mind wall

A few paragraphs back I mentioned surrounding yourself with inspirational goodness. In the movie *A beautiful mind*, about the life of mathematician John Nash, the director, Ron Howard, employed a visual device that showed us the inner workings of a schizophrenic mind. It took the form of a wall covered with clues, scraps, numbers, visual reference, and lengths of string that connected points and isolated relationships. It showed us a 2D version of a 3D mind. Make one for yourself. Anything that you can tack, tape, stick or pin to a wall that relates to whatever you are working on and, as important, doesn't relate directly, put it up.

Trust your choices, many picks may not have immediate apparent relevance but the subconscious mind is always at work, so, the crazier the better... unless you are schizophrenic.

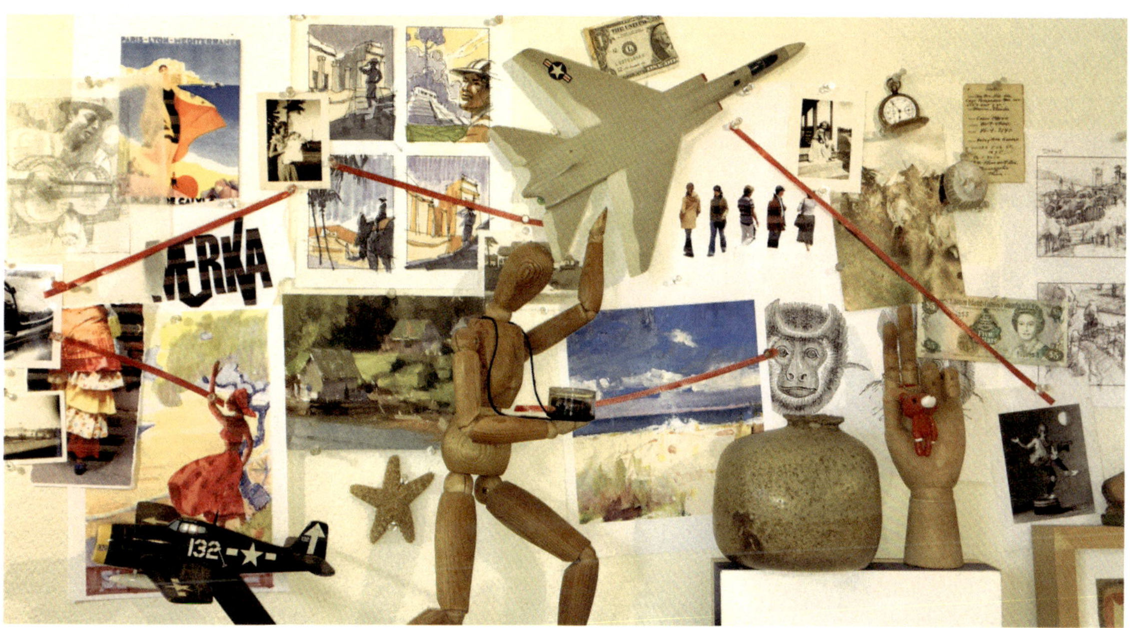

A beautiful mind wall

This method can be used for ideating on a specific project or when you just got nuthin'. If it's a specific thing you are after, gather up all your sources that relate and a few that don't, as wildcard notions. Stick to a wall and look for connections. I use red string or ribbon to form connections randomly. If you are just flat stuck and looking for a story, more random source material choices (the subconscious mind guides you way more than you think) will give you a bounty of new ideas. Apply "Is like" and "What if" thinking to the connections that show up.

In **Acquisition,** I suggested that you collect things that you respond to, things that conjure feelings and sensory response, or that are just plain cool for whatever reason. This is the place for them to exist. Anything that can access and trigger your brain compartments, like the five senses, photo memories, inspirations, textures, patterns, odd found things, scents (like exotic teas), acorns, pieces of paper, old letters, postcards, tribal clothes, whatever ticks for you.

Pick up a box of push pins and a spool of red string from the clothing store or GiftMart and get your crazy wall on. This is like a dimensional free association list. It can be an elaborate construct or a simple one made of stuff that relates and stuff that doesn't, as long as it pings on your radar. Think of it as method acting for the visual artist.

The illustrators of the Golden Era (circa 1910-1950) used this method of reference gathering to inform a new piece of art. If there was a painting of Roman gladiators underway, clippings of period architecture, metal shields, leather garb, Neoclassical paintings cut from museum catalogs and figure sketches would adorn the walls around the canvas. If it wasn't possible to fly to Rome, rent the Colosseum and fill it with actors in fighting garb, the only way to recreate that kind of scene was with as many information pieces as possible.

Building ideas needs that same kind of effort and input. The wall becomes a viewable flat screen of the mind where you can physically make connections with push pins and red string between two or more items. It's a powerful way to kick the brain into connection mode.

Connectivity, intellectual synergy, is the name of this game. The interaction of two or more unlike things can lead to the sudden formation of a compound idea. Sometimes that idea can relate to whatever you are working on and sometimes not, but it's the process that is important. Of equal importance is writing down all ideas, relatable or not. They can serve a purpose later by leading to another concept or being placed in the someday jar in your library. The subconscious mind, the internal muse, is always at work, I've learned to trust what comes from it and believe that we do a lot of our best work without directly thinking about the problem at hand.

Check your assumptions and resistance

There are many assumptions artists make about the creative process, about the right way to do something, perhaps because someone else taught them the "correct" way or about where talent and ideas come from, about what good is or is not.

What others think, like, believe, can have limiting effects on the authentic creative self. While some assumptions can work fabulously on an ongoing basis, like the proper way to tune a piano or stop at a stop sign, some can be just flat outdated or wrong, without the user even realizing it. While following time-honored traditions and methodologies is a perfectly acceptable place to be, sometimes a simple, subtle shift in an existing process or in content can completely alter the context and impact.

You don't always have to reinvent the wheel to get to where you wish to be. At the least, an all-points assumption validity check can help you to know that you are on the right track and spark a renewed enthusiasm for your modus operandi.

I'll be recapitulating some of the items from the **Resistance** section because I know that some of you (and you know who you are) need the refresher. I've compiled a few assumptions about the art thing that may or may not apply to your path. The main idea is to always question what you think you know and to identify your motives, as well as the motives of those that influence you, something we will work on in the **Intent** section.

Bear in mind, while I speak from the point of view of a confirmed life-long visual communicator, these assumptions apply to any form or expression of creativity.

Assumptions sampler platter

1) **I got nuthin.**
   At times, you may feel that there is nothing showing up on your brain screen or flowing forth from your muse, but creativity is a learned skill that requires a process and a concerted effort to let go of resistance. Take the mountain in small steps.

2) **People are born with talent.**
   Nope. Sorry. No one is born with such a skill set. What you are given is the desire to acquire. The "Want-its," as a friend of mine, who is living proof of this, puts it. Maybe a handful were blessed with a savant-like aptitude in their area of expertise: John Singer Sargent, Wolfgang Amadeus Mozart, Jane Austen, Picasso, Da Vinci, Mary Cassatt, Albert Einstein.

   Generally, talent isn't given, it is earned. But the drive to strive must coincide with a confluence of conditions; ability, opportunity, support, connectivity, The Medici's, etc. What if Michelangelo had been born into a family of Siberian elk herders? One must assume that great talent occasionally lands in the wrong environment and never gets fully realized.

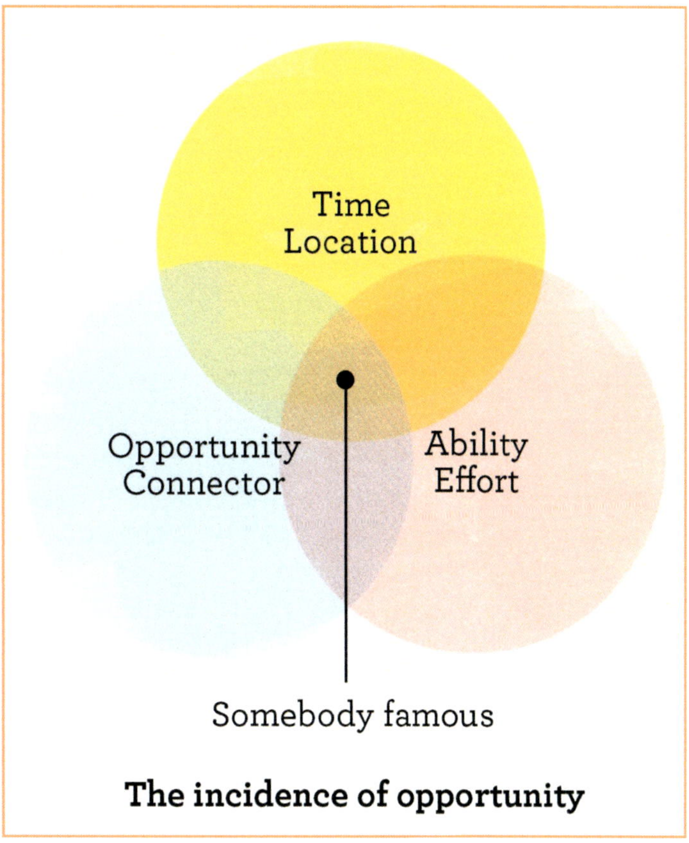

The incidence of opportunity

3) **Technique is everything.**
Technique is half of everything. Concept, idea, motive, thought comprise the other half. You may be able to paint the hell out of a vase of flowers. But, unless you are Matisse or Chardin, you are just another flower painter. You need to strive to bring something new to that table. There are a ton of hyper-adept technicians out there. It's what you do with that skill that counts. Ability is cool. Ability plus thought is transcendent.

4) **It's okay to use the stuff off the internet, right?**
This one is like snow in the Arctic, it's everywhere. Borrowing, using others work or intent, stealing. People do this without being conscious of it, or worse, justifying it as their own. We are inspired by someone, so we learn from them. Mentor / apprentice relationships are a time-honored tradition, but just copying someone doesn't get you anywhere. There are always prominent artists who have copyists and those copyists get copyists and claim it as their own.

Some may not be aware of it but, but trust me, others are. Learn from the masters and then snatch that pebble from their big hands and move on down the path. It's better to be a first-rate you than an ersatz somebody else. Also, copyright infringement is still a thing. A realistic guideline is this: If an impartial viewer can see any similarities between two pieces of art there is infringement. There is no acceptable percentage of similarity.

5) **The path of least resistance, following the trend.**
There are always dominant trends and, because they are so pervasive, they are very easy to fall into. Tattoos, Art Deco, bell-bottom jeans, gluten-free cookies, plein air painting, country music. Nothing wrong with doing things the way the majority does them. That's a natural hard-wired response to group pressure (real or imagined), but that doesn't mean you can't push it a little and then a little more -- and then right off the proverbial cliff.

6) **I'm too left-brained to be creative.**
Albert Einstein was pretty darned left-brained, would you not agree? Do you know how he came to his theory of General Relativity? Thought exercises. The math came later. Leonardo DaVinci, right-brained or left-brained? I'm going to say both. As it turns out, very few of us are only one or the other. No matter your proclivity, bringing curiosity, play and exploration into your process is for everyone. Bring your strengths to the table. Believe in yourself and don't be afraid to fail.

7) **To be successful means all work and no fun.**
Negatory. Success means a whole lot of work, but all forces need their counterpart. Work needs fun, pattern needs rest, peanut butter needs jelly, right brain needs left brain, play needs structure, warm / cool, Lewis / Martin, Yin / Yang, yada / yada. To be a better creative, be a well-rounded person.

8) **I am already unique.**
Being unique is a relative thing. There are probably a few thousand people in the world with exactly your personality and your abilities. The good news is, you can be different and unique. Almost everything you think about, want to learn or master, has been done before. But if you really push for it, no one will do it like you.

9) **I don't follow any rules; therefore, I am creative.**
See #7. Creativity needs guidelines and structure. At the very least, you need to understand the rules to know which ones to break. Launching into a free-form creative endeavor without thought is like sailing without any ropes. You won't end up anywhere good.

10) **Jackson Pollock just threw paint at a canvas, that ain't art.**
The counterpart to #9. Many look at Pollock's work and say, "Well, any monkey could do that." Might be true to a point, but he did it first and he did it with intent. And sometimes the intent is simply to break the rules.

11) **If I dip myself in paint and roll my naked body on a canvas, I am an artist.**
Perhaps when it was done the first time, as in example #10. After that, it's an idea without intent. It's a gimmick... unless you are a Playboy bunny, then, yes.

12) **Being an artist is easy.**
Making one painting for your main squeeze is easy. Coming up with a lifelong oeuvre is tough. Art is hard and the better you get the harder it becomes. If you think making abstract art is easy, take one of my classes.

13) **I will be an overnight success.**
Just like every musician wannabe in Nashville or artist in New York. If you are in it for the long haul, sooner or later you may get to be an overnight success... or not. And if the latter is true, you'd better enjoy the journey and not the destination, or be prepared for a life of disappointment. Matt Damon had a SAG card for years before he was "discovered" in Good Will Hunting. Way more important is this, how about just being great for the sake of being great? The list of standard-setting creatives who never experienced that validation in their own lifetime is long. Do this for you.

14) **If I'm good enough, I will be respected and accepted.**
No matter what you do and how well you do it, there will always be someone out there who won't like what you are doing. The realists don't like the abstractionists. Classical musicians don't get the heavy metal bands and the Sharks don't like the Jets. It's the way of the world. Work on not caring because worrying about what people think will hold you firmly in the place of zero growth.

15) **The best materials / equipment make for the best creative output.**
The masters work with the best materials because they know how important they are to their process. Good work needs quality paints or well-made instruments and such. But the truth is you can rock the house on a Ukulele made from a cigar box, make luscious paintings with old house paints. It's how you do it that counts.

16) **I am an artist (musician, poet).**
This is actually a good assumption (in my opinion). The second you apply paint to canvas for the first time and make that commitment to learn and grow, you are an artist, maybe not a good artist, but you bought your ticket and have embarked on the good ship Artannic. Own it. Staying in this frame of mind is the trick. In the beginning, you don't know what you don't know. Then you figure out what you don't know and spend the rest of your life trying to learn so much that you won't have to think about it. Spoiler alert: You never completely get there.

17) **My school / mentor / tribe / guru said that there is one way to do something.**
Is there a better way to say BS? Misinformed, no way, so not true... nope. Everyone who is far enough along has developed their way of doing things, which they've learned from someone else. Rules seem always to come in conjunction with a specific methodology. I learned my craft through no one in particular, and everyone, and the truth is that there are hundreds of ways to go about a thing, unlimited solutions to any problem.

18) **I am an awesome creative genius.**
I'm going to tell you what everyone else already knows. You are never as good as you think. It's a peculiar thing, but I find the greatest talents to be the humblest, and the ones who believe they are the shit, aren't. Convincing yourself that you've arrived is the death of growth. But, sadly, you probably won't be reading this.

Free association: Creative alchemy

And here we are at the kitchen of ideas. If you give 10 chefs the same 10 ingredients in 10 identical kitchens, each will cook up something unique, in part because they know that their counterparts are cooking up something new to out-chef their competitors. This is when each asks the big "What if" question.

It's the quest for a new way to do it. Necessity might be the mother of invention, but curiosity is the father. Without it, we would still be hunter gatherers. With this in mind, I'm starting the academy of What If University with a master's in **Voicefinding** and I'm handing you your own campus.

So. *What if ...?* How can this one simple question move you to a new place? It is the wonder of curiosity that can lead you anywhere and everywhere. "What if..." can get you out of the soft sand quicker than calling AAA. Once you give yourself over to exploring your curiosity you become open to a multitude of options, which can lead to a multitude of other options, which will lead to more and better solutions.

This process of thought applies to anything you wish to achieve, you may have already used it in your life without considering it as a creative source. "Honey, what if we move the TV to that far wall so we have to use theater glasses and replace the lounger with three tractor farm stools and make a table out of that old cask and paint skull and crossbones on it?"

And Honey says, "Yeah, I don't think that's going to work. Who wants to watch TV with theater glasses? And our home is Post-Modern...How about we move the TV to the far wall but make it really big, get a nice post-modern couch and redesign the cask table to fit?"

"Okay, that works."

In this unusual suggestion/response dialog are two parts of the creative equation; considering the options and weighing the outcome, which then leads to part three, assessing the ideas for a better solution.

The first part of the equation is the *what if*. And the second part is considering the solutions against the parameters of the problem. Having the skills – and the willingness -- to look at options without judging too soon is necessary to free up the creative process. It's called *Blue Sky* thinking, lateral thinking, divergent thinking, or open-source imagination. If there's a problem to be solved, then ultimately the parameters of said problem have to be considered, which is the left-brain aspect of solution finding, *convergent thinking*.

Convergent thinking is the analytical side of problem-solving. After all, what value is a great idea that has no relevance and can't be applied to anything? Consider Honey's response above.

But having the freedom to look at seemingly ridiculous ideas can lead eventually to more refined and workable conclusions. Doing so without parameters is like walking to work with your eyes closed. The trick is knowing when to be free with Blue Sky thinking and when to look at the ideas with discernment. Too much judging too soon is a kind of idea contraception. Let's focus in on the first part and then we can see how it fits into problem/solution applications.

What if exercises

The point of these mental excursions, in case your inner police force shows up, is to use your brain in a way that is unfamiliar and seemingly superfluous, so that you can become accustomed to bringing it when you need it. The more you have this freedom to think *Blue Sky,* the more it shows up when you least expect it. I live in the realm of the what if. Ideas flow freely because I'm free to allow them to happen. I don't judge them as they come out. I don't assign a level of importance or workability. I just write them down for a time when they may be applied to something later.

I truly get the concept of the muse as it has appeared throughout history, or the creative spirit, or the dream fairies, or whatever the preferred nomenclature is, because often it just seems as if ideas mysteriously show up without conscious effort, usually after the preliminary homework is done. I choose to accept the notion of a creative spirit, because doing so separates the ego from the process of creation. And this way, I can blame the bad ideas on someone else, plus I get the holiday off. The creative spirit comes in two parts: 1) the subconscious mind at work on a problem in which the groundwork has been laid and; 2) being open without ego or judgment to everything that comes your way, either as a direct inspiration for a current puzzler or as something inspiring to put in the acquisition library for later. The creative spirit is the internal voice that only a few have the courage to listen to.

It's trusting your gut.

How does one foster the use of the subconscious mind and at the same time develop the trust needed to listen to that little voice? Practice. You can certainly work on these two skills with a current project or give it a go on something that carries no weight or repercussion. With that said, here are a collection of thought exercises to work on.

It's not an IQ test or a psych test. These are just mental playgrounds to work out on. Spend a little time on each problem, sketching or writing and really burn it into your brain. Jot down solutions that seem worthwhile. Be open to an idea that can lead to another idea. There are no correct answers listed on page 93 of this book, so the more imaginative the better.

Once that's done, let them stew. Don't even think about it, work on other stuff. While you aren't focused on the problem consciously, your subconscious mind is running the app, it can make a connection between the two realms without effort. Just like remembering a name in the shower. Keep a notebook with you always, something you should do anyway, so when your baby Ah Ha! arrives, it can be committed to paper. Learn to trust these connections.

You can do some of these thought exercises in your head. But, if you are able, sit down with a piece of paper (instead of your laptop) and write or sketch multiple answers to each scenario or exercise. Thinking is good, but doing is better. Also, nothing inspires like a deadline, so give yourself a time limit. You can come back to these anytime. If you journal on a regular basis, and you should, this is good place to work on these. Remember, for the true creative mind, there is no box to think outside of.

"What if" exercises

Exercise 1: Imagination time

What would life be like right now if, since the beginning of time, all land was submerged under water for 2 hours each day.

What if Neil Armstrong stepped in an empty swimming pool when he put his first step on the moon?

What if cows were 40 feet tall?

What if every single human being was sea foam green?

What if we evolved just as smart, but with dog paws, how would our tools be different?

Reframe your perceptions day. Spend a day noticing stuff, assign new meanings for things or find relationships to unlike content.

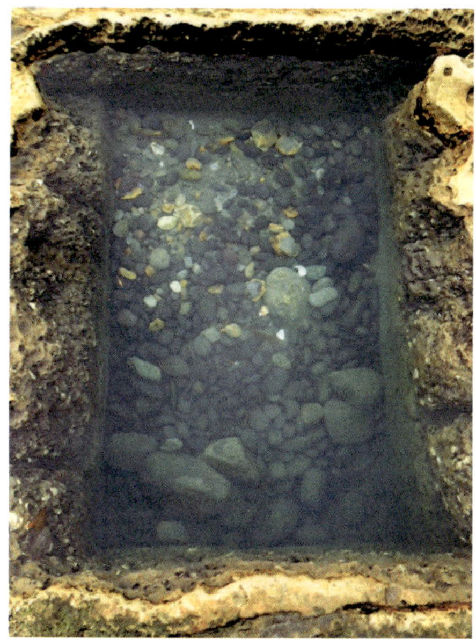

1. Best guess

This 3'x 4'x 2' rectangular hole was found in a flat rock about 15' from the crashing seas in San Diego. Not a natural occurrence. We could Google it but where's the fun in that? Come up with 5 possible answers, the sky's the limit.

List

Why go through this silliness? Because applying this kind of thinking to any problem can take you to a place you would never have thought to go, and from the unusual scenarios that develop can come brilliant AND plausible solutions. Often, people don't consider themselves creative because they stop at the first level.

The use of divergent thinking to solve a problem isn't a focus in school. We are trained to think linearly and often go for the more logical or comfortable ideas, the first level stuff. Good ideas are rarely the first out of the gate. Usually the initial round is something based on the familiar or something that's been seen before. The second level requires a bit deeper digging and pushing out from the regular responses. The deeper you dig the more authentic to you the responses become. The *trick to this whole process is not to judge* what comes in the early stages, be open to what shows up. Your logic brain can kill a potentially great idea so fast it'll make your head spin.

Here's an example of how this works: Imagine a brain club meeting for a statewide restaurant chain. The problem at hand (parameters) is that there are a lot of smaller communities that are not within a convenient drive to their popular fresh foods establishments. It's too far to deliver and too small to build there, but you're missing out on a lot of untapped customers.

Person 1 says, "What if we make the meals and shoot them out of a big cannon and they can float down on little parachutes with our logo?"

Person 2 says, "That's just idiotic!"

Person 3 says, Well, what if we prepare the ingredients and send the boxes using an existing delivery system and they can cook them themselves?"

Person 1 says, what if we build out a semi-trailer and put in a full kitchen to go to these places?"

Person 2 says, "What are you stupid? How is that thing going to corner the back roads?"

Person 3 says, "Well then, how about we use smaller trucks, about the size of a Charles Chips truck and we take prepared meals to be cooked on-site at the big small-town events? We'll call it a food truck!""

The boss says, "Hmmm, mailable meals and a food truck! Persons 1 and 3, you get a big raise, Number 2, you're fired."

A small idea can lead to bigger and better ones.

Exercise 2: What would you do?

A big oak just fell in your back yard. The tree people came in and cut it up into 20 four-by-three foot sections and they're returning in a week to haul them off. You are looking at a veritable woodhenge waiting to happen. What could you do with all that wood? Write down /sketch out 10 ideas, any application, plausible or not.

List

Sketch

Exercise 3: Book trouble

You've just inherited 400 hard-bound school books from the 70's that are sitting on your back porch. The library doesn't want them and you can't sell them. What could you do with this mountain of printed words and covers? Write or sketch 10 concepts, dig deep, be open.

List

Sketch

Exercise 4: Public art project

You've been invited to create a large, 8'x16' piece of art to hang on the main lobby wall for the local hospital with the theme of knowledge and growth. You are not terribly gifted at drawing and painting and there's not a huge budget for expensive art supplies. How many ways can you inexpensively represent these concepts. Remember you also have that big pile of wood in the back yard and the 400 old school books!

Blue Sky, What If ideas lead to more ideas that can be refined to fit the parameters of the problem. Use it in coming up with rough concepts and work on polishing them later.

List

Sketch

Free association, listing, word/visual clusters: the art of the connection

You were just given a series of thought exercises that may have been a little tough to dip your brain toe into. How to get the ball rolling, you may be wondering? Free association is a seemingly simple concept that psychologists use to gauge their patients' state of mind.

It goes like this: I say cat and you say ______. Dog, of course, is the usual response. But what if I repeated that same question 10 times and each time you had to come up with a different answer? Try it. Write down 10 responses and change the context each time without repeating a category. Like this: cat = dog, eye, woman, scratch, liger, Egyptian, night vision, box, stealthy, allergic.

Child's play you say? Give it a shot. Here's your trigger word of the day: mountain

List

Notice that it gets harder as you go? The obvious responses show up first, but then you have to come up with different associations in different categories. You have to dig a little more with each word. It's good mental exercise. Now let's open it up by adding in, not just word associations, but simile associations as well.

For example, I'll use the word *library*. A library *is like* the human mind in that it stores information. So, our list will look a bit more descriptive. Remember do not judge the associations that pop into your head, just write them down.

Library =
books
homeless people
a quiet place to go
Alexander the Great
Gutenberg, movable type
stories
quiet
history
storage of information
human mind
the Oracle
a forest of words
a house of paper
antiquated technology
the wisdom of the elders

There's some good stuff in there. A forest of words. What? Where'd that come from? Sounds downright Shakespearian, sort of, almost.

Let's go back up to exercise Four, the art with the theme of knowledge and growth and the backyard full of logs and 400 old books. I could use this word image, a forest of words, for the hospital problem with ease. I'd pay the tree people to rip-cut the logs length-wise into four-foot planks, cut the books up in little chunks and glue the pieces to form a forest from the torn pages, cut the covers into leaves, mount those suckers on the wall and Bob's your uncle.

It's a cool idea, taking books that used to be trees, reforming them back into word trees and mounting them on planks that used to be trees. Knowledge, growth, recycling and a bit of poetic irony to boot.

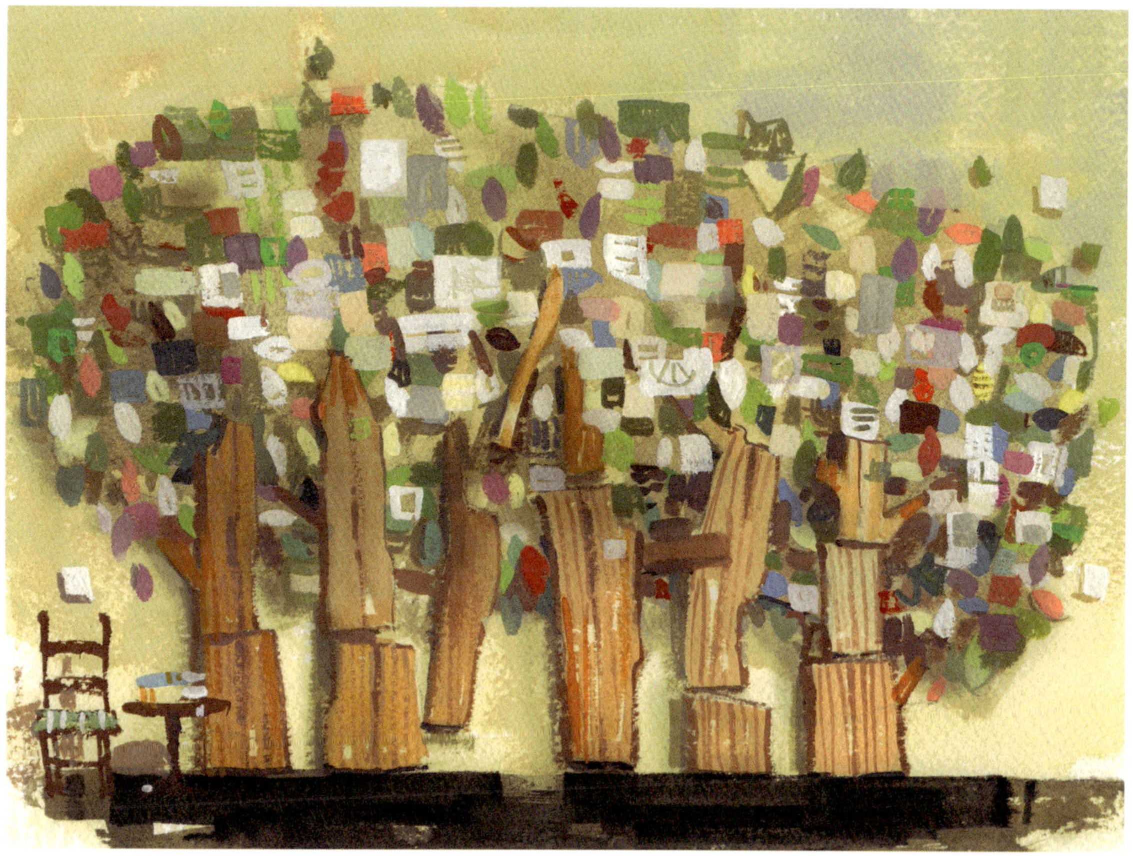

4. A forest of words

This gouache sketch shows how this installation might look: cut wood stumps, old book covers and pages cut and torn into leaves. A little connectivity can go a long way.

What just happened was a series of associations, a cluster of connections that occurred almost without thinking. It nearly solved itself because of this simple process, which, FYI, can be applied to just about anything, from cooking to poetry to public art. Well, perhaps not rodeo.

This is basic creativity, the synergy of two or more ideas combined to create a new concept. In the last paragraph, you'll note, there was an assessment of the idea, the rational part of the brain, the logic, judgment, left-brain consideration of the idea. It fit the parameters of the problem AND made a subtle statement about ecology.

To ramp this method up even more, we head over to an extended form of free association called listing. It's the same process as above. But we use multiple trigger words, creating a list from each word and then looking for cross connections in the results. It's a technique I've used extensively as an illustrator when I just could not come up with the insta-idea.

It worked great with editorial assignments for magazines to find a way to visually represent the over-arching concept of an article without, hopefully, going for the obvious and, in the best of cases, being wonderfully clever and winning national awards. I was simply using the word-association process and then turning those words into a visual narrative.

To show you this next stage, here's an illustration assignment from a few years back, the free association lists and the resulting visual. It was a cover for a regional magazine on professional creativity that went out to advertising and marketing people, photographers, designers, art directors, illustrators. No pressure at all.

The issue was their annual new technology review that featured things like state of the art cameras and video equipment for the industry. My word lists went something like this:

Creative	Technology	Review
art	camera	consider
create	video	compare
think	lens	see
print	record	eye
person	capture	rank
mind	reproduce	best
combine	machine	business

By going through the lists of associations, I could connect certain words, sometimes random choices, to see where they would lead. After considering a series of three-word groupings, the ones that inspired were sketched out the old-fashioned way. The resulting cover symbolized the mind's capacity to consider the tools of the trade with a comment on our dependency on technology. I chose gouache (opaque watercolor) as the medium because it allowed for tight rendering and was perfect for the machinery and techno-stuff. The choice of the medium was as intentional as the solution.

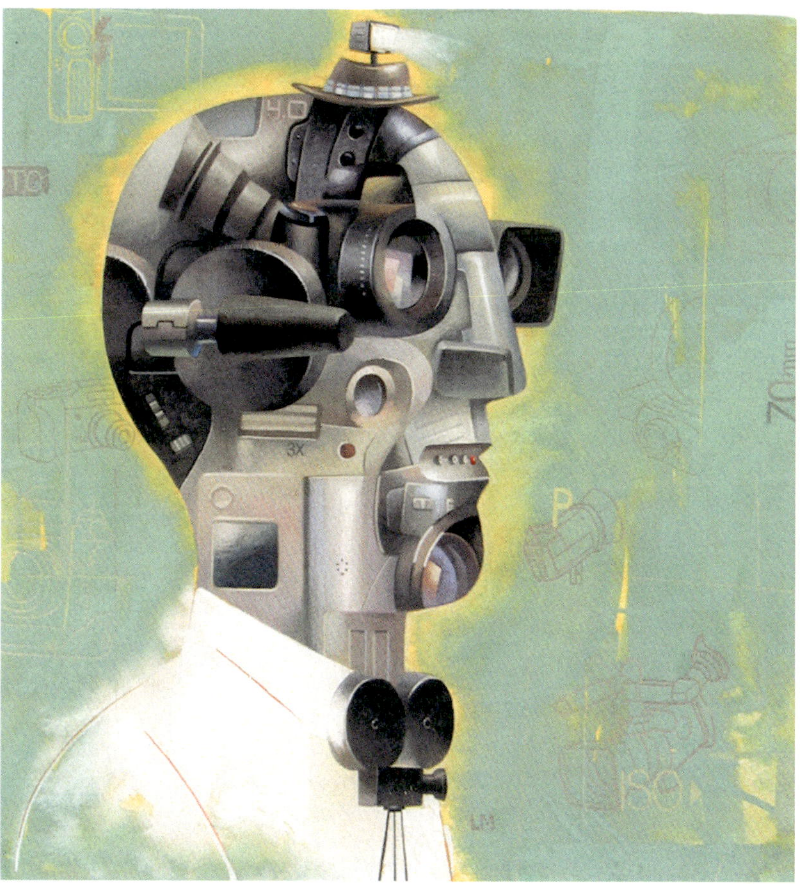

Final cover for Create Magazine, the new technology review.
Gouache 16x18 in.

Give it a try. Put 3 key words at the top of each column, they can come from a project you are working on or you can pick them randomly from this book. Write down whatever associations come to mind and connect one word from each column and see what shows up.

Thought Molecules

Also known as a mind map, this aptly named method models the word associations we make as we go through the thought process. It's a powerful tool to conceptualize and capture synaptic connections.

When I first started to tackle this subject of creativity and its components, I needed to visualize what the various stages and pieces parts were, and the relationships to one another within the process. It's just in my nature to have to see it all in front of me at a glance. Some people can do this in their heads, like math. Not me.

I started with the goal of creativity at the center and reverse-engineered it on a dry erase board, editing, moving and reorganizing until it started to feel like the groupings were in the right place. It felt a little like trying to figure out how DNA worked as a structure. I had the ingredients for the most part. I just needed to see how they fit together. You can view the outcome in **chapter 3, The molecule.**

By working this way, I could see the general flow chart at a glance, which provided a way to organize and see the relationships. This is just another way to trigger connections and hold onto them for later use. A difficult reality is that the flashes of connections and genius can be just that, momentary and fleeting. If they are not captured immediately, they are lost for good... like a dream from the night before.

Exercise 5: Building your own thought molecule

How the heck does this crazy thing work? It looks like a family tree or a chemical compound... It's kind of both. Making one of these models can assist in seeing the big picture in a non-linear form so that you can look at, say, how the many parts of city planning work, or something simple like trying to build a unique new pizza. You see the whole exploded pizzapalooza at a glance.

It's a great tool for analyzing, planning, connecting, reframing, brainstorming and, you betcha, creative pursuits. The thought molecule is a nearly three-dimensional, free-association list... more like 2.5 dimensions. As the example of the creativity molecule is rather complex, let's try something easier.

Let's take the pizza premise. Apply the 2.5D molecule and see what comes from it. A horizontal format is usually best. Start in the middle with a key word and let the sub-topics fly, branching out to wherever they lead. Incorporate icons, symbols, words, phrases and doodles. You can even glue things down. The multi-tiered structure can help push you out of linear thinking and into the creative compound.

When a pizza is run through this thought processor, it turns into everything from pizza flavored communion wafers to The Amerizza, a new 4th of July party treat. Stupider things have made loads of money for somebody.

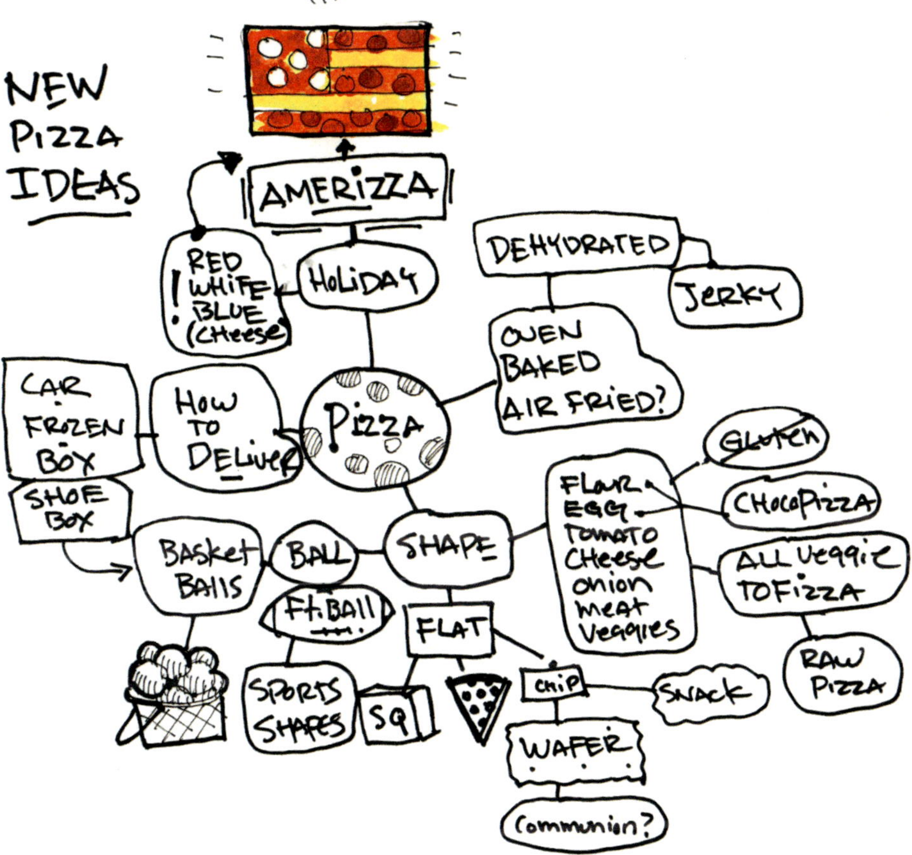

5. Thought molecule

Pizza is just pizza.... or is it? Just let your mind wander and see where it goes. It's a bit like taking the pet bear for a walk... you just go with it.

Seeing things differently

One of the great joys of being in this state of verbal and visual connectivity and synthesis is the constant arrival of inspiration from the everyday, the ordinary. It's a state of openness to anything that can be compared with, applied to or morphed into something else. Like the free-association process using words and visuals.

The two go hand in hand. I can get an idea by joining words and phrases but, because I am a visual person, the ideas present themselves in visual forms. Likewise, visual concepts and associations can be churned into words in ways that are way more powerful than a straight forward observation.

Her skin was like alabaster. A statement that compares the cold smooth, sculptural qualities of a translucent stone with that of a beautiful (or dead) woman. Visuals can be combined to give birth to more synergetic, symbolic and thought-provoking images and ideas. A falling apple spawns the notion of gravity. The visual of a mountain floating impossibly in the sky among the clouds alludes to the power of God. If you cross a man and a spider you get a super hero. Ripples on the water are like waves of sound or light.

To take this idea even further we can add another layer of tools; the photo, the thumbnail sketch and the symbol. Words do what pictures cannot, and vice versa, so why not combine them on the same page? A small, quickly jotted down symbol placed alongside a variety of word associations can lead to a whole new Narnia closet of ideas.

A symbol or simple visual element can be processed a little more quickly and more easily than words, not to mention it's a more universal language. For example, writing the word constellation and drawing a constellation are two very different presentations of the idea, with differing synaptic paths that fire off each. This is where paper is better than an app.

constellation

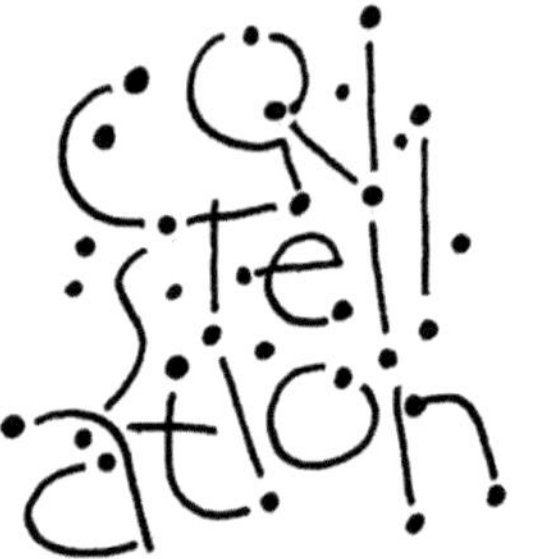

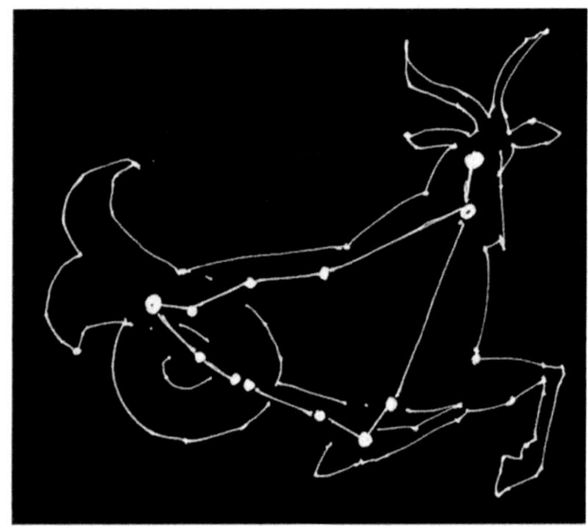

Alter the context of how you see a thing.

Looking at the two side by side you quickly get the concept of more is more when searching for connections. My first response to the word "constellation" is to ponder other meanings or simile based cousins. When I look at the sketches I think about the *What Ifs:*

A constellation is like a connect-the-dots drawing with stars.

There's a ship called a Constellation, maybe there should be a constellation of a Constellation.

You can arrange the letters with lines so that the word looks like what it is

Remove the vowels, it still reads... cnstlltn or Cnstll8n

Movie stars could have their own. "See that up there, son? That's Leo, and that over there is DiCapritus "

Why do constellations have to represent mythical beings? Why not a telephone or a bunny?

The lines that connect the dots in real space are millions of light years apart. That's a big bunny.

Stars are like grains of sand and every beach is a galaxy. Each grain is its own universe. So perhaps there are multiple universes after all.

What if we had some of the more famous trademarks located in the sky in constellation form? How much would that cost? A lot of Starbucks.

Dots and dashes... that's like Morse code. What can be done with that?

What if I took people in glow-in-the-dark suits and put them on a beach at night in the formation of Orion or the Little dipper and filmed it?

If two planets are just friends is that called plutonic?

Again, these may seem like a bunch of silly, random associations. But when you apply this kind of thinking to a set a of parameters to solve a specific problem, you will get a lot more relatable associations and potentially viable solutions than you would have gotten by staring at a blank sheet of paper or thinking in a linear fashion.

Exercise 6: Reframing (Guess what this isn't)

Look at the six images on the following page See them for what they are and get that out of the way. Then make a list of at least five ways each image reminds you of something else and how the nature of these interpretations can be applied within a different context. Altering the context can go a long way towards reframing, a great trigger term to use for this is "Is Like."

Much of advertising is based on "Is Like", a leaky kitchen pipe is like getting a swimming pool in the living room. Having a Merkan Credit card is like being the king of your own country. Wearing Sof-Tee underwear is like wearing a sheep for pants. A traffic jam is like a clogged artery. The mind is a portal into a new universe. It's a figurative association and not a literal one.

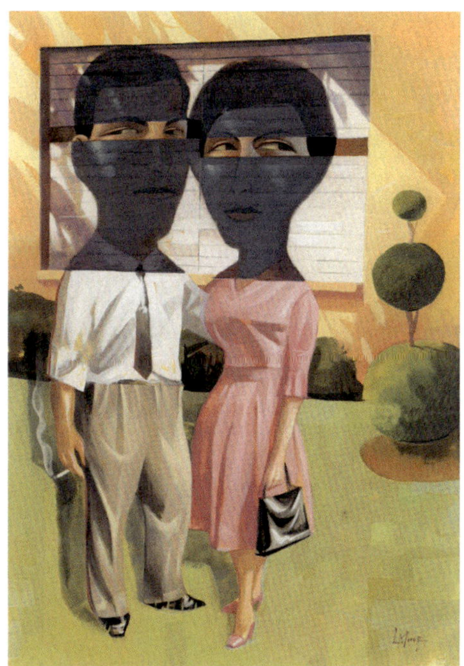

This illustration employs duality to express two states of being at the same time. The couple, key characters in the play *Pack of lies,* is depicted as being both outside and open and inside and secretive.

One of the most powerful communication tools in the arts is found in the term *duality*. A state in which two things exist at once, either in a synergetic sense where two or more elements are combined to form a unique message (i.e. fishing for elephants), or when two or more components are opposed to one another, as in the Joan Baez song "Diamonds and rust". It's found in the above example of pants made of sheep and is the foundation of some of the most thought provoking works in art and literature. The first step to developing this tool is to learn to interpret what we see in new ways.

Consider what each of these images are like and jot down the associations. I'll do the first one and you get the next five. Remember, there is no right or wrong answer. No one is watching. What do these make you think of? If you have the wherewithal, go to 10 per list and see what shows up.

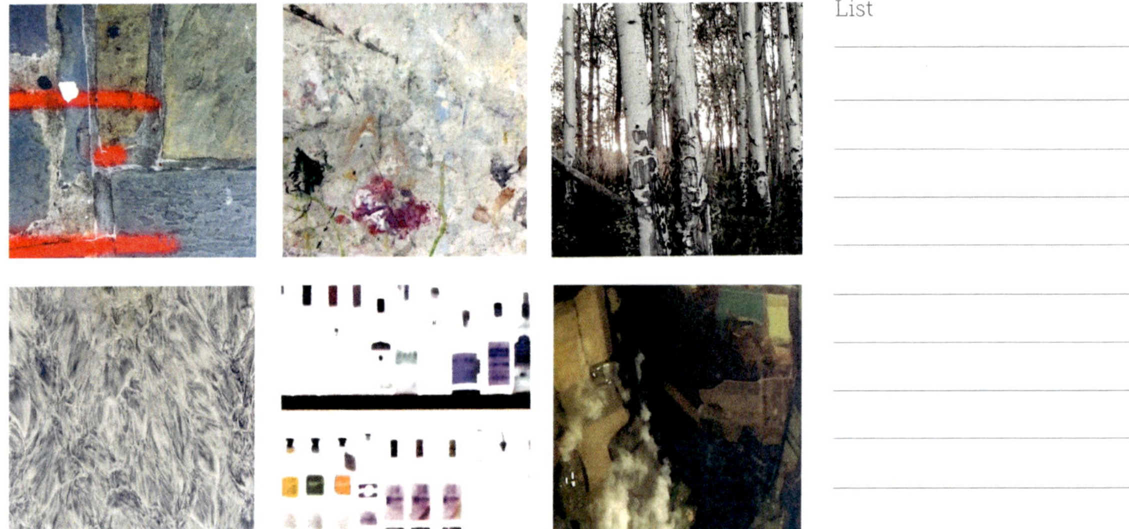

6. Guess what this isn't

Apply other contexts and meanings to the known, think "is like", as in this is like aggro geometry, rock music in 2D, slate windows, etc.

One of the best places for a cornucopia of visual connections is a collection of antiques where everything can be reframed and ideas from the past can be noted, absorbed and applied to something new. Looking at old quilts could inspire appliqué-based painting methods in which chunks of painted canvases are sewn together to make something new. Wallpaper sample books can deliver loads of ideas. An old tin toy can become fodder for a large-scale sculpture and vintage travel posters inform compositions for paintings.

From a creative viewpoint, this collection of vintage stuff can be viewed in a variety of ways:

- Old friends
- A library of the obsolete
- The beauty of the everyday object
- A pattern of color and variety that makes for great painting subject matter (abstraction of shapes and patterns)
- A collection of discarded souls with stories of their own who team up to make new stories.
- An archive of family history.
- A still life painter's dream come true.
- Juxtapositions of unlike things that are randomly placed together.
- Antiquated patterns and decorative motifs that can be borrowed and adapted.
- An IdeaMart for different ways to design a piece of furniture.
- The Universalist Utilitarian Orchestra

This way of seeing a place, reframing, can be applied to anywhere and anything. Walk into a shoe repair store, a grocery store, or your closet, and in this open state you will become aware of more than the things themselves. You'll see ways of arranging patterns and groupings, textures and colors, forms and shapes. The way shoes are organized in a shoe store could be applied to a software or a routing issue. Patterns in a fabric store might be inspiration for a new kind of sheet music language. A carton of eggs can lead you on a fantastic journey of life forms that are repurposed. If you are a creative of any sort, this way of seeing is your currency.

Exercise 7: Story time, your turn

It's better if you do this on your own, by going to a place where you can find an odd assortment of unfamiliar stuff and single out a cluster that you connect with -- an old plantation estate, a library, the house of a well-traveled individual.

Or use this visual prompt to write a story. You can take this trigger concept anywhere you wish. Apply a unifying prompt -- they came on a boat, had a past life, are in group therapy. Use your methods of free association and your imagination. Throw in some key words and get to work.

By doing this on a regular basis, by being aware of associations and staying open to the idea that they can be more than the common perception, you can constantly be in a place of wonder and imagination. It's your very own self-amusement park.

Frank L. Baum wrote the Wizard of Oz based on his immediate family. Vincent Van Gogh infused patterns into a world where they did not exist and the Greeks assigned gods to explain the unexplainable. It's all creativity in action. The next time you roll into a big city like New York, imagine you are from a primitive tribe with no understanding of how it got there. What explanation would you come up with?

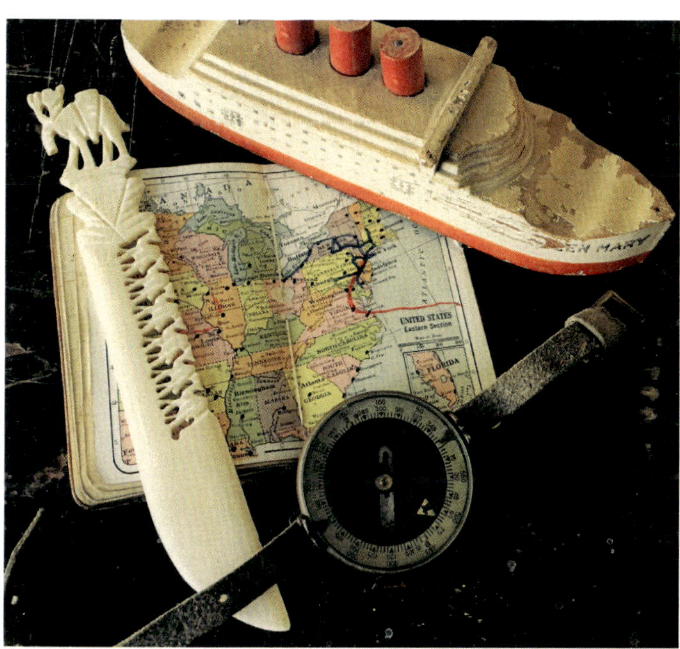

Whatever your creative passion is, be it writing fiction, poetry, painting, music or decorative cake-making, this is fuel for change in your work. Observe it, absorb it, adapt the idea of it and apply it to what you do. It's how a lot great ideas are conceived.

7. Trigger props

A toy Queen Mary, a pocket calendar/map book with a trail, an exotic letter opener and a vintage military issue wrist compass... where can these artifacts lead you? Use your "what if" skills to reframe each item. Think like a child, a soldier, a pirate or from the vantage point of an evil witch. Is it a toy ship or is it a real ship? Is the story about the things at all? Even if you don't take the time to write it down, close your eyes and visualize a place where this collection comes to life.

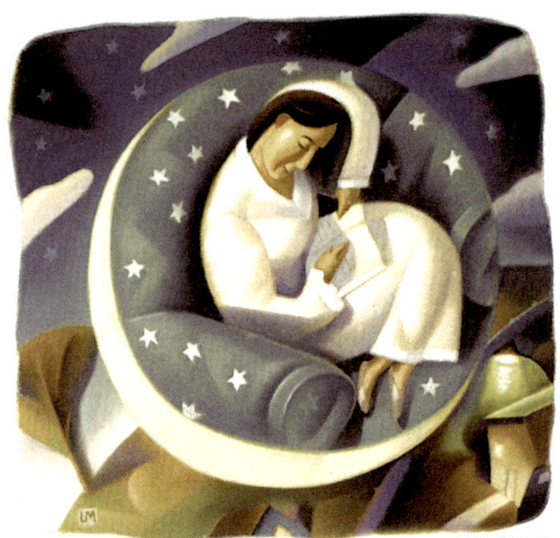

Exercise 8: The dream catcher

Everyone dreams, even if you think you don't. You just don't remember them. Many are aware of their dreams but can't recall the specifics. But if you are lucky enough to remember your dreams when you first wake up, it's time to start a dream journal.

Each morning as you are starting to wake, usually before your alarm goes off, you enter the in-between state of the unconscious and conscious called hypnopompic. It's right about there that whatever you had been dreaming is still hazily in your mind. Your journal is for those fleeting moments. Write everything -- from the time of day to the kind of light that filled the dream, who was in it, what they wore, how you were feeling and what you were doing in that space.

As you wake, it becomes easier to connect these details back into the whole story. Do this for a month and you will be amazed at how inventive your mind is, without conscious effort.

What's so funny?

We all like funny. I like a good laugh and enjoy making other humans laugh about as much as having someone respond positively to one of my paintings. Coming up with a good verbal pun is every bit as enjoyable as creating a visual one. But I couldn't come up with a standard joke if it attached itself to my shorts.

Humor is making an unusual connection to a truth and a joke is just a metaphor in clown shoes. Some make a left turn visual that takes the audience by surprise and runs them into another world. Many jokes are situational, and their success has a lot to do with relevance, timing and delivery. The figurative "Is Like" is prominent in humor. A good comic will conjure a visual using two unlike things that represent a common truth or take a common thing and make it uncommon.

Many times, a good chunk of funny comes from a simply absurd association presented in a very deadpan way, an unexpected combination with a nonchalant delivery. "I love my underwear, it's like having sheep for pants. So, I'm going to open an underwear store called "Love Ewe." Listen to a good comic and ask yourself what it is that you are laughing at.

And next time you need a little inspiration or would like to see lightning-fast free association in action, go to improv night at your local comedy club; better yet, sign up for an improv class. Thinking on your feet is just another learned skill that requires self-awareness without self-consciousness. Train your courage muscles while sharpening your brain.

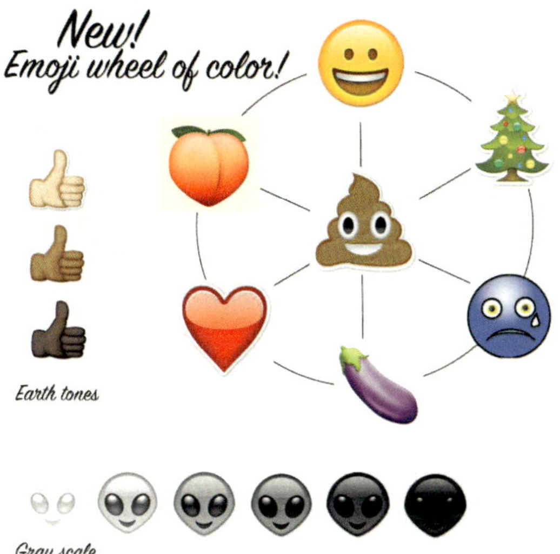

Ever wonder why funny plays such a big part in TV commercials? It's to keep people from turning off the sound or flipping channels. Often, they don't sell a product directly. The intent is simply to generate top-of-mind awareness for the brand. Humor was the foundation of the successful insurance company campaign with the line, "So easy a caveman can do it".

Divergent thinking: the path of creativity

Divergent thinking is the ability to take something and expand on it in different directions.

Free association, listing, and using two unlike things to conceive another are forms of divergent thought. We're playing with ideas without discernment. We are thinking like a child, Blue Skying without a net and without the usual boundaries of judgment that accompany an idea. Once enough idea clusters are generated, it's time to sit down and sift through the pile of inspirations and make decisions about which can be applied and which won't make the cut.

That part, of course, is important. But, for now, we will go further with creative play.

Key to this process is taking the new connections and associations and seeing where they lead. It's a mitosis of ideas, allowing each new thought to divide into other new thoughts. It's a lot like heading down a new path and finding more new paths along the way.

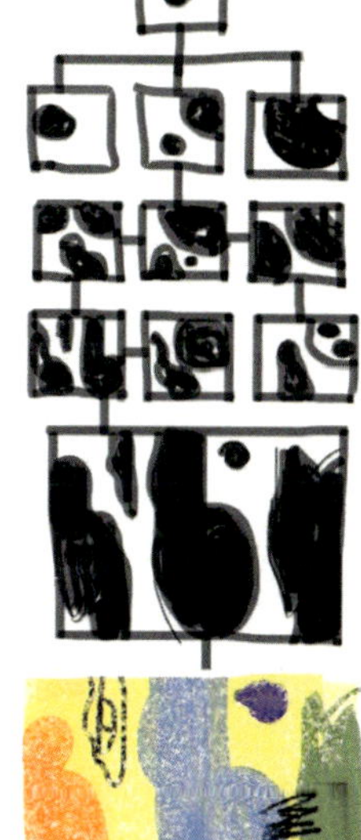

This idea tree is just one example of divergent thinking. A parent idea spawns lots of baby ideas, the best ones have babies of their own and so on until the best solution shows up.

We need to be fearless because discovery is the name of the game and the more we dig around in our treasure hunt the more we are likely to turn up. You must learn to turn off the judge part of your brain, disabling the "this is stupid" kinds of thoughts that may nix a direction. There's plenty of time later to parse out the stupid.

We can extend our word play even more by adding visuals in the form of sketches, symbols, words, textures. In architecture, they use a charrette, which is a team effort, to flesh out a concept as it relates to a specific architectural solution; photos of sites, architectural styles, marker sketches, patterns, textures, color swatches, all on one long continuous roll of paper, so that a viewer can see the linear progression and thought behind each consideration.

Many creatives use this same technique to explore more in-depth catalysts for inspiration. For 35 years, I used this tactic to come up with visual solutions to solve countless clients' commercial needs. Now as a fine artist, I employ this technique to get me past the craggy crevasses of creative problem-solving.

Adapt-transform-alter context-rearrange

Modeling terms are additional sparkers to assist in seeing anything -- object, solution or problem -- in a different light. Even the best of us get used to looking at a subject in the obvious ways. A monkey is just a monkey. We see it from the viewer's standpoint, at least until we start modifying our frame of reference or reframing the known by altering the context. Sift through some of these lists and apply them to anything you wish and see what shows up. I'll present some examples in the **Voicefinding** section.

Adapt: add wings, restyle, mechanize, change color, alter hue, value shift, add pattern, pimp it, make it funny, absurd, edit, sculpt it out of clay, add, subtract, repurpose, isolate, make alien, deconstruct, mobilize, emoji.

Transform: Warp, melt, aerial view, worm's eye view, scale, robot, gender, repurpose, fast-forward, evolve, reverse polarity, upside down, multiple viewpoints, simplify, mutate, Streamline, Japanify, super-power it, add layers, marginalize, personify, propagandize, '60's psychedelia.

Alter context: Under the sea, Byzantine, "Is like", Film noir, make political, religious, period (Victorian, psychedelic, surf culture), science fiction, cartoon, primitive POV, exploded view, fairy tale, French provincial, peace, love, war, Medieval, evil, mythologize, swap, put it in an infomercial.

Rearrange: take apart, reorder, reassemble, transmogrify, reverse, inside out, reprioritize.

Using divergent thinking and doing multiples (creating many versions of an idea) generates a bigger net in which to capture the elusive and rare ivory-billed idea. So, how might this look in action?

Story time: I was assigned the glorious task of coming up with imagery for an opera poster series. Each painting would represent one of the four operas of each season, and there were many seasons. This was a dream job because, as an illustrator and a graphic designer, I had a passion for storytelling and this was the perfect opportunity.

Mozart's *The Magic Flute* is a Lord of the Rings-like tale with way more going on than could be represented at once. Where to start with this crazy story? Research. Books on Mozart, photos of the opera from Italy and New York, a synopsis of the libretto and a one line condensation of the whole thing. "Boy with a magic flute conquers evil and finds love."

With my visual acquisitions spread out before me, I began writing key words and sketching thumbnail compositional ideas, sometimes just making interesting designs before content was even added. If I came up with an idea that was good, I would try as many variations on that theme as I could muster (multiples). Once I felt satisfied, I moved on to the next little path and developed that. Just for fun, I would throw in a wild-card solution to see where it might lead. Often, I played the music to add to the mood as I sketched.

Without this thought methodology, I might have just stopped at the first obvious solution I came to.

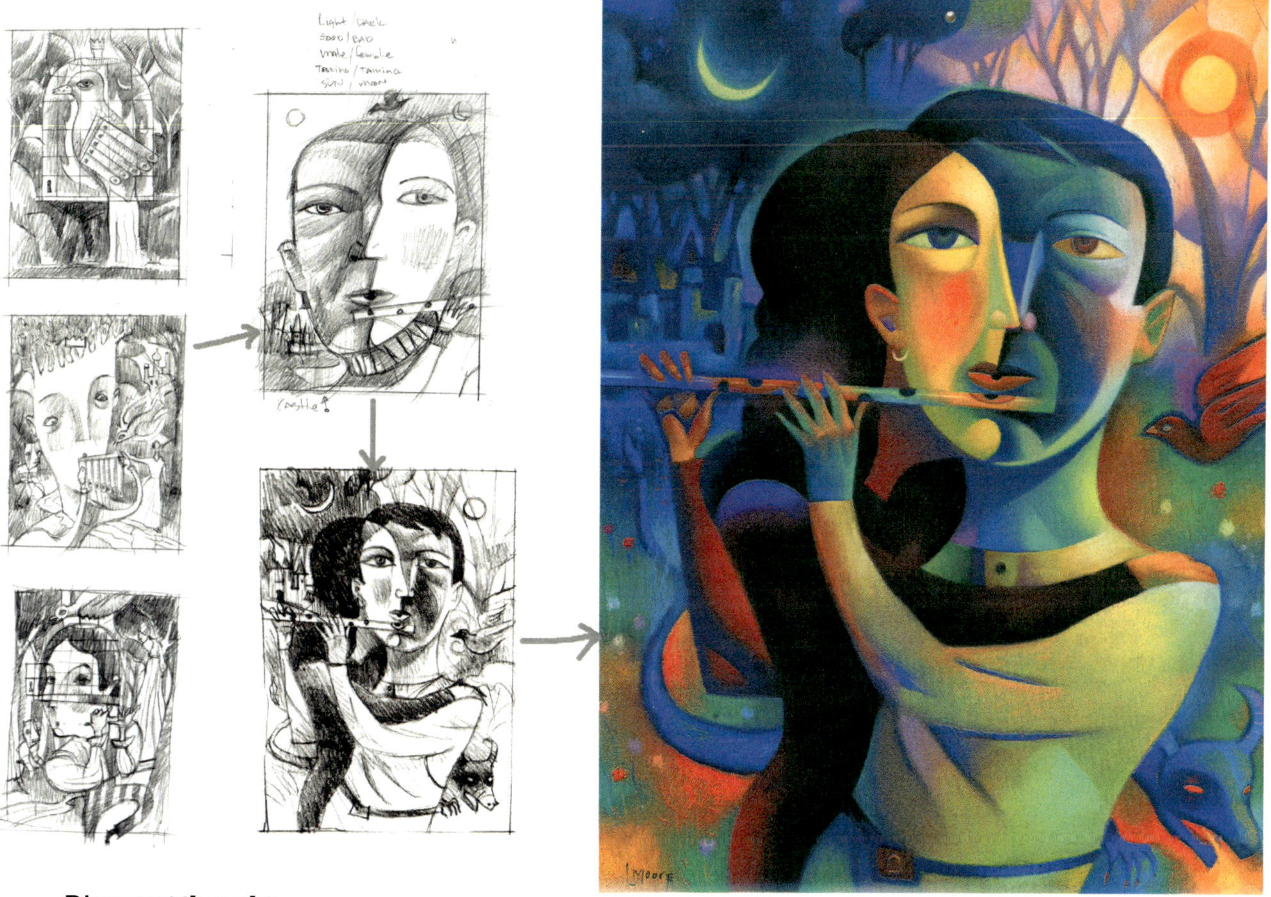

Divergent thought

***Magic Flute*, is a very complex mix of story and symbolism. In order to explore ideas, I use something like a family tree concept with two or three originating notions (parent ideas) and then allow the offspring to grow up and produce more ideas.**

Linus Pauling said, "The best way to have a good idea is to have a lot of ideas." And the best ideas are usually the simplest ones. And working small in thumbnail form helps to keep the TMI syndrome at bay. I then worked up a tighter sketch of each potential idea, choosing the best for even more development, adding color ideas when needed.

Breaking the search for a solution into chunks allows more brain power for each component of content, design and then color. All this effort to come up with one idea. Why? Because that's what it takes to develop a strong, unique, inventive approach to anything.

Whenever we see greatness in the form of a painting, sculpture or building design, we see only the top layer, the finished project. We aren't privy to the countless hours of development or the piles of abandoned solutions.

For the artist readers, there are exercises in the **Voicefinding** section to help with application and exploration.

Feeding the parameters (convergent thinking)

Now that you have an idea on how to think way outside of the cubicle -- and into a cubicle in another universe -- you have to know how to put it to use. Playful divergent thinking eventually requires thoughtful convergent thinking or it's just fun play (not that there's anything wrong with that.)

This setting up of reason boundaries is what I call feeding the parameters. Define the rules first and look for the ones to be bent, broken or improved. Go way, way beyond the outer limits of ideas and then use these parameters to guide you back in.

To come up with a genius solution, you need a problem to solve and you need to understand all its facets. I've experienced plenty of spontaneous ideas dropping like pennies from heaven, but a random idea that fits rarely lands in the right place at the right time.

This technique can be applied to a specific set of needs, such as a new public art idea for the airport, a logo, a themed gallery show, a unique take on a story, a new fashion design, an ad campaign or a ground-breaking something-or-other.

During my time in advertising, we used a client/campaign info sheet, which we were handed by the project manager, who got it from the account assistant, who got it from the account supervisor, who got it from the client. The chain of command was why I got out of advertising. Loved the problem solving, hated the chain; too many chiefs.

The info sheet addressed the nature of the client, the thingy they wanted to sell, the demographic they wanted to sell it to and the method of delivery -- print, radio, TV, magazine, trade show. Welcome to Parameter City, population 37. Once we figured out how the gizmo worked, we could find how to make it seem different and amazingly life-changing to the prospective buyer/user. Without the parameters, we would be bunch of monkeys typing out random letters and hoping a campaign would show up.

I've discussed this idea of building parameters with enough artists that I have realized very few who are creating for themselves apply this kind of thought process to their work. By modeling their efforts into the form of an assignment to be solved, the solutions could be that much better.

Now's a good time to provide you with an all-purpose worksheet for your personal or professional creative assignments. To make this specific enough to be useful, I'm using what I do for a living -- fine art, specifically, gallery work. You can take this idea and adapt it to your modalité du jour, be it photography, glass blowing, painting, rock guitar or writing a book on creativity.

LifeForm F4E-PW Parameters worksheet

You can't solve a problem unless you've really looked at it.

What is the problem at hand?

What form might the solution take?
(2d, 3d, medium, mixed media, digital, installation, print, etc.)

Who is it for?

What are the restrictions? *(size, ability, audience, money, etc)*

What does it need to express/communicate?

What do I hope to receive from this?

What should the recipients receive from this?

Is this part of a larger solution *(a campaign or body of work)*
or a unique problem?

What can I bring to this? *(strengths)*

What are my limitations? *(shortcomings, weaknesses)*

Assumptions check. (Does it really have to be ______?)

The best way to present the parameter process is with a few assignments where the boundaries are defined so that you can do this for yourself. I used this same client/problem info sheet in my illustration classes presenting actual jobs and situational info that I had dealt with in the past. The entire class was given the same assignment so that we could all see the variety of solutions that can come from one problem.

The most successful solutions, of course, considered the infrastructure of the assignment (objective). The students who just went from the gut (subjective) without the parameters did not fare as well. The rare few that got A's did so because they solved the assignment in a unique and compelling way that communicated the message clearly. They dug deep and with intent.

These exercises are designed to push you into different modes of thought and solution-finding. I'll do one to get you started and provide a few what-if cues to help you solve these your own way.

Try the ones that are the most different from anything you do and stretch your brain muscles a bit (you might even end up with a mental six- pack). When you have the process down, you can apply this to any of your own issues. No Googling or YouTubing.

Parameters worksheet for a specific problem

Exercise 9: Illustration assignment

Portrait of a famous person. Create a recognizable 2D or 3D depiction or portrait of a famous person of your choosing. Mick Jagger, Albert Einstein, Margaret Thatcher, Steve Jobs. The viewer must be able to "get" who it is.

Assumptions check: *Does this have to be a painting?* Nope.

Does this have to be a portrait type likeness? Nope.
Can I just print something off the internet and copy it?
A) Where's the challenge in that? B) Copyright infringement.

What can I bring to the table? If you're not so good at drawing you'll have to come at it another way. And even if you are, you should try a different approach. Collage. Assemblage. Play-Doh. Mixed media is fun... glue and collage and found objects that relate to the subject, e.g. using circuit boards to make a likeness of Galileo doesn't fit, but it might if it were for a database of the universe called Galileo (parameters).

Now let's apply some list-making and free-association and see what shows up.

Person: I'm going with Charles Darwin

Wrote "Origin of Species", developed the theory of evolution, Scopes monkey trial, pondered natural selection and collected a variety of animals. Spent time on the good ship Beagle, was lampooned as a monkey. Was enthralled with the diversity of finches on an isolated island in the Galapagos.

How many ways can I convey a likeness? Direct vs implied, sculptural, association, written, rendered portrait, interpretive, combo, mixed media.

Preliminary thoughts: A likeness forged out of pieces of monkey faces. Finch wallpaper with silhouetted cut-out of Darwin, monkey showing through cut-out. A silhouette made from finches and/or other animals.

What does it convey and will viewers get the idea?

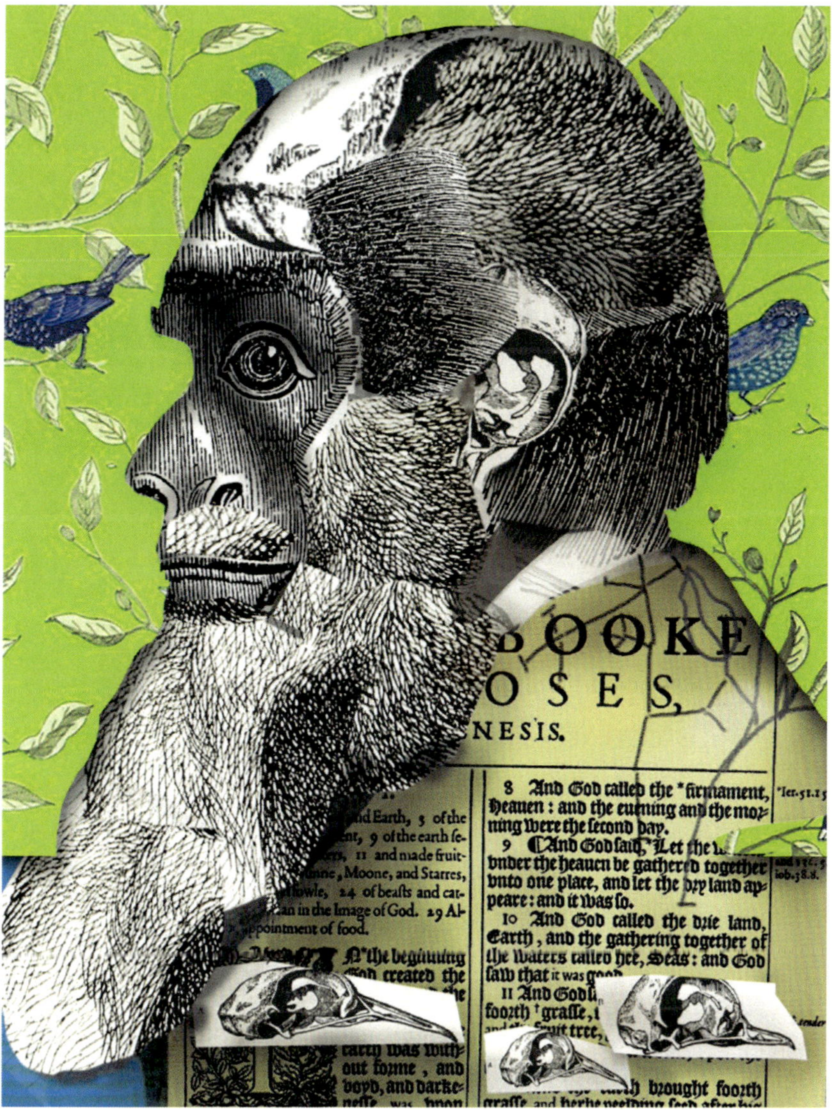

9. Non-traditional portrait

Charles Darwin made with an assemblage of wallpaper, chunks of primate etchings, a section of Genesis (relax, it's a print), and clippings of bird skulls. No drawing, no painting. The duality of the parts aids the story.

Your turn. Pick someone you would like to depict.

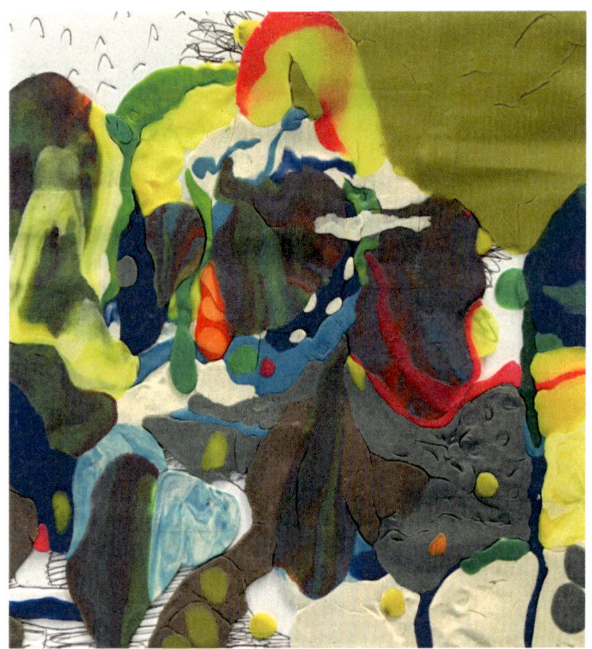

10. The Play-Doh challenge

A particularly playful Play-Doh painting by artist Victor Bokas. Once you realize this medium's potential, it's not just for recess anymore.

Exercise 10: The Play-Doh challenge

Playing with play-doh. How fun! I'd love to just let you go with it, but you need some parameters. Your challenge is to depict some aspect of nature; a landscape, a flower, water, a tree, and figure out a way to do it without using it in the obvious way. Don't just make a flower, communicate flower. You get triple bonus points if you do.

Assumptions check:

Can it be a sculpture? Sure.
Does it have to be? Nope.

Can I use the medium in some really inventive way? Yes please.

Should I just make a landscape? Not if it's the first thing to come to mind.

What can I bring to the table? What skill set do you have that you can allocate to this? Perhaps a Vincent Van Doh painting, or flattened and cut into pixels like a quilt, use your free association skills.

Exercise 11: Ad campaign assignment

This exercise can be about something you love, something you feel passionate about and know backwards and forwards.

Maybe your fave subculture is lacking in the idea department, or maybe there are a lot of ads out there for fishing or dressage that really miss the mark. You can do better.

Did you know that Harley Davidson's comeback was due to an extremely successful ad campaign? Create a series of three full-page ads for your product (or cause) for your fave magazine. One ad is easy-ish. A campaign is tough.

Work in thumbnail form, ink on paper. Think about the product. Think about the market demographic (perhaps you) and an appropriate mag and come up with something powerful. Hint: Keep it simple and make it different. Words first, visual second. Avoid the obvious.

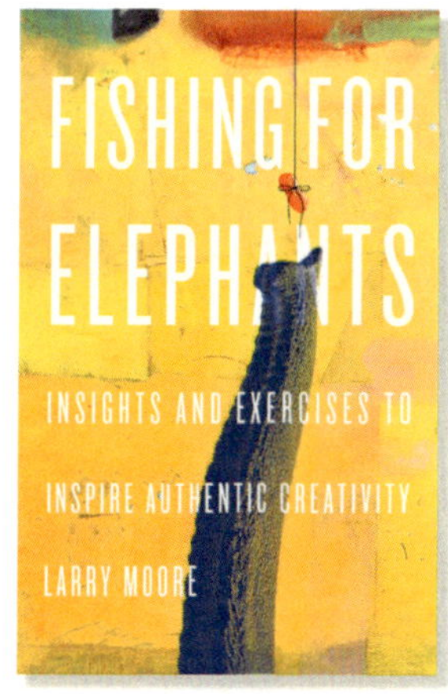

Creativity for smarties.

You 10.0
Available on iBook, and Amazon.com for Kindle. $24.95

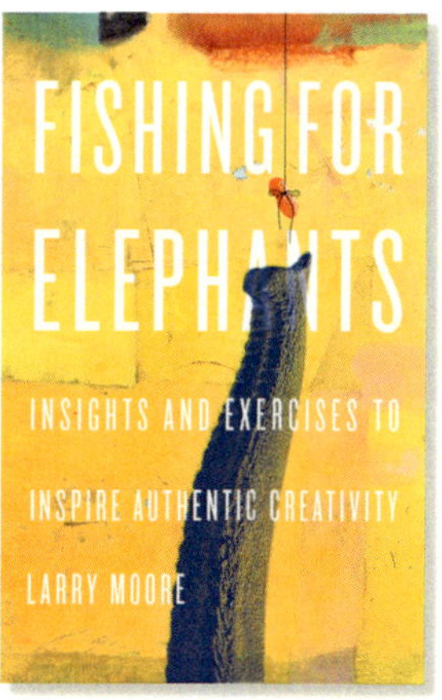

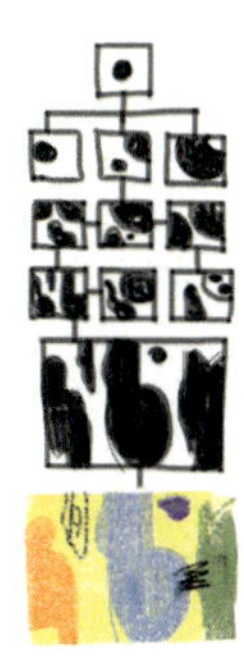

Creativity explained.
Available on iBook and Amazon.com for Kindle. $24.95

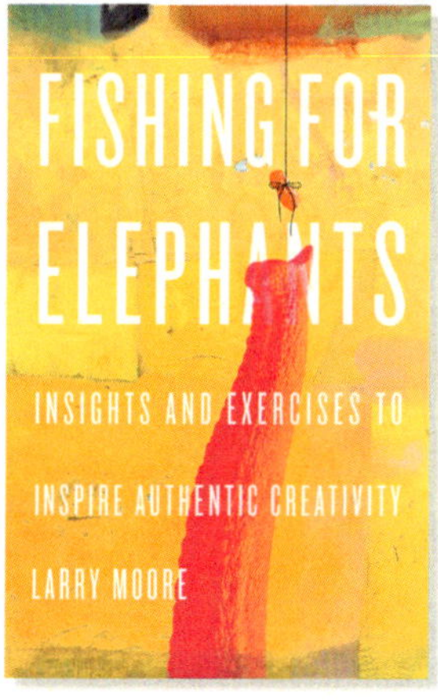

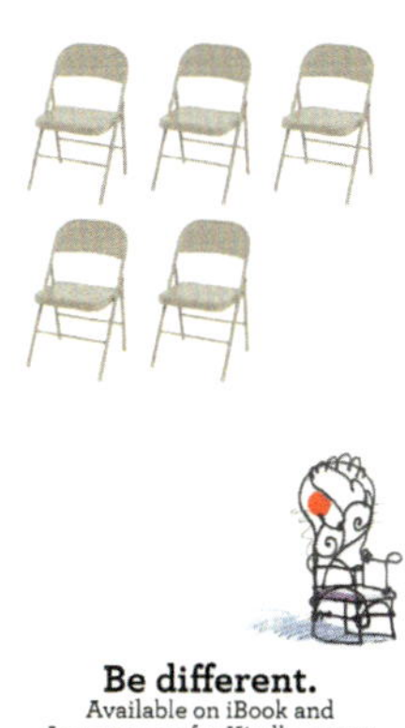

Be different.
Available on iBook and Amazon.com for Kindle. $24.95

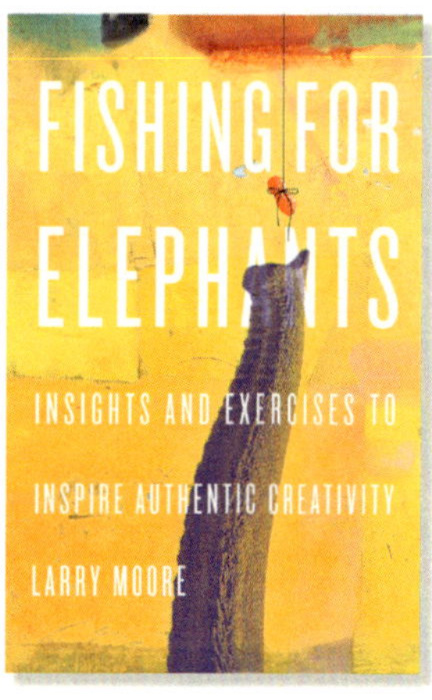

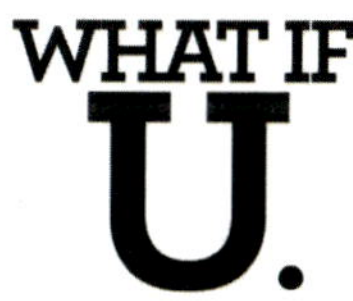

The portable creativity lab.

Available now on Amazon.com for iBook, Kindle and Nook

11. Ad campaign assignment

4 of 20 ads created to promote this book. Maintaining a consistent message and being creative with a series is tough work.

Name 5 topics, causes, or products that you feel strongly about. What do you have to say?

List

Sketch

Furniture design assignment

Unusual couch or chair design using unconventional or repurposed materials: Cardboard, garbage, deconstructed reconstructed furniture, old car parts. You don't have to make the thing, just sketch it out. But building a small model out of cardboard, heavy paper, x-acto knife and glue sticks gets your brain moving on a whole different level. Sketching something and figuring it out in 3-D are completely different ways of thinking. Consider the "is like" method when developing design ideas.

Travel poster assignment

Space travel to Bella Luna Resort on Mars. It's 5-star! A good headline goes a long way toward solving a visual problem and vice versa.

Haiku assignment

A Japanese non-rhyming poem of 17 syllables in 3 lines (5-7-5 syllables) that evokes some image about the natural world, a great opportunity for brief verbal symbolism. Or you can just write about your day.

How hard can it be?
Just seventeen syllables
I am too busy

Your turn

Song lyrics assignment

Everyone at some point in their lives has wanted to write a song, usually surrounding a broken heart or falling in love, or both, and beer. There are a host of well-known musicians who have made their names from the work that came out of a break-up. This is a great opportunity to access emotion, dig deep, use metaphor and simile and make a word picture to express some past or present heartfelt emotion.

Try comparing the feeling or event to something else. "You cut me like a bad razor." And you don't have to start in the beginning, just start with key phrases and tie them together.

Gadget assignment

You know there's a problem you've encountered that you have a genius solution for, sketch it out.

Story quilt

What can you make a quilt out of that tells a story? Think unusual materials. If you're an artist you should have no problem with this... push yourself. And if you are not an artist, you should have no problem with this because everyone knows what a quilt is. Just do the opposite. Don't go for the usual.

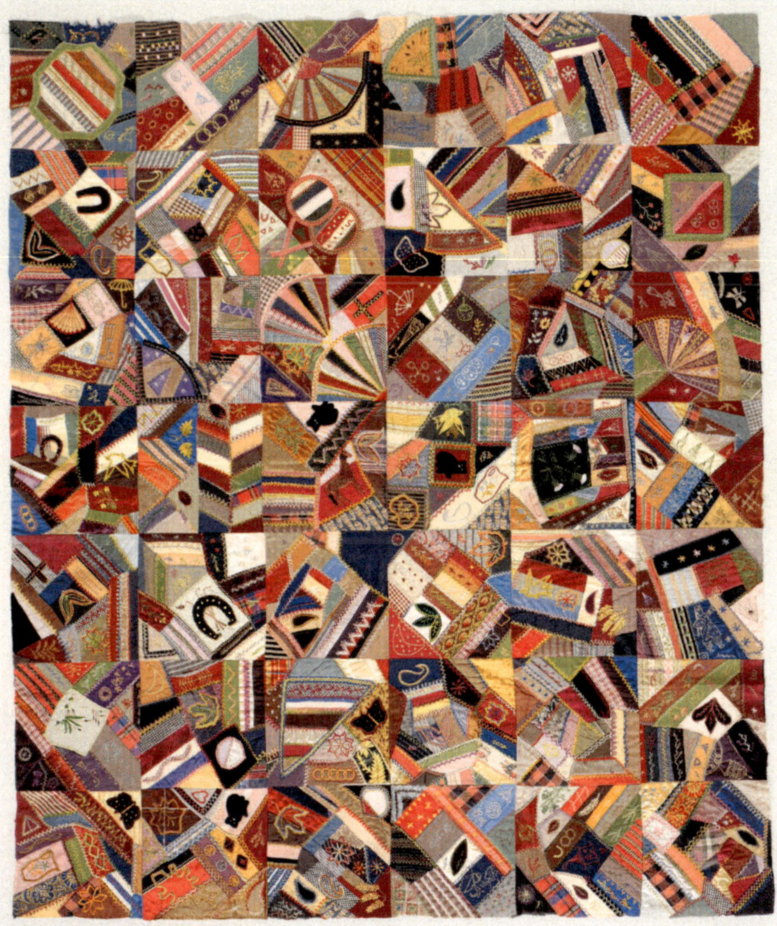

Quilt top, Crazy pattern. Artist unknown
Image courtesy of Metropolitan Museum of Art

Conscious and subconscious

Your subconscious is always at work. Even when you aren't consciously assessing away on an issue that needs a solution, somewhere in the recesses of your cranium the neurons are firing away at it. Case in point, the memory game, and I'll bet $1.45 this has happened to you.

You are at a party and your love bunny says, "Remember that TV show? You know... the guy with the rifle, gunslinger and town protector, son named Luke or something... black and white? What was his name?" And you say "Ummmm oh it's ummm... it's something like Blaine or something."

Your brain is starting to piece together the answer. It's sorting through file cabinets and slowly cracking the code by putting together the parts you are fairly sure of. Maybe you don't get it right then. But that night, as your head is about to hit the pillow and you are on some other thought train .... Wham!, out if comes. "Lucas McCain, The Rifleman!" So much for winning on Jeopardy.

I use this behind-the-scenes form of problem-solving all the time. It's part of the trust I have in the creative spirit, the muse, the subconscious mind. I am always open to what it has to offer. After I define, review, absorb the input and the restrictions (as in the above exercises), I do some research, make key word lists and a few sketches.

And then I just forget about it for a day or two and move on to something else. It feels often like I'm sending the problem upstairs to the creative department, because while my noggin is consciously working on other problems. Something happens.... a solution lands on my frontal doorstep. While I'm running other apps, like the driving the car app or the doing the laundry app, the internal software is quietly whirring in the background connecting the dots and sorting possible solutions, and then, out it comes. My own little subconscious Eureka plopped out from the id.

The trick is to really burn the parameters into your mind. Study them, write them down, diagram them, sketch and list and free associate and get familiar with it inside and out, so that it's still floating around when you stumble on the connector, which could be something completely unrelated.

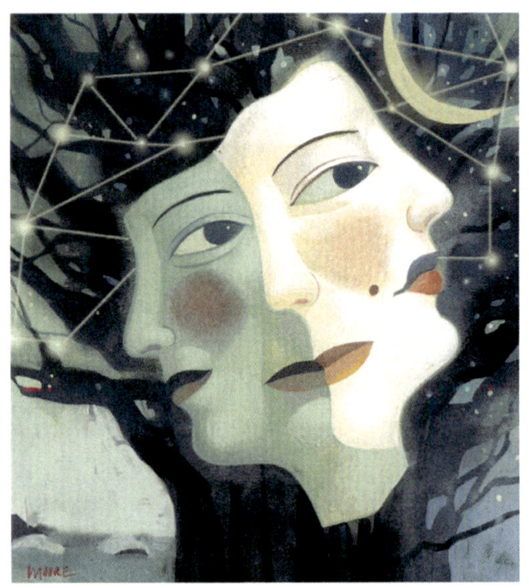

Your subconscious mind is always connecting the dots.

But it has some aspect that can be applied to the problem, a missing link to help solve the puzzler. As an example, out star-gazing one clear night, a writer sees a familiar cluster of stars and makes the connection that the stars are points that form a character or a symbol in a story, which leads to a new way to connect key plot points of a project that was stuck in the mud. The subconscious mind does automatically what we are learning to do here consciously.

Many great minds have experienced this backroom method of problem-solving. The state of being open is 24/7.

It's a fascinating process that involves a great deal of trust. One critical factor is the deadline. Without it, we can continue to whir on a thing until the other more critically on fire apps take over and put this particular problem into a file cabinet marked "Never mind."

Creating a visible reminder, like a big dry-erase calendar or setting a schedule of events on your iMachine so that it's right in front of your eyes and more prominent than the "Don't forget to feed the iguana" or "Recyclables go out Tuesday" post-it notes. Keep the deadline in the fore of your mind.

Intent scaffolding

The sibling of Feeding the Parameters, Intent Scaffolding is a way to tier what you want to do with goals that you set. It's a structure for creativity and process. To show you how this works, let's say as an artist I want to represent nature in a loose, richly colored palette. Then my Intent Scaffold will look something like this.

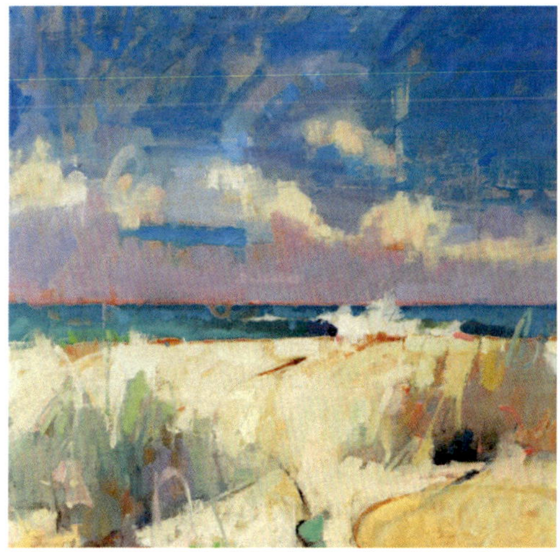

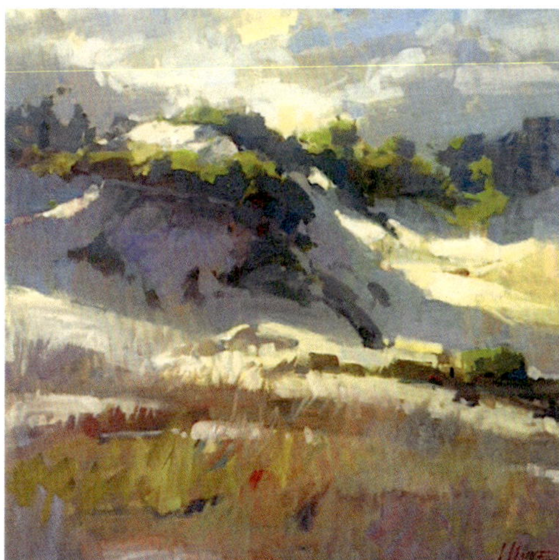

Statement:
I want to express the awe of nature in a more abstract and loosely described way with strong but realistic color.

Color palette:
full chroma / full value

Drawing:
realist with some interpretation of shape.

Edge:
lots of lost edge, hazy depictions.

Surface:
thin/thick, textured and drippy paint.

Impediments:
Paint too tight, can't get loose enough, need to work on values more.

Strengths:
Drawing, non-traditional solutions, understand abstract principles.

Exercises:

A) Small loose studies from life.

B) Paint without drawing, use unusual tools and large brushes, out of focus method.

C) Study color mixing: Use limited and unusual color palettes.

D) Use different surfaces and tools to force looser paint, use lots of paint.

Method:
Acrylic, oil, cold wax on wood.

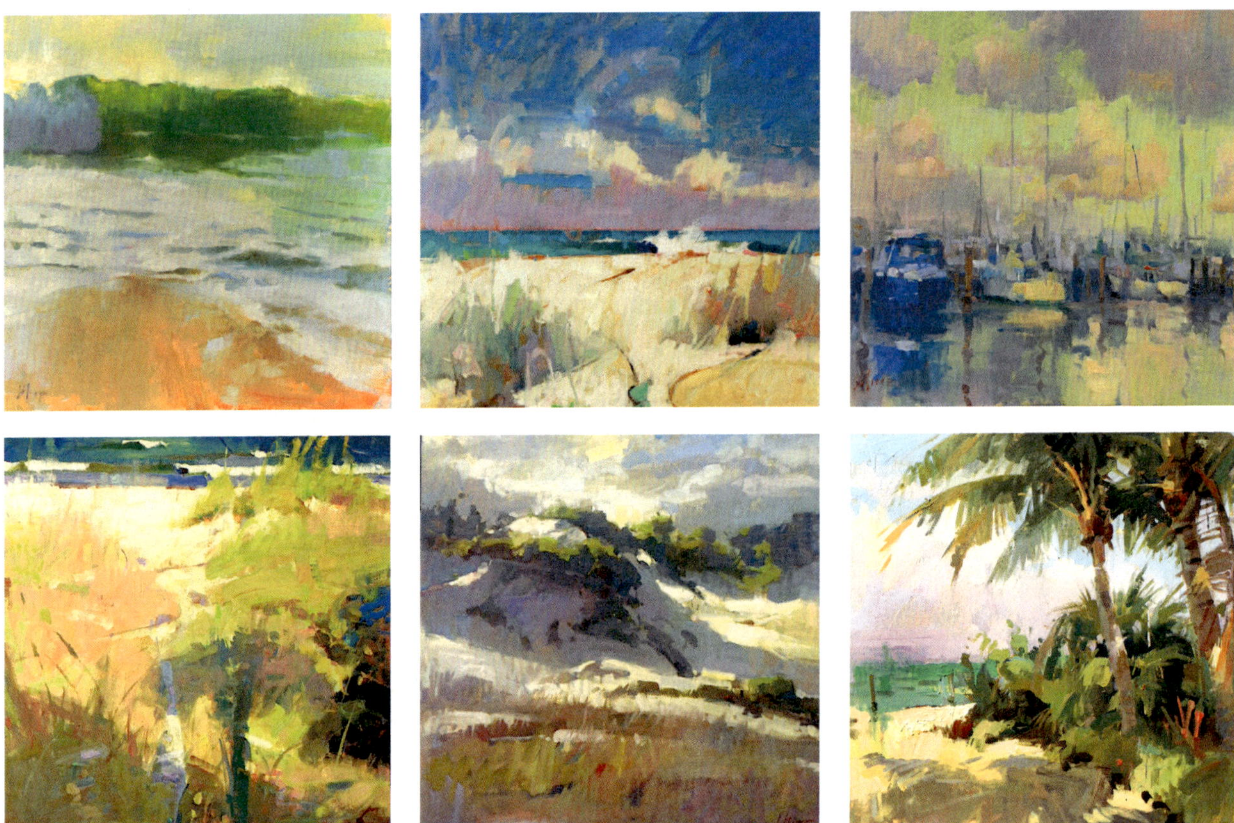

State your intent

Stating intent for the what, why and how of an endeavor allows the creator to stay on task throughout the work. Coastal theme, check. Loose with high chroma, check. Consistent approach and style, check.

You will find a lot more on this in the **Intent** section.

If I were to boil this whole creative process down to three basic components, they would be: Play, Intent and Discernment. Intent drives everything from product design to poetry. Without a path, it's all just aimless meandering and play is just play. Use the Intent Scaffold forms in **Intent** to design your road map.

The problem solver questions the problem

The creative mind isn't just waiting for an assignment. It's on the hunt and always in the state of openness, the 24 & 7 Brain Club. It's just waiting for the creative spirit to whisper, "Hey, check this out, it could fit." and "This is like....," and "Wait, why isn't there a better way?" Once the creativity threshold has been crossed, you are the hammer and everything is a nail. You've probably gotten a taste of it when you were in the middle of creating something. That magic part of your brain was switched on and doesn't get unswitched until something else takes precedence. You are experiencing a heightened state of mind, what is referred to as "flow." Inspiration emanates from all things: light, air, shapes, textures, the way a passing car is designed and, yes, even that problem child of a trash can that needs the genius touch.

And the ideas flow... so many "what if" scenarios, they are hard to filter and file. It is a wondrous world, the creator's playground, a room filled with things that can be adapted to fit another need, and a place where a need can be reframed.

The cognitive alchemist wants to experiment, solve and produce. But this isn't just a solution-oriented sport, it applies to the problem as well. One of the greatest instigators of change and adaptation doesn't lie in solving the answer to the puzzle. It is in questioning the problem itself. The world's shortest question: Why?

So often there is the assumption that an immediate solution is the critical thing, but the initial issue that started the whole mess is overlooked.

Conversation 1

We need a road over the mountain.

Why?

To get the people from here to there.

Why can't we go through the mountain instead of over it?

Because they said so.

Wait, why does the road even have to go there at all?

That's where the water is.

Why can't we bring the water to the people? Wouldn't it be better if we just ran a pipe?

I'll ask.

Conversation 2

We need a new TV ad for Merka jello products.

Why?

To promote Merka's Vegetable medley Jello

Why?

Because it's not selling.

Why?

Because it's vegetable medley flavored.

Why don't we rebrand it and sell it as Mirepoix stock for fancy French cooking?

I'll ask.

If you are open, everything gets questioned, reframed and converted into an "Is Like" or a "What if?" It may be annoying to the people you work with, but tough noogies, this is about making brilliance.

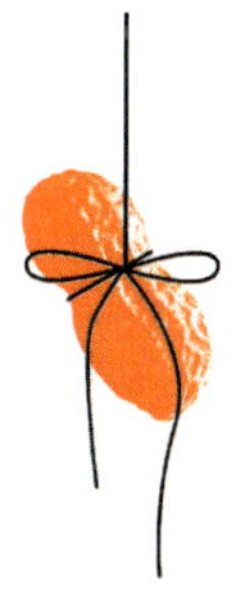

7. Intent

Intent is both the sextant and the compass of your vessel. Identifying not just where you are and the why of your journey, but also *where you want to go*. That's paramount in setting your path to authenticity and ensuring your creativity is your own.

Defining intent on both a big-picture scale and on a detailed level means you'll make more informed solutions, not just from the surface emotional responses or the imitative stylings that surround us. Intent builds the framework for a strong, unique voice. It allows for the planning of goals, action steps and the best use of your time. It's wheat from chaff time, ladies and gents.

Truly deciding on a direction, whether it's that first step or the voyage to Youtopia, means facing less internal resistance (putting aside the external ones, like family needs, financial needs, time availability). It stokes the fire in the belly, the want-its, the desire to do what is necessary to progress.

Winston Churchill once said "Never, never, never give up." No one knows for sure how many nevers he actually used, but three is pretty good. Even if you simply land on something that just piques your interest, rather than your radiant beacon of happiness, it's as good a place as any to start.

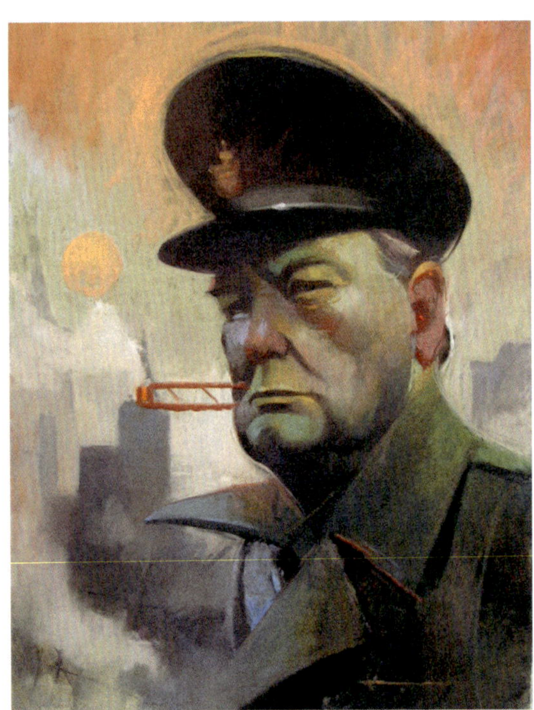

Winston Churchill, 18"x24" pastel on paper

"Feeling a little anxious about not knowing your intent? Don't sweat it. Just do, experience, observe, play, until something rings your bell. If you don't already have a bliss in mind to follow, then go and do and it will find you."

You may be a little stuck, or a lot. You may have only a notion that you want to do something creative, but not know where or how to start. You may already have set your clipper ship on its course, but you've decided to reroute just a little to visit some neighboring islands and frolic with the natives. By the way, try the ceviche, it's fab. All types are welcome here.

In my classes, I see people with all levels of desire and direction. Some know what they want and are already forging their way, learning as much as they can from whomever they can. They work from the larger intent of, say, finding their voice as a great landscape artist, to the micro-scale intents of mastering specific rudiments of painting.

Some come in not really knowing yet what they don't know. And when I show them the process, a way of self-discovery, it opens the door for the creative spirit. It doesn't happen to everyone in a class, but it always happens to someone.

For some, that takes a while to sink in. Often, the spark shows up in someone who is in the state of openness, willing to face the new or uncomfortable and ready to do what it takes, accepting of all information and prepared to do the work. The clear, bright light of intent means zero resistance.

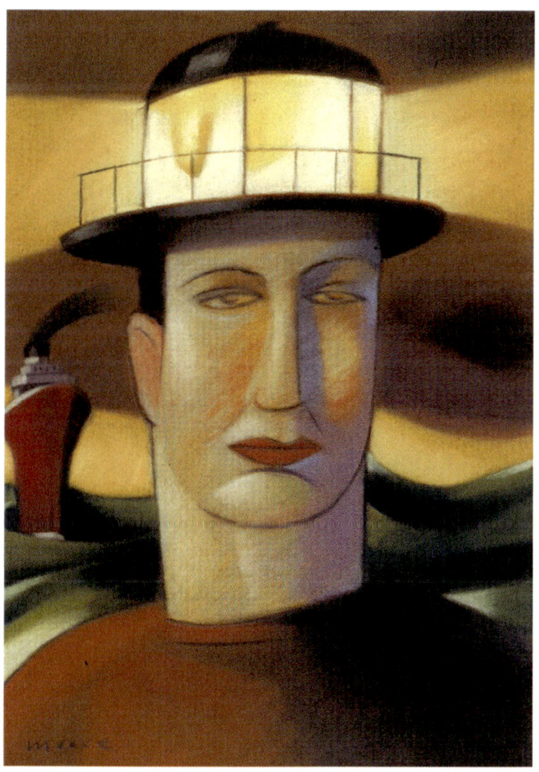

Be your own beacon. 10x16 in. pastel

Defining intent should occur first on a personal level, then on the bigger level of path and direction, and then to the more granular issues specific to the direction of the orbit.

Here's the general rundown on what is needed:

- **Your story - Core values, strengths & weaknesses**
- **Figuring out your *why*, your motivation**
- **Defining parameters of problems / solutions**
- **Learning every aspect of the how, the mechanics**
- **Nailing down what you have to say**
- **How do you want to say it**
- **Honing your path to authenticity, micro granularity.**

Decades ago, I had a conversation with a good friend, the extremely thoughtful and gifted artist Tim Beall, about the nature of my work. He asked about my process, why I painted what I painted and which methods I used to get there. I thoughtfully said, "Ummmmm, I don't know. I never really thought about it."

And he said, "Oh... the School of Pokenhope." I, of course, looked at him like he had just turned into a kangaroo.

He continued, "You are just pokin' and hopin' it's going to turn out." I bristled... and for a good while, I shrugged it off, because I had won a few awards in my time, so, obviously, I knew something. (I am capable, dammit.) But his words had started to seep in around the edges. I began to wonder why I didn't have a plan, a path for the larger stage, and for the smaller stages around the perimeter. It felt a bit like having a big circus tent without knowing what to put inside.

I thought just painting stuff was enough. Now, in mid-career, I saw that I did not yet know what I did not know. How was it that I didn't know why I was doing what I was doing? It dawned on me -- knowing myself and knowing my goals, my life's work, motives, paths, might be just a skosh important, unless, of course, I just wanted to wander around in increasingly larger circles until I accidentally fell into the magic well of success. As a commercial illustrator, a battle plan and a process was fundamental. Perhaps as a fine artist I should have one as well.

In the early days of my painting career, I believed I was pretty darn good. Sure, I had skills from my illustration days and, in fact, I was kind of a big deal in that realm -- at least in my zip code -- with a drawer full of awards and accolades. But that knowledge didn't necessarily translate over into the fine art realm.

The chat with my painting buddy had put a burr under my chaps, and had made me realize that I had a far piece to go up into them thar hills. Coming to the realization that I needed to know more about how and why was the second stage of learning, referred to as *conscious incompetency* or as I like to call it, the "Oh Crap" Stage. Now what?

The next move was to find ways to figure out what I knew and what I needed to know to move forward. I hadn't really determined which trail to take. But at least I was shopping for the horses to pull the wagon.

Although I did not realize it at the time, I would be switching horses in a lot of streams along the way. And, that's okay. What I had first thought was simply an inability to commit was really me flitting from one flower to the next to find which one I liked most.

I landed on plein air painting for many years, during and after my illustration days, which went well until I started to feel that I was missing the narrative part of visual art. Time to move on, but where to go? Next step: What did I have to say?

The act of painting an object realistically is a form of visual communication. It's a language. And when you alter some of the parts of the style so that it becomes more intensely colorful, for example, that becomes a dialect of that visual language. If you choose to add a story line, you add yet another layer and elevate the work, which creates another dialect.

All are conscious choices and the more conscious choices that are made about the creative endeavor, the more personalized and original it becomes.

If your current way is still not satisfying the authentic core self, and you decide to comment on the human condition by making morphed art-deco style cement figurative sculptures, that is an entirely new language with which to become fluent. Painting realistically = English. Painting brightly-colored figures fishing for crabs on a boat = Louisiana dialect, Art deco cement sculptures = Innuit eskimo.

A lot of the evolution of the creative is landing on an authentic language and learning it backwards and forwards. This is as true for music and writing as it is for art. Some are adventurous enough to create entirely new ways to communicate an idea by hybridizing methods and going outside of the known. This is known as scary art, (but after 50 years it will be called revolutionary.)

The driver

Lots of people hope to accomplish lots of things. Hope is not enough.

My brother is a guitar virtuoso and I thought it would be fun to learn to play so that I could accompany his brilliance and we could go on tour. After years of thinking about it, I finally went out and bought one! Hurrah! But I have yet to consistently pick it up and practice.

Apparently, I am not yet at that place of *fire in the belly* sufficiently to make me pick it up and work at it. Not that it won't come. There are just other things I want more.

How many of the exercises in this book have you done so far? That's a pretty good tell.

You'll do them when you're ready.

You have to do the work and do a lot of it. Talking with a psychologist about what gets people to change, or do something to initiate change, she said, "Well, showing up is a good start, but I can't change them, that takes action on their part."

I'm going to guess that you have already embarked on your craft and you're a diligent worker. Now is the time to take it further, and the best place to start is by understanding yourself.

The most important questionnaires you will ever fill out. Ever.

You may think you know yourself pretty well. But if everyone really knew themselves, there would be an ice cream counter instead of a self-help section at the book store.

Of all the things you can do to improve your skill set in any arena, picking a path, defining goals, and developing intent -- with an action plan and specific strategies to back it up -- will help you way more than a couple of how-to workshops. You'll choose more carefully the components you need to focus on, and make more thoughtful considerations of content and context, to spend your time wisely. You can watch all the how-to videos you like. Until you sit down and make a concentrated effort toward any goal, it's just entertainment.

To help you get to the specifics of who you are and what your intent is (for now), I give you the Life Forms: Life story, Core values, Personal goals, Resistance, Intent scaffold and Parameters worksheets.

This will help you gain clarity in your work by getting clear on yourself. Fill these out as if no one will see them. Be completely honest. When done, highlight key words that can trigger new movement in your creative endeavors.

Make multiple copies of these forms before you fill them out. You'll change over time, so date each one. What you want today depends on who you are today. And that evolves.

Life story

Start with a brief synopsis of your life. Include important events that have defined you and your world view, both good and bad. Rather than making this a Tolstoy novel, bullet-point the events, which can be anything from your first trophy to the nature of your upbringing, even the seemingly meaningless memories that still resonate with you.

LifeForm F4E-LS Life Story Date

My story to date.

What's my story to be in 1 year.

What's my story in 10 years.

Core values

List the principles and standards that matter most in your personal and creative life, along with the five or so most important things in your life, from a loved one to a cause to ice cream. The resulting keywords can inform your efforts and your path.

LifeForm F4E-CV Core Values Date

Define your core values as they pertain to your personal life and then to your creative life. They can change over time, hence the date.

My creative purpose in the short term is:

My creative purpose in the long term is:

Core values that are important to me in my life: *Think in terms like courage, honesty, intelligence, defending nature etc. Be honest, this is for your eyes only.*

And in my creative endeavors:
Think in descriptive terms like unique, adventurous, informing, motivating, challenging, financial producing, fame, etc.

In order of importance, list 5 (up to 10) things that are of utmost importance to me.

1.
2.
3.
4.
5.

Goals

Playing Madison Square Garden to a sell-out crowd is a dream. Performing to a full house at a decent local venue is an attainable goal. To get there you need to be honest, realistic and diligent... but a dream can be a great driver to attain your goals. Here's what you'll need to do:

Identify your current skill level and the skill level you want to reach.

Rate your abilities in key skill components. (Singing, grammar, drawing, wood-joining).

Which skills are most important?

What do you need to get there: Time, equipment, money, and what you'll need to learn – education or training.

List any specific accomplishments on your wish list: MFA, MacArthur grant, Pulitzer, article in your fave magazine, just wanna be good. These things give your decisions direction.

Consider your most important goals and write a promise to yourself, a contract, a commitment to follow your dream. There's a big fat line between a wish and a goal.

LifeForm F4E-PG Personal Goals Date

Big changes or little ones? Set your life and creative goals in an honest way. Identify your ability level of your preferred skill from 1 (low) to 10 (high), identify the skill level of where you want to be on the same scale. Use a master artist benchmark as your 10.

Skill components that are important to my work.

My current skill level:

In 5 years:

What are my life goals?

What will I need to have to get there? *Materials, financial, emotional support*

What will I need to do to get there? *Action steps. Specific skills to focus on.*

1.

2.

3.

4.

5.

Which accomplishments are important for me to achieve and why?

This is my promise to myself: *Make a clear commitment in writing, a contract with yourself for what you want to achieve.*

Motive/Resistance:

Identifying your true driver is as important as it gets. Knowing this can streamline your most important decisions and action steps. List the external and internal forces that hold you back. (Fears: Read the **Resistance** section) List which forces you can change, reframe or drop and which you have to accept.

LifeForm F4E-RM Resistance/Motive Date

Defining your why. No matter what your goals are, being honest about why you do what you do or want to do is critical. Identifying what holds you back is too.

My motives for creating: *i.e. Not starving, self-expression, learn my craft, meet cute girls/boys, etc.*

Identifying resistance: *Reread the Resistance section if you need a refresher.*

What are my fears:

I am held back *(internal resistance)* by:

I am/my work is affected by these external forces *(what prevents you from being your authentic self)*

These are the external forces I wish to keep (important) and why:

These are the external forces I wish to put aside and why:

Intent scaffolding

Scaffolding is not a new concept. It describes tiered-learning in education. Here, it's a way to state your intent and create a hierarchy of importance for ideas, actions and goals. It's a way to figure out what you are going to do next, what you want to say, and how. It's a structure for creativity and process, a mission statement with a workable plan attached, the passport for your journey.

What are your strengths?

Your strengths can come in the form of personality traits, like diligence, problem-solving and humor. And they can come in the form of technical strengths -- drawing, engineering, coloring, narrating, shape-making and abstraction. Even skills that have nothing directly to do with your goals count.

Or you can make it just like a high school year book: Most likely to draw stuff, captain of the scrimshaw team, tallest in the band, most personality disorders.

What can you bring to the table?

This will be a distillation of all the forms down to a couple of clear, thoughtful phrases to discern the you in your creative endeavor. Look at who you are, what you can do and your motives for getting on this crazy train.

Mine would be along these lines:
I love telling a story with paint. I draw well and paint well. I have a black belt in creative thinking skills, am highly adaptive and have a strong work ethic. I want to represent nature in an unconventional way, go large scale with high price points, make a good bit of moolah, travel the world and encourage the next thing to show up.

Note, please, that I am writing in a language that I would never use in front of another person, except you, because I trust you. It's too braggy sounding, but this is for me. I am owning it, so that I can believe in myself enough to follow through.

What do you have to say?

This comes from your core values, strengths and your life story. It can be an artist statement or a description of what you want to express on the large scale and small.

What are the components that comprise your vision?

Words? Mixed media, weaving, trombone, realist painting, installation art with sand, salt and found shoes, a combo platter of these? Not required in the beginning, but as you progress, pick a method and really work it out. Stay the course.

"The more conscious choices that are made about the creative endeavor the more personalized it becomes."

Actions

Use your goals, values, strengths and resistance forms to identify a plan of action. Be realistic. Becoming the best violinist in the world is not a goal or an action plan, it's a dream. Finding a violin tutor and making the time is a plan. Think short-term, mid-term and long-term and, again, be realistic. I would like to be a black belt in karate in six months but that is not possible.

LifeForm F4E-IS Intent Scaffold Date

What are my strengths:
The things you are good at, include skills/passions that don't relate directly to your path.

What I can bring to the table:
Say it like you mean it.

What do I have to say:
Everyone feels strongly about something, what's your passion?

Mission Statement: *(personal)*
A formal statement of your aspirations and core values.

Artist statement: *(body of work)*
State to the best of your ability a description of intent for your work. Address issues or elements of your expression that are important to you.

Components of creating that are central to the direction:
These are going to depend on what you are after, i.e. narrative, interpretation/style, etching, rhythm, mixed media, history, juxtaposition, found objects, color... etc.

Training goals *(stuff you know you gotta work on):*

Another example: I have an ongoing series of paintings that represent animals in an unconventional narrative style with a theme of man vs nature. If I were to sit down and write this out with the **intent scaffold** for the body of work, it would read like this:

Statement:
I want to express the conflict between nature and man by juxtaposing animals with industrial spaces. Who is intruding on whom?

Color palette:
Natural color, somber, lots of darks

Drawing:
Realistic but with some interpretation of shape.

Edge:
Lots of lost edge, hazy description countered by tight detail

Division of space:
Unusual breaking up of canvas, off kilter compositions, use color, mass to create asymmetrical balance.

Surface:
Texture variety, thin and thick.

Impediments:
Need compelling ideas that aren't obvious. Don't have exotic animals in my back yard. Need to practice my drawing of animals.

Exercises:

A) Draw animals. Go to zoo and draw from life. Gesture drawing. Take photos.

B) For ideas, multiple thumbnails of unusual combinations of animals in spaces. Not fantasy-based.

C) Take photos of gritty abandoned building interiors.

D) Paint technique: selective focus method. Thin wash layers and areas of thick paint. Use different methods for under-painting; pour, unusual tools, experiment.

E) Work on color: Develop color combos. Use limited or unusual color palettes.

F) Surfaces: Wood, linen, masonite, heavy gesso, more texture.

Methods: mixed media, house paint, acrylic, oil, and cold wax on wood.

Goals:
One man show in major gallery, go large scale. Higher $$'s. Sell stuff.
Elle Macpherson as a girlfriend or similar.

Action steps:

List of animals, 35-50 finished paintings, marketing and branding, small book. Two shows per year; contact specific galleries. Big coffee table book when done. Shoot repro quality pics of each painting.

The Intent Scaffold on pg. 118 is for *Intrusion,* an idea that began as a single sketch, the result of a search for a narrative that was unique to my core values and turned into an ongoing body of work. Developing a series in this way is a process of growth and self-discovery. As I progressed through the series a very personal narrative hidden in each piece became apparent.

These were about me, not just nature. I chose the animals, for the most part, randomly, but I found the subconscious mind hard at work. Only by staying with a concept can an artist fully explore the true depths of an idea. From one simple notion can come a lifetime of work.

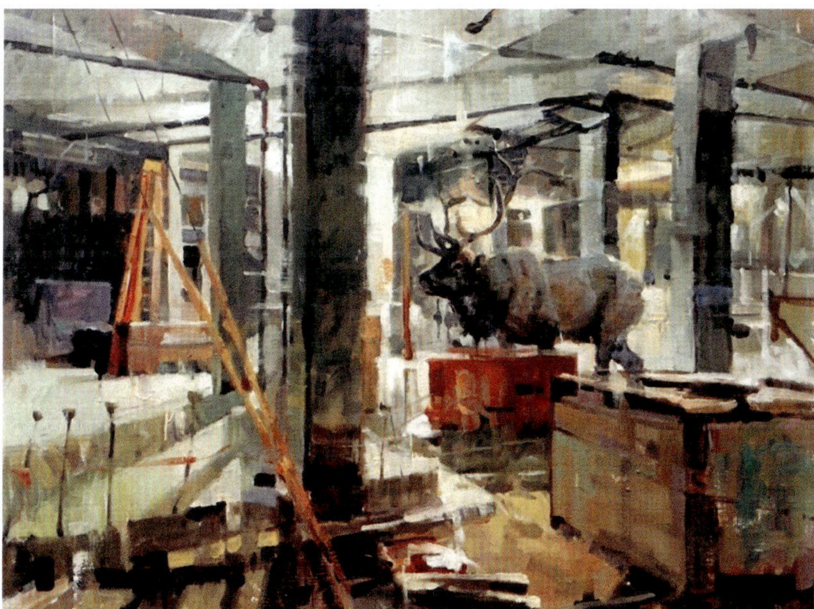

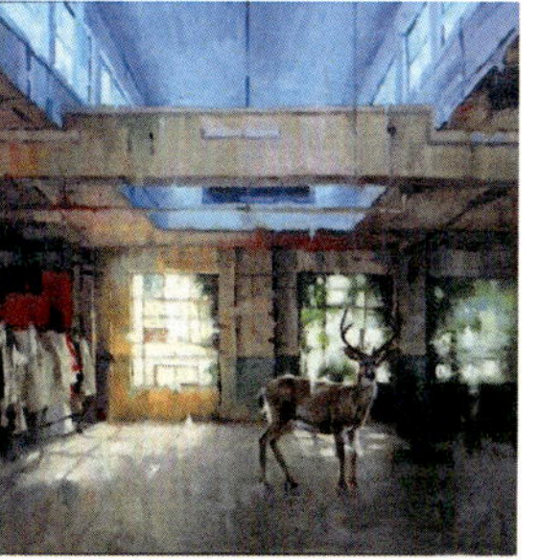

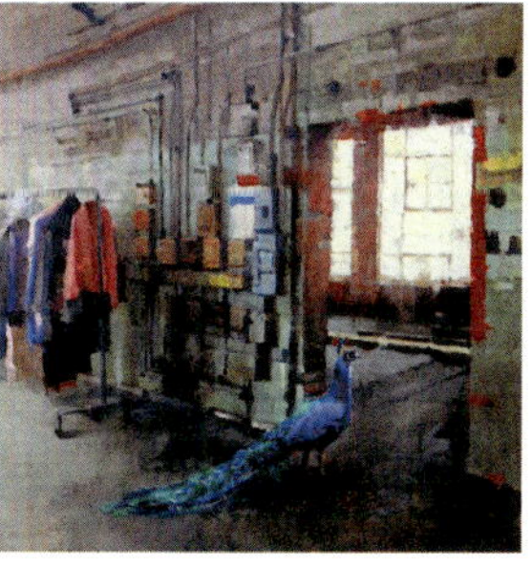

7.1 Intent: Man vs nature

The theme that drives the engine. One good idea is fine, but a series allows for more in depth exploration of a thesis. Various sizes, oil on wood.

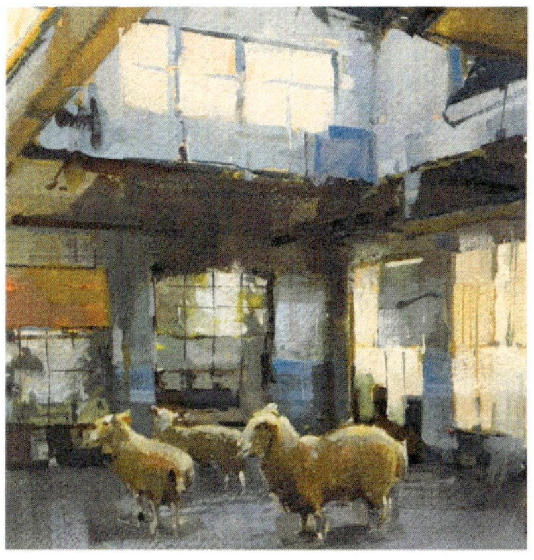

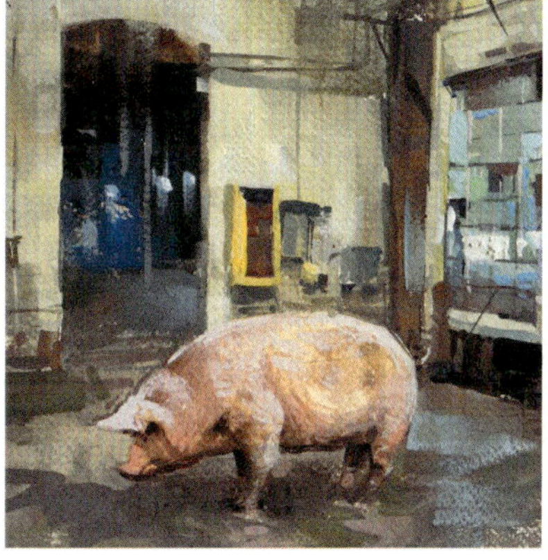

To get to the big ideas, lots of little ideas were developed and considered. These exploratory 8 x 8 in. gouache paintings were enjoyable because, at this scale and with this medium, I was free to take more risks.

Granularity

Whatever stage you are in as a creative -- beginner, intermediate, advanced or super-secret 10th-degree black belt ninja master -- you should aspire to a constant honing of the blade. In the beginning, the path is not always clear, so there are more knives to sharpen than at a Dansk outlet store.

Laying out the Intent Scaffold helps guide your efforts toward which elements to practice. In the intermediate stages, your skill set should be forming up and moving toward sharpness as the areas of necessary training become even more clear, i.e. which components require the most focus.

If you are stronger in one component than the others, concentrate on the weaker ones to bring them up to par. This is a good time to address your *why* and further define your voice, developing the artist statement, personal goals and what it is you want to communicate with your work, if you didn't already have an idea to begin with.

This process is the formation of self, the gradual bringing into focus of one's authenticity, as if we, and, by extension, our efforts are walking slowly out of the fog and into light. While a few are given the gift of this comprehension at an early age, most aren't that fortunate and have to wait for the distant call of the creative spirit... what it is we are to do with who we are. But the more you apply yourself, the clearer that voice becomes.

As the artist moves into the more advanced stages of craft and concept and the path is, for this time, laid out ahead, the skill set acquired over years of concerted effort and practice begins to naturally evolve. Certain components of the voice begin to grow in levels of importance and others begin to go dormant, becoming less a part of the overall intent.

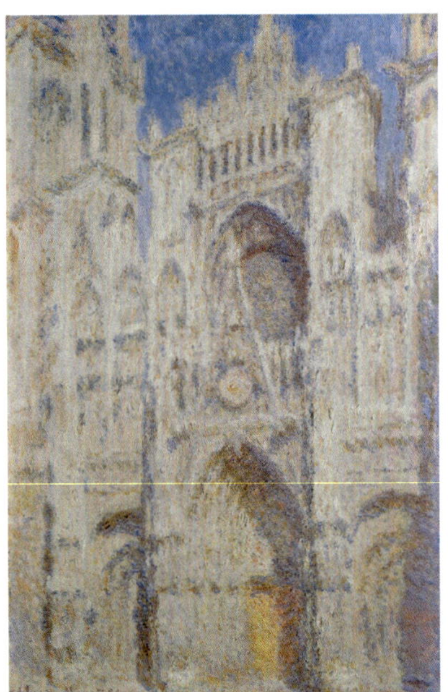

Claude Monet *The Rouen Cathedral: The portal (sunlight),* 1894, 39 1/4 x 25 7/8 in. oc Image courtesy of The Metropolitan Museum of Art

It's here that the concept of granularity comes into play. At some point, after all the work has been done on the larger levels, just as in a great painting, the important areas of process that are key to that intent become your most decisive focus.

"I want to paint the air which surrounds the bridge, the house the boat, the beauty of the air in which these things are located."

- Claude Monet

This is where the nuances of the intent and the components of the process are placed under the microscope. If the artist stays on the path and the big solutions have been explored, the obvious has been done to a fault, the need to go deeper arises from within, the call to climb further into the well and see what muse lives there drives the intent of the creator into more subtle and sophisticated relationships of the parts.

For the figurative painter who has mastered drawing, value and color components, it may be that the drawing and color come to the fore, with more attention on narrative or edges, or the same artist could become fascinated with brushwork and spontaneity and that becomes the emphasis of the work.

For a musician, the hours of covering other artists' songs build the requisite understanding of song-making enough that it comes time to hone the writing blade. It is this nuance of the components and the story behind the creator that comprise the voice of the artist.

It's at this stage that many creatives take a sabbatical from their usual calendar to focus on their voice. They dig deep to give 100% to their creative spirit.

Here, the exercises of guided play and multiples in the **Connectivity** and **VoiceFinding** sections can be employed again and again to finesse on a small scale the micro-relationships of components.

This evolution is in constant motion. Just as nature bends and adapts to refine herself over eons, it's up to us to move and flow and make the change according to intent. We don't have eons.

Authentic change should take time, but it can be manipulated and sped up, once the priorities of intent are set.

It works a lot like elementary school, periods of intense learning interspersed with guided and purposeful play. Then rest and repeat, (then milk and a nap.)

Over time, a circle of acquaintances and friends has formed around me, or I should say, we formed around one another. A tribe of independents brought together by a common aspiration, to progress as artists. While soaking in nature, we grow together.

It's an activity that can be experienced in a small group while focused on one's improvement and the voice of the creative spirit. It has been a big part of my learning experience to gather with my tribe on painting trips and work alongside respected peers and come together over dinner to discuss theory and applications of nuance.

We are all at that place where we focus on our own specific components. But each artist has a different set of priorities, so everyone brings something to the table and we all learn.

This stage of granularity is also a time to push the boundaries of learned process and become open to all things for additional inspiration, letting stimuli filter through the heightened *flow*-state of the artist.

In this elevated level of awareness, all things can inform the work, like the crisp notes of a bite of apple pulled from a stray tree or the rhythms formed by a grouping of stanchions in a boat yard that are vaguely reminiscent of sheet music, or the stories of the sea-faring workers who live in the extreme locations of the North Atlantic. This is how inspiration comes.

8. Discernment: CRITICAL THINKING

The world is full of ideas that arrive like the Saturday taxis in Times Square. Coming up with a few is the easy part. The hard part is figuring out which work, identifying why they do or don't, and filtering out or refining the parts that underachieve. Only then can you move forward with whole-hearted belief that your solution is the best it can be. This requires one part ruthless judge, one part courage and, of course, a model.

Now it's time for assessment, the most challenging stage:

- **Define the parameters of the problem to be solved**
- **Set up your Intent Scaffold**
- **Play: working with multiple solutions**
- **Assess solutions based on parameters**
- **Application: Implementation and presentation**

Your exploratory play time is over and there are stacks of ideas to review and pages of solutions to sift through, and perhaps a nearly finished execution staring at you. How do you figure out what works and what doesn't?

There is no universal barometer. Every creative problem is different, as are the solutions. There are only the subjective and objective responses from which to work and judge. So, let's do a quick review, because both are essential. But, depending on the problem, one may be more important than the other.

The objective, based on facts, data, rules and guidelines, is impartial. The subjective, based on or influenced by personal feelings, tastes and opinions is, well, partial.

An artist's work can and should be highly subjective. The content, the color choices, the method of application, all originate from the creator.

But even the subjective can and should be built on an objective platform. The solutions require thoughtful consideration. Does a painting work compositionally, based on known compositional constructs? Does this tie go with my shirt and pants? Does the song fit into the generally accepted framework of song-writing (if it is within the intent of the artist)?

I know from many years as a visual communicator and instructor that maintaining objectivity about one's own work is nearly impossible. We get so wrapped up in the pieces / parts that we can't see the whole, looking through the wrong end of the telescope. That's when we call on a trusted colleague who has fresh eyes or hire an editor who actually knows how to write or, perhaps, tell a joke to a crowd of unfriendlies to get an honest response.

As a means of starting out when we are in our formative years, we use the masters who have gone before us as our personal touchstones to gauge our work. But it's the rare artist who, once influenced by these masters, can then separate from their once-guiding beacon, with only the light of their own intent to go by. Like running in the dark, a little light can go a long way.

And that brings us back to the original parameters of a problem and the intent scaffold (hopefully) created before all the fun began. The best criteria for discernment is the framework / research created before play time started, remembering that we need both the objective and the subjective viewpoints. The yin needs the yang for balance and the left brain needs the right to not be so boring.

While there is no single unified method of discernment, there is a way to check and assess your own work to filter the wheat stuff from the chaff stuff by using the same Parameters and Intent Scaffold that guided the solutions to begin with.

Assessment and evaluation

Using terms of inquiry and questions can help you reach an objective judgment. Useful keywords for these steps, like *analyze, contrast, simplify, function, motive, survey, inference and conclusion* can be used as guiding terms to assess and appraise the concepts, filtered through the parameters from which they came.

With this, just like in the NFL, we make the first round of draft cuts and on into the second and third rounds. Bear in mind that solutions are always a work in progress, a series of corrections. In the case of more subjective output, where there is no definitive right or wrong answer, nothing to compare it with, the deciding factor can simply be a deadline, as in, time's up, put your pencil down.

When is a book done? When the publisher must go to press. A painting is never done, no song is perfect in the eyes of its creator. At some point the artist, writer, inventor comes to a place of decision and says; This is as far as I can go, based on what I know right now.

Inquiry

The necessary counterpart to play and thoughtful exploration, examining the creative results through a series of questions, comes when all the "what if's" have been birthed and it's time to appraise the spoils, using a series of questions to filter, refine, rework and push forward. Bringing these steps in too soon can limit the outcome, much like the weary traveler getting 90% down the trail and turning back for fear of making a mistake. Separating the subjective and the objective viewpoints allows each to better perform.

As I guide my students in developing their own inquiry and assessment approach, or the inner critic, I've noticed that the answer is often presented in the question:

Student: *Do you think I should make this color less intense?*

Me: Yes.

Student: *Do you think this piece is too confusing?*

Me: Yes.

Student: *Is it okay if I try to...*

Me: Yes.

Often students know what to do before I try to pry it out of them using inquiry, because they have already identified something that doesn't work. I don't have to always agree with them because it's their solution and not mine, though I may ask them to consider the intent and suggest additional alternatives.

If they go with their gut and it doesn't work then they've still learned something -- what not to do.

Ultimately, you must satisfy your creative spirit or suffer the niggling sensation that something isn't right. Identifying the problem is key. You don't always have to have a solution right away. That can take time and, for the record, solutions don't have to be permanent, they can always be amended or withdrawn.

To bring this book together, I started with a rambling collection of thoughts and notes, like a pile of rocks that I slowly arranged and rearranged and edited until I was satisfied that I'd built my rock pile into a home. It took time, because I was in a constant state of assessment. What seemed like pretty good stuff in the early stages ultimately went through a lot of change, but those original ideas were the building blocks. Bringing in a good editor as an objective writing mechanics coach did not hurt either.

Heart and intuition

I know what you're thinking, "Where the heck is heart in all this assessment crap?" Ya gotta have heart, passion, intuition, emotion. You must believe in yourself to the exclusion of anything that may stand in the way if you are going to succeed.

But it's important to understand, as much as is possible, these different methods of discernment – and how they work -- because sometimes the heart is wrong and other times intuition may be all you have to go on.

Play, exploration and implementation -- that's where the heart is.

Using inquiry, seeking clarification through thoughtful questioning, will allow for the objective to enter into the equation rather than, "I like it, it's kinda cool."

Here are a few questions to mull over during your assessment. Answering these one at a time and to the best of your ability is your best form of discernment. Also, employing a second set of eyes doesn't hurt.

Is the outcome in keeping with the parameters?
What assumptions am I making?
What changes would I make?
Have I edited this to its simplest form?
Is it practical, based on the criteria?
Do I feel satisfied with this/these? And after three days?
If this were someone else's project, what would my opinion be?
How would I rate the solutions (1-10 scale)?
Can I assess the value or importance of the best concepts?
What would I say about this in a presentation?
Why is it better than __________?
Which solution would I select and why?
Can I validate or test the results?
Are these concepts authentic to me?

As an example, listed below are a series of solutions that we can review based on the problem parameters and assess from objective and subjective frames. In the **VoiceFinding** section for painters, I'll use more specific measures to gauge a predominantly subjective painting. One major consideration is whether the solution needs to communicate a message, satisfy a need or appeal to a broader group than just the creator.

Some art is just plain unknowable. Some work is created more to confront than to inform, whereas designing a full-page ad in Garden and Gun, which costs around 55G's per page, damn well better sell some product or heads are gonna roll. Conversely, some things are just done for fun, or compulsion, or to zag when others are zigging, and as such need only satisfy the one who makes them. Different intent requires different forms of assessment.

We are drawn to the visionaries, those zaggernauts who paddle furiously upstream while the rest flow happily down to the delta, coming up with something that is just plain different, compelling or completely new. The new idea. There is always room on this planet for the intrepid explorer with big ideas that stand apart from the regular, pretty good ideas that comprise the norm.

Elon Musk develops Paypal, SpaceX and Tesla. Andy Goldsworthy makes ephemeral sculptures from nature and transplants them in urban settings so that people can watch them disintegrate. The architect Frank Gehry decided that buildings no longer had to be formatted as rectilinear and could be rounded or shaped like crumpled pieces of paper. And somebody came up with FedEx, an international overnight delivery system for which there was no infrastructure at all. Gutsy. These are concepts that had no yardstick, they were new and, at the time, became the prevailing benchmark... until the next explorer pushed the boundaries further still.

"Critical Thinking narrows and creative thinking expands, but they must work in tandem for problem solving and decision making."
- Pearl Zhu

Discernment by parameters

In Intent, we discussed *"feeding the parameters."* Let's look at a variety of problems and subsequent solutions to see how this works. I'll start with a well-known problem/solution story and then move to more uncharted territories. First, we go to the objective settings of a well-known problem to be solved by one Thomas Edison, circa 1870's:

Problem 1: New light source

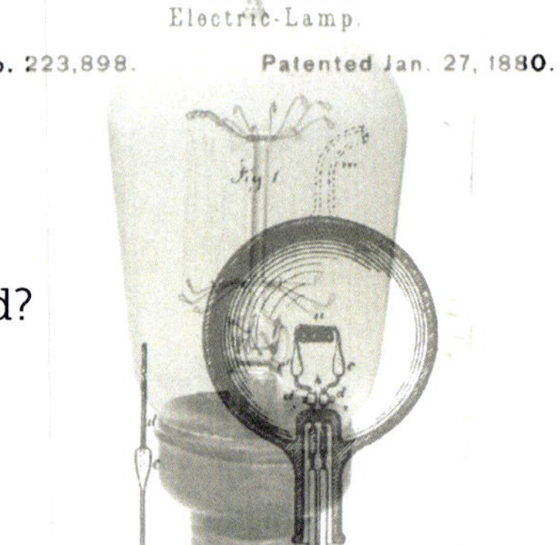

1) A light source for mass use that does not rely on directly burning carbon fuels.
2) Is there a yardstick to measure by?
3) Energy source: Please, anything but whale oil.
4) Can the light emitting contraption be mass produced?
5) Is it commercially viable?
6) Is the energy source accessible?
7) Positives and negatives.

Are the original parameters of the problem satisfied?

1) Light source. Yes (after much trial and error). An incandescent light bulb that works on electricity.
2) Yardstick? Yes, Humphry Davy's bulb from 1800. Does this one exceed the original? Yes
3) Viable energy source? Electricity, though still working out the bugs and supply system on that.
4) Mass producible? Yes
5) Is the concept commercially viable? Yes and no. Great idea but no infrastructure yet... working on that too. But a huge demographic of people who like to see in the dark.
6) Energy source infrastructure. Lots of bugs on that one, AC vs DC, home plant vs power plant, power lines etc.
7) Pros and cons. A couple of pros (light for everyone) and a ton of cons. Breaking the cons into separate problems helps. But, problem 1, light bulb, solved and patented!

Overall rating 4 out of 6. Plus, the target demographic is anyone with eyeballs, so the obstacles are worth overcoming.

You get the idea, test the solutions against your own framework, run it by some trusted brains for their responses. The light bulb had a lot of practical criteria to fulfill. But what about something with a little different subjective / objective mix? For that I'll use my wheelhouse of illustration, where there were both O&S specifics to satisfy. And for this I'll use one of a series of cruise ship posters I created a few years back.

Problem 2: Period travel poster for cruise ship

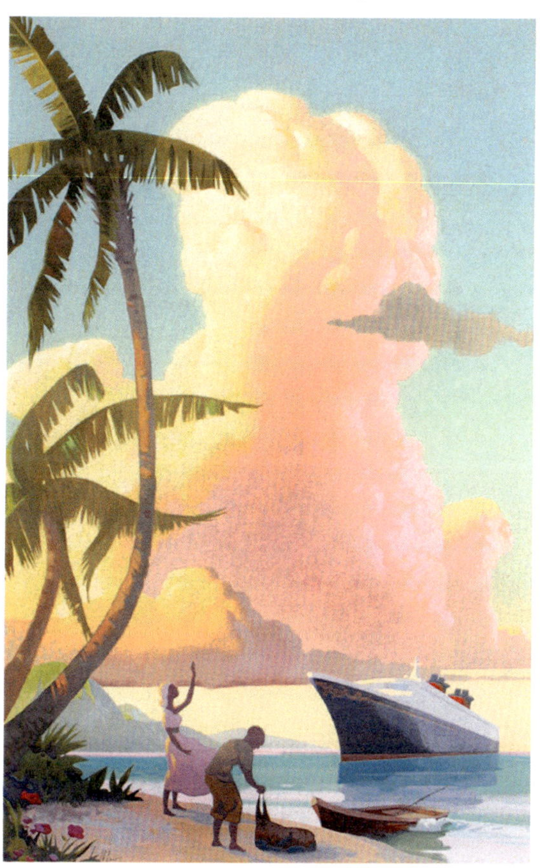

Parameters:

1) Create original painting that has a vintage cruise line travel poster feel, circa early 1900's.
2) Must communicate a specific tropical destination, be warm and inviting and include some portion of the ship.
3) Is there a yardstick? Yes. Highly recognizable existing vintage travel style poster art.
3) Must satisfy client, in this case, the Creative Director for the cruise line.
4) No size restrictions, but there is a deadline, so medium sized art is better than large
5) What can I bring to this? Ability to work in any medium and mimic a style, graphic design background, and a love for narrative art and vintage anything.

First steps involved a bit of research (acquisition) in the form of vintage travel poster books, safaris to antique malls for travel stuff, a gallery of stone lithographs and vintage travel art, an extensive internet search of anything and everything that related.

I gathered up applicable images, samples and ship reference and created my *Beautiful Mind wall.* Worked through multiple solutions in thumbnail format (connectivity), picked my faves and refined for preliminary approval (discernment).

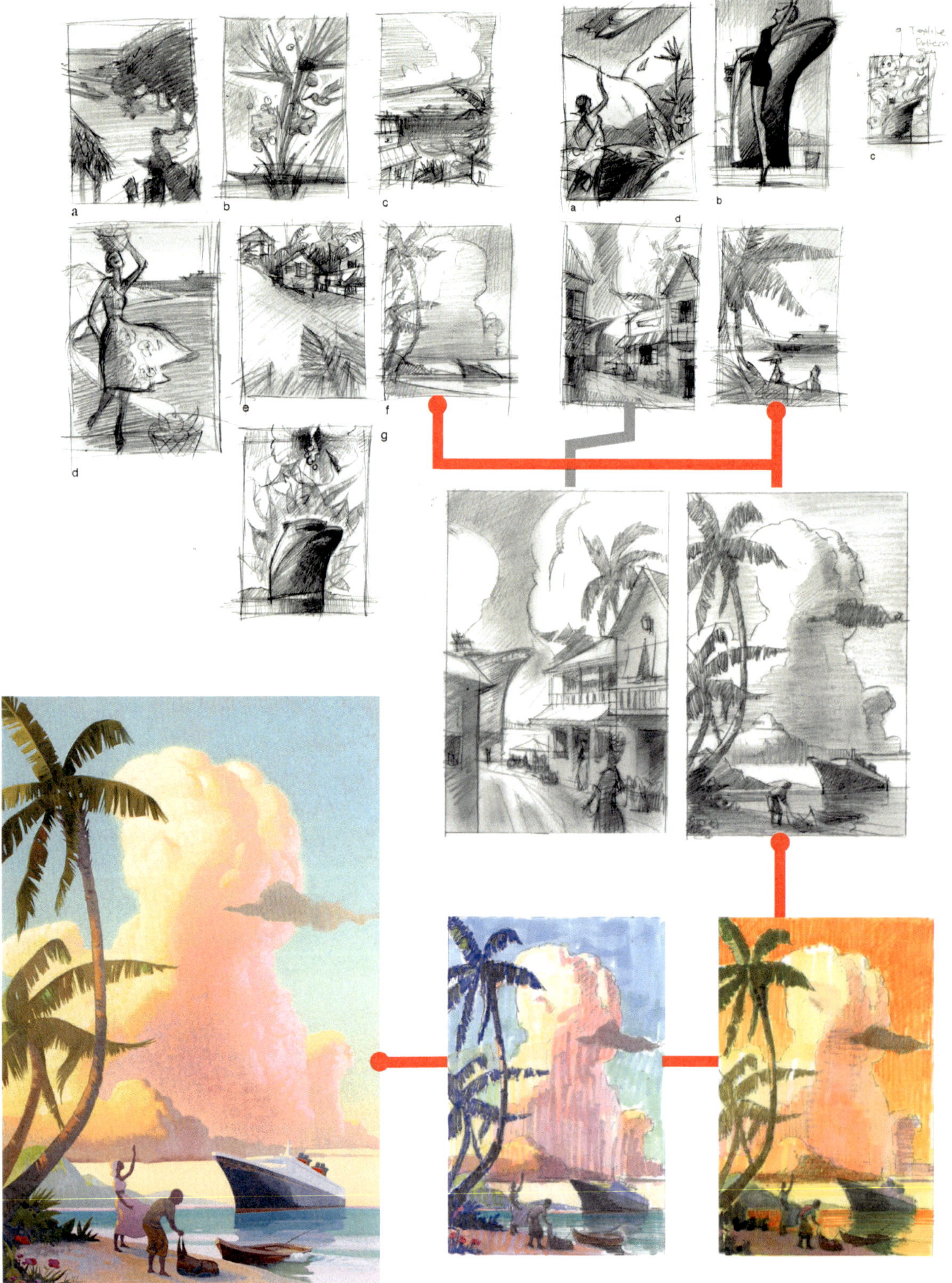

Travel poster

Assessing the work against the parameters. Has a vintage feel. Yes. Tells the right story. Yes. Thoughtful design with room for type. Yes. Satisfied clients needs and expectations. Yes.

Solutions (multiples) review, refine, assess and submit for third party approval. By "chunking" or isolating the stages, my brain power and efforts could be focused on one stage at a time. And by using a tiered form of assessment I could quickly decide on a solution. Notice that I didn't say, "the right solution." As I've mentioned, if you gave 10 people the same assignment you might get 10 different answers. The one that gets picked should be the one that best meets the Intent criteria or the parameters in a compelling way -- and the more obvious ideas are filed under "S" for Seen it.

A bad idea or even a near miss may not work for its intended use, but *may* work for another. Never toss a bad idea.

Case in point, a scientist working on a specific kind of adhesive discovered one that didn't stick very well. It didn't solve the problem at hand but, but as it turns out, it could be applied to a problem that didn't even exist (somebody was a problem finder). Low-tack adhesive on small paper note pad equals Post-it notes, and you know how that went.

Problem 3: Design for a chair

Parameters:

1) People have to be able to sit in it, for home use.
2) Must be simple, functional and practical to produce.
3) Must be aesthetically pleasing.
4) Contemporary in design but with mass appeal.

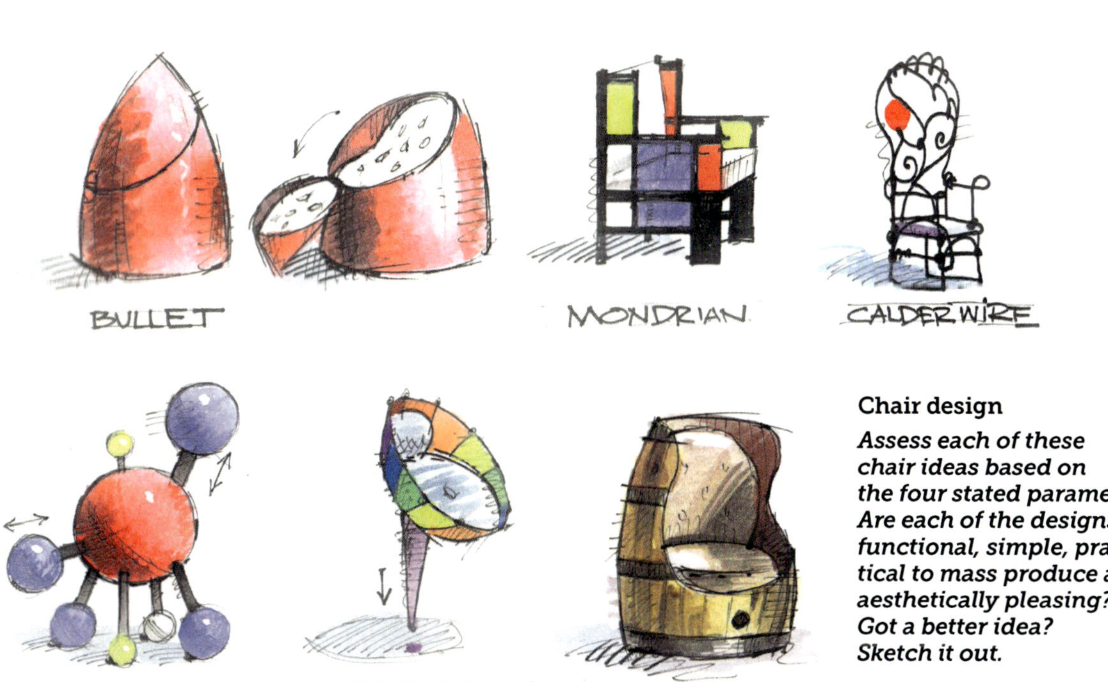

Chair design
Assess each of these chair ideas based on the four stated parameters. Are each of the designs functional, simple, practical to mass produce and aesthetically pleasing? Got a better idea? Sketch it out.

Problem 4: The painting that didn't fit

Now for something with more subjective criteria. Keep in mind that this painting emanated from my hands and, as such, will have my subjectivity all over it. You may or may not like it, or you may disagree with the choices, but when dealing with personal work we make our judgments as best we can from our own intent and personal aesthetic.

Parameters:

1) Must convey some aspect of nature, landscape.
2) Colorful and inventive, because people love color and inventiveness.
3) Strong, unique voice.
4) Fits the venue of realist gallery in Santa Fe, NM.

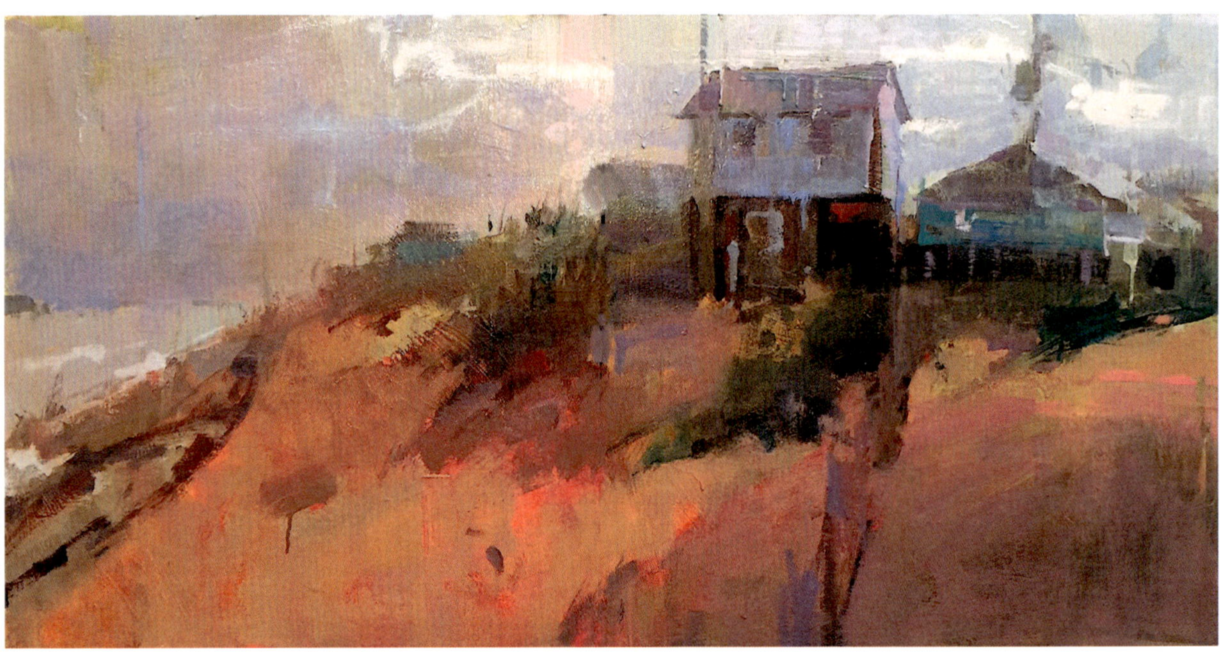

Right fit?
Art for a gallery in Santa Fe.
Colorful and contemporary. Yes. Unique style. Yes.
Content. No. A little too coastal in imagery.
The right message won't work in the wrong market. Were this a painting of a pueblo with buttes in the distance then sure. But this one is a no.

Problem 5: A painting that doesn't work

It's not quite fair to pick things that are known to have worked, so how about something that doesn't? An obviously bad painting (I know...subjective). I've done plenty, but I'm smart enough never to show them. Here's one that went on the chopping block and why. Again, this is from my point of view.

Parameters:

1) Representative of and consistent with current body of work, according to my criteria.
2) Strikes the balance between loosely painted and finished.
3) More realist and less abstract.
4) Has appropriate levels of hierarchy and eye flow.
5) Looks like I know what I'm doing.

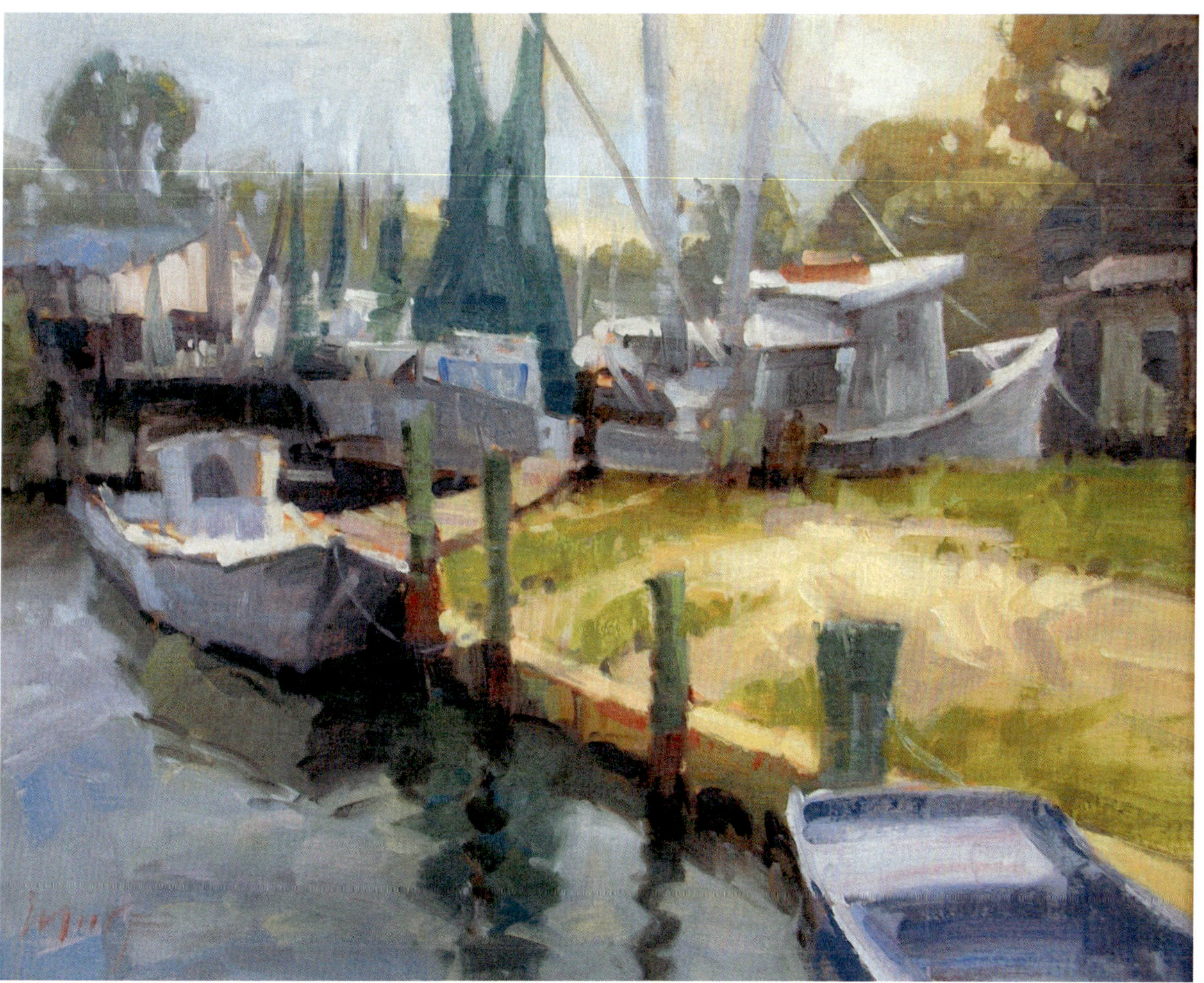

Bad painting

This one wins by losing. A 16 x 20 in. plein air in oil, created in 2009, I would not show this publicly today. Biggest issue is no hierarchy. My eye just does not know where to go because too many parts are battling for the dominant spot. It's boring. It's klunky. Same strokes everywhere, brushwork is too consistent and every shape is awkward. I did try to rework it to no avail. After a while I tossed it on account of it being so insolent.

Problem 6: Recreation center public art concept

I submit for a lot of these and have won several projects. Methodology-wise, these are pretty open-ended, so the solutions can go in any direction. They just have to be good, functional, hopefully interactive, long-lasting, adhere to construction criteria and stay within the budget. And survive a panel of 12 judges.

Parameters:

1) Budget of $50,000
2) Wall hanging/sculpture art
3) Must do the following; Convey aspects of rec center; health, mind, fitness, fun appeal to kids and adults and be able to withstand little fingers and weather.
4) Can either hang on an interior wall that is 15'x30' or hang on exterior wall or both for a combined 50' span.
5) A profit should be made.

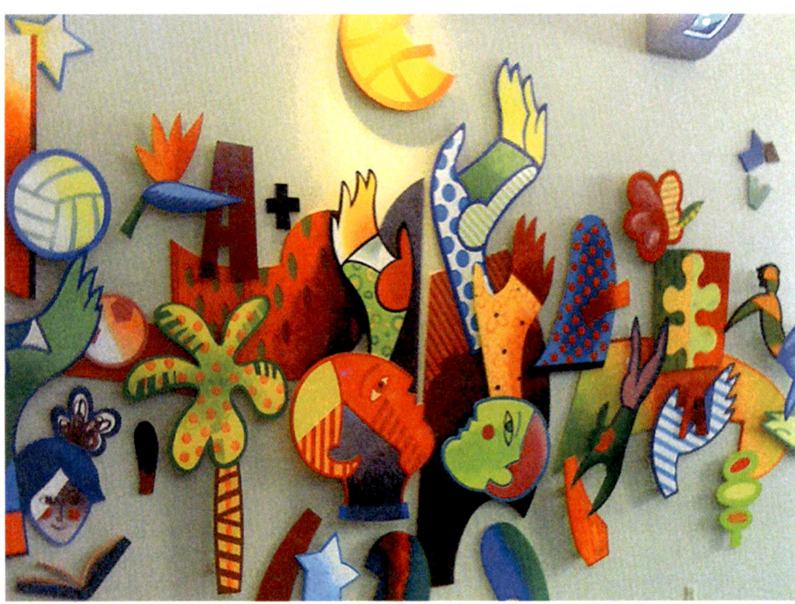

6. Public art for Recreational center

1) Budget of 50K for design and install. Yes

2) Wall hanging/ scultptural. Yes

3) Fun, represent the function of the space with rigid construction. Yes

4) Profitable. Yes, thanks to a rather clever application of sign-maker technology. Out of pocket costs at 15K and 35K in profit.

The solution for this project came from a meeting with a friend who had a sign-making business. He owned a CAD router that could cut shapes out of pvc, aluminum, wood, whatever. Mostly used for cutting type. When I asked if it could handle any kind of shape, like those from a sketch, the answer was yes. An idea was born. The production cost was only about 20% of the budget. Though I am not a sculptor, I, with partner Martha Lent, came up with a sculptural expression by delegating production to someone else.

Problem 7: Book title and cover design

Coming up with a title and visual direction for this book was tough. After all, if this is about creativity in action then the first thing you see better sell that idea. From the beginning of this venture I wanted to keep a 3rd party publisher out of this process in order to maintain the authenticity of message and purpose. Last thing I want is a "How to" feel or "Change your life" ring to it.

Parameters:

1) It's a book on creativity, so it sure better reflect the contents.
2) The umbra market is realist painters, but the penumbra market is anyone looking for new ideas on how to be more creative. So – hopefully -- everyone.
3) Should be serious, but not too. Reflect the tone of the book.
4) Can't tap into any of the other already taken strings of six words or less, which is really tough, here were a few titles we came up with:

General Theory of Creativity - Play on general theory of relativity. Cute, but doesn't connect.

Dig Deep – (From writer Jane Harrison) Supports the theme of the book, works well as a title that sells.

A Way of Seeing - I like it but it's been done... a lot.

Blue Skying or Blue Sky - Like it a lot. It references both painting and Blue Sky thinking, another term for "out of the box," but no one seems to know it.

Fishing for Elephants - To my surprise, everyone's favorite. Intended to conjure up an image of something both difficult to attain and rare. And probably not taken by someone else.

VoiceFinding – (Jane Harrison) Very strong. Using it in the book, considered for the title but felt it was a little too narrow.

Ponderlust – (Jane Harrison) Great catchy word but does it convey enough?

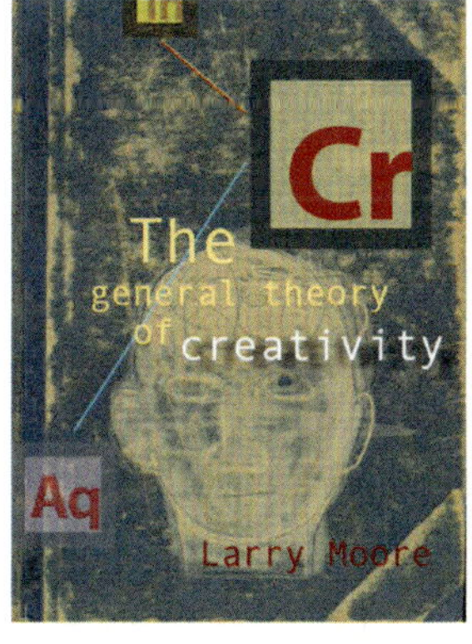

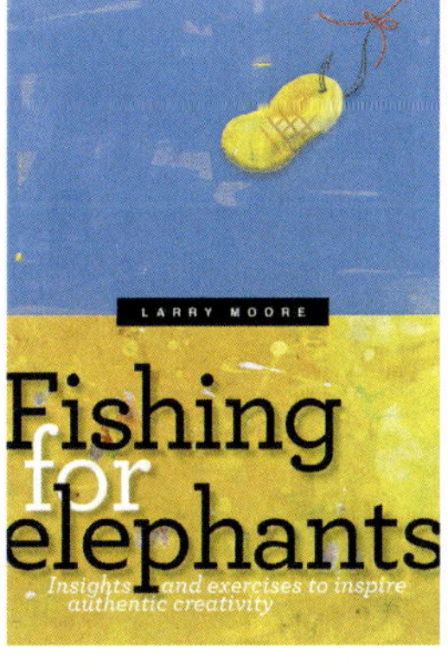

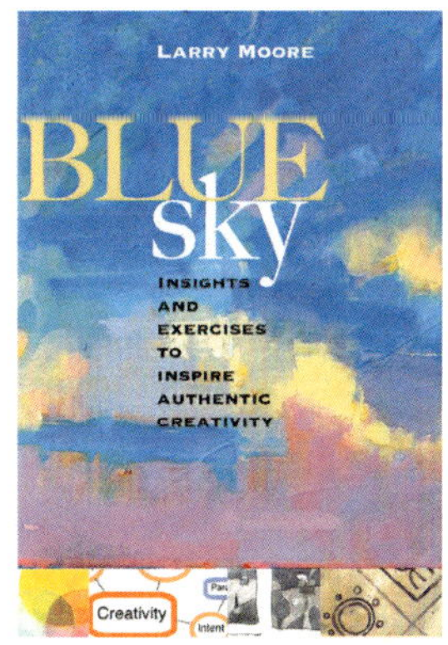

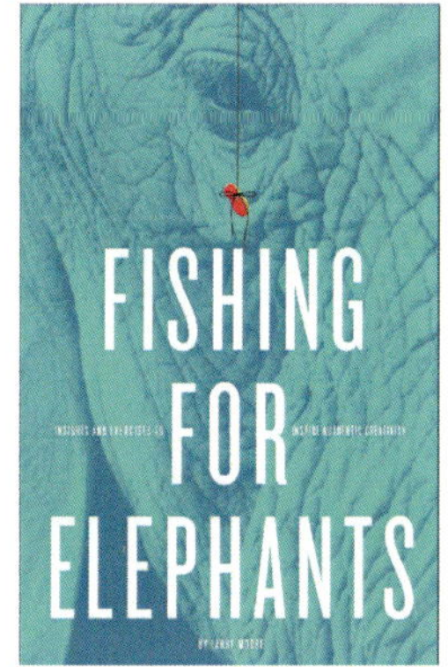

Book covers

1. The original direction. Too scholastic in feel.

2. Okay, but the hook doesn't work. Feels cruel.

3. No. Feels average in every way.

4. This one is by Jeff Matz, as is the final cover. Good looking, but the elephant in the title is meant as a metaphor and the photo alters the meaning of the title.

Problem 8: Opera poster

In 1999, I walked into the Orlando Opera Company's office and offered to do the art for their season's posters for a nominal fee. This began a 10-year, 40-poster relationship where I was able to put my visual communication skills to the test. Each image had to tell a story in as clear and compelling way as I could muster.

Parameters:

1) Illustrated wall poster for Faust.
2) Must convey the theme and feel of the libretto (narrative).
3) Should reflect the period of the original opera.
4) Producible within the abilities, time frame and budget.
   No time to paint an entire battle scene.

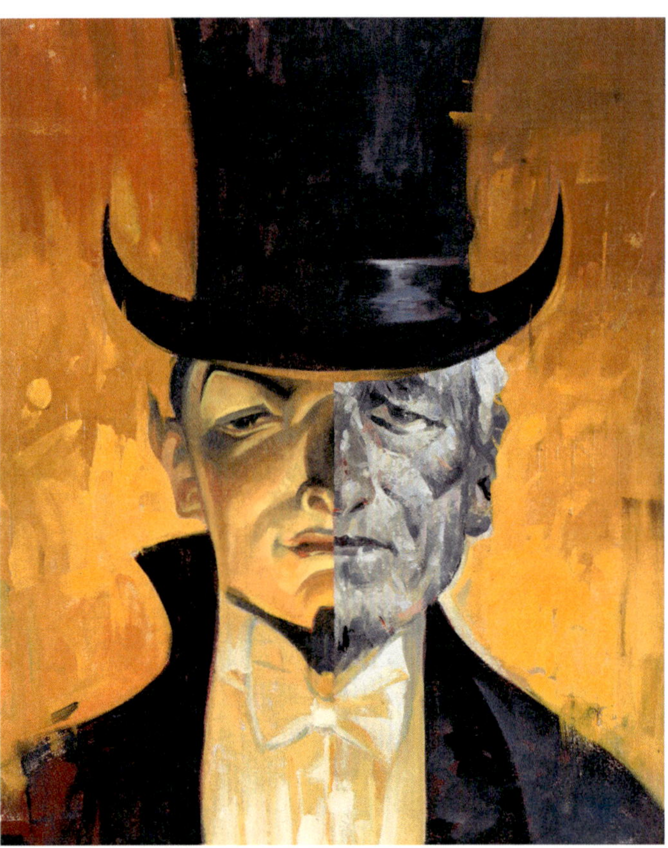

8. Opera poster

- ***Faust. Old man sells his soul to the devil for youth and love.***
- ***Message conveyed? Yes***
- ***Reflect tone/time/intent of the opera. Yes***
- ***Producible within the time constraints. Yes.***

Simpler visual solutions communicate better and take less time to produce.

The optimal components of a compelling outcome: A clear intent from a distilled set of parameters combined with a better than average understanding of the visual communication process. If you are authentic in your efforts, only you can know if your solution works or not.... unless it's a light bulb or a rocket. Then pretty much everyone will know whether it works or not.

At the end of this book you will find case studies by unique and talented visual communicators with their take on the "why" of a piece they created, for a glimpse into intent application.

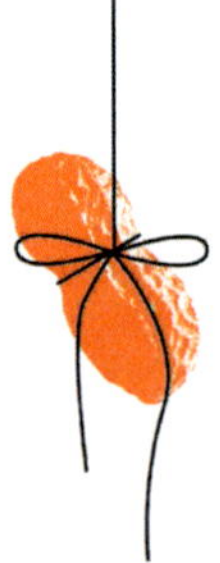

9. Implementation

It's a general failing of many creatives -- coming up with ideas but not following through. I am as guilty as anyone of having stacks of ideas and inventions that haven't been realized. How many times have you heard or said, "You know what would be a great idea...?" Conceiving an idea is the fun part, but raising it is the trick.

Getting that golden egg to fly is the hardest part. If you don't go in with a realistic plan and big chunk of effort, it's not going to happen. Do or do not; there is no try.

- **Think like a big dog**
- **Say it like you mean it**
- **Get help**
- **Develop an action plan**

The chihuahua effect

Have you ever seen a chihuahua facing off against a much bigger dog? They don't blink; they don't back down; they don't care. As far as they know, they are every bit as big and tough as their opponent, who usually is the one to back down. It's just like two guys facing off in a bar. One blinks and the other does not. Non-blinker wins.

This kind of thinking can win your cause 93% of the time. Remember the book "The Secret"? If you put it out to the universe you will get what you desire, because you are the master of your domain.

Personally, I believe the universe cares not a molecule for your happiness. You need it way more than it needs you. BUT, if you go after anything with the dogged belief that you are right, or that your solution or idea is the best and you are worthy, then you will have a much higher chance for success. This is the chihuahua effect.

If you want someone else to receive your efforts with any credulity, then you sure as heck better act like you believe in it. Believe it enough to present it well. Make a commitment to the direction, frame it nicely, print it on quality paper, hire a designer or an editor or producer, promote it professionally and send it out like an invading army. Put forth a professional image because **perception is reality.**

Perhaps, you have had this response to a piece of art in a high-end gallery or a big museum or a song in a high production TV show. You wonder: "Why is that considered good?" It's in front of you because someone with credentials or money thought it was good. And so, it's good by association.

That said, any good idea is worth fighting for and that means overcoming the negative influences or the fear of a negative response. If you have done the hard work and you believe in it, you will hurdle over the nay-sayers with ease.

If you are not sure, go back to the drawing board and refine... or throw buckets of money at it. Consider the current trend in auto insurance marketing. They aren't directly selling insurance or saving money. They are spending big bucks selling the brand. When it's time to look for insurance or get a pill for low testosterone, you will know which one to ask for.

Be a big dog and sell it like you mean it.

It's no secret that great creatives often want nothing to do with selling their fruits, and that's why so many are just scraping by. Those who succeed have the double whammy of creative ability and Type A salesmanship, or they take the financial risk of hiring someone to help them.

This second option is a good one for those who are business-impaired or shy about their work. If you can't be the tiger in your circus, hire one. At first, it may seem like a ridiculous notion: "I'm going to spend money I can't spare to hire someone? I can't afford that."

The successful people I've come to know have people, or are married to people. Not surprisingly, these assistants not only pay for themselves, they multiply the income, because the creator has more time to do what got him or her there in the first place.

There are two easy steps:

1) Do amazing work.
2) Hire someone who is smart, eager and won't siphon money.
   Simple as that.

Aim for the stands

So many great ideas are left to die because of poor planning or no planning. Babe Ruth pointing to the stands. This is the state of mind to have when you plan. Aiming deep isn't just for baseball. It means thinking big and following through with authority.

This also applies to getting your work into the best possible setting. I have seen, so many times, artists miss the incidence of opportunity by thinking small or staying local. You can have an amazing, unique voice, but if you are in the wrong venue it will go unnoticed. Many artists give up because they were singing to the wrong crowd.

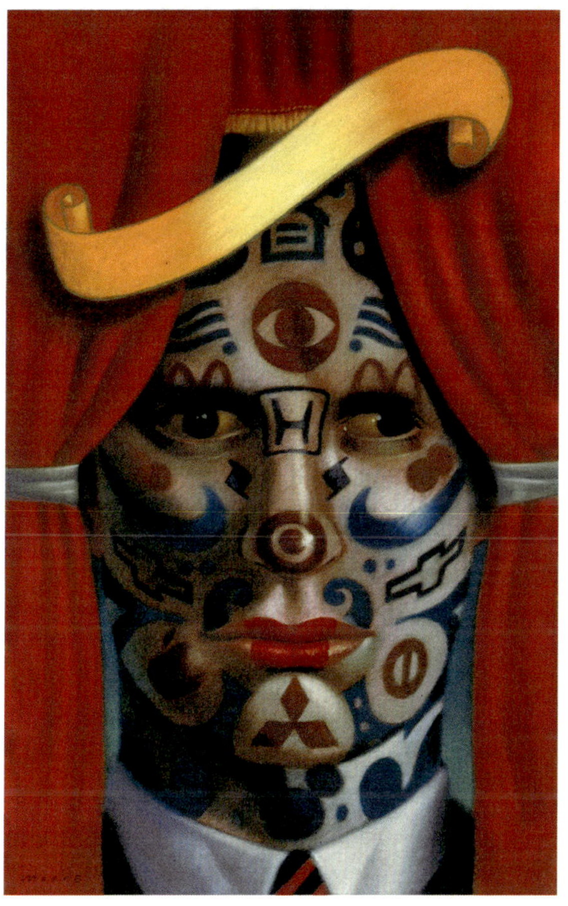

Pastel on paper, 14 x 20 in.

Use the goal-setting and Intent-scaffolding methods listed in Intent to make a workable plan with achievable goals. Create a calendar and break down your plan into realistic and attainable steps. Delegate where possible. Remember that Meyers-Briggs personality test? This is where that info comes in handy. How you set your plan depends on your personality type.

Bear in mind that disappointment is guaranteed at some point along the way. The best creatives don't let disappointment slow them down, because they are creative. They use their super power to overcome the obstacles. And they don't just have one idea; they have many.

Presentation and brand

So, my years in advertising and design are good for something after all. The lessons -- concept is king, thoughtful design, parameter-driven thought processes, the power of perception, and the move into a more self-expressive realm of visual communication.

I've learned a few very important things that I just assumed everyone knew about selling an idea... but apparently not:

1. You can be successful without being good, with the right marketing efforts. Perception is reality.
2. You can be good and unsuccessful, despite your best efforts.
3. Just because you have the technology to do your own promotion does not mean you should.
4. Hire a pro to do your promo work. I mean a real pro, not your nephew who does obits for the newspaper. Good design is, sadly, a nearly lost art, but it will help you stand out if used properly.
5. Marketing and inspiration gurus sell the dream. **Just use common sense.** A multi-tiered, multi-media plan works if you have something unique and compelling to put out there. Figure out that part first.
6. Nothing stands out like true authenticity, though it is riskier.
7. Less is more. Avoid TMS (Too Much Shit) in any presentation. Remember the billboard analogy. This applies to ads, biz cards, brochures, websites, book covers, menus, paintings.
8. Edit. Just show the good stuff. You are remembered by your worst efforts.
9. If you are doing something that at least one-quarter of the planet is also doing, you damn well better be original about it. Bring something to the table.
10. If you are in this for the notoriety and success, good luck with that.
11. Pick the right venue for your work. Be consistent in your work and be prepared for rejection.
12. Don't send your Alt Grunge-Country-Metal-Rap-fusion music to a Christian recording studio.
13. Don't walk into a gallery and show them artwork on your phone and hope to get picked up. Think about your presentation from the recipient's point of view.
14. Social media. Don't confuse your professional persona with your personal one. Make a choice. If you publish a strong opinion, be prepared for the shit storm and know that you are the one who opened that door.
15. Go where the money is. A hand-crafted lamp made from a lobster pot and heavy rope for sale in a sleepy coastal MaPa shop will net $75. Same lamp in the high-end design stores of the Chelsea District will go for $3,200. **Perception / reality.**

16. Have a lot of work in the can before you go pro. A website with three quilts and a pet portrait will not be helpful.
17. Do your research. If this is a creative enterprise, know your market, know your venue, understand the rules of engagement, pricing, competition. Don't open your dog portrait stand in the desert.
18. Don't quit your day job unless you have: a trust fund, married rich, two years of reasonable financial return and saved income, balls of steel, a yurt to live in, children who are doctors.
19. Understand that most returns on investment of time, money and effort are rarely direct. Often the positive rewards show up way down the road.
20. Some people say follow your bliss, I say follow it at a safe distance until you are sure it's the right bliss.

Nothing inspires like a deadline.

Even the most professional procrastinators cannot avoid the inevitable. If you work best under pressure, and many do, create your own by making something happen. If you are in a venue already, like a gallery, set up a show and set the parameters just a little past your fingertips... 20 pieces of magnificence to open in six months. That will get your planning butt in gear.

If you aren't already in a venue, find two or three people to do a collaborative effort and find a space. If you are a painter, grab a sculptor, a maker of repurposed functional art and a beat poet and rent a place. Make it happen. And when it does, you will quickly figure out a battle plan because you have to.

Mark all the important benchmarks on a calendar: Finish studies date, five pieces done date, 10, 20, order frames or similar, ship or drive-to dates. Multiply your anticipated anything time by 1.5 and add an additional .5 for safety reasons. Everything takes longer than you think.

The old days of Peggy Guggenheim discovering you and making you a household name are kind of over. It's on you now.

Create a project. I like to make my own trouble. Because of my illustration roots, I love creating narrative art and, late in the last century, I wasn't getting enough of that kind of work in my life. So, I went out and found it.

In 1999, I approached the local opera company and offered my services as an illustrator to create art for their upcoming season at a greatly reduced rate. They agreed and the relationship lasted 10 years, culminating in 40-plus paintings, each turned into a poster edition of 250. Many of the pieces gained recognition in national competitions.

At the end of the run, I approached a gallery about a show, framed the 40-plus paintings (ouch) and had an opening. One man bought them all. I approached him later about a book on the series to give provenance to the collection. He agreed and financed half of the production. I financed the other half (ouch).

A book was born, *Poster and process, The opera art of Larry Moore.*

A collection of 40 paintings / posters, a one-man gallery show, a permanent collection and a prolific patron... none of this would have happened had I not taken the initiative and the risk.

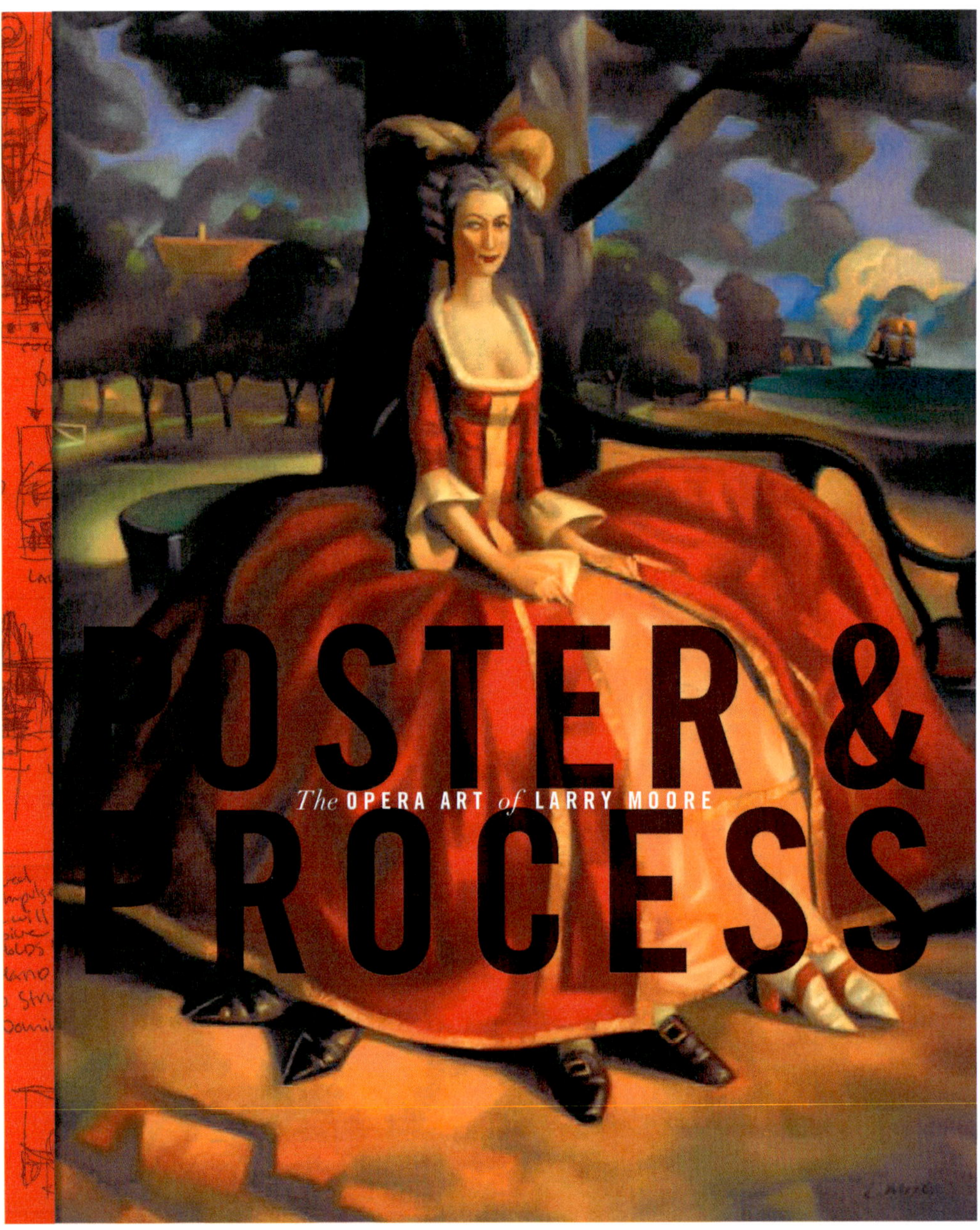

9. Poster and Process
11"x14" Designed by Jeff Matz, Lure Design Inc.

Submit for a public art call for entries. They are open to all walks of creativity, from sculpture to painting to Italian glass mosaics and interactive digital displays. Many are open calls with nominal requirements.

The submittal process is a pain and the odds are slim. But if you get one, and you've read this book, you will be golden. In this realm, the idea is king.

Start with the small ones and work your way up. Small budgets are in the thousands and big budgets are six figures, sometimes up to 500K or more. I've done several, each vastly different and a remarkable learning experience, with trial by fire immersion in battle planning.

But if you can dream it, you can do it. Why not you? And if you are a black-belt problem solver, you have a leg up on the competition. Here's a hot tip: This is the place for presenting it like you mean it. If you do get your foot in the door, you will be judged only by your shoe, so it better be a really fine shoe.

"Everyone who's ever taken a shower has had an idea. It's the person who gets out of the shower, dries off and does something about it who makes a difference."

- Nolan Bushnel

Battle plan

There is no universal battle plan for every creative engagement. Moving ahead with your dream work should be more than just pokin' and hopin.' A good place to start: Adapting the goals form from **Intent** to develop achievable objectives and schedules. Identify clear steps and assign deadlines. Break those down into smaller deadlines.

Example:
Success goals:

What will I need to have to get there? *Materials, financial, emotional support*

What will I need to do to get there? *Action steps **with** schedule.*

1.

2.

3.

4.

5.

Which accomplishments are important for me to achieve and why?

My promise to myself: *Make a clear commitment in writing, a contract with yourself for what you want to achieve.*

Often, with most big (and medium) ideas, one person can't go it alone. Employ people who know what they are doing to help. The sculptor Claus Oldenburg --whose large-scale work fills the halls of contemporary museums and the corporate grounds of the Fortune 500 -- was an idea man and a great delegator. He and partner Coosje Van Bruggen conceived them. But they didn't make them; they hired the right people to construct and install.

1) Get an idea.

2) Make a plan with a schedule.

3) Set attainable goals.

4) Delegate to people who know what they are doing.

5) Do it like you mean it, from the bottom to the top.

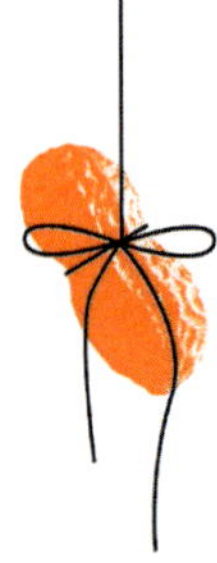

10. VoiceFinding:
THE ARTIST'S PORTABLE LAB OF GENIUSNESS

If you are searching for new inspiration, looking for the spark that lights your fire, you aren't going to find it by doing things the way you always have. This section is about discovery for painters, venturing into uncharted waters to see what is out there.

Here is what you will learn: The key to re-invention is to look at the known components of what you do and arrange them in a new way, focus on what matters and disregard the rest. First, we look at a few training ideas, then spotlight on what makes a painting tick followed by a series of non-traditional exercises designed to push you into new ground where growth lives.

The finale presents a series of exercises that put the entirety of the contents of this book to work toward developing your authentic self.

- **Chunking: training in pieces**
- **Know your components. Creative cross-fit.**
- **Know thyself. Intent and the artist's statement.**
- **Discovery and invention**
- **Divergent thinking and multiples**
- **Convergent thinking and the inner critic**
- **Seeking authenticity**

Paint and process: the voice of the artist

By now, you have no doubt noticed that this isn't a book about how to paint something to look like something. There are thousands of resources and instructional videos available out there; that territory has been covered. This book is about how to think for yourself, move forward, get out of your comfort zone, get out of your own way, define your voice, refine your voice, focus on those characteristics of creating that are authentic to you and try new directions.

The first section was to give you more intellectual tools in problem-solving, whether you are a painter or a needle-pointer -- beginner or advanced -- to free up and shore up the imagination, find direction and develop your personal vision quest. Innovation requires developing the mental capacity through practical techniques to solve ordinary problems in extraordinary ways.

This second half is more specific to artists hoping to push their assumptions, skills and techniques and to practice the application of idea development. It's geared toward painters, so, my apologies to the needle-pointers. But these ideas apply to any form of visual communication.

Learning how to paint a portrait well is no easy feat, but what happens once that skill set has been developed? What do you do with it?

Art is hard. Okay, perhaps not laying roofing tiles during a Florida summer kind of hard. But it's still hard. The process of applying paint to canvas to get a realistic result is a hard-won and highly-respected craft that most people can learn to do proficiently, given enough study, brush hours and proper instruction. But the real art comes forth when you've mastered the components enough so that your voice can arise unfettered.

The artfulness is in the *idea*, coupled with a mastery of the medium. Another example can be found in performing a song, which most of us have tried at least once or twice. You know that you want to play "Blowin' in the wind" with all your heart, singing the melody to the guitar's harmony and conjuring wistful tears from the eyes of all your friends, followed by rapturous applause.

It's easy to dream up in fantasy, but it's not so easy to do. It takes years to learn the rudiments of chords, notes, strumming and picking, reading music, singing and playing at the same time.

You may be familiar with Malcolm Gladwell's premise about 10,000 hours... the general measure of time it takes to master something. It's not until you are at a level (about 9,242 hours) where you no longer have to consciously think about where to find the notes that you can play the music in your head without effort.

It's what the karate practitioners refer to as "No mind," or muscle memory... what Maslow referred to as unconscious competency. At this stage, the heart is free to explore and express without being distracted by thoughts about technique.

But how, exactly, should those 10,000 hours (5 years, 40-hour work weeks, 2 weeks vacay) be spent?

Chunking

As I've learned from many years of teaching, painting well is so difficult because it's like juggling 10 balls. And, to add to this mental cross-fit course, each ball is completely different; one is a pumpkin, one is a golf ball, one is a cotton ball, one is a long-bladed knife.

If you happen to attend my three-day, 10-ball juggling workshop in the bucolic Tuscany region of Italy (wine and pasta included), I won't be throwing all 10 balls at you on the very first day and saying, "Okay, now commence to jugglin'." You wouldn't be able to do it.

I am going to give you one ball to practice with, then two to throw upward and catch with the other hand and then, when you are comfortable with that, here comes the third. And there you will stay, practicing your three in Cortona until you are ready for four, and so on. When you have the 10 down and can tell jokes at the same time, you are ready for phase two, learning better jokes.

This is known in many learning circles as "chunking," breaking a process down into learnable, digestible portions. The old-school realism ateliers used this methodology on their students. The instructors had the attendees draw from casts and from life for four years or more before they ever got to hold a brush. If you couldn't draw well, you sure as heck weren't going to be able to paint.

One of the winningest basketball coaches trained his team this way (only with a basketball). Chunking means to practice the rudiments separately. The students who come in to any painting class hoping to come out with a realistic portrait of their grandchild playing with the family puppy are in for a bit of disappointment. There are a lot of chunks. Why it's not an Olympic sport, I have no idea.... but if we added a rifle, maybe. At the end of this section there are a series of chunking exercises to help you learn better and faster.

Sameness

If you walk through 20 galleries or flip through the art mags, you will see the trends. The one constant about anything in art is the trend du jour. You'll see a kind of sameness throughout. From the pre-Columbian era, up to the end of the 19th century, movements have always clumped by regional *schools;* Renaissance (Italy), Japanese wood cuts (Japan), Tonalism (Tonalville), Cape Cod colorists.

It's a consistent part of the human experience to fall in with the like-minded. Though the 20th-Century held massive changes in the art realm, many followers stayed within the lines of their "school" and only a few broke free, asking the "What If" questions and seeking answers through their own explorations.

Nowadays, artists can still fall into following without realizing it. If someone is doing a certain thing or if several artists are doing the same thing, there must be a good reason, right?

The current movements in realist representational art have a few dominant trends and a few dominant leaders that have spawned hundreds and hundreds of followers and imitators. What was once referred to as the Golden Line seems more like a golden leash, lots of great technique with a suitcase of borrowed solutions. If you pay attention, you can see the influencer, then the copyists, then the people who are copying the copyists, until it becomes a mannerist movement. Where is the authenticity of the individual?

While the movement/master/apprentice model has been around for a very long time, most apprentices eventually achieve their own master status and move on. They add something to the mix of what they learned and they evolve and grow. Some, however, just adopt someone else's voice and pass it off as their own. Borrowing heavily from another is part of a learning curve, but many eventually recognize that it's time to leave the nest.

Why be an ersatz somebody else? It's always better to be a first-rate you. The big trick is to trust one's own ability to solve creative problems in a way that is unique. That is true authenticity.

Admittedly, borrowing from another artist is seductive. It's downright easy to go online or flip through a magazine and hear the sirens' song... "I'll just do that."

But that is not the creative spirit; it is just the opposite. As a training tool, copying from the masters is a time-honored practice, but claiming borrowed concepts of color, shape and narrative as one's own is plagiarism, especially when money is involved. Similarly, it's really easy to pull an image off the internet, perhaps a photo of a sunset or a bird in flight. Who is going to know? But, it's still considered copyright infringement.

The general rule is this -- and as an illustrator I know what I'm talking about -- if you place the original next to the copy and see any resemblance as borrowed, it is infringement. There's no acceptable percentage. Borrowing a style is a little harder to prove in court, but it's still a risk and... people will know.

In many ways commerce drives sameness. Many galleries are filled with similar regional ideas because that is what sells. However, some venues do seek out the young pioneers of style and content. The movement toward more progressive means of expression, like installation- and electronic-based work, has swelled considerably. A trip to Art Basel in Miami, which I highly recommend, will show you what the contemporary scene is up to. And even there, if a good idea is not present in a work, it's just an execution or feels like one.

Similar but different

An interesting thing to consider is this: Think about any memorable museum you've visited. The Metropolitan Museum of Art in New York is a good one. Now run through your memory banks the vast variety of two-dimensional paintings you've ogled over the years, your favored inspirations, maybe the Ashcan School, Sorolla, Calder, De Chirico, Frankenthaler, Monet... whomever and whatever. Each is unique, but, amazingly, they all share a rather important set of commonalities.

1) Rectangular format, with few exceptions the parallelogrammed paintings are king.
2) Flat ground with hand-applied pigments, usually with a secret magic brush.
3) Crazy-ass frames.
4) A color palette that is some variation of yellow, red, blue, brown, black and white, and many of the colors in between.
5) Emphasis on one or more of the following components listed.

So how is it, with the five (okay, four) listed commonalities, that each painting can be so completely different from its neighbor, even in the same hall of the same wing? What separates one artist and one movement from the next is the emphasis on one or more of the components listed below. This conscious choosing of elements, components and thought comprises the unique voice of the artist, with the key ingredient being **Intent** -- the thought or the why behind the work. The truth is, the slightest shift in a component -- edge, for example -- can completely alter the feel of the work, the message of the work, and send it into a different camp.

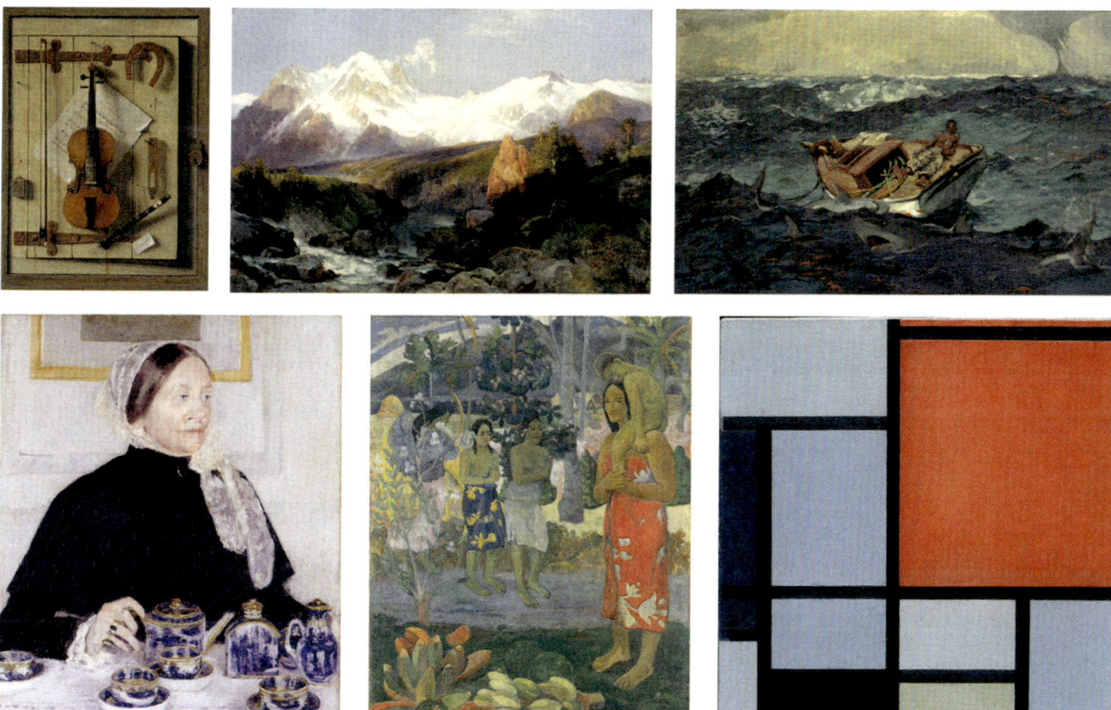

Six very different paintings that share some surprising characteristics.
(Top) *Still life – Violin and Music,* William Michael Harnett, 1888, *The Teton Range,* Thomas Moran, 1897, *The Gulf Stream,* Winslow Homer, 1899. (Bottom) *Lady at the Tea Table,* Mary Cassatt, 1883-85, *Ia Orana Maria,* Paul Gauguin, 1891, *Composition,* Piet Mondrian, 1921. Images courtesy of The Metropolitan Museum of Art, New York.

Primary components of picture making

Intent / concept / narrative - story, motive or idea.

Interpretation - the level or degree of abstraction or interpretation of form.

Drawing - one's ability to accurately portray proportion and shape relationships.

Value - the relative light or dark of two or more colors.

Color - from quiet warm / cool shifts to full saturation and intensity.

Shape - shape tells us what we are looking at -- box, ball or elephant. Black-belt shape skills add poetry to the ordinary.

Form - shape plus light-side and shadow-side.

Edge - hard edges come forward, soft recede, edge identifies form (think pine tree versus apple).

Mark making - line, brush work, the use of notes to pull the eye independent of subject.

Division of space - surprising the viewer with unusual ways of dividing up the canvas.

Juxtaposition - Energy is created by two opposing forces – light / dark, hard / soft, color complements, bright / dull, pattern / rest, chaos / harmony.

Pattern and rest - most paintings need both, pattern to excite the eye and quiet areas for the eye to rest.

Composition / hierarchy - *All the a*bove components in service to eye flow, where the eye starts and where the eye finishes.

Layers / surface - Build-up of paint, use of substrate creating tactile response.

Methods / materials - from glazes to squeegees to mixed media, the methods support the message and sometimes *are* the message.

The same is true for music, photography, dance, the written word, sculpture and so on. It's you and how you handle these components that reveal your distinct voice, from John Cage to Martha Graham to Ernest Hemingway to Auguste Rodin, all clear and decisive voices based on mastery of nuanced components. Finding that voice is the hard part and that takes time. But it's a process like any other, one that involves the two-part catalytic combo of a command of medium and method with constant searching and thought.

The conductor

We, as visual communicators, are conductors of all the components in service to the music, the intent of the work. Our role is to pay thoughtful attention to each piece, each player, each instrument, listening for the flat notes and off-tempo rhythms floating up in the sea of performing parts so that the overall intent of the work is not compromised.

Understanding the full capability of the parts is as important as having a clear vision of the whole. A good conductor knows the music backwards and forwards, the intent, the message and meaning of each passage, how the underlying lines of melody and mood resonate throughout and how the range and capability of each player affect what they can do with their instrument.

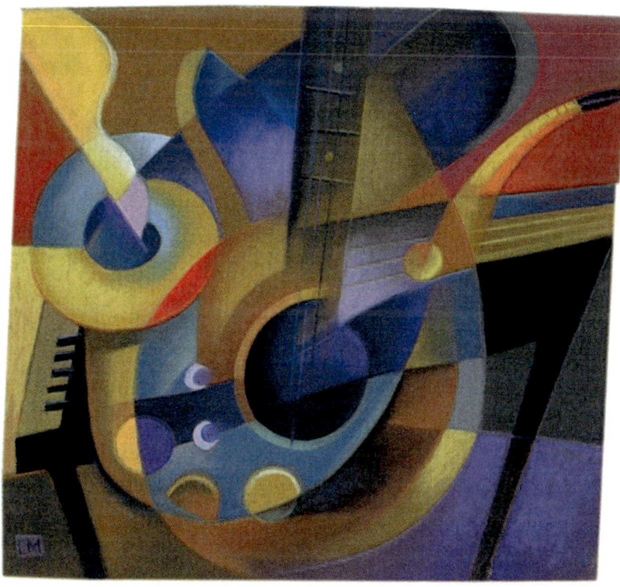

As artists, we are both singer and songwriter, composer and conductor, we are responsible for conception and delivery, making sure that the idea emanates from our core and has an orchestration in service to the whole of the idea.

Igor Stravinsky said of Bach, that "...there should be a careful balance in the music between variety and unity. Too much variety causes chaos and too much unity causes boredom." Both the composer and conductor seek a dialogue between the parts.

The visual artist, the interior designer, choreographer, architect all have the same charge: to direct, manage, manipulate, edit and balance each element so that the work functions in its entirety. Most people who believe painting is easy haven't tried to wrangle all the cats.

It only looks easy when the artist has finished the effort in a thoughtful and practiced way. In truth, it is a herculean task of manual skill and mental ability bound together by the idea or intent. Prioritizing intent is essential to progress and growth, starting with the whole, then breaking it down into attainable and digestible chunks to avoid frustration and indigestion.

Paint and process

While the chunking concept is an impactful tool for learning, the first segments of this book, Acquisition / Connectivity / Discernment / Intent, *in conjunction with* mastering the fundamentals, adds up to a lot of chunks.

In life, we learn all the chunks simultaneously. We don't spend two years figuring out the fork, knife, plate and table concept and *then* a few years more getting the eating thing down. If we did, we'd never make it, the entire species would die off and ants would take over the world.

We acquire it all, little by little, gaining understanding while we learn to handle a fork, a brush or a chisel or that red pearl accordion inherited from your Dad. And who doesn't love the accordion?

This is a life-long school, not a four-day "Painting the Guy DuJour way" workshop. You may learn a trick or two in a workshop, but once back in the comfort of your studio, what do you do with those tricks?

Rather than poking around blindly on your creative path, start with a plan. The best place to start, no matter where you are in your life-goals flow chart, is to establish your intent in the broad sense and then in the narrower bands of making the art that you want to make (see **Intent** section).

Realize that these personal creative mission statements evolve and adapt, are refined and then evolve again and again as you go along. So, it helps to start somewhere specific before you embark on the dusty Art Trail, especially if you are going with your entire library of knowledge in tow.

The beginner's mind

A few words for the beginner. Starting is hard, daunting in fact. But it can be mitigated by the simple fact that the beginner is usually in the lyrical, blooming, rosy, joyful stage of creating. Just like a relationship -- really fun in the beginning, and then it's hard work the rest of your life.

It takes only one belief to get you through it all, "I can do this" or, just as good, "I want this with every fiber of my being." That drive can push you through all the tough spots. If you are in love with the doing and not with the results, you will always be content in your journey.

Be ever aware of what is going through your mind as you progress. If you concentrate on learning the rudiments, assimilating the building blocks, you will have a house soon enough. One thing you will realize is that, with each step conquered comes the awareness that there are more steps than you had realized. Get used to that; it's what keeps you in the game.

If you take workshops and classes, now the popular model for learning, take from people you admire. But also try something very different from what you normally would choose. Different experiences will inform your work in surprising ways.

Be ever aware of your "style" source, that is, from whom you are modeling, to learn your process. There is a risk in borrowing solutions from a single source. It's tempting, but one can become a copyist rather than an apprentice. Rather than adopting solutions from another artist, adapt them. Find a way to make them your own. Analyze more than one source of inspiration, paying attention to the intent of the source, rather than the technique.

If someone is making beautiful paintings using an ink roller and wallpaper collage, look for methods that are similar but not the same. The viewer can spot it a mile away. A musician may be an ardent follower of Bob Dylan, but why borrow his voice?

If you are worried about disappointment, take the weight off. Think small. Don't make a goal of having a gallery show in one or two years. This is a long-haul. Make sure you have a comfy chair and plenty of water.

The intermediate mind

From conscious incompetency into conscious competency. By the middle stages, the stairs to conquer have expanded like a Hitchcock camera effect. Once you see what's ahead of you, if you have the fire in the belly, it is nose to the grindstone, simple as that.

Develop a plan, that's what this book is about. Know that you will change as you grow. Be open and work through getting stuck when you occasionally veer off road. Continue to separate the components out, especially your weakest ones. Identify those areas that need the most effort and bring them up to speed.

If you want to be a realist painter and you are fantastic at color, but suck at drawing, don't pretend no one will know, practice your drawing. Nothing gets past the critical eye. Be careful that you are not overly influenced by what is shown or published. It's easy to do. The world wants to see something different and unique. Be authentic, be real and always hold yourself to the highest standard.

Expectations. These are the killers. They show up early and stay late. If there is one truth in the world, it's that expectations are evil. "That artist is selling or winning stuff and I am not. I deserve better."

While success favors the hard worker, it is not a given. Constant reframing of your point of view is a must. As your friend, I'll tell you this. It's not about you, it's about who you want to be. When you do get recognition, take it in stride. It's like a dozen roses... feels nice but they don't last. If ego gets in the way, progress stops. Walk the fine line between believing in yourself and believing that you are awesome.

The advanced mind

Clarity of vision and ability. Refinement and perfection on micro levels. By this time, hopefully, the ego has dissipated and there is even more focus than ever before. It is exciting at this stage to be so good at something, so nearly done with the sculpture that it's almost time to polish the stone. And so it is in the creative life; constant polishing and perfecting. It is at the same time less complicated, because paths are set and goals are met, and infinitely more so, because of the knowledge that everything will change when a single component is changed.

The nuances make all the difference. The advanced creative is more sensitive to the things that aren't working, while the beginner / intermediate can more easily gloss over the shortcomings.

The advanced creative can get pigeon-holed, which can be good or bad, depending on how you look at it. It's either rapturous or a chore to do the same thing each day over the long haul. And there's a big difference between change and advancement. Often, what is needed is enough change to make what is already sound work that much better. That is advancement. The master artist seeks this growth continually.

Developing Artistic Intent

Intent is imperative in every single facet of art-making. We've talked about defining your core values, writing your story. But intent also helps to refine the characteristics of your art that comprise the language of your authentic voice and the message you want to convey. This voice is the fingerprint of the creator, the signature of the individual. It's how you can tell Salvador Dali from John Singer Sargent.

Now let's figure out how to get it to come out of your hands.

To start, identify the components of intent in other artists' work, or your own, that you respond to. Most of us can spot a unique voice a mile away. They tower over the others in the crowd. We are sometimes assisted by pundits and historians, so, it doesn't take a lot of research to understand the intent of a Pollock action painting, a Monet water lily masterwork or Frederick Remington's pioneer western narratives.

But figuring out your own intent is a tad harder, because it's easier to be objective about another artists' work than it is your own. Developing the inner critic is essential. You'll find more on that at the end of this section.

Artist's statement

Let's start with your artist statement for the big picture, then on to some of the components of painting and see what feels like a fit. Here are some key points for you to identify in your statement. For more detailed forms, go to the **Intent** section. Even if you think you know the answers, write them down. The act of writing illuminates the thoughts and makes them accessible and easy to edit.

1) Where does your work fit within the broad spectrum of contemporary art? Is it 2-D or 3-D? Is it Realism, Abstract, Impressionism, Tonalism, Pop-Surrealism? Plein air in and of itself doesn't really cut it; it's a method not an idea. But you could say Plein Air Luminist as an example. It's good to know all the isms of art so you can figure out which one(s) you fall in with. In other words, if you were invited to a group show, who would you want to be hanging with? Remember this is just a starting place.

2) What is the why behind your current body of work? As discussed, this is a rather important thing to identify. It doesn't have to be deep just yet. It could simply be that your intent for now is to learn, to paint still life like your current art hero. But as you progress, your why will become more specific. You could have your intent stated as "I would like to make a living doing what I love," or, "my work is an on-site recording of industrial decay in America" or, "with this body of work I am exploring the duality of memory presented as everyday objects remembered incorrectly, obscured by foggy glazes of wax" or "I am concentrating on shape / color relationship by depicting the Southwest in flat geometric forms."

Or the noncommittal way out, "I just want to express myself." Nailing this down, even if it's just for the immediate future, helps to keep you on track.

3) Which method, medium or technique is integral to your work? Is it oil, cold wax, acrylic or clay, or some mixed-media combo? Does the medium inform your process or do you control the outcome from the start? Which key techniques are important to your work? Something to consider... it doesn't have to be the way everyone else has done it. Remember the What If University motto? You be U.

4) What are your sources of inspiration? Another artist? Nature? Art Deco patterns? Some quirky aspect of the human condition? Light? Unicorns with extra-large eyes? Cultural icons? All the above? If so, I'd love to see it.

5) What message do you want a viewer to receive?

Now repeat the same for your future body of work. This is where you wish to be in one, five or 10 years, without restrictions. Be clear and concise. This is not a poetry contest or an art-speak slam. A good thought exercise at this point is to sit down and ask yourself, "If I were the last person on the planet and no one else would ever see the work, what would I paint?" Would you even paint at all? This simple premise can go far in helping you configure your direction.

The Artist Declaration

What is the message of my work?

What is my motive?

What will be my method and materials?

What inspires me?

What do I want viewers to receive from my art?

What do I wish to receive from my work?

Once you are done with these questions, break out the key highlights that you want to focus on. Always know that these things can evolve over time. Take those key phrases and words, write the focus points on post-it notes and stick them around your easel and studio as constant personal-trainer reminders of your current and future path. Muscle memory is attained through repetition and application. Drawing takes a pencil and a piece of paper. Becoming a master (a greatly overused term these days) draftsperson requires 500 pencils and a small forest of sketch pads. But once a high level of competency has been achieved, what's next? Have a vision for what you want to do with it.

Training, practice and muscle memory

Knowledge-Comprehension-Analysis-Synthesis-Application-Evaluation

It's not a big secret that practice improves, though never perfects, the how of the process. I can't tell you how many top-notch artists I've spoken with who are in a constant state of honing and sharpening their skills. You have to learn where the notes are, how to pluck the keys, the songs of the past, before you can freely play the songs in your head. Practice, practice and more practice, not to sell or impress, but to learn. Practice so that you can freely play the music you want to make.

Students in my classes often have drawing issues (I'm not saying who, but you know who you are), and so the other components of painting get left on the side of the road like stray shoes. Best thing to do is to start juggling with the one ball and get comfortable with that. Draw and draw a lot. Work on learning one component at a time, but be aware of them all. I can't think of too many instances where a piece of art is purely a one-component event.

One very popular comment by passersby when I'm out painting is, "Boy, I wish I were born with talent."

To which I reply, "Yeah, me too. I could have spent those 35 years of practice making a living." Or, "Thank God you weren't. There are enough of us already." Talent is earned, not given. If you like snappy comebacks for similarly stupid remarks, I have a bunch for cheap.

From broad strokes to nuance

If you are a beginner, work and study are your best instructors for each building block of visual communication. Workshops are a wonderful way to cram info, but you will find that learning it all is impossible. You don't go home with the abilities of your instructor. Being able to factor in all these parts at once is like working on Quantum Physics equations. It's 8th-degree black belt stuff. Direct and analyze each of the components, exploring them for new possibilities instead of assuming another artist's process is right for you.

Don't just practice drawing, play with it. Look for new ways to train yourself. Consider your intent against the methodology you choose. Don't just practice mixing pigments. Find new ways to combine and layer and apply to get a desired result. Not every painting should be created with paints and brushes and canvas. Make compositional motifs out of cut paper and fabric. Intertwine components, mix them up, add new elements in to your process, new tools.

Creating is like math. At first, it's simple math, then it progresses to more and more complexity -- algebra to geometry to calculus -- as your brain absorbs the exercises and practice. Working this way, isolating two or three components, is akin to cross-training for fitness. It works in sports and it works in art. There are a range of cross-training exercises for you to work on in this section.

If you are at an intermediate level, it's time to assess where you are on your journey. Isolate your strengths and weaknesses from the list below and figure out which will help you get to where you want to be.

Look at your early work. Now look at your current efforts. Check for growth. Note the areas of progress. It's hard to see short-term spurts, but long-term, it becomes clearer. Growth is slow. Now analyze a favorite artist (or similar) who has some of the qualities you want to adapt to fit your tool belt and write them down.

It's easy to look at a John Singer Sargent painting and wistfully say, "I want to be able to do that." But what is "that?" Which pieces of the jigsaw puzzle are you missing? Find them and practice them.

The goal of this dimensional form of self-actualization is to break the big parts of study down into smaller and smaller parts, just as a painting is developed from big shapes down to small. The master focuses ultimately on the sub-atomic levels.

Characteristics of great painting

The voice of the artist

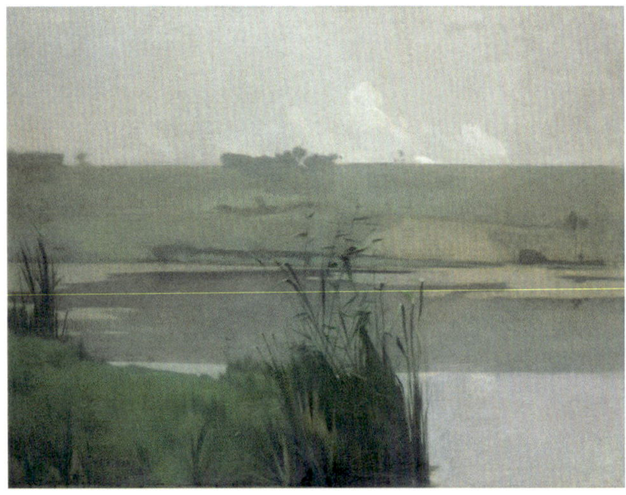

John Henry Twachtman's work features these components: tonalist, atmosphere, shape and seamless paint transitions. *Arques-la-Bataille,* 60 x 78 7/8 in. oil on canvas. Courtesy of Metropolitan Museum of Art.

The characteristics, listed previously, comprise the unique visual signature of each artist. It makes painters like Thomas Hart Benton, whose emphasis was on the narrative and shape, readily identifiable from across a room. Franz Kline's voice was in mark making, edge and positive/negative shape relationships. Nikolai Timkov was shape and color. Klimt was pattern/rest, shape and division of space. The Ashcan School focused on stories of the human existence during their time. John Henry Twachtman's oeuvre was based on tonalist, atmospheric methods of materials and surface... I could go on.

Presented for your self-assessing considerations is the list of components of painting. When you begin to understand these features, pull out a book from your library on your favorite artists to see if you can identify what makes up their unique voice. You'll gain more insight into your own work.

We don't always know what we want or prefer in our own work, so another way to come at this is to discover what we don't want. Sifting through your own work or reviewing your favorite creators can help to discern those things that aren't a part of your aesthetic. This also applies to solution finding. A cursory look at 10 ideas will show the four or five that don't work; once those get culled, the refinement process gets that much easier.

Components abilities chart

Consider where you are currently (one low - 10 high) and identify which areas you need to develop to move up to the higher levels. Keep in mind your intent as an artist. If you are an abstract artist, then drawing is not your top component. Mark-making, shape and color are.

If you know an accomplished artist or two, have them look at this for you. They will be more objective in their ratings than you would be, unless you owe them money.

Overall competency	1----- 5 -----10
Intent / concept / narrative	1----- 5 -----10
Interpretation	1----- 5 -----10
Drawing	1----- 5 -----10
Value	1----- 5 -----10
Color	1----- 5 -----10
Shape	1----- 5 -----10
Form	1----- 5 -----10
Edge	1----- 5 -----10
Mark-making	1----- 5 -----10
Surface	1----- 5 -----10
Division of space	1----- 5 -----10
Juxtaposition	1----- 5 -----10
Pattern and rest	1----- 5 -----10
composition / hierarchy	1----- 5 -----10
Layers	1----- 5 -----10
Methods / materials	1----- 5 -----10

List the three primary components to focus on:

If you already are a master painter, you may simply be looking for a little push in your work. You've gotten down to the nuances of what you excel at, but perhaps you feel stale, safe, pigeon-holed, trapped by the dark forces of resistance. This is a natural phase of the growth process. It's healthy to always question your work, as long as it doesn't stop you from creating.

The state commonly known as writers' block can lead you into new territory. If you aren't getting bored with yourself, you are not growing. Drop your resistance and become open to busting a move and break some damn change loose in your work. And if you still aren't sure what that is going to be, read on, the chain-busting exercises are comin.'

This period of pre-growth does not always mean you need a completely new approach in your work. Change should be slow and gradual. Trying new techniques and pushing out because you are bored with you can sometimes simply lead to a new excitement level for what you have always done, which leads to a higher-level of understanding and perfection of nuance in your work... evolution.

Maybe the beak of the finch doesn't evolve in a week, but sometimes the smallest changes can kick-start movement. A simple change of tools, a new surface, or a different subject can initiate change. But taking some big risks in the privacy of your studio is really freeing, pushing way past what is comfortable to assimilate the lessons back into your current method.

Discovery and invention

Triggers, prompts, motivations and inspirations (or Dr. Frankenstein takes an art class)

A huge part of this growth will be in the trust and permission aspects of the creative process, allowing your creative spirit to encourage you to take a chance and wander into deeper waters.

The eminently powerful force of the creative spirit shows itself when you are not trying so hard to control what you are doing. By relinquishing control, even for a little while, you open a portal and allow it to flourish. Trust that little voice that whispers in your ear, "Try this." or "here's an idea..." or "That's it, that's what I wanted." And off you go to see the Emerald City, skipping through the poppy fields... the ones without the flying monkeys.

Let's start with a few challenge exercises in *permission, application and analysis.*

You'll have to turn off your inner-adult default app... "This is a waste of time..." "I don't know what I'm doing..." "I've got other stuff to do..." "My mani-pedi is in two hours..."

Toggle it off. It's a judgment that may feel responsible in the short term, but is dumb like rocks long-term. And, let's face it. What you are experiencing is the "what if I do it wrong" syndrome. Guess what? There is no wrong. There's stuff that works and there's stuff that doesn't.

Accepting that and doing it anyway will free you up. The learning comes as much from the mistakes as it does from the successes. This is guided play and the goal here is to look for new ideas that work for you. Remember, your secret mantra is: *All Play and No Judge* (that comes later), and don't tell anyone else what your secret mantra is. Pinky swear.

Note: Thomas Edison did not view the 200 light-bulb attempts before he got the one that worked as failures; he simply saw them as a record of what not to do.

Trigger exercises

Here are a few trigger exercises that are designed to push your routine way of thinking by changing the way you approach a problem. The premise here, and in my classes, is that by challenging a participant's assumptions and usual methods, the ever-resilient brain will find a new path, a new way to solve.

1) Inspiration station.

On the following page, with your Artist Declaration printed out (pg. 154) as a reminder of what to work on (either the where you are, or the where you want to be list), make a connections list by writing down trigger words and prompts. For your word groupings, make at least three columns, with about 10 words per line. The groupings can be in categories like Random inspiration, Paint tools, Components.

Another example; Paint tools, Motivations, Palette. The prompts can be visual reference, pictures, artists' samples, and objects that can work as jumping off points. This is trust your gut stuff, I can't write it for you. It's got to come from your inner recesses.

Take a pen and connect a trigger word or prompt reference from each column and do it several times so you end up with three or four seemingly random connections. This is the same free association listing process that we covered in the Connections part of the Play section (pg. 92).

The difference here is that your choices will be influenced by your intent statement that is sitting there under the cup of coffee.

Take a few of these Christmas light clusters and start sketching from the seemingly random associations, whatever comes to mind. You can also write a paragraph or a story. If you find something that really gets your juices flowing, let your creative spirit play. Take a sketch or two and do some color roughs. This is the blueprint for your painting (not a photo).

This is the process I used for 35 years as an illustrator. It works. It may feel uncomfortable because you are working outside your usual method. And what does your usual method bring? You know...the usual. Do it and thank me later.

2) Simple listing and word clusters.

If you want, you can use the list of painting characteristics and add a list of random words, combining three. For example: color, shape and robot.

Just from these three words a myriad of associations pop in to my head, so here's how that looks to me. For more on this approach go to **Connectivity.**

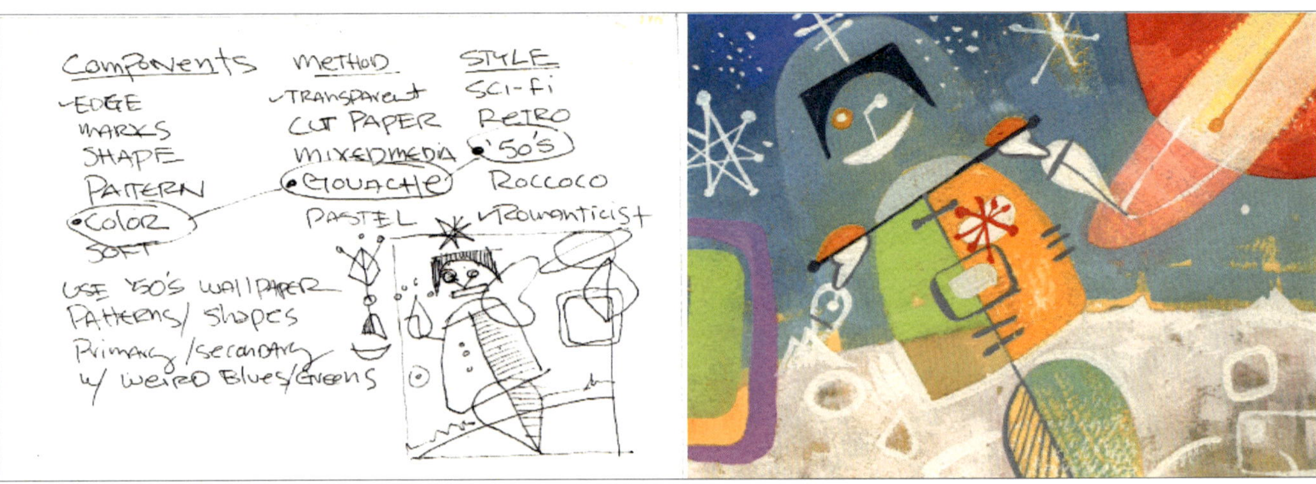

1 & 2. Trigger list and results

By placing 2 or 3 unlike terms together, a whole range of ideas can show up. Color, shape and robot. From the above list came several different solutions to the trigger words.

Inspiration station trigger words

Sketch

3) Antique stories.

Head over to the thrift store or your local antique mall and pick out four small, quirky objects that you respond to and are affordable. Place in bag, place bag in car and go to studio.

You can use some of your own personal collection as well. Put them in a pile, pick three randomly or that somehow go together and allow them to conjure up a story. Be open to combining these elements in unusual ways. If you found a ceramic bull and a cigar box, you could paint some pastoral scene on the cover and glue the bull to the top.

Hang cigar box. Instant story.

Or you can write a folky tall tale about Segundo the giant cigar-smoking bull who dug the Rio Grande Gorge with his horns to keep the cowboys and Indians apart. Paint it. Give me an antique store to play with and I'll come up with 50 different series and three years of work to do.

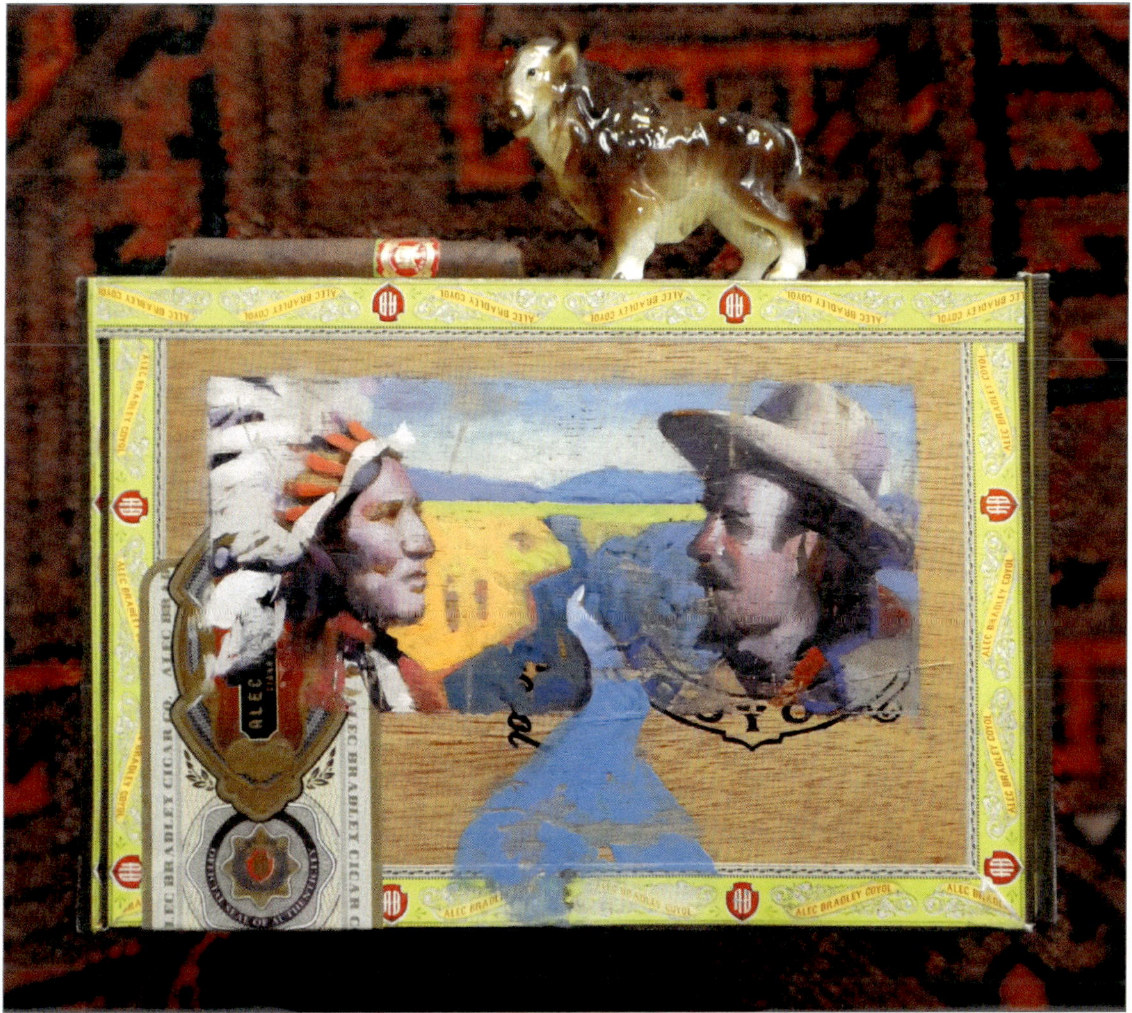

3. Antique stories

Any two or 3 unusual objects can inspire a story and can sometimes become a part of the story. Mixed media assemblage with oil, cigar box, ceramic bull and cheap cigar. It's even wired on the back to hang on the wall.

4) One-person Telephone.

Doing multiples. Try the Telephone approach (from the campfire circle days) working from life or photo, create a small color sketch, or use an existing painting. Make it as detailed as you wish. Have at it, all your usual tricks, the more the merrier. Put in every window and every friggin cow, all the reeds and every leaf.

Now, put your original reference aside -- and no peeking -- remember to trust in yourself. Create a new painting from the sketch you just made and then do another one pushing some of the components (i.e. color, shape). Put the original sketch aside and paint another one from the second and so on.

With each new painting, concentrate only on the things you like, not how closely it resembles the reference. Keep going and keep pushing. Make conscious choices as you go. Try to go five rounds at least and then compare the first with the last.

"The best way to get a good idea is to have a lot of ideas."

-Linus Pauling

The farther you get from the rendering, the closer you get to your authentic voice; if not your intent, perhaps the components that assist the intent.

I can't stress how important this process is. It's how ideas are born. (When a man idea loves a woman idea, yada yada). You aren't necessarily trying to reinvent yourself. Just find out who you are.

Once done, decide which parts of the outcome to bring back into your work or explore on their own merit... and which to discard.

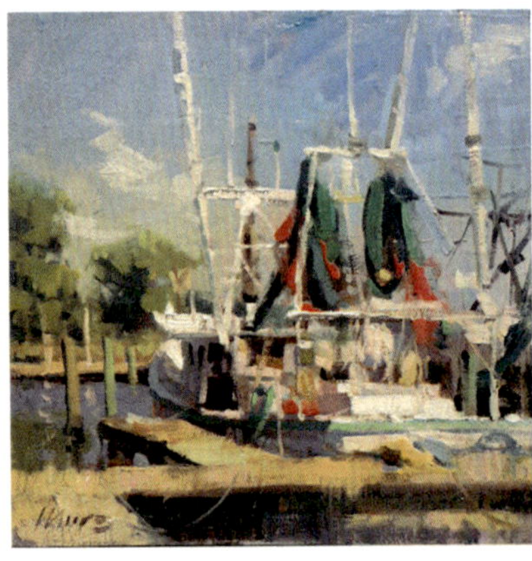

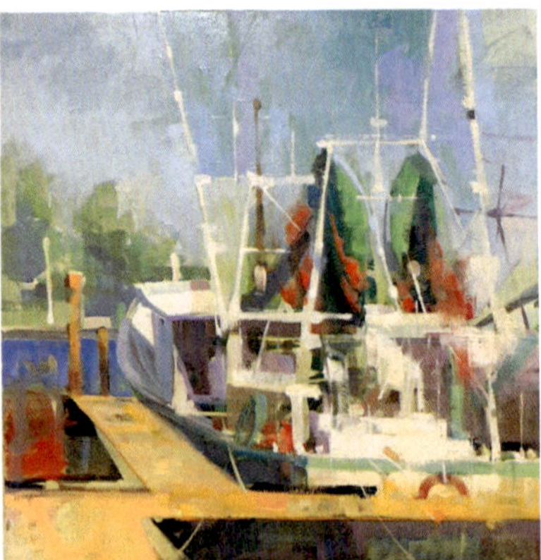

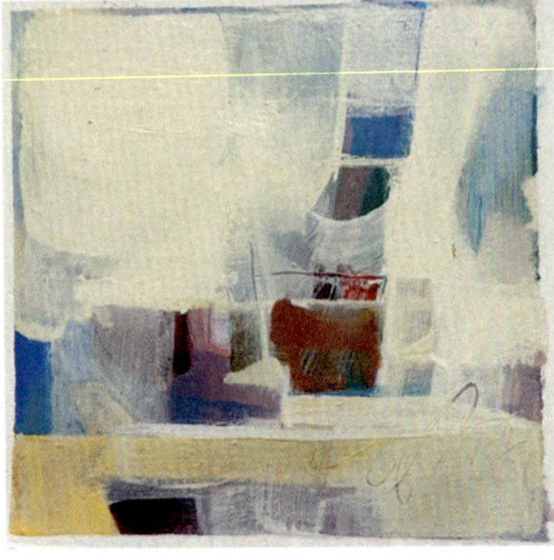

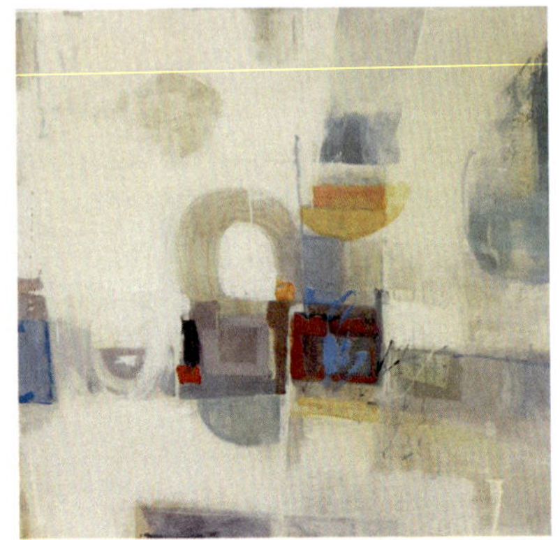

4. Telephone; progression series

UL First 12x12 study in oil. UR Second version from the study, 20x20 in oil. LL 5x5 acrylic study from version two overpainted with warm white. LR a 30x30 acrylic/oil piece created from version three, editing things I didn't need and emphasizing things I did.

You can speed up the process by taking an existing painting, some white artist's tape, and section off parcels of the painting that you find compositionally or conceptually interesting. Use these cropped portions as ideas for designs and proceed with fervor, add vim and/or vigor to taste.

5) House paints.

Go to your local hardware store paint department. Pick a variety pack of eight to 10 *random* colors in the small tester size... lights, middles and darks.

Grab any cheap primed surface and a set of cheap brushes and a platter to mix on and go to town. Just move the paint, feel it, see what it does. Pour it, spritz it, smear it. If this doesn't inspire new thought, you need to work on being open.

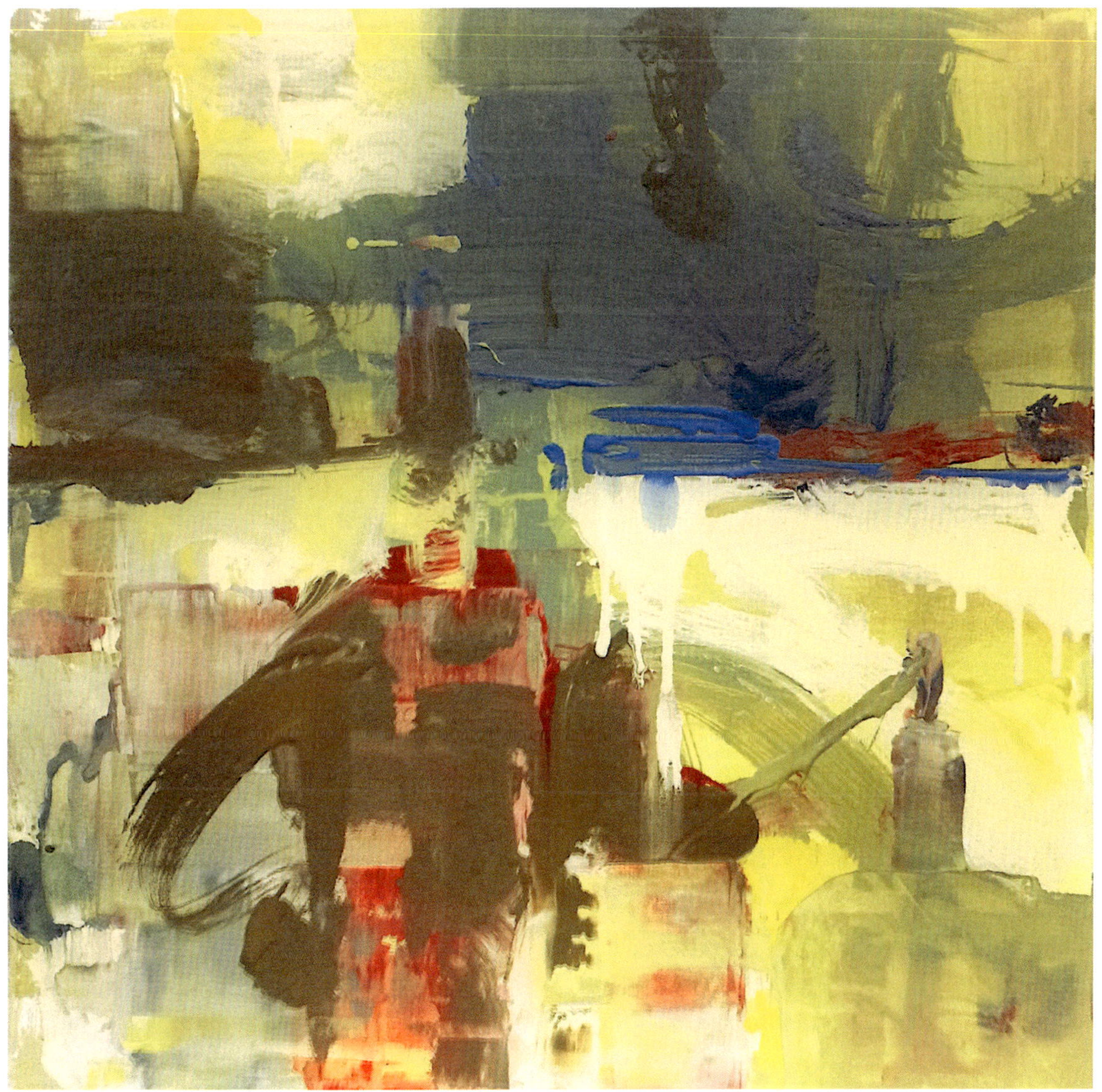

5. Discovery

My secret weapon of discovery... house paints. It's not like those fancy paints, it's drippy, cheap, and way more fun. This playful experiment was created with about $4 of hardware store color samples, picked at random just to see "what if." When you don't care about wasting paint, you throw it around like candy at Halloween. It can set you free.

6) Mix-downs.

Related to exercise #5, Mix up eight or so large puddles of values and colors with no intent, just colors you like in your favorite medium, stuff that makes you say "Ahhh." Arrange your new fave colors by values of light to dark.

Find a subject of interest with no resemblance to your color piles and paint with only those premixed colors. Put your usual palette aside. Paint by value. What shows up will amaze you.

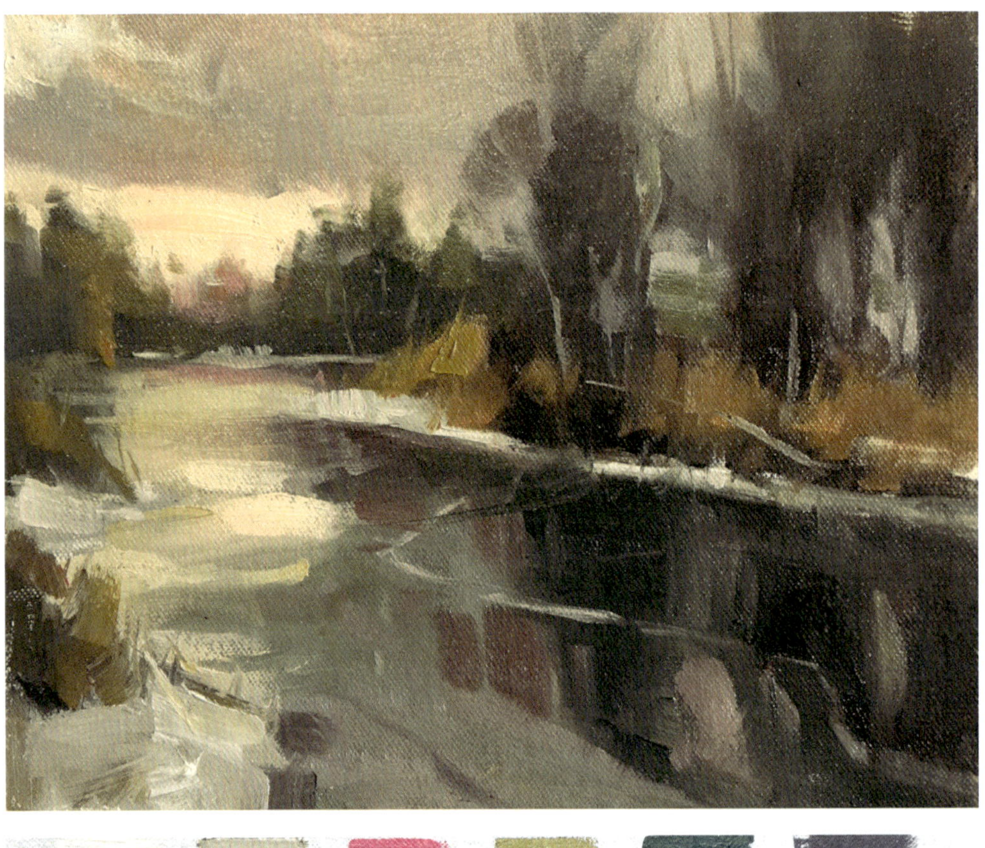

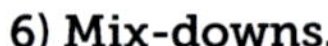

6) Mix-downs.

Mix a range of random colors you like, colors you would paint your living room with. Create values of light, middle and dark, some warm and some cool. Pick a subject independent of your color choices and paint by value. Use your dark color for the dark stuff and your light color for the light stuff. It always amazes me how nicely these things turn out when I'm not chasing color around. 8x10 oil.

Methods and materials

If you are expecting a lengthy discourse on the ways to best create an archival piece of art using the finest Moroccan linseed-oil-based pigments on the perfect flax linen surface hand woven by Lithuanian virgins, read no further. This is the opposite of that.

To encourage play, experimentation and growth, I recommend using all sorts of unusual methods and materials and preferably the inexpensive and plentiful kind.

People do two things with expensive stuff. They tighten up and they scrimp. In countless classes, I have seen participants show up with palettes that look like little rainbow mice left presents on them. Tiny portions mean tiny movements and no risk-taking. Using cheap stuff is another way of tricking the brain into becoming less resistant to learning something new.

Mid-century modernists, like Robert Rauschenberg, used all manner of odd materials, Toulouse Lautrec painted in pastel on cardboard. Picasso used anything that wasn't nailed down.

Welcome to *Camp Free Yourself,* where anything goes. I'm not suggesting you present these odd experiments to a gallery, as eternal productions of your genius. This is for experimentation. Beginning and intermediate students ask me all the time about the permanence of certain mixed-media pieces, to which I say, worry more about making good art, there is nothing worse than a bad painting that won't die. And I know what I'm talking about.

After this is said and done, you can go right back to doing what you were taught to do, but with new ideas on how to tackle the process.

Note: Don't write me to ask what's the best cheap paint for whatever surface. Just pick one. Same is true for brushes. There is no magic brush, except maybe for the #4 sparkle brush.

Divergent thinking, multiples and the search for truth

We all like to make handsome paintings and post them on the internet to gather ebullient praise. Who doesn't?

The thing about an external reward system... while it is perfectly good and helpful, it can motivate you to keep doing the same thing. And then the quiet voice starts saying, "There has to be more in me." And, of course, there always is.

Building trust in your own decisions is key. It means relying on one's intuition and knowledge, combining a personal aesthetic with the power of discernment. It is the essence of critical thought, basing a conclusion on evidence and reasoning, inferring a solution from the available body of information.

And what the heck does this have to do with creativity? Once you do the divergent work, producing a host of solutions, you can eliminate those creative suspects that don't fit the problem at hand, and sort out the one or two that are guilty... of being awesome.

The creative person takes all that good information about resistance, free association, play and intent and puts it to work, reviewing whether it's right or wrong as a solution.

For most artists, this should be easy. But, surprisingly, it's not.

That's where doing multiples comes in. It allows for a bit of guided serendipity, rather than trying to control the process. It's the process of doing ***just to see what shows up.*** These six words are among the most important in this book. They require faith, diligence and courage.

Working in multiples is not new. We do them for a bajillion reasons -- to improve through repetition and muscle memory (i.e. figurative sketch books) and to explore ideas on smaller scales so there's less of an investment to risk (thumbnails) and explore new ideas in their simplest form, making a flock of unusual suspects to be considered.

Both as an illustrator and a fine artist, the preliminary thumbnail is *de rigueur,* the thought of engaging all those masterful faculties in a larger painting without some kind of map is a bit sketchy. No pun intended... (Oh wait).

So, why not use it to see where we can go instead of where we have been?

Chunk Fu: Art Ninja Warrior training ground

Intent: To discover new ideas, break old habits, explore compositional motifs, component possibilities and just plain explore.

You tried the free-association techniques in the **Connectivity** section using key words, combining those key words to get new associations (digging deeper).

Now try the same idea with paint (or whatever your medium). Many people do thumbnails, but they stop way too soon, because they already had an idea of what they were after... and that is usually the obvious.

This method is about discovery, a start with no finish line; at least, at first. We'll take the Telephone exercise and amplify it, turning it upside down, making it blue, adding wallpaper patterns, you name it (apply some of the adaptation key words from the **Connectivity** section).

I should point out that one form of resistance shows up as preciousness. If I give you a nice canvas and say, "Mess it up... have at it", it might be hard for you. Fear of screwing up or losing what has been accomplished prevents us from moving forward through taking risks. Remember, if you got it once, you will get it again. The work is not precious, the intent is.

One way to trick your brain and shut down this resistance is to break up a page or a canvas into smaller quadrants or rectangles. You see each quadrant as a study, an exercise, and the efforts become less treasured. They get done faster and are less labored.

More work gets made, more ideas are generated and progress happens faster.

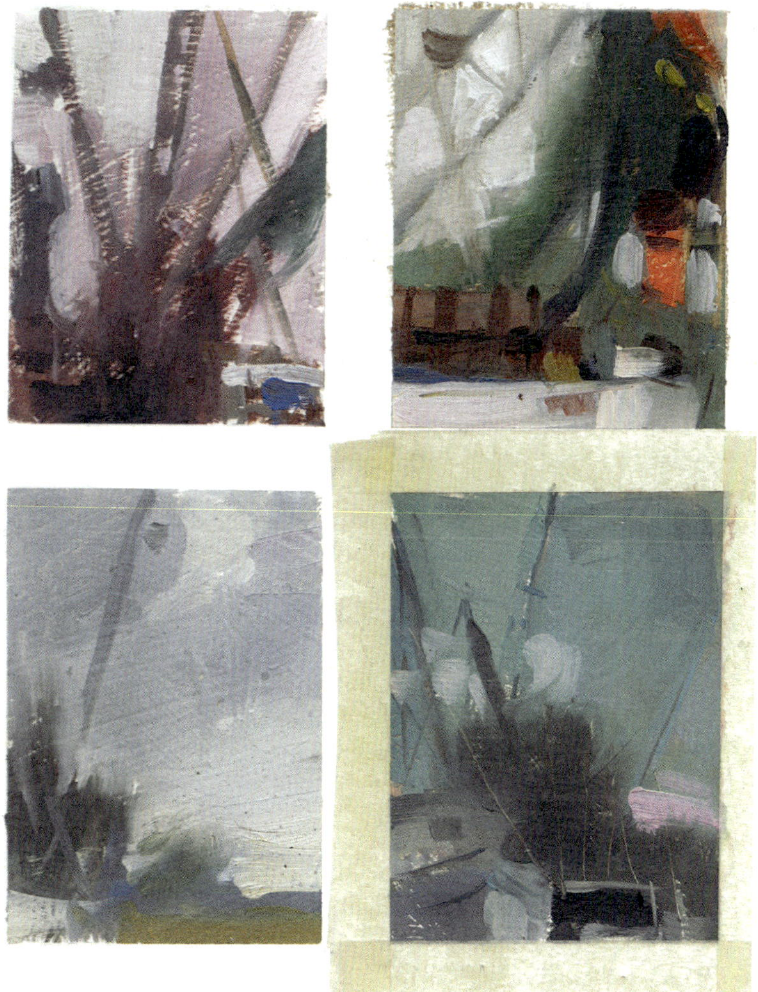

Lose the preciousness and you lose the fear. By taping even a small canvas into quarters you send an automatic signal to your brain that says, "these are just for study... I will not beat them to death".

Breaking out the individual characteristics of painting by isolating and practicing them is a sure-fire way to get better more quickly. Look at your personal components chart and see where you fall in the pretty darn good vs not so much spectrum, which elements you need to work on most, and which are your strongest?

Which are more important to you in your authentic voice? Decide what you really want to focus on and get to work. By making a note of what you are going to work on, you are making a small contract with yourself.

There are suggested exercises for each category, but you can also come up with your own. This is Multiples, so one idea just don't cut it. Fill a sketchbook or three or 30.

Note: Energy requires two opposing forces. It's a tenet that runs through every aspect of the creative process. Everything requires its counter to operate. A color note needs a different color against it to gain energy. A value requires an opposing value to be placed in context. A soft edge needs a hard edge to work.

1) Concept/narrative/intent.

The idea is king. Great art has a story to tell. Without it, it's just something nice to look at... or not.

If you were to address a theme or an idea and express it visually, what would it be? The working man, the ephemeral love note, dreams, nature and her glory, the symbolic power of the buffalo?

Monet said, *"Other artists paint a bridge, a house, a boat, and that's the end. They are finished. I want to paint the air which surrounds the bridge, the house, the boat, the beauty of the air in which these objects are located."*

This was his purpose, and each haystack or lily pond he made was in service to this idea. Developing a message, a story, is vital to a cohesive body of work. Revisit the **Intent** section for more on developing personal concepts.

Perhaps your motive is more materials-based or interpretation-based, an assemblage of unlike things to make a new reality. You'll know more about this when you get to the methods and materials exercises, if you don't already. Identify for now what is paramount in your work and build a story around it.

A) Write. Write short stories and vignettes. Make poems about whatever you have responded to in a specific moment or object. List key words that matter to you relative to a subject you wish to create around. From these short vignettes, make thumbnail sketches, adding notes to the side to aid the idea, should you go further with it.

B) Movie frame. One thing missing in contemporary genre painting is a compelling story. A cowboy on a horse isn't much of a story, nor is a woman on the beach in a flowing white dress and floppy hat. It's a borrowed, meaning-less piece of genre.

If you want to tell a story, think like a movie director and build a narrative that goes beyond a moment in time. Some of Americas greatest storytellers were illustrators of the Golden Era. Look at how Norman Rockwell, N.C. Wyeth and Dean Cornwell (page 169) depict a story. Every piece of each scene carried weight and held meaning, all aided by brilliant compositional designs.

If you don't know where to start for this exercise, pull a section from a favorite book and create multiple versions and points of view in thumbnail form.

C) A metaphor is like a summer's day. Okay, that's simile, but metaphor is the underpinning of much of the world's great literature, film and fine art, because literal is boring. Make the viewer think a little.

Go through a few of the free association methods featured in **Connectivity** to jump-start your process. Pick a topic that is important to you, something you have passion for, and make a connection to something that it is like. Read some Shakespeare, he was the master of metaphor and simile.

For example, a good day of fishing could be expressed as "It was raining fish out there." The phrase, Iron Horse, a moniker for the steam engine train, can now symbolize industrial decay and be extended to the computer age. Go for it. The world is your oyster.

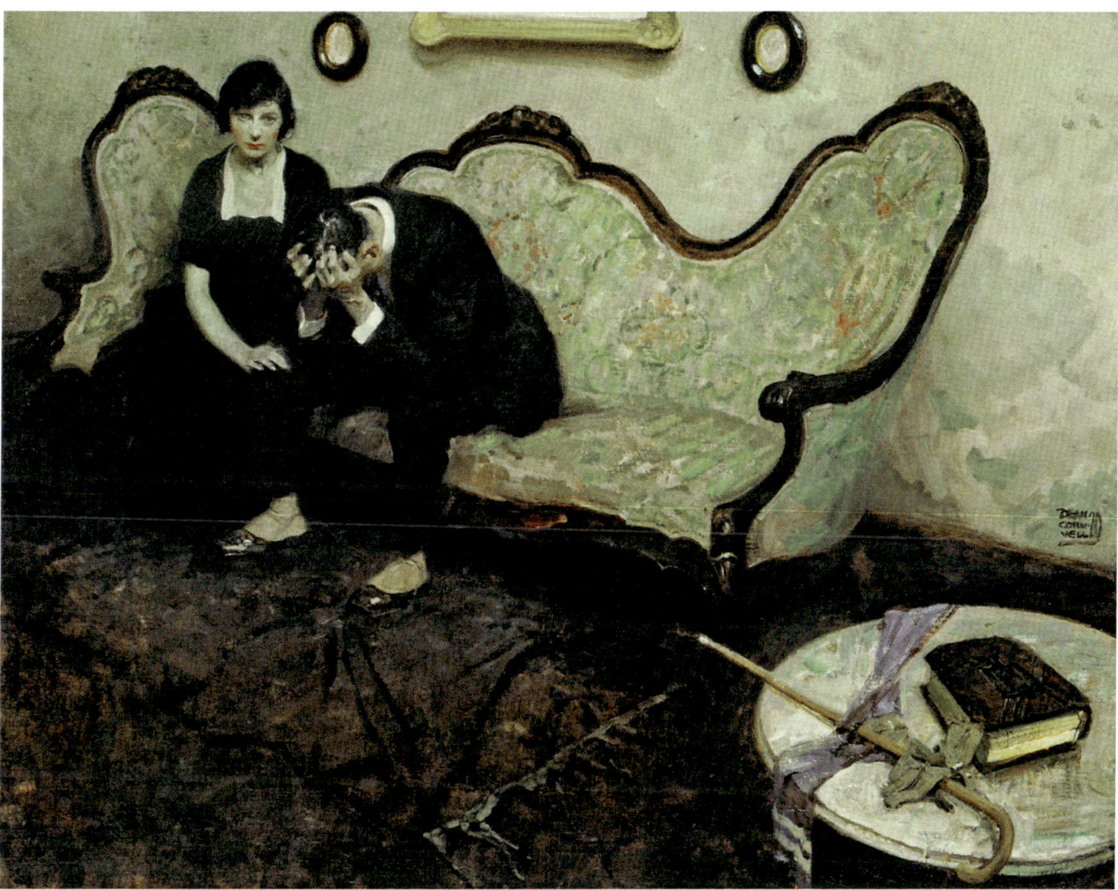

Dean Cornwell
"It's pretty hard to explain murder, isn't it?," 1920. Oil on canvas, 28" x 35"

"Find the Woman", Arthur Somer Roche, Cosmopolitan, January 1921, p. 72.

SYNOPSIS: Clancy goes to the big city to find a career in show business. A friend she meets at the boarding house sets her up with a very unscrupulous agent who offers to only help her if she is nice to him. The young man in the painting has just confessed that he has murdered the agent and they are waiting for the police to come.

D) Paint your time. The Ashcan School, active from 1908 until WWI, painted their time and focused on the grittier sides of class differences in New York. What gave their work authenticity was not a reliance on photography as reference. They worked from life, from drawings and studies.

What stories can you tell about your time? Next time you are stuck sitting and waiting somewhere like the hair salon or the DMV, have a sketchbook handy to draw and write about the experience. Make quick, simple gestural drawings and note colors and observations.

In the studio, make more refined drawings from the sketches. Stay away from abused themes like chefs in a kitchen, ballet dancers or American Indians doing anything. Apply that energy to something that matters to you.

E) Dreamscapes. As discussed in **Connectivity**, dreams aren't just a rich source of imagery, they are a fount of story and narrative ideas. Use the same methods described on page 90 to capture these mini-movie concepts and apply the distillation process below to boil the dream story down to its essence.

F) Distillation. This is a big one. Take a story you have written, a painting or a movie, yours or anyone's and reduce it down to its simplest elements. What is it really about? Write it down. "Man keeps hope alive in prison." Boiling a plot to its bare bones gives you an opportunity to find another way to reframe it by using metaphor.

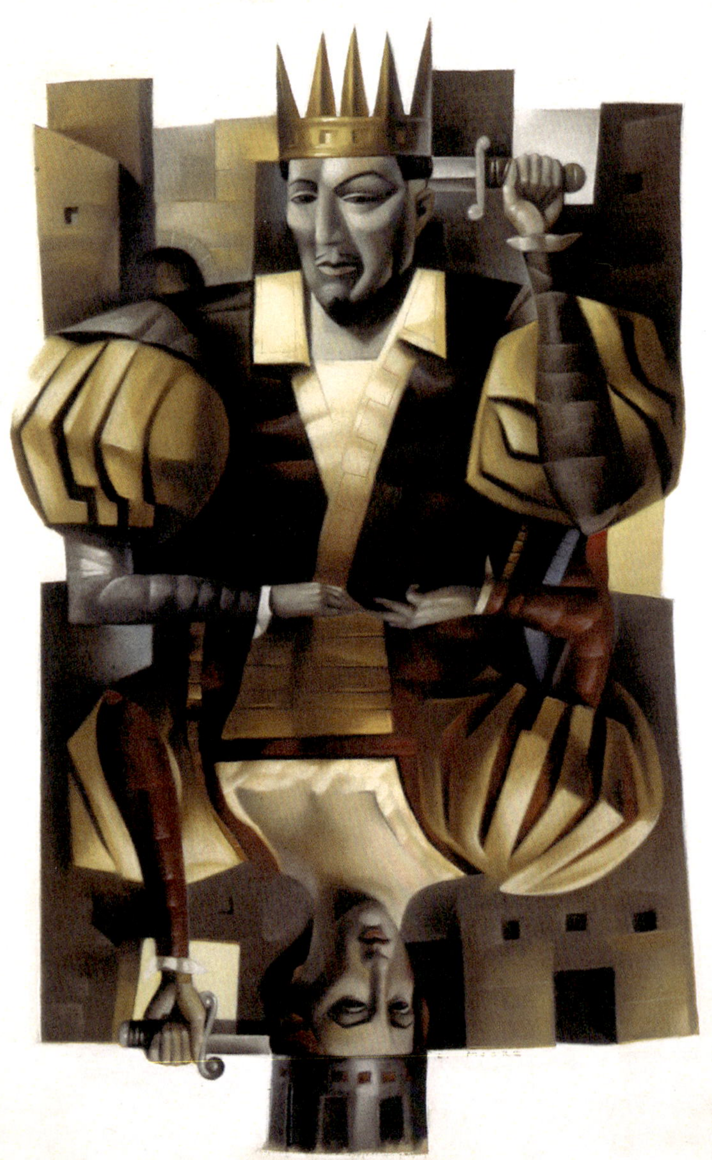

This kind of reframing permits the voice of the artist to come through. Considering the essence of idea makes for clearer motive in the production of a painting and adds greater potential for interpretation. Macbeth: Dysfunctional power couple self-destruct, the suicide king and queen, as in the playing card, King of Hearts.

1F Distillation

Boil the theme down to the bones so that you can reframe it. Macbeth: Dysfunctional power couple self-destruct. Or the suicide king and queen, represented by the playing card king of hearts.

2) Interpretation.

Knowledgeable painters can identify their favorite artist's work in the blink of an eye by the way said artist interprets the elements of shape / style / color -- often without having seen the painting before. Which is to say that the most recognizable artists have developed a recognizably unique visual language. Georgia O'Keefe, Andrew Wyeth, Thomas Hart Benton and Maynard Dixon are great examples.

An architectural illustrator handles elements (trees, people, buildings) in a very graphic way; the architectural model builder, another way; a botanical artist, another still. How you express an element expresses your point of view. Take an object, anything with a little bit of complexity to it and see how many ways you can morph it.

Use some of the trigger words in **Adapt-Transform** section of **Connectivity.** I don't think I should have to say this but... be creative. For most of these, black and white sketches will do, unless you get really inspired.

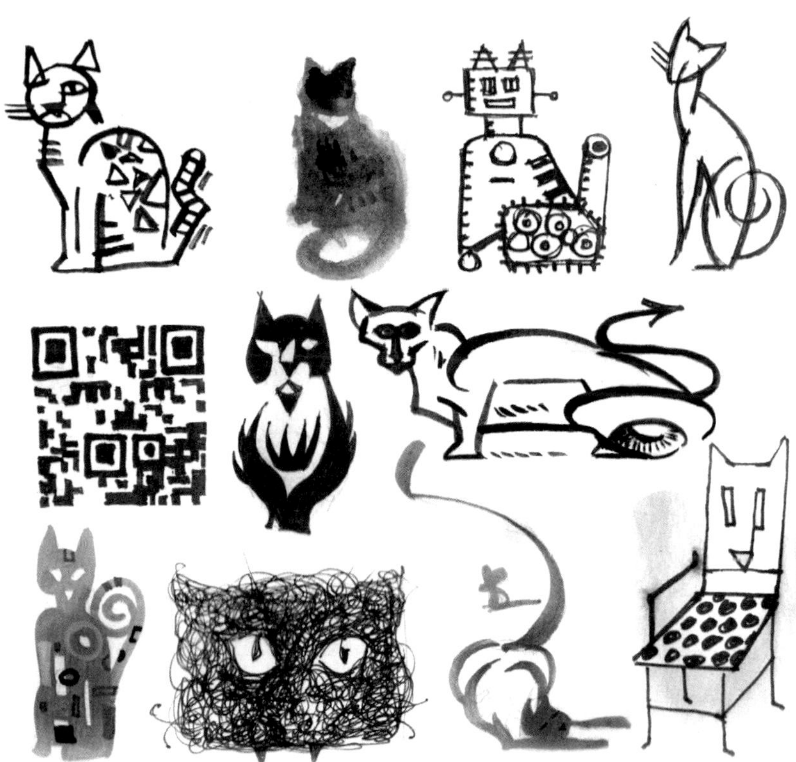

A) Trigger-happiness. In the **Adapt-Transform** section is a list of prompt words (pg. 92) to pull from, like mechanize, worm's-eye view and French provincial. Take your chosen reference and randomly select two words from the list (or make up your own) as filters for how you see the object. Try this four or five times with one object and force yourself to visualize.

B) Fractured image. This one requires some sketch paper and tissue or vellum and you will have to switch off the desire to over-control the image. Start with a small drawing area, 4"x5", and very light random-line breakup of the space. Working from your reference, start a key-line sketch of the most basic structural elements. Don't over-draw or connect every line. Once it is loosely (and lightly) blocked in, put the reference away and allow the random lines to influence the drawing. Rework using darker lines adding random values where lines intersect.

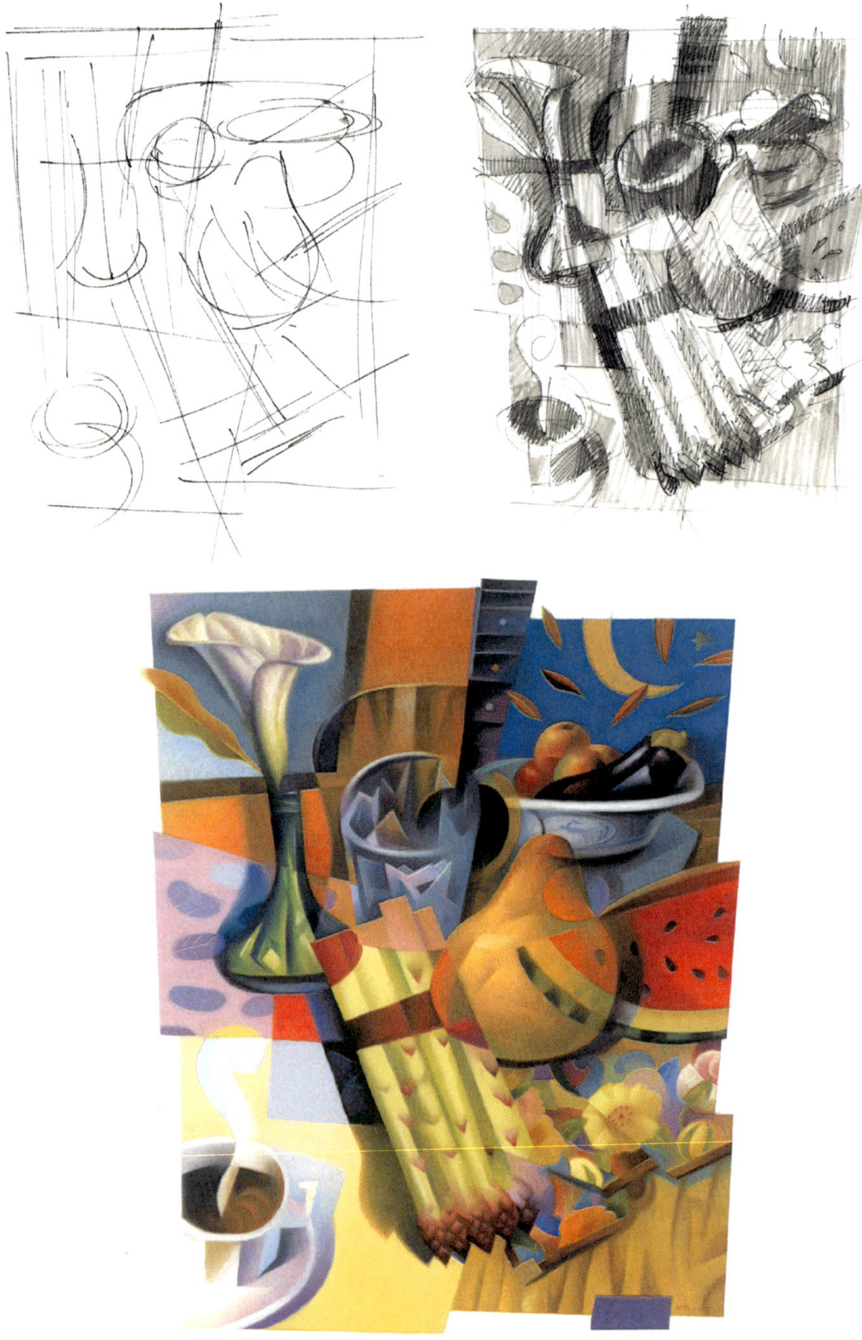

2B Fractured image

Start with a few random key lines to break up the page, add loose descriptions of the elements you want and then put the reference away. Place the values where you want them. Follow up with color.

C) Altered state. Change the context of the reference. Put a fish in the sky, a meteor in a fish bowl, a caterpillar smoking a hookah on a mushroom. Contextual change plays a powerful supporting role in many great works of art. Even a simple shift of background content or sky color can be enough to alter the impact or meaning of a piece. Painting a pear on a table is a pretty straightforward act, but dropping the shadow so that the pear appears to levitate above the rest of the still life provides for an entirely different outcome. Same goes for recreating the Mona Lisa in a silkscreen comic book style. Utilize some of the trigger terms on page on page 92 to adapt and transform whatever you wish to apply them to.

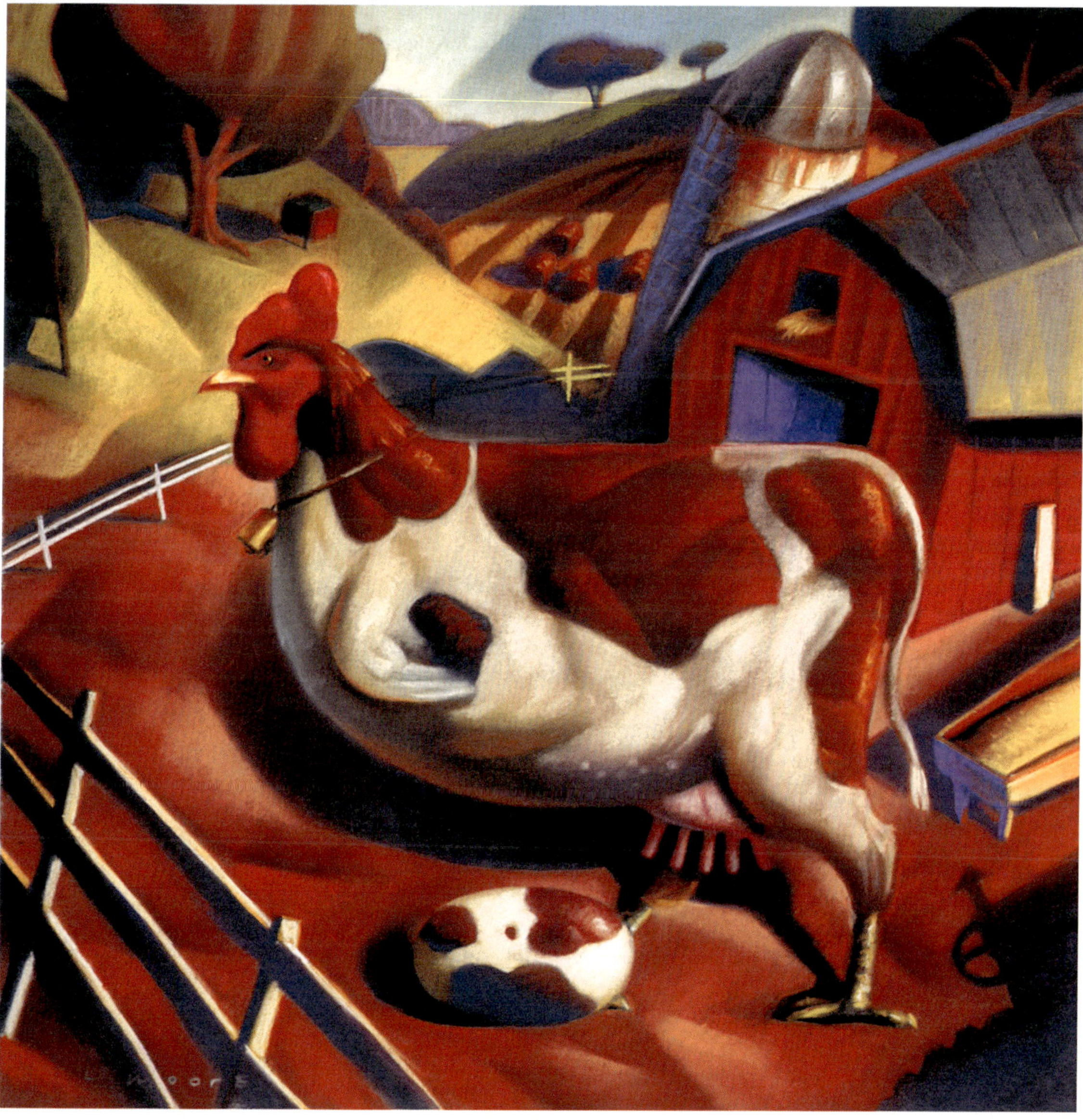

2C Altered state

Interpretation comes in many forms. The term "hybrid animal farm" led to this unusual change of meaning. Pastel on paper 16x16

D) Mixed planes. This is a good exercise for making chaos out of order. We get to create Bizzarro world where nothing works right. There is a saying, "The drawing needs to either be spot-on or intentionally way off. Just a little off don't look right." I know this because I said it. Do this one from life. Set up a still-life and start by drawing a portion of one object, move and complete the object, move again and draw a portion of the next thing, move again and so on, allowing forms to overlap and morph until the whole setting is done.

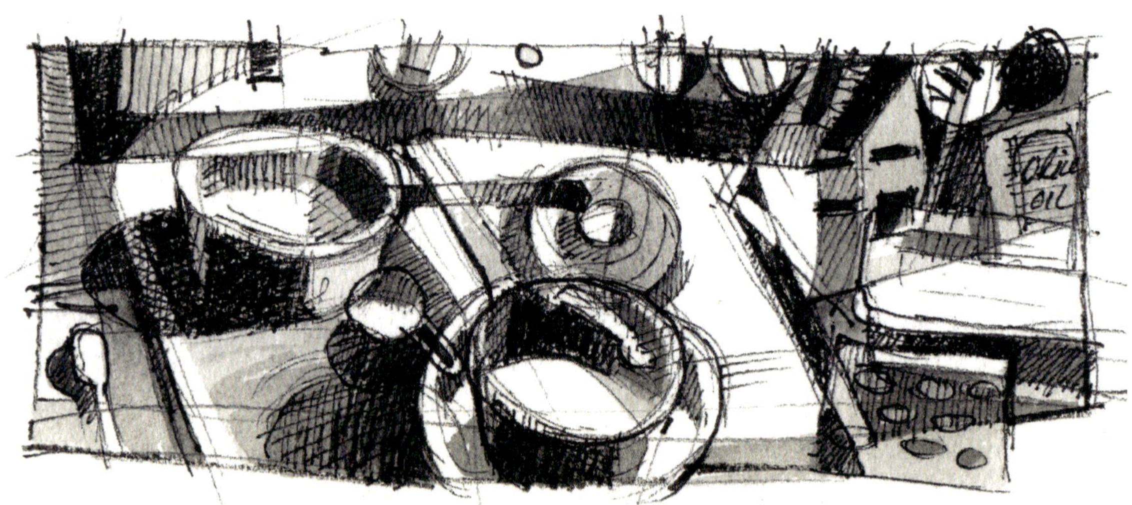

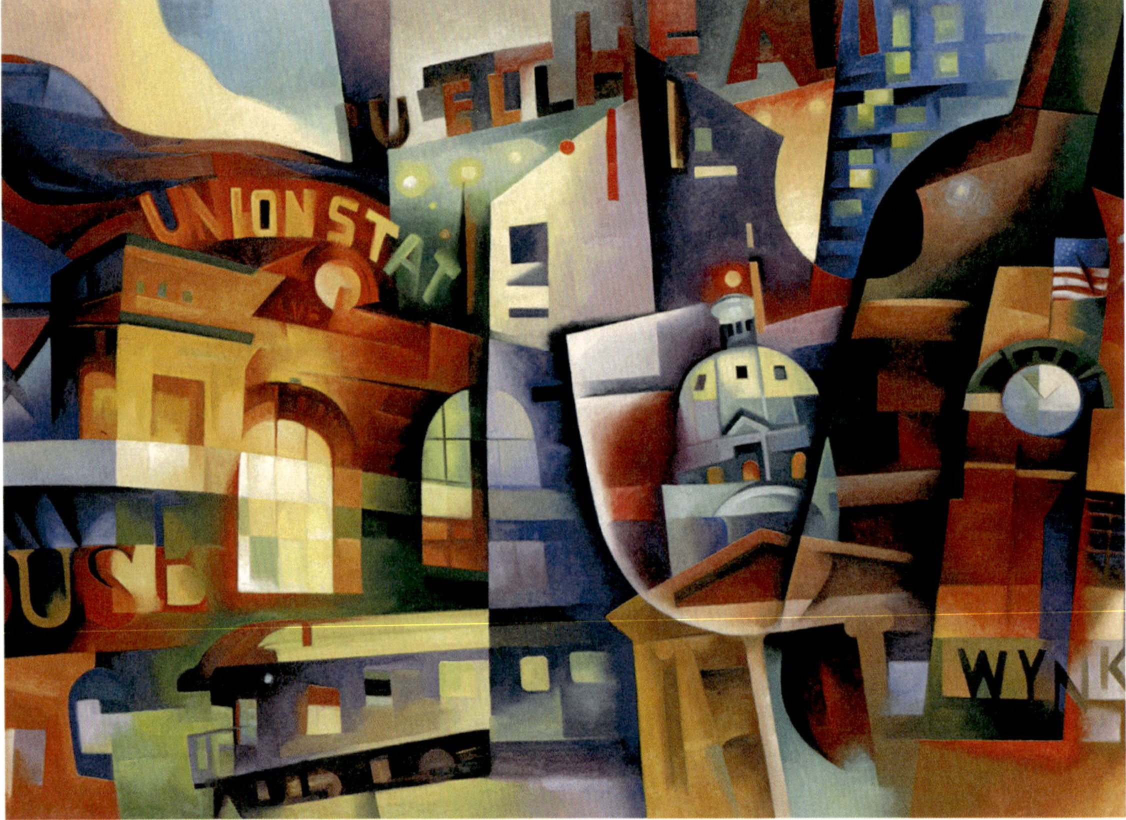

2D Mixed planes

An ink/wash drawing of my kitchen using the mixed planes concept and a section of a mural painting (oil) with the same principles. Let go of the boring physics of perspective. It's your world after all.

E) Color me crazy. You know your usual palette? Don't use it. Pick an assortment of pigments you would never think to put together and paint with. If you tend toward bright color, go neutral. If you are a local color person, go with primary and secondary. Just because you learned a certain way doesn't mean you can't try another.

Warm white Cadmium green Dove grey Transparent red oxide

2E Crazy color

This odd mix is made up of colors I never use. Because I'm not trying to match color I'm free to explore other possibilities. Try any color combination that is not red/yellow/ blue based and see what you do with it. It helped to gray-scale my photo reference so that I was not in color chasing mode.

3) Drawing.

Spoiler alert: If you are an artist, you should be drawing every day, no matter what kind of artist. Not just working on how to draw a figure, boat or horsey, but also sketching little thumbnail ideas while you watch the Tonight Show. Drawing people in the park or at the airport, quick gestures, interior settings, little vignettes, more is better. Go to the art store and buy five portable sketch pads. Fill them up and repeat. Draw with a pen so that your brain knows there's no erasing. Though you can intellectualize drawing. It must emanate from your hands and that creates the muscle memory. Practice. Practice and more practice. But, to make it more fun here are some different ways to draw that will keep you in the game. Fill the page with little rectangles to draw in just so you don't turn it into a full-page novel.

A) Traditional line gestures. Great for quick sketching people and reading the dominant shapes and lines. Fill your pages with lots of little people, just like in The Lord of the Rings.

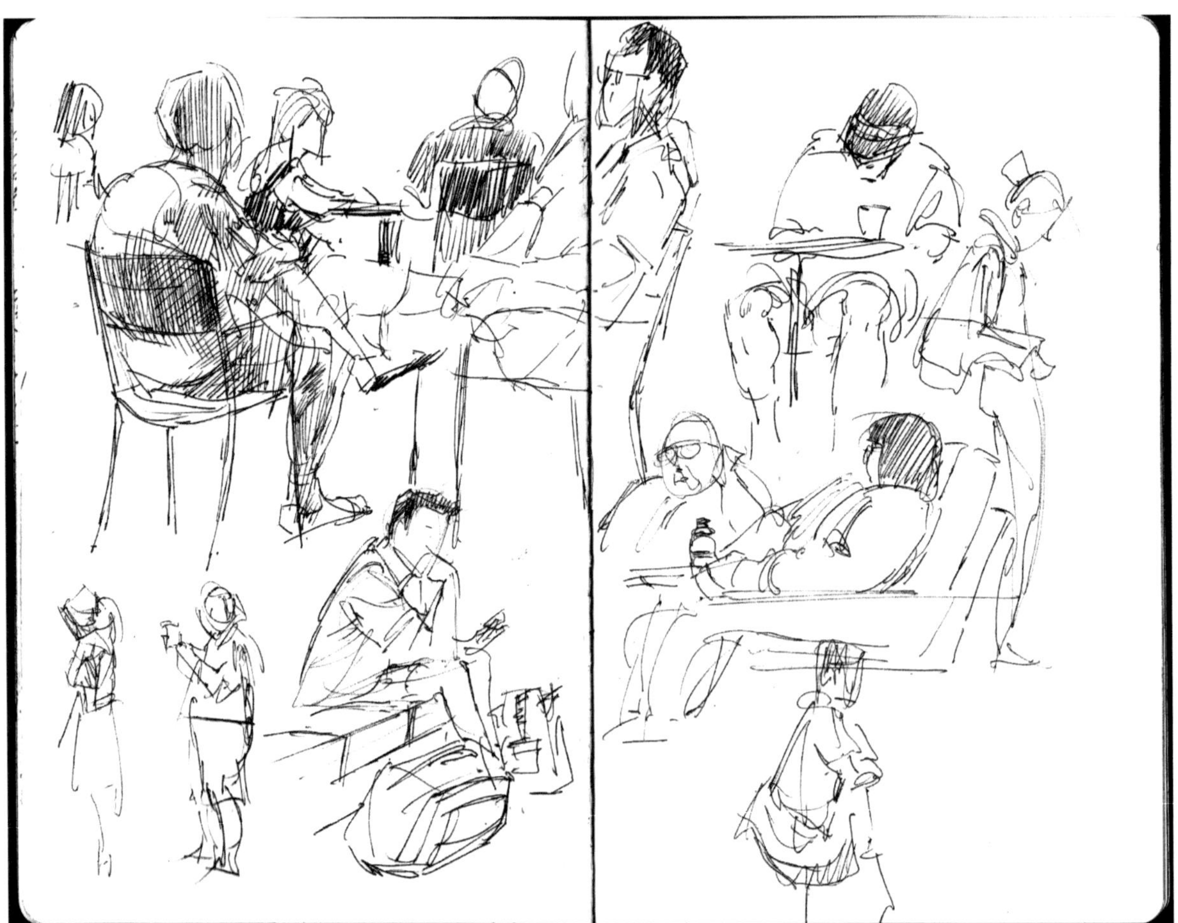

3A Gestures

The contemporary realist Terry Miura has done his share of these quick sketches. They aren't about polish or line trickery, they are about study, gesture, implied movement, and expression of form through line. There is no shortcut, just miles and miles of line.

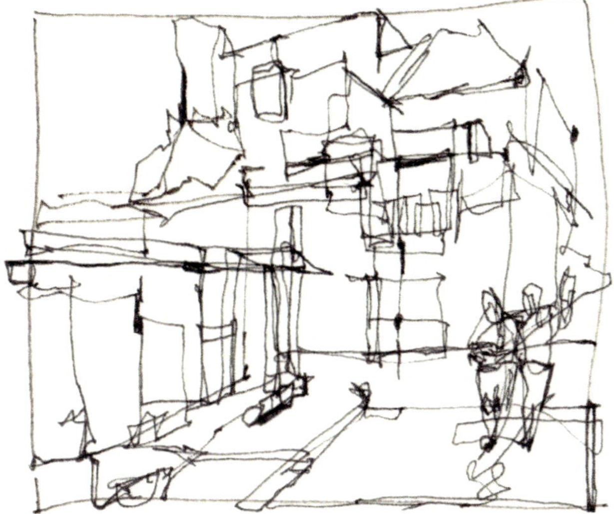

B) Continuous line. Place the tip of the pen down and don't lift it until your drawing is done. Let the line "draw through" other shapes to create unintentional partitions and sub-shapes.

C) Notan. See only what is in light and only what is in dark, sketch in with black angle-tipped markers for the shadows and leave the rest as light... great for combining shapes, simplifying and editing.

D) Broken line. Line is more than a dot that went for a walk, it skips and jumps and slides happily around like a puppy on caffeine, but it's only as playful as the hand that makes it.

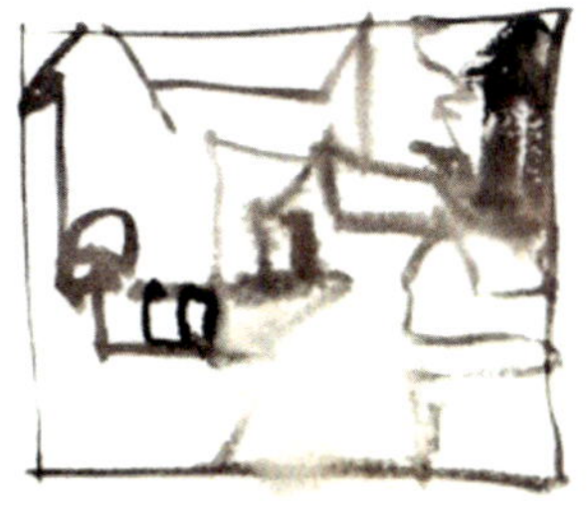

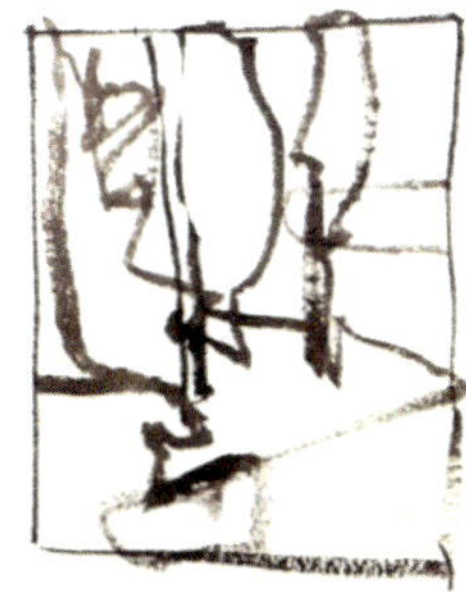

3B Continuous line

Draw a box and once your drawing utensil hits the page, don't pick it up until the drawing is done. Work fast, loose and let the shapes overlap. It's like Etch-a-sketch only faster.

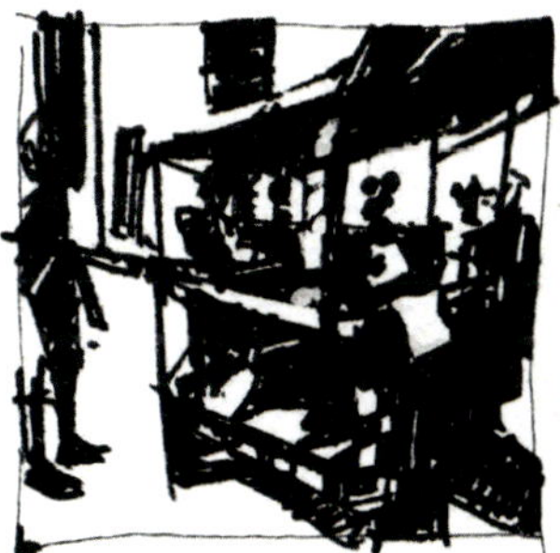

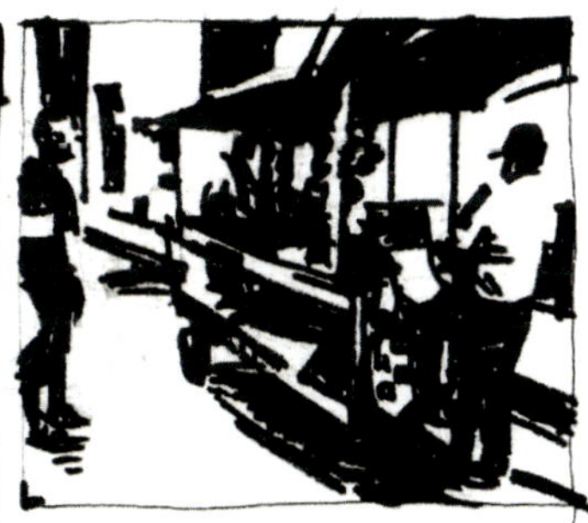

3C and D Notan and Broken line

Two different ways to explore spatial relationships in black and white through shape and line. Notan is the combination of 3 of the most important compositional elements; shape, positive / negative, division of space. Utilizing this simple tool will greatly simplify the way you see and compose. Black marker, felt tip pen, or pointy round brush and black ink on paper.

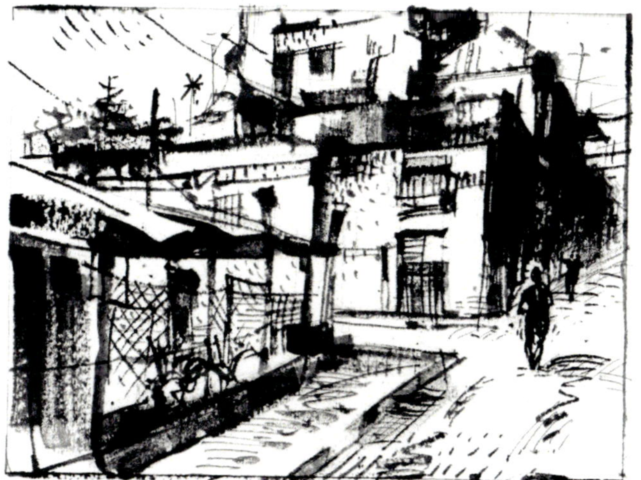

E) Blind contour. A way of drawing that encourages interpretation. Look at what you are drawing but not the drawing itself. My best work is done this way. (It's kind of embarrassing.)

3E Blind contour

Place pen or pencil to paper, look at the thing you are drawing but not at the page, just feel your way around, hence the term blind contour. Add color randomly or through aesthetic choice and watch what shows up. Ink and watercolor.

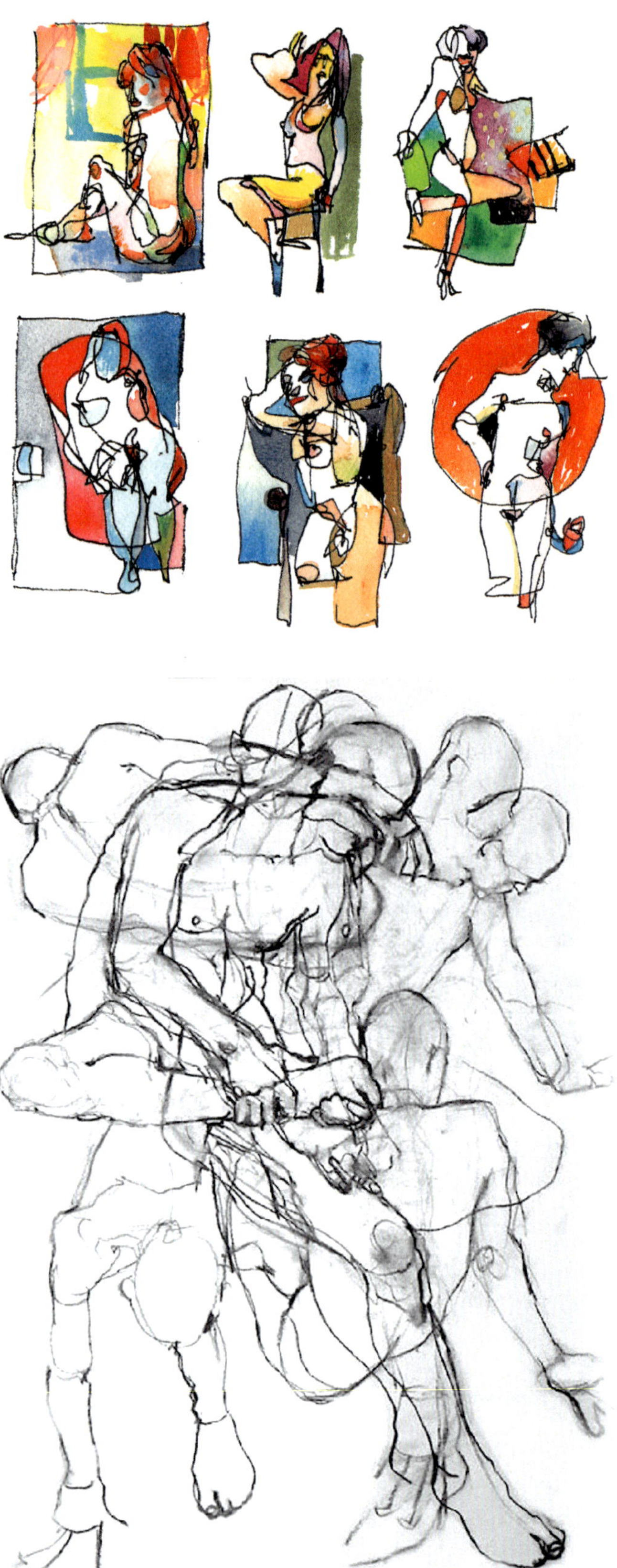

F) Moving lines. There is something really interesting in seeing the history of thought in an artist's drawing. The series of corrections and adjustments, left for the viewer to see, includes the viewer in a way that a perfectly executed drawing does not. And what if the figure moves as you draw it? Got a cat? A dog? An antsy child? Begin to draw a figure loosely, emphasizing key lines and, as it shifts, redraw on top of what you have. Get a model to walk or turn slowly and capture all of it. It's like a still movie. Charcoal on paper and kneaded eraser or soft cloth to knock down and blend.

3F Moving lines

The British artist, Dee Berridge, captures a figure's *movement in layers in what she calls a "composite drawing." Each time the model moves, the next drawing is begun over the last, replicating motion while visually expressing the passage of time. Herdrawing style reinforces the theme of movement through its thin to thick calligraphy and use of seeking lines to define the edge of the form.*
Yoga man, 13.75"x19.5"-- charcoal on Fabriano paper.

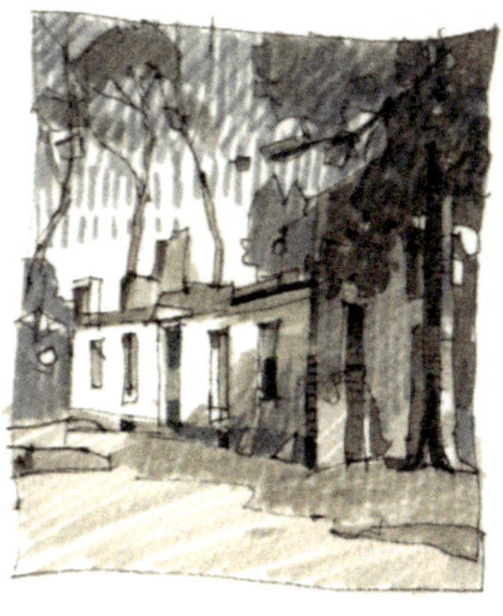

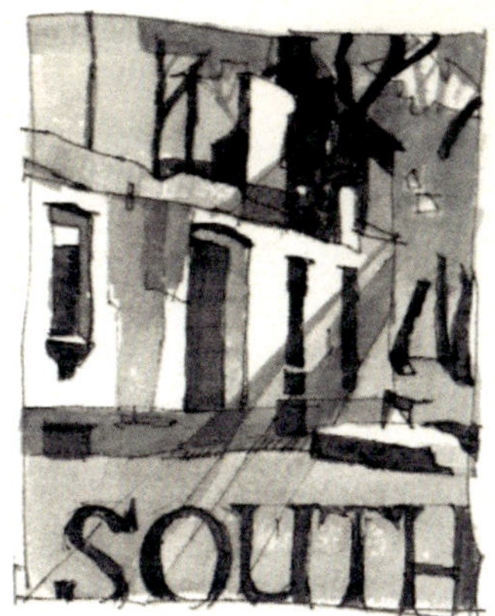

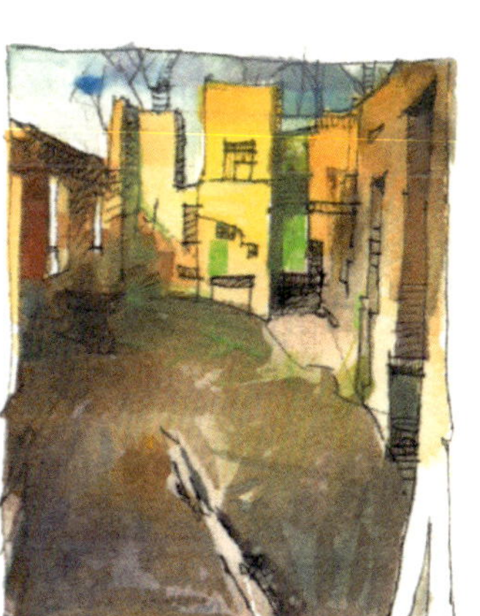

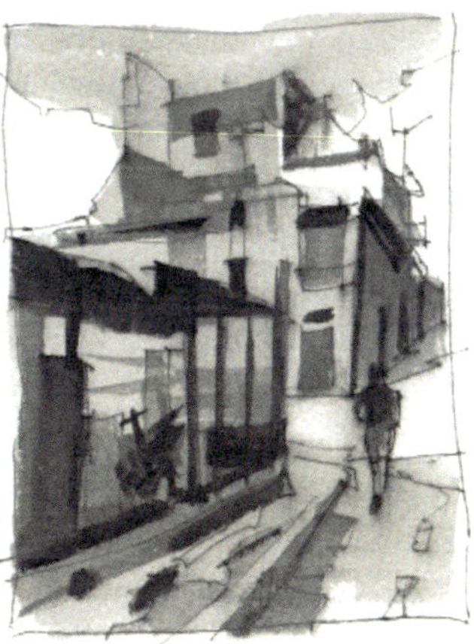

3G Posterize

Think vintage travel poster. Simple graphic shapes with simple, flat color / value relationships are the best foundations for great design.

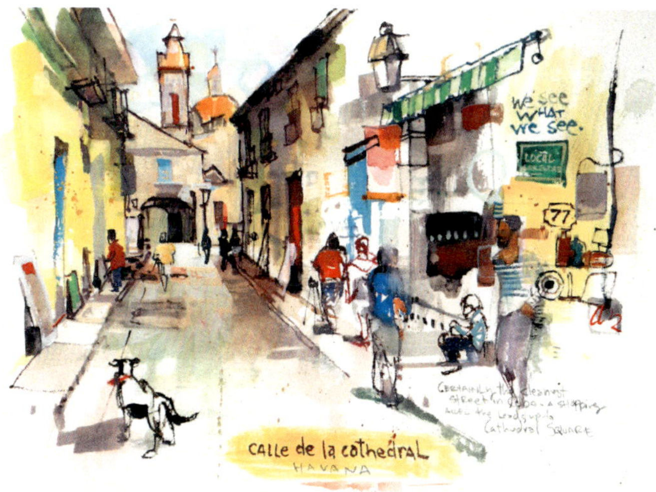

3H Reportage

Pick a scene, any scene, but make it a busy one. The white of the page plays a big part in this style, leaving room for serendipity, additions, text and the occasional dog walking into the scene. This piece was created in Havana, Cuba where our tour guide stated quietly that, "we only see what they want us to see".

G) Posterize. Think holiday train poster for the Grand Canyon circa 1950's. See and draw the shape (exterior line of the object) and the shadow shapes. You can bring out the watercolors or value markers or gouaches for this one. This kind of shape simplicity is how you need to be seeing. It's a good exercise.

H) Reportage. A method of expression that could be filed under drawing, interpretation, intent, or narrative. A style that has its roots in wartime reporting where brave military artists would risk their lives to record not just a moment, but a series of moments, an event. Usually (though not necessarily) ink and watercolor, the artist combines drawing, written word, glued down ephemera and creates a combination of visual references to make a story.

I) Really totally hammered. Okay, I'm seriously kidding. Don't drink and draw, kids. And also, don't drink and draw kids.

4) Value.

Three-value marker sketch: draw with the lightest, place your middle values, put in your darkest notes, leave the white paper as the lightest light. Most of the very best paintings are laid out in three or four values, just like a good blues song-- three chords and the truth. My personal favorite for these exercises is gouache, cheap, small and opaque (like I like my women). Use black, gray and white gouache, mix three values or use a three- or four-value marker set. Or just good old black and water.

A) Soft and light wash. Using either soft charcoal or watercolor and a single value color, like black or Paynes gray and watercolor paper or similar, taped off into small rectangles. Start with a very light value wash and, working from life or photo, slowly develop the study from light to dark in three to four values, no more. Pretend you are developing a black and white photo. Allow for one or two hard edges for contrast.

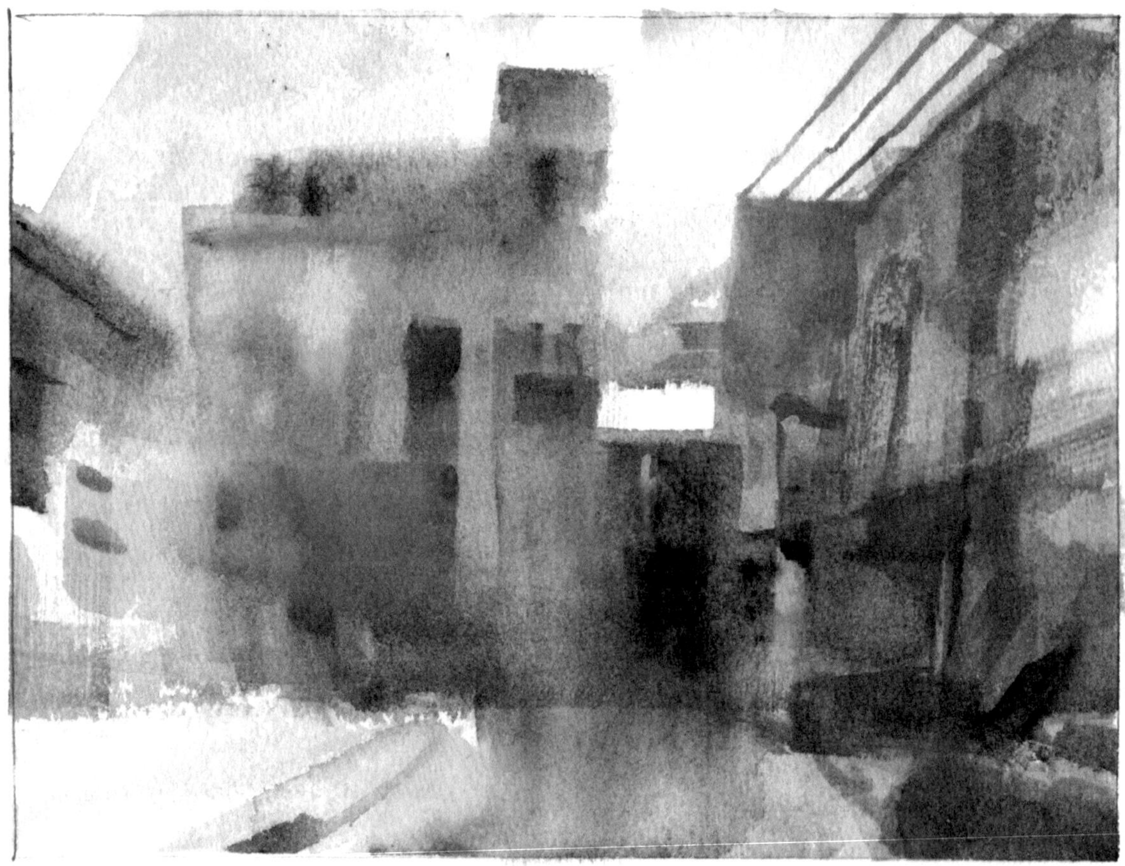

4A Soft and light

One color wash-in starting with the lightest values and slowly working darker. Wet into wet allows for a lot of soft edges, pick the edges you want to be crisp. It shows how little information is needed to explain a thing.

B) Hard. Taking a more cut-out approach, any medium including mixed media is fair game. Using one color, like black or a dark warm gray and white, premix three to four values or use cut paper or both. Work on a gessoed board of any description, whatever your reference, think in terms of cut-out shapes. Play with mechanical- and organic-form relationships, dominant-value plans, using the two values and the third for accents. Try translating a favorite piece of reference or painting into simple forms. Feel free to incorporate cut shapes from newspapers or magazines, especially the old black and white ones you've saved for absolutely no reason. Cut 'em up and stick 'em down with a glue stick or use acrylic medium and a flat plastic scraper tool to press them flat.

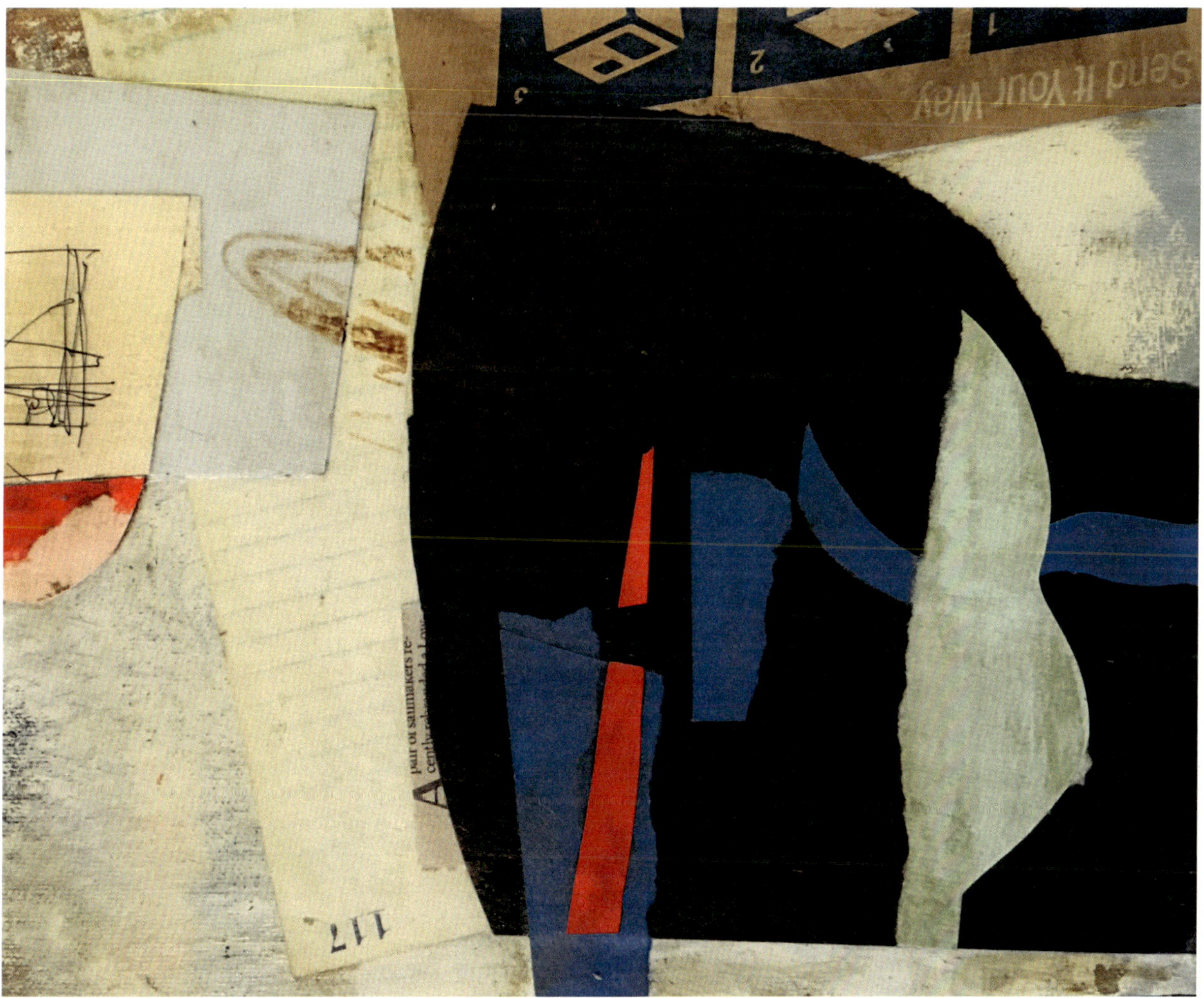

4B. Hard shape assemblage

This playful approach to composition is also a powerful learning tool. Torn and cut paper in a variety of colors, ink, crayon, magazine/newspaper clippings and Modge Podge or Gloss Gel Medium, with some acrylic colors for glazes and accents, are all you need. This piece started as an old 9x12 acrylic painting on a gessoed canvas panel with a few sketches for direction. Cut or tear the paper, brush the glue on the back and use a small plastic squeegee to press the shapes down. A final glaze of acrylic brown gave it a nicely antiqued finish.

C) The value plan. Whatever is in light is the white of the page. Whatever is in shadow is black, whatever is middle is gray. Push the dominance of one value over the other. When it's an even split, it's boring. Concentrate on dividing up the space in different ways using the same reference. Focus on the relationship of shapes and edges.

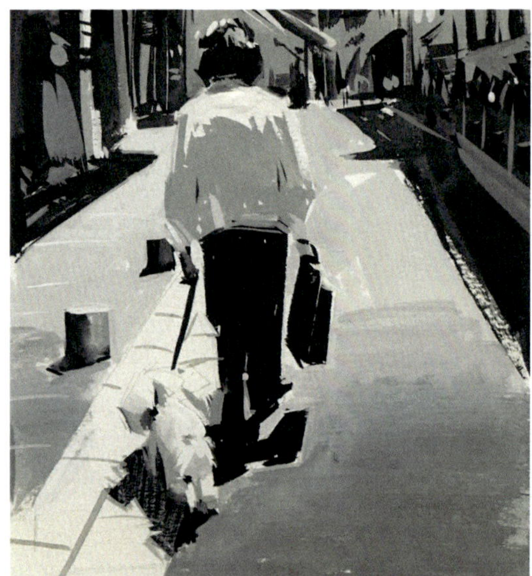

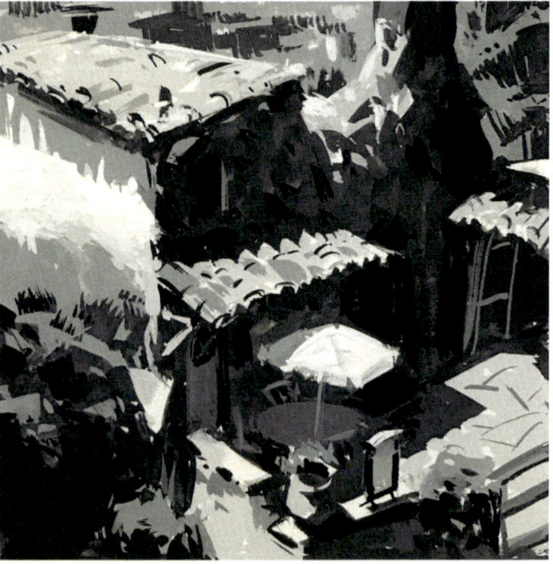

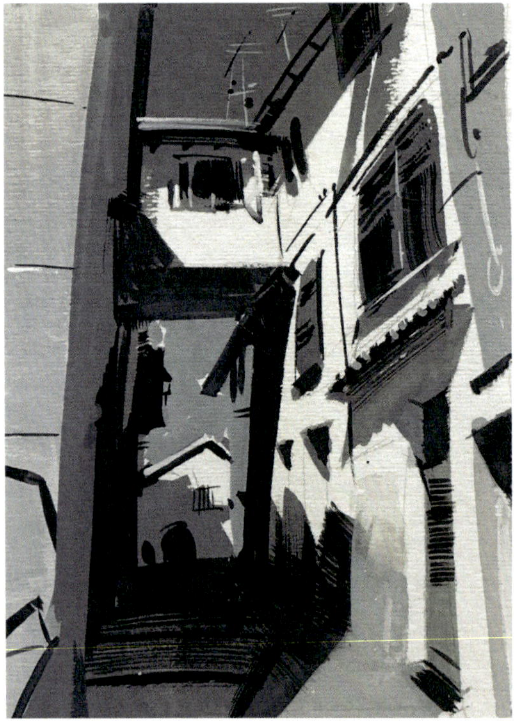

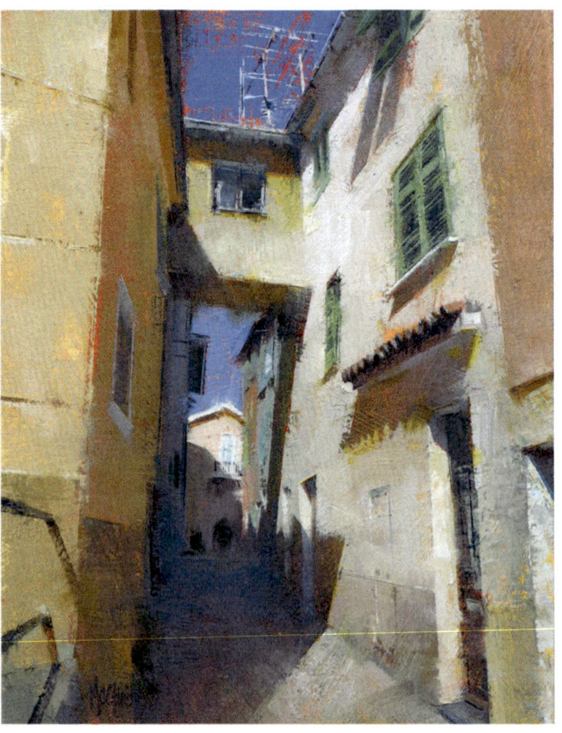

4C Value plan

Train yourself to control value rather than the other way around and you can do the same with color. A simple premise that supports a lot of noteworthy art. These brilliantly designed 3-value gouache sketches, and the resulting color piece, are the work of California artist, Jennifer McChristian. Thinking only in light, middle, and dark values simplifies the construct and allows for more freedom in color choices.

D) Continuous line and counter-intuitive values. Using the continuous-line technique in the drawing components exercises, add in values randomly just to see how they work. Good art is like a good joke, starts with a great idea and takes a left turn to surprise the recipient. Fine ink pen and watercolor on watercolor paper are great for this.

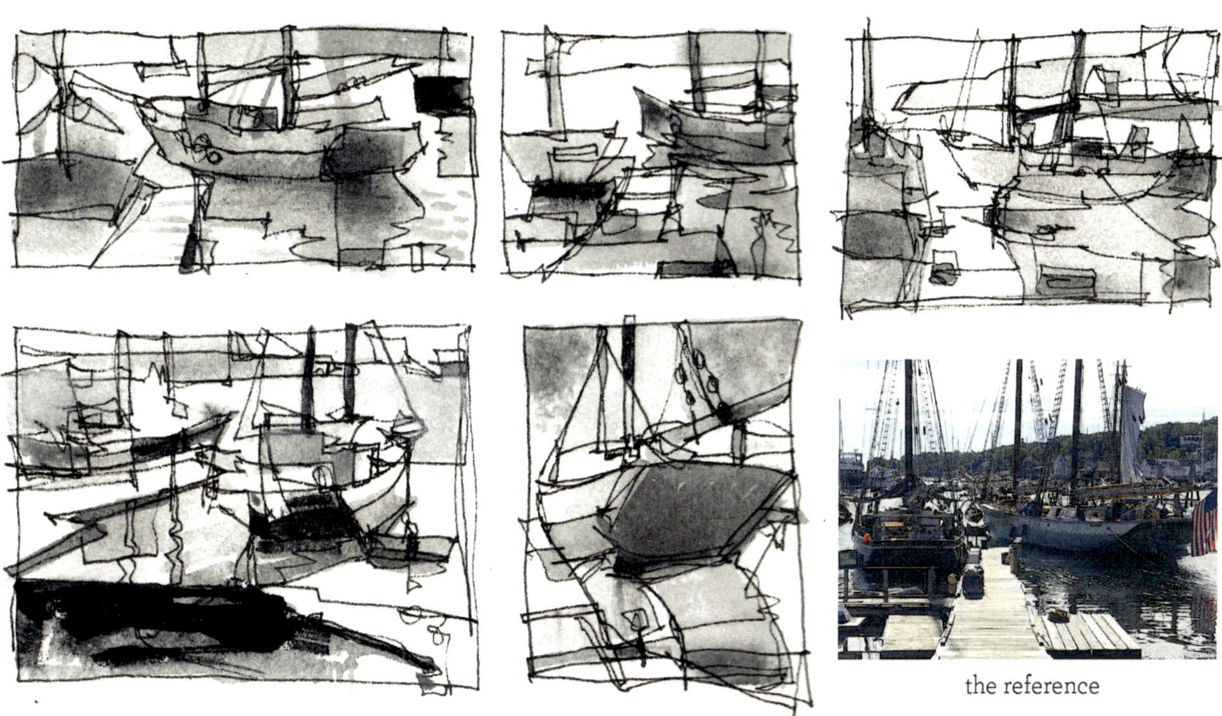

the reference

4D Random values

After the first stages of drawing and light value block-in, don't look at the reference. Place the values where you want them, work intuitively and move the eye where you want it to go. Ink and watercolor.

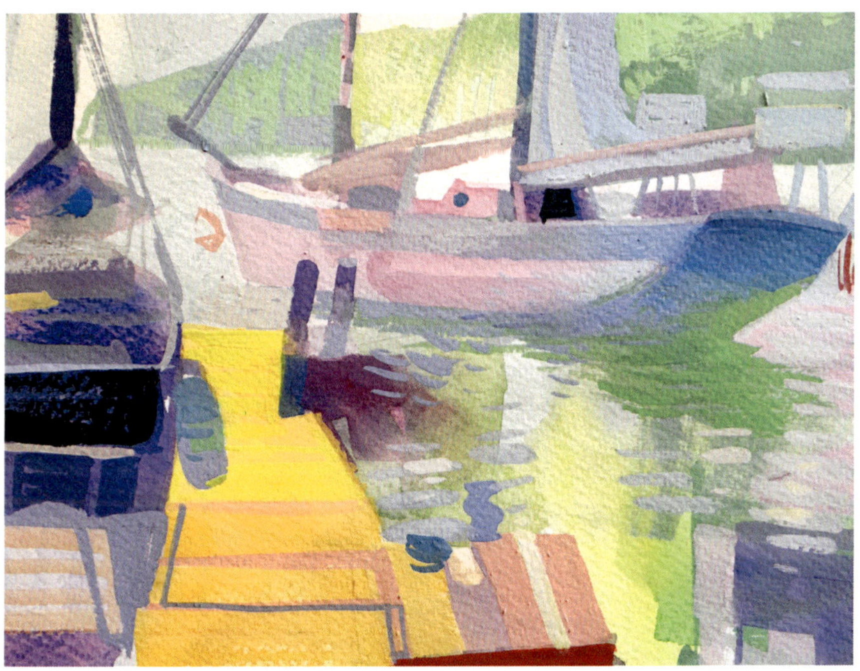

This 4"x5" gouache study was created from the value sketch in the upper right corner. Because I was not locked into the photo, I was free to explore color and value.

5) Color.

The number-one troublemaker in painting is color, or the inability to see it. First, we learn to understand and see value and then we learn to replace value with color. In most painting classes, it messes with everyone. Here are a few sure-fire ways to learn to see it and use it.

A) Color mix. The Paint Chip Challenge. The very best exercise for mixing color. Head over to your fave hardware paint store and grab a couple of handfuls of color picker cards with the multiple values. Grab at least 10 color cards, tell the paint guy you just bought a mansion. Back at the studio, match each color with a limited palette of a warm and a cool of each primary (yellow, red, blue) in oil or acrylic. And yes, you will need white. Use a smallish tapered tip palette knife. If you do enough of these, you will start seeing everything as color notes and you will know how to make those notes without thinking.

B) Color note. You will need the outdoors for this one. Grab your portable easel, favored paints and a limited palette of a warm and cool of each primary and white. Mix and then place the colors you see, note for note on a small, business card-sized chunk of taped-off canvas. NO drawing. Charles Webster Hawthorne said (paraphrasing), "Put the right color note in the right place and the form takes care of itself".

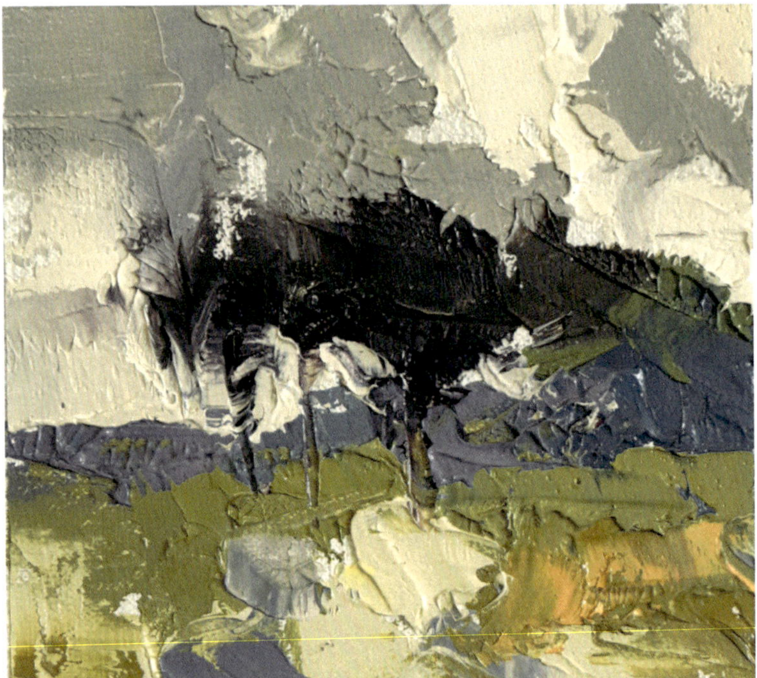

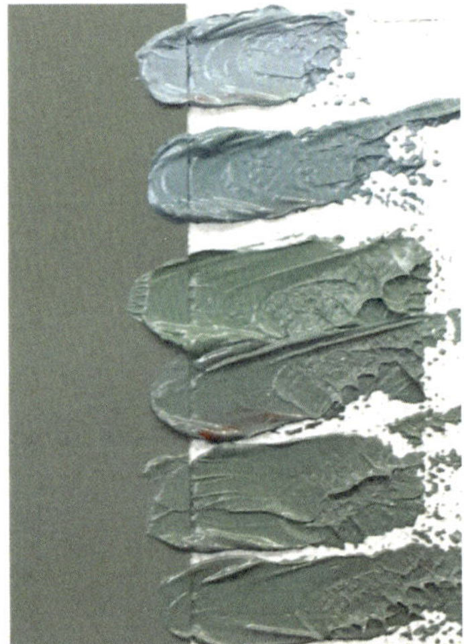

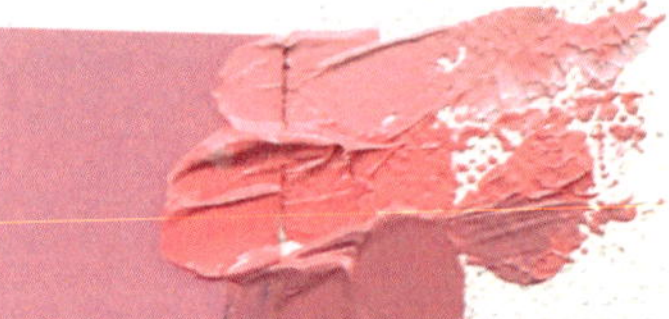

5A & 5B Color mix and color note

Learn to mix and match a variety of color chips and you will realize that the world is just a bunch of pixels.

C) Printers primaries. Cyan, Magenta, Yellow, Black (CMYK) and the white of the page. These are the colors that every single magazine from National Geographic to Cosmopolitan uses to reproduce such rich, luxurious photos. You can do it to with the right pigments and white. If you are a watercolorist, use the white of the page, just like in printing. Here are the pigments you will need: Cadmium yellow light, Quinacridone Magenta, Pthalo Cyan, Black and White.

D) The really odd three-color palette. The really odd three-color palette. Take three or four off-primary pigments, something to act as the blue, red and yellow. Experiment. Use colors you would not normally use. Amazingly, paintings come out better because they aren't confused with too many color choices. One trick to choosing an off-primary palette lies in where the pigments are on the color wheel. If two of your "primary colors" are warm then the third needs to be very cool. Conversely, if two of the pigments are leaning to the cool, then the third needs to be very warm.

Pigment suggestions
Manganese blue, Burnt sienna, Indian yellow and white
Manganese violet, Prussian Blue, Indian Yellow, Transparent red oxide and white
Yellow ochre, Vermillion, Black and white
Warm white, Yellow Ochre, Viridian, Burnt Sienna, Blue Black

Indian yellow
Prussian blue
Burnt Sienna

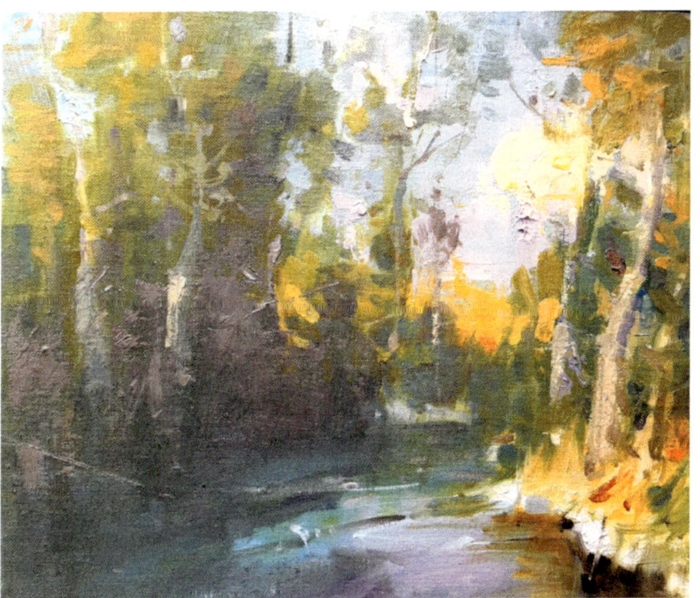

5D Odd color palette

Transparent red oxide, Manganese Violet, Pthalo blue, Indian yellow, and white. An uncommon palette can render uncommon results. Oil 10"x12".

E) Warm/cool interplay or color vibration. This one is the biggest diamond in the collection and is found in just about every master work. An offshoot of pointillism, where small color notes are placed next to one another to create the illusion of a color field, allowing the notes to merge together in the eye of the viewer. As opposed to flat color, the vibration in the color field creates energy, it hums with life. Almost every one of the impressionists, French, California and Pennsylvania, as well as anyone of the colorist persuasion, have used some version of this. There are so many ways to do this. It's easier to show you than tell you. Just play with color.

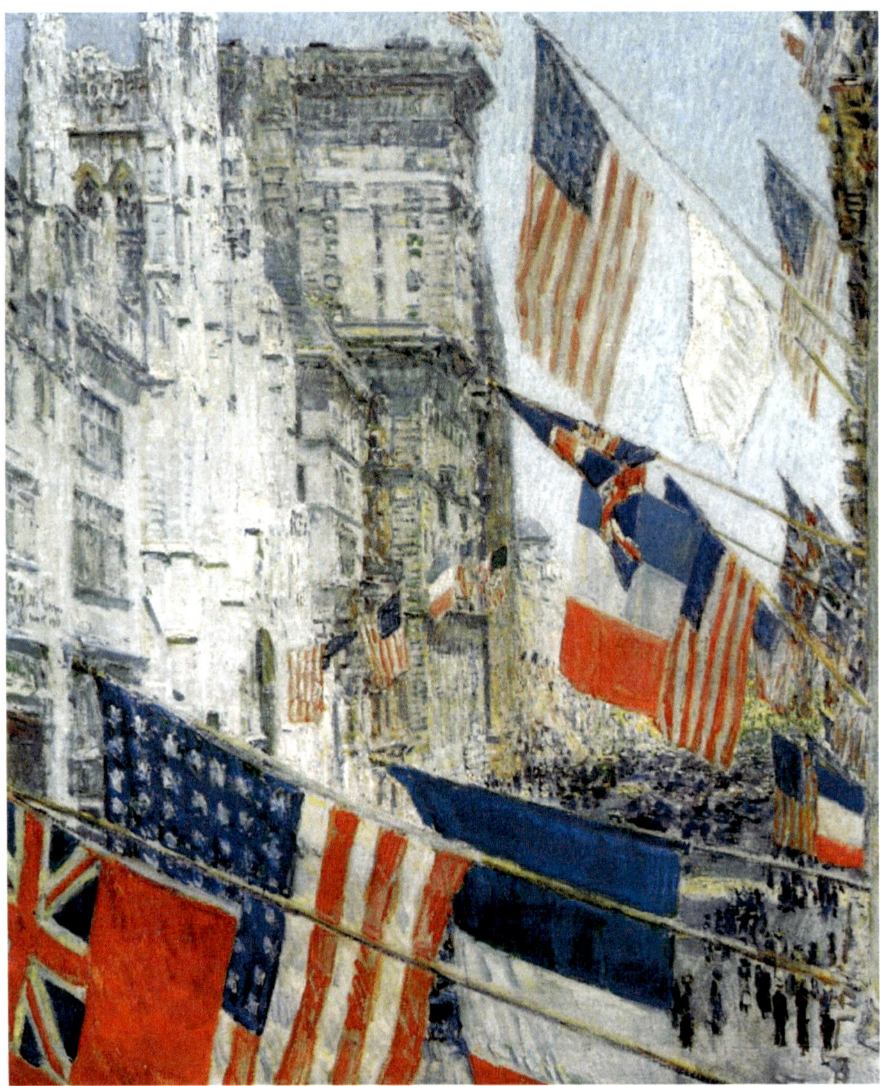

5E Color vibration

Speaking of master works, this oil painting by Childe Hassam epitomizes the warm/cool vibration technique. Rather than placing accurate but flat colors down to express a scene, he places small notes of color that shift from bright to dull or warm to cool. This action creates a more energetic expression and pulls the viewer in.

Allies Day, May 1917 93x77 cm, oil on canvas
National Gallery of Art, Washington

6) Shape.

Good shape-making skills are rare, probably because most people don't isolate and practice it. While everything in a painting is a shape, from a color note to a cloud, generally artists who are beginning to intermediate don't really think about them. A beautiful shape should have the variety of big, medium and small sub-shapes. However, our natural tendency is to move toward symmetry.

By placing any shape on a page, an instant tension is created; the anti-shape, also known as positive and negative shape. Both are of equal importance. In addition, we all have an inherent shape preference from organic to mechanical. Look at Georgia O'Keefe. Her work is almost entirely organic in nature, all rounds and few straight lines. The stylization of shape / form requires a specific purpose and intent as to the level of adaptation. Whichever method of interpretation -- whether through shape, color, paint application or other -- should be consistent throughout the work. Each component expressed in this way should be authentic to the creator and not a borrowed device from another artist.

Find your signature shapes.

The positive / negative shape interaction is why creating any design is difficult. All shapes create a space around them that become a shape. Clouds are tough like that. You make one and then you have to deal with the sky... what shape is made when one or two or many are placed in the sky? If you cut out two pieces of paper and lay them on a canvas, how they interact is altered when you move just one a little. Move one to the left --more boring, move one to the right -- less boring. It's a chess game that takes practice to master.

How many ways are there to manufacture an object or likeness using any variety of shape styles? Let's see... 14, carry the 1, times Pi ... like, a lot.

I use the tree as an example of shape opportunity, because many artists have their own unique expressions of it. Everyone knows what it's supposed to be, so there's no guess work. From realism to abstraction to mixed-media assemblage modalities, it is ubiquitous throughout the world. From Japanese woodblock to Mondrian paintings, the tree has been articulated in every conceivable way with only three major components to describe it; shape, edge and color. Countless articles written, video demos, step-by-step articles on the making of a tree. Being a designer is as (or more) important than being a "painter." That is to say, it's your world, your universe, you get to describe it any way you wish. So, take the helm Captain Design.

The trick to drawing or painting anything is not to identify it as what it is, but by its shape components. If you get the shapes right, the object appears in correct proportion and relationship to the rest of the painting. You have to trick your brain a little in art. That's not a sheep, it's a rolled-up pair of socks with four toothpicks and a triangle on one end.

Note: A skilled shape technician will look for repeating shapes and alter the scale, so that none are repeated exactly. Always keep in mind this important credo: Variety in all things.

A) Build compositions with just shapes. Make up a variety pack of your own signature shapes and fill each with one of four values (white, middle light, middle dark, dark) using a pen and value markers or watercolor. Feel free to overlap and alter the overlapping values and pay close attention to the negative shapes that are formed. Set up multiple rectangles in each page of your sketch-book; work small, 2"x3" thumbnails, not full page.

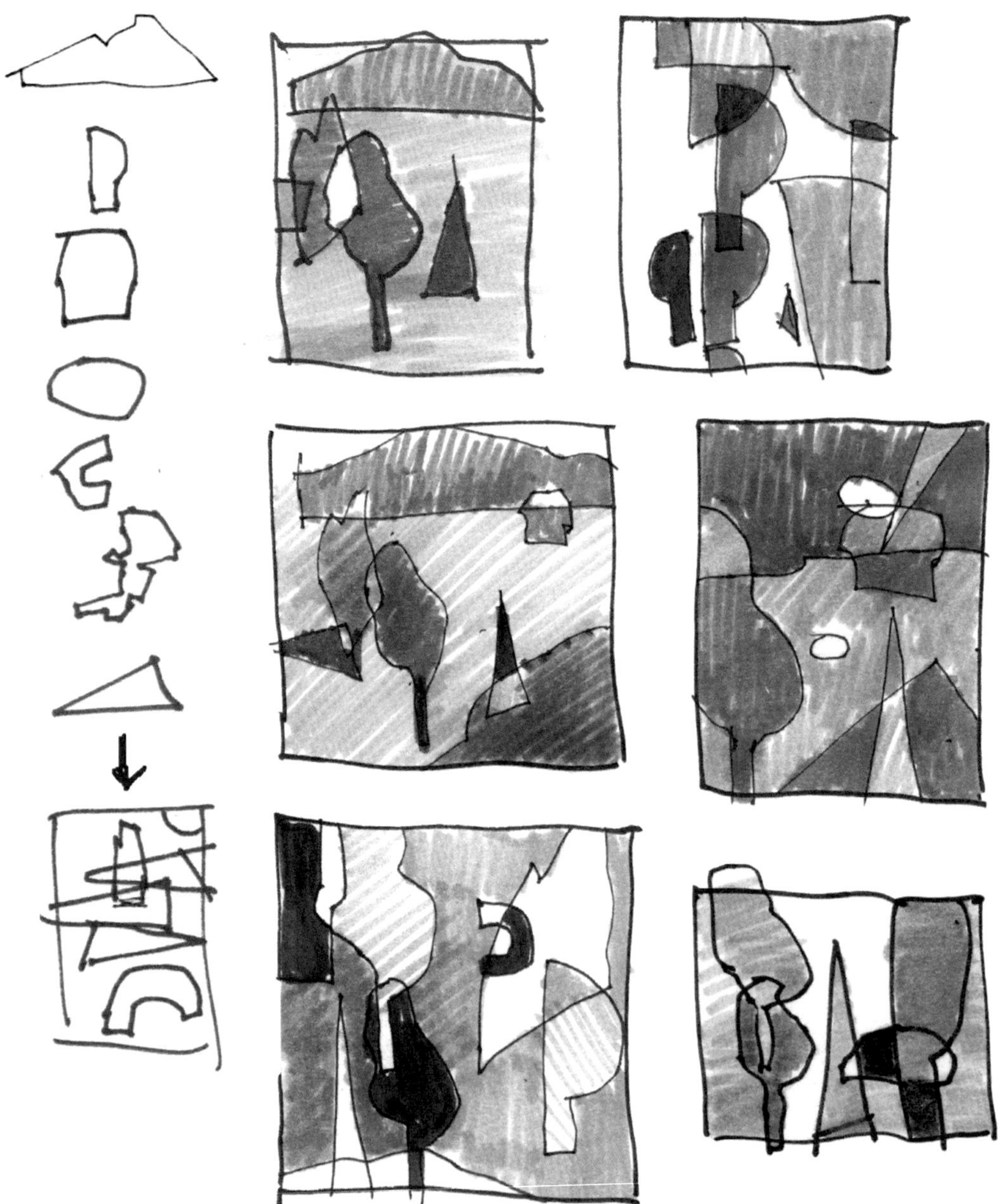

6A Shape compositions

Create designs from a range of shapes that you like; round, angular and mixed-bag using a limited value range of light, middle and dark.

B) Doodles. Seemingly mindless shape-making, but, is it really? Doodling facilitates free thinking and encourages absorption of dull information (it's why we doodled in school). Though the outcome is generally unpolished, there are always lessons to be learned from the act. While you are on the phone or watching tv with your mind otherwise occupied and your drawing hand free, doodle without thinking. It's like daydreaming with your hands. And if dreams mean anything, these do too. See what shows up as your inherent shapes, look for ideas that pour from your subconscious. From these you can create color thumbnail concepts, altering scale, value and edge, and method for an encounter with the real you.

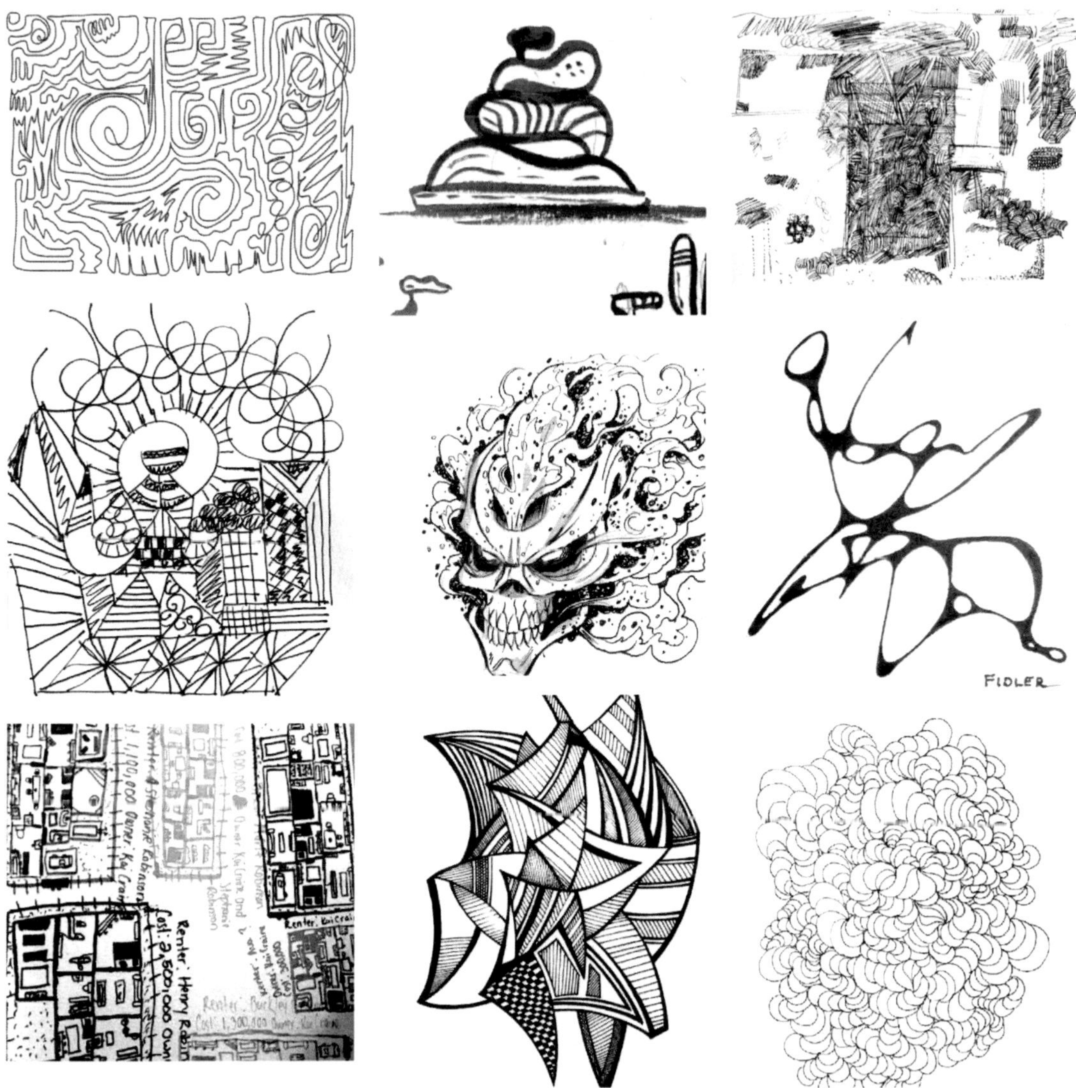

6B Doodles

A variety of examples of mindless thought in black and white. Doodling works because the creator knows there's no right or wrong way to do it. There are plenty of insights and ideas to be gained from what our school teachers commonly regarded as inattention.

Contributors from upper left to lower right:
Barbara Stroud, Brian Demeter, Connie Rigdon,
Dottie Leatherwood, Dres 13, Joe Fidler,
Kai Craine, Mark Horton, Shannon O'Dunn

C) Shape and color. Same exercises in A and B. But this time, add color and texture. If you need photo reference to start, that's fine. Simplify everything in your reference to basic shapes without trying too hard to draw. Mixed media works well for this -- cut paper, fabrics, and old mags. Go to town and don't forget the milk and eggs.

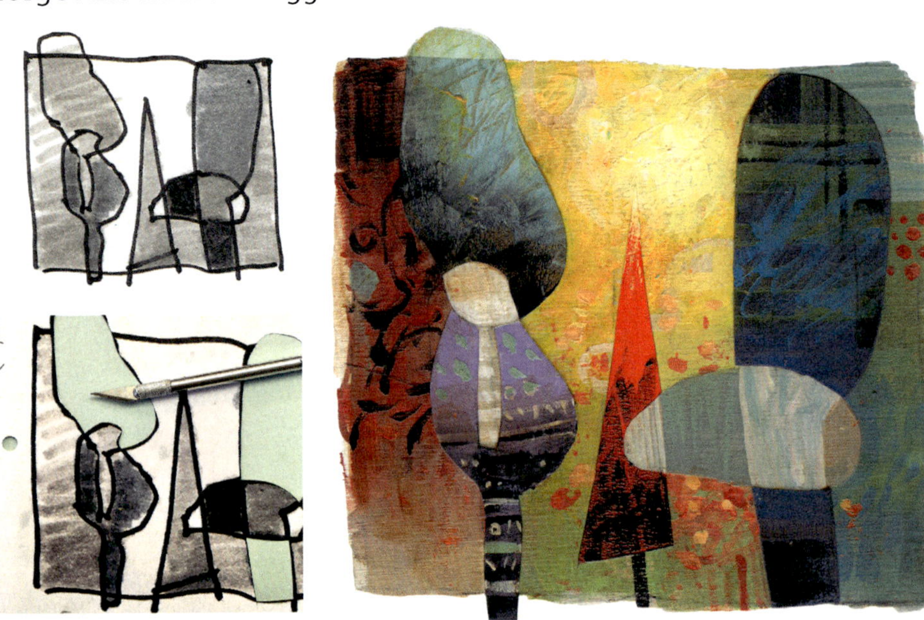

6C Shape and color

UL, A design from exercise 6A. LL, A to-size print/copy to overlay on whatever paper or fabric to be cut up. To get to the final I traced the shapes from the copy onto a gessoed wood panel and used the same copy to cut out shapes from painted and printed papers. Background is acrylic paint and the trees shapes are painted paper glued down with Modge Podge or similar. The outcome is always a surprise, never underestimate the power of What If.

D) Work on creating variations in mass and weight of shape in a composition. Daddy mass, Mommy mass, older brother mass and lots of little baby masses. Mass has gravity, but large things aren't always the boss, a large light value mountain can sit next to a small dark rock and the little rock will win. (There should be a moral in that story.)

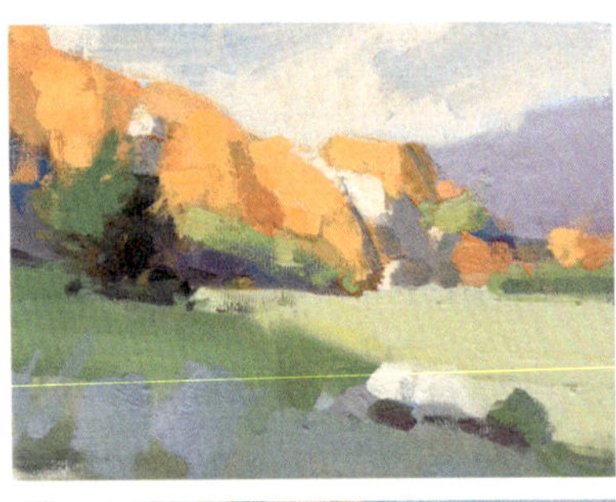

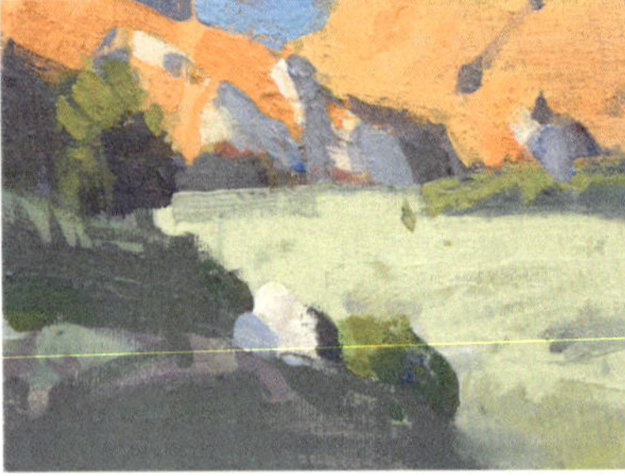

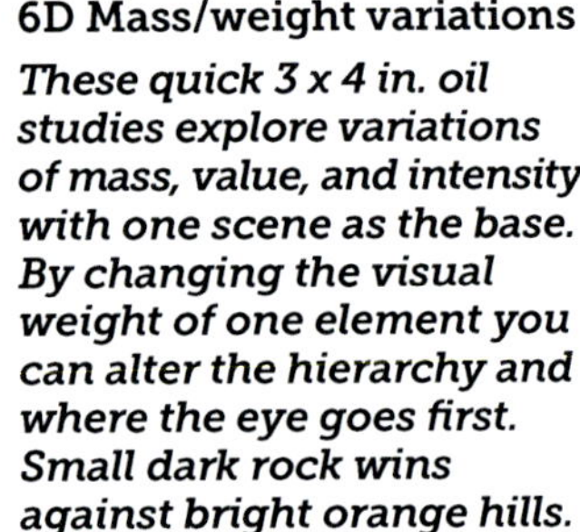

6D Mass/weight variations

These quick 3 x 4 in. oil studies explore variations of mass, value, and intensity with one scene as the base. By changing the visual weight of one element you can alter the hierarchy and where the eye goes first. Small dark rock wins against bright orange hills.

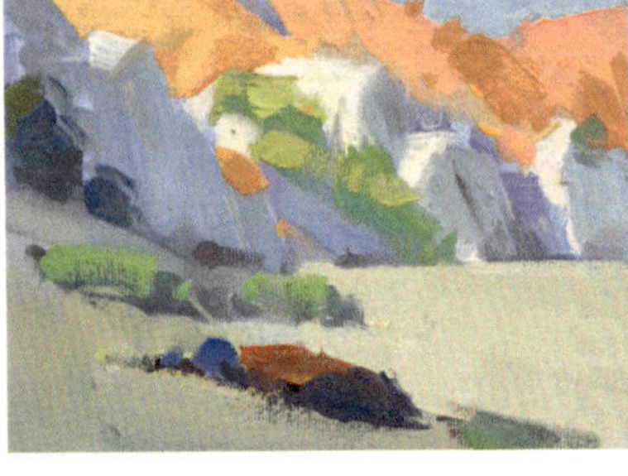

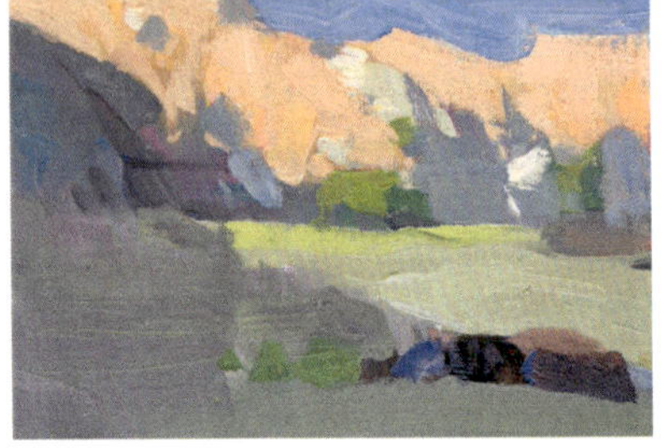

7) Form.

Form is the shape of an object, its perimeter line, combined with the clear separation of light and shadow within that shape. Think pear in strong light. Some of the best paintings are built on this basic tenet... shape, plus light side and shadow side, equals form, with vibrating color (warm to cool) in both. Many Southwestern and California impressionist painters painted in this graphic way. The light / shadow shape relationships are carefully designed and simplified, and the color variations within each value zone suggest the detail. It is often said that the color can be whatever you like, if you get the drawing right and the values clearly stated.

A) Take any scene from life or photo reference and break it down into the simplest graphic components of value. Think in three or four values. Play with color in the value sub-shapes in your medium of choice. Work in small vignettes, a grouping of rocks or a simple boat on water, and push the color relationships. See how far you can go with color.

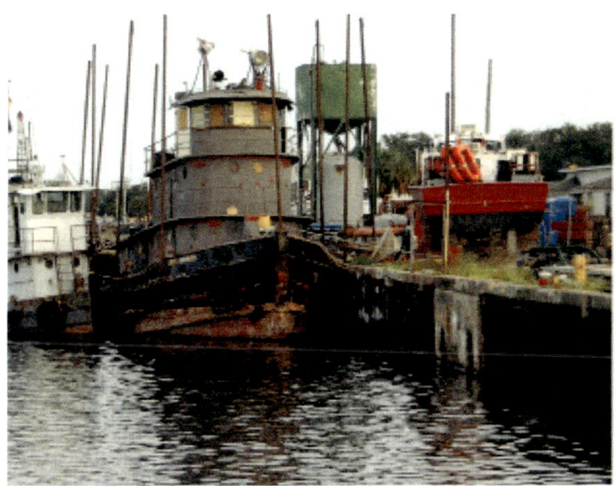

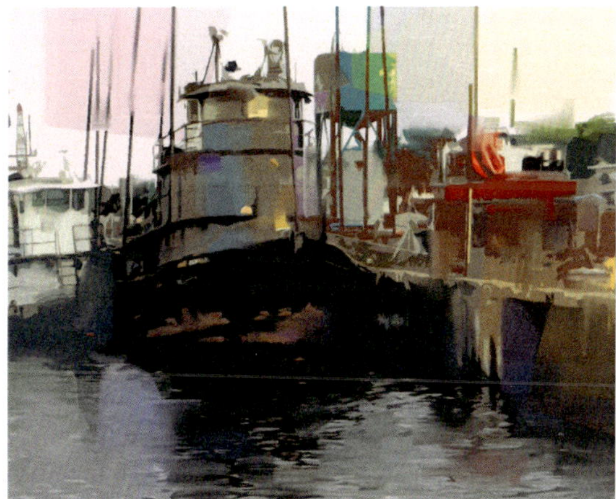

7A Keep the form, change the color

Maintain shadow and light and make the colors whatever you like. Start with a cut-out shape approach and modify the color zones to taste. This color translation was created in Photoshop.

B) Colortan. Combine the notan (#3A) shape idea with color. Pencil out only the shadow shapes from a given piece of reference, playing with color variations in each shape, and see how far you can push a scene or object and still have it read. Lighter / brighter colors in light shapes, darker / intense colors in shadow shapes.

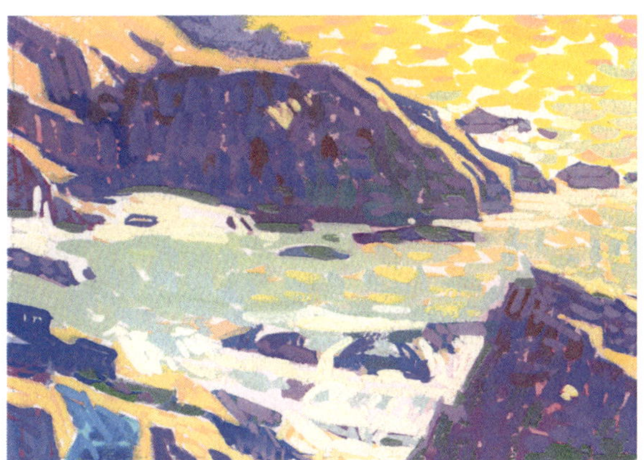

7B Colortan

A simple premise, what is in light is light/ bright color and what is in shadow is deep/ intense color with color variations in each zone. This is similar to how many great Southwestern and California painters have approached their work.

C) 100 ways to make a tree... give or take. Pick a tree, any tree, perhaps several different kinds, to see how many ways the forms can be expressed in the medium of your choice. Combine one or two of the component variants with form, changing the combos each time, like chroma / hard edge, tonal / soft edge, random color / poured paint or interpretive shape / expressive brush work. See how many ways you can articulate the tree form, including the shadow shapes. If you run out of ideas, add in some of the trigger words from the **Connectivity** section. Once you do this exercise, you will have a better awareness of what makes each artist unique.

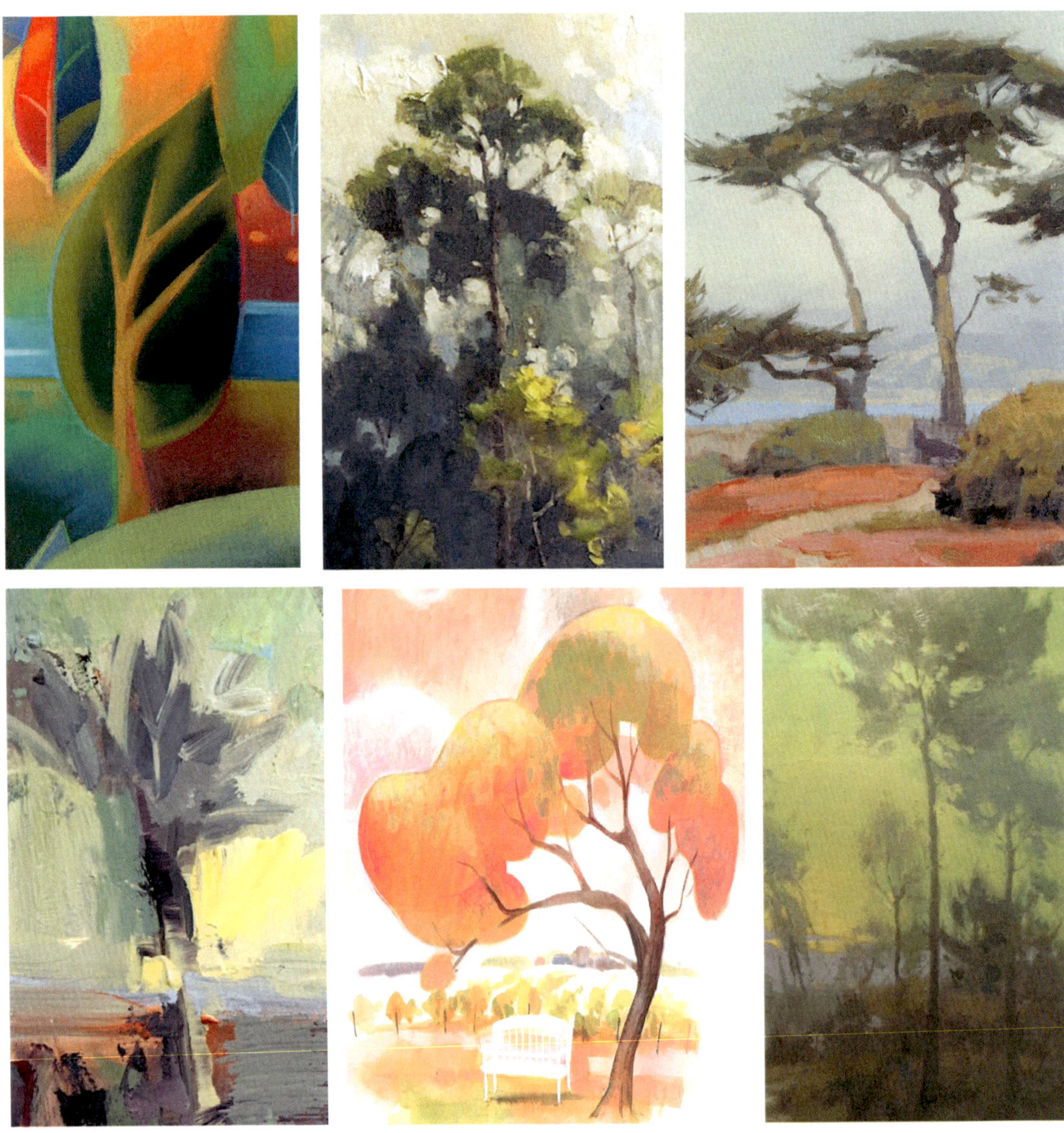

7C Trees come in every form

There are as many ways to say something as there are languages. The mediums influence the approach, so try several, finding your signature style takes exploration. The trees shown here are created in pastel, oil, acrylic and watercolor.

8) Edge.

Edge pulls a lot of weight in paintings. Soft edges recede, hard edges pull the eye. Work with simple abstract shapes and play with hard- and soft-edge qualities. Pay attention to how they influence movement and hierarchy relationships. Work or rework a realistic painting by losing edges that are less important or by softening edges contrary to the physics of the subject, to enhance the hierarchy of the parts. Edge also helps to define an object. Trees are a great example -- an Italian cypress is hard-edged and a cottonwood soft. A Florida cypress and a palm have completely different edge types. Each artist of merit develops a unique way of expressing the outer perimeters of an object. Some interpret a soft-edged thing, a cloud, for example, as a hard-cut shape. Find new ways to express the everyday things. Who says buildings have to be represented with hard edges only?

A) Hard and soft forms in three values. Again, I'd recommend gouache on watercolor paper for this. It's a versatile medium on this surface, with crisp, clean lines and soft or textured edges if you vary the ratio of water and pigment. Use three values of gouache; white, middle gray and black. Work from reference or any of the sketches you've done to date.

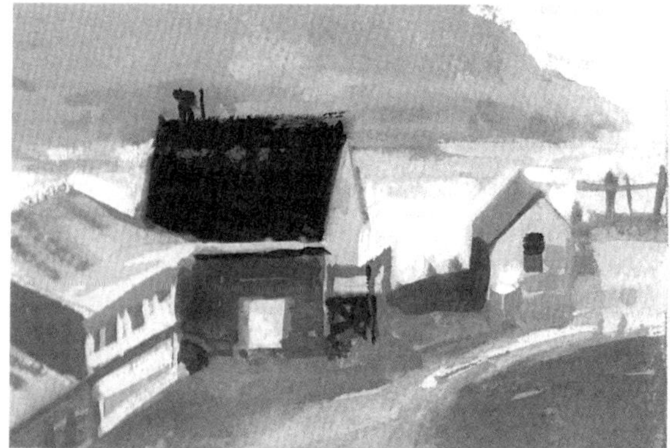
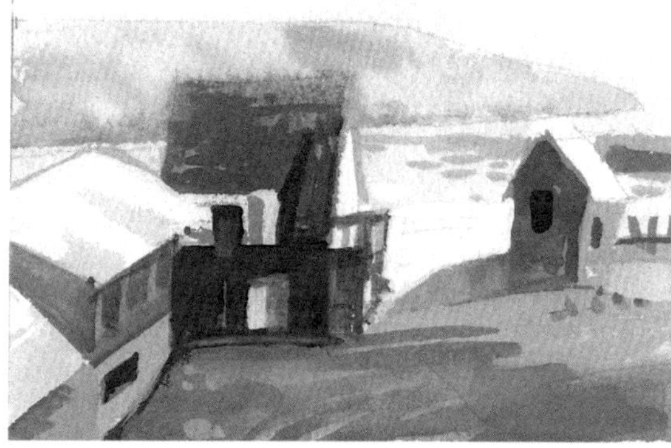
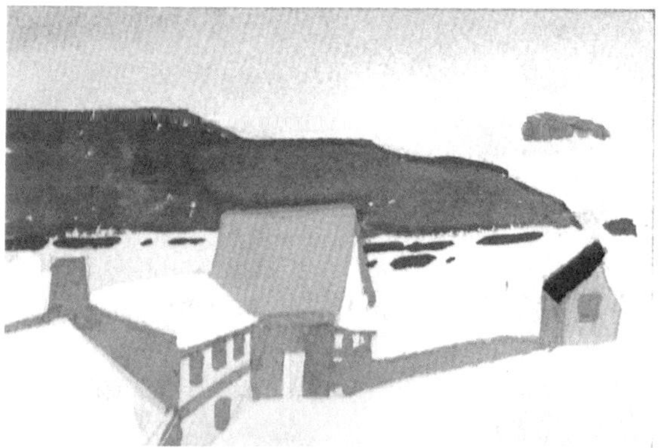
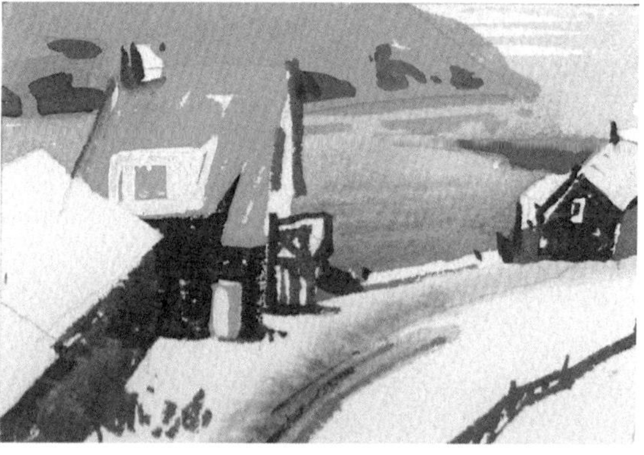

8A Hard and soft shape

Explore variations on a theme in simple values. With these basic shape constructions, without color, we see how shape, edge and mass move the eye and alter the tone of the effort. Hard edges pull the eye, soft edges recede.

B) The Richter effect. Gerhardt Richter, a prominent modernist, has gone through a variety of permutations in his work. One was to complete a fully wet painting and then run a soft brush across the top, obscuring the image while keeping its legibility. Seek out unusual tools to move paint and break edges. Select those edges that are less important to the theme to soften. It helps to think how the eye sees the world. Whatever is looked at directly has a defined edge and what is not in the center of focus is soft. Explore the concept of random focus, where elements that might be important are softened, like a photo where the featured person is soft and the background is sharp.

This effect, broken edge, is showing up in a lot of contemporary work. If you choose to employ it, take care not to overuse or it can become a gimmick.

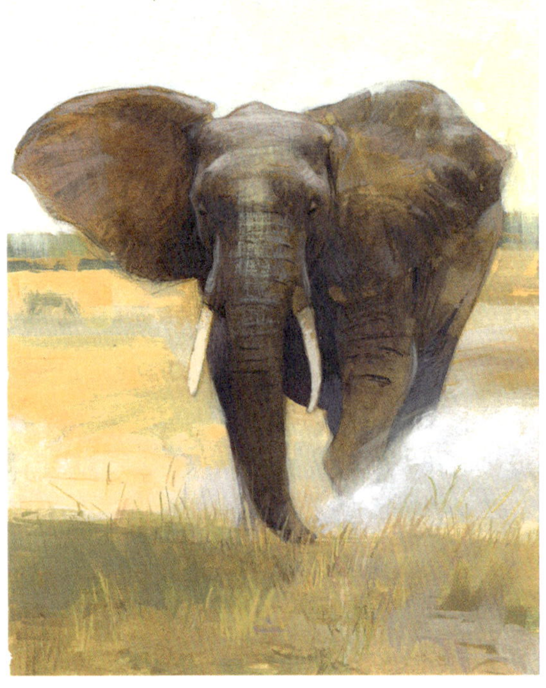

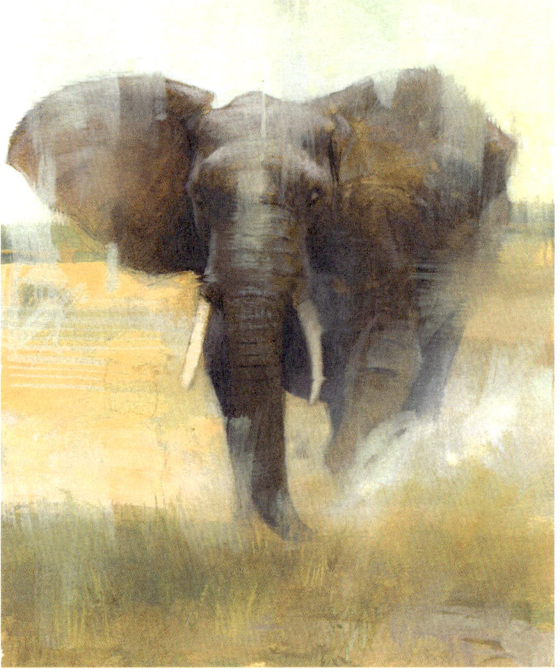

8B The Richter effect

On your left, a perfectly good elephant painted in gouache. Straightforward and just a little boring. By rewetting the medium I was able to move the paint around and break up the image with a soft, flat brush. This can also be done with oils but you have to add a slow drying agent like poppyseed or safflower oil.

Note: John Singer Sargent employed a technique that simulated the way we see, to direct the eye to the important places in a portrait. The eyes, mouth and hands were sharp and in focus, and the rest was implied or suggested. This is how we see. Not everything has to be a hard edge, unless that is your intent.

C) Tool time. Experiment with a variety of unusual tools to create different paint handling and morphing effects. You don't have pay $25 for The PaintSmudgeStick at the art store. Use a batter paddle, a sponge, Q-tips, a squeegee, and old credit card, a roller. Look around your house or in your garage. I love good brushes, but there are just some things they can't do.

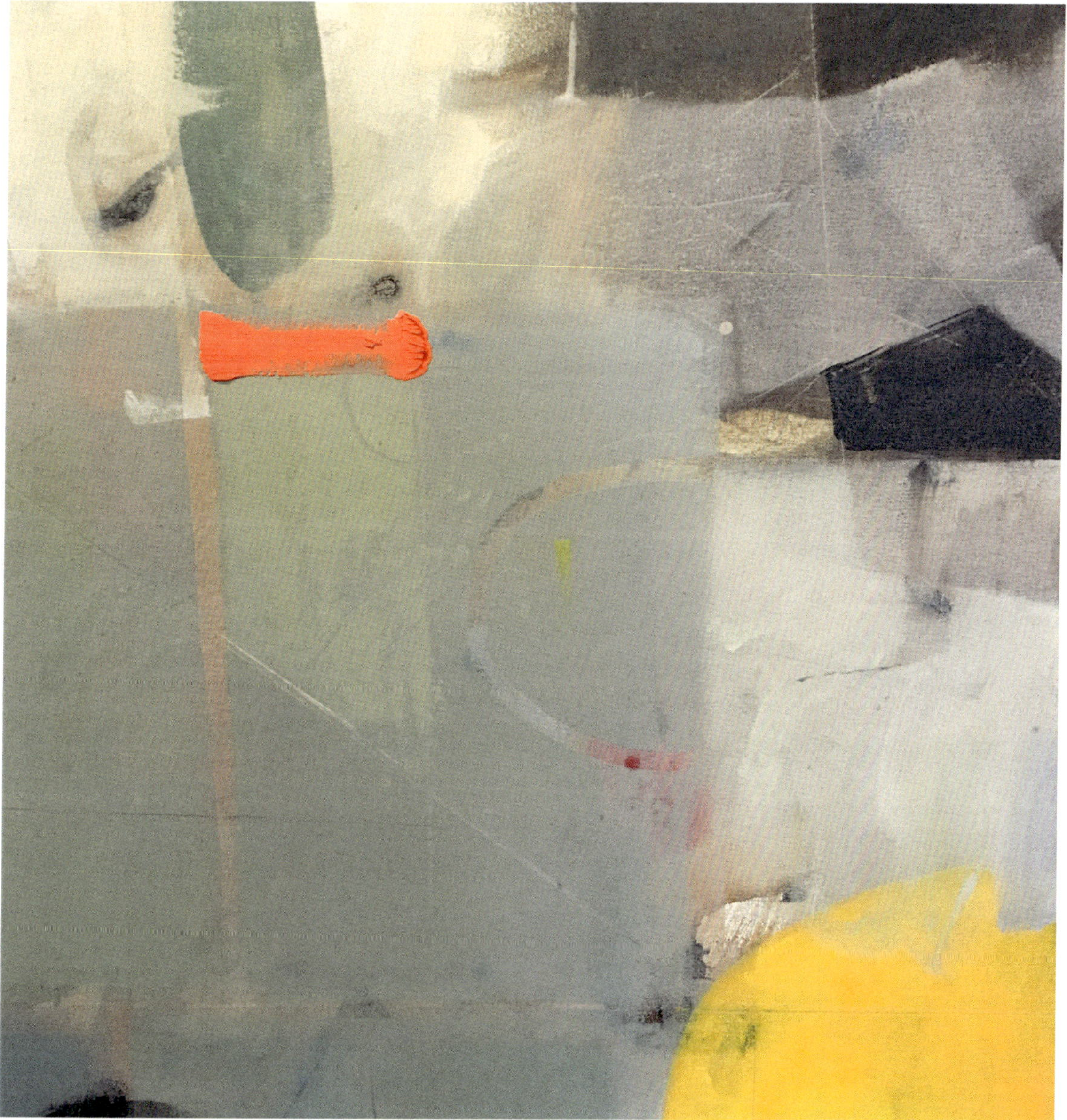

8C Tool time

Sometimes a fancy brush just does not cut it. Using unusual tools to apply paint can infuse the work with mystery as to how it was done. This 16x16 oil and cold wax painting was created with a brayer, knockdown knife, squeegee, screwdriver, and brush (red note).

9) Mark-making.

An entire piece can be comprised of a series of marks. Practice mark variety by using different tools: squeegee, sponge, palette knife, credit card, crusty brush, whatever you can find laying around that can apply paint. All paintings are just a collection of marks, some distinctive and some softly blending in with their neighbor. Marks bring energy and life, revealing the hand and mind of the artist. Work on variety of mark-making, even within the mark itself, using the brush as a calligrapher might, thin and thick, square or round. The brush, the tool, is the accent of the artist's voice.

A) The accidental mark. Mark-making, the hand of the artist, can be an integral part of the language of the painter. Most students in my classes try so hard to control the brush that they never get to what it is truly capable of. Don't choke up on the handle. Hold it at the back and use your whole arm. Stand up, move. Push, pull, scrape, roll, twist and shout. One color, any medium.

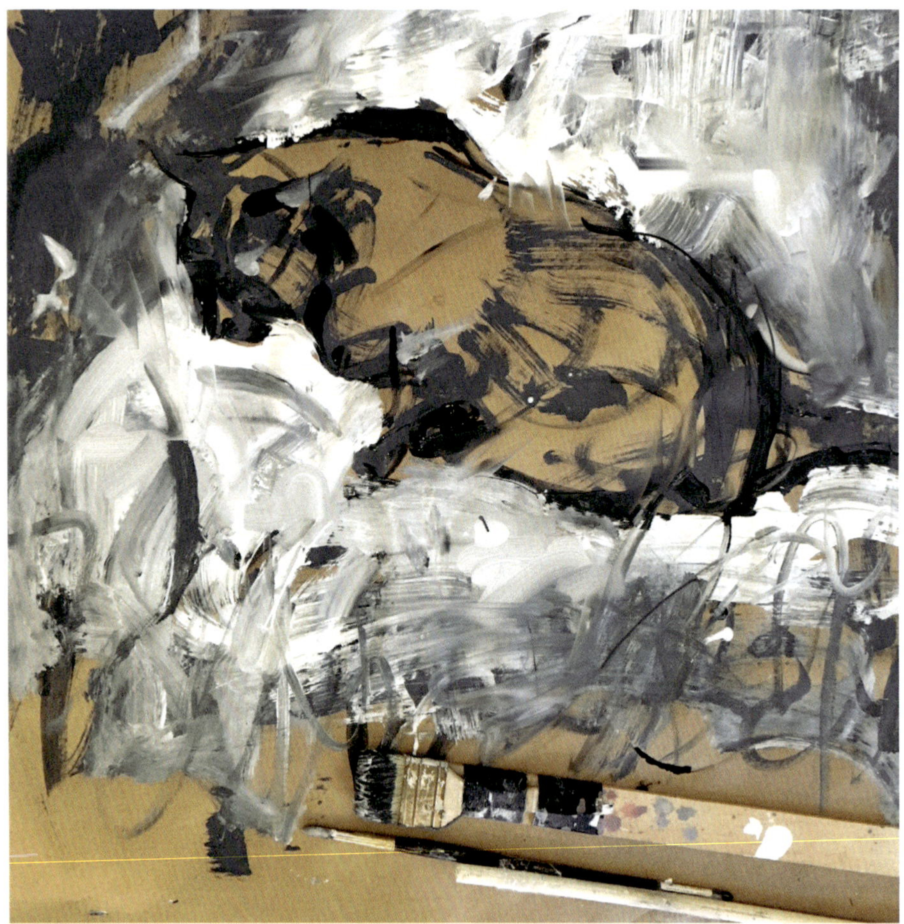

9A&B Brush on a stick

If a brush with a 2 foot handle doesn't loosen you up, nothing will. Go to the hardware store, pick up 3 or 4 1/4" oak dowels and some decent tape, tape brush to dowel. Pick a subject, one or two colors of liquidy paint, and a roll of brown craft paper. Hold the brush at arm's length and see what happens.

B) Brush on a stick. This will require large sheets of paper. A couple rolls of heavy craft or butcher paper works well and is affordable. Ingredients: a variety of brushes, push pins, several two-foot lengths of oak dowel from the hardware store, duct tape and black ink consistency paint. Pin a large sheet of paper to your wall, 30x40-ish, fill a medium container with black thinned paint or ink, tape a different brush to each of the lengths of dowel and start drawing. Blind contour figure is a good starting point. Look at the reference but not at the drawing and strive for a variety of marks. The dowels force less control into the equation and allow brushes to do their job. Work from the shoulder and get your whole body in it. Put on your favorite upbeat tunes and aim for the stands. You'll find way more possibilities in a brush by not controlling it.

10) Brush work.

The smarter sibling of mark-making with a more distinct purpose, usually in describing an effect, an edge or suggesting a pattern like the sparkling light on water. One of the fingerprint components of voice... anyone who has studied the masters can identify the creator by a small section of a painting. One of the reasons there are so very many unusually shaped brushes on the market today is because the design of the tip, the length and nature of the hair / fiber used makes unique marks. The masters learn the language of the brush, how to short-hand an effect like the edge of a cloud or the tall thin grasses of the low country marshes. If you've ever watched someone worth their salt paint, the language of the hand is unspoken but vital to the work. This is an important component to chunk out and practice on its own.

A) The intentional mark. Black and white or color. Without the tricks of visual short-handing through brush work, a palm tree can turn into a wet cat event, an explosion of unfrondly strokes. For the realist painter, especially the plein air painter racing the clock, learning the entire vocabulary of even one brush is vital to a readable work. This is why they have distance alarms at the museums to keep the knowledge-hungry artists from breathing on a painting while trying to figure it out. If you have an area of interest -- boats, palms, birds, clouds -- work on little descriptive vignettes of your favorite subjects to suggest a texture or effect. Try the same event with different brushes. Synthetics, bristle, flat, bright, filbert, rigger and round.

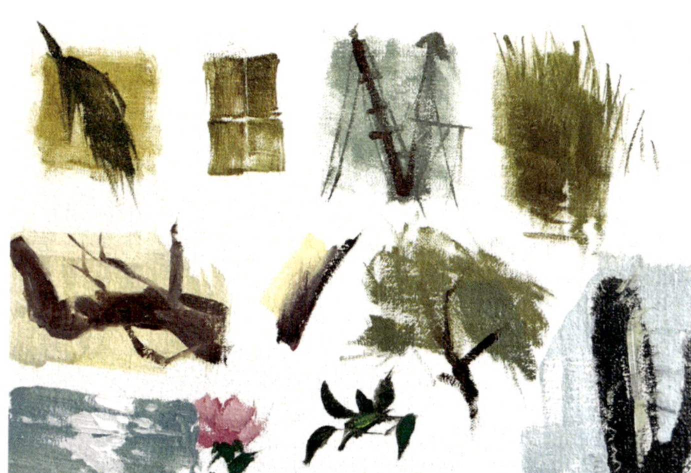

10A Intentional marks

A big chunk of what makes a great artist is the intimate relationship between hand and instrument. The language of the brush is unique to the artist. When you combine surface, brush and pigment you get a lot of variables to become familiar with.

B) The book of marks. Devote an entire notebook just to mark-making. Fill it up, both sides of each page, even the bleed-through to the other side is fair game. Use fabrics, patterns, nature, tattoos, desk-top scratches, tribal patterning as inspiration and see what you can come up with. Use every tool in the book. Black ink on paper.

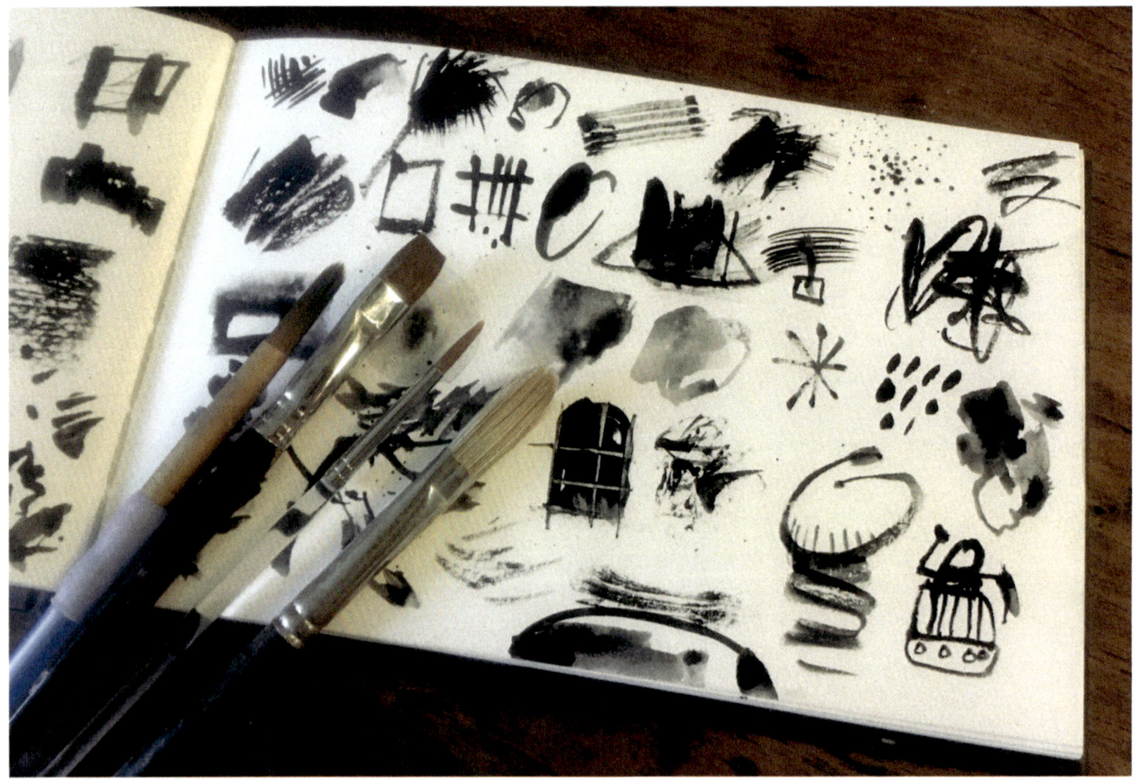

10B The Book of Marks

If you happen to watch a master painter at work, the thing that rarely gets mentioned is the language of the brush. This is a good way to learn the differences of each tool in your art bin; round and soft or flat with course bristles, flats, brights, rounds and filberts. Train the hand the way you train a dog... repetition and treats. Watercolor, ink or gouache.

11) Surface.

Surface is the last bastion of the two-dimensional original work of art. No matter the method, from oil to mixed media, the tactile, textural qualities reinforce the intent -- smooth vs textured, chunky broken ridges vs soft wet into wet passage, thin and thick, glossy and matte. Anything can be recreated via software these days, even better in some cases than the original medium, but surface can't be faked. The nearly hidden multi-layers beneath the surface combined with surface variety are unique to the hand-made. In BFA graphic design, during the Taft administration, our instructor assigned a project of experimentation with every medium and surface and tool we could get our hands on. Now there are so many more options.

Don't assume that all the materials that can be applied to a surface have to come in a tube or jar from the Artrageous store and have to cost $37 or more. Just because a respected artist says he uses only yak hair linen mounted on planks of tiger maple hewn by forest nymphs doesn't mean it's right for you.

I get a lot out of used house paints and unusual painting surfaces found at your local hardware mega-mart, as well as repurposed tools. The surface you choose informs the outcome of the art. Absorbent, toothy substrates soak in the pigments faster and allow for more layering and broken color, while smoother, less-absorbent surfaces make for more scratchy paint striations and cleaner marks.

Finding the right one for you will change your world. I promise. Try anything and everything. An unusual mix of materials and surfaces can greatly influence intent and impact. And there are two kinds of surfaces, the one you start with and the one you end up with.

A) Home Depot challenge. You can only create with materials from your local hardware store, preferably from the cut-out bins. From brushes to paints to surfaces.

B) Smorgasboards. It's all about that base, so you have to try different kinds. If you could only eat one kind of food, that would get boring quickly, so variety is better. Collect an assortment of surfaces, trade with friends or buy the variety pack from an online art panel provider. Go with one size for each. Get out all your favorite mediums and apply them to each of the boards in the same way and place, so you can experience the differences; blend, wash, scumble, wet into wet, wet over dry. Send me 5% when you get rich and famous.

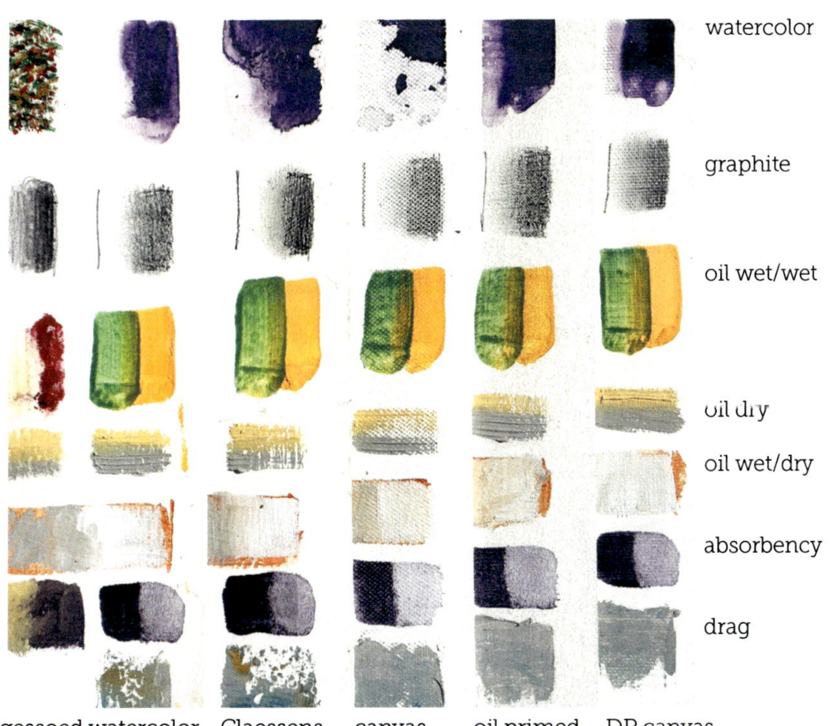

11B Smorgasboards

The surface informs the start, which influences the finish. The right one will make you happy and the wrong one will make you frustrated and sad. Test every possible kind of painting substrate for absorbency and texture until you find the one that works for you.

C) Layer builds. Great paintings are rarely done in one layer, even alla prima paintings get two or three passes. Good studio work means the chance to let under layers dry and to build history into the surface. Working on gessoed wood or cheap canvas boards with acrylic or oil or house paints, throw down some heavy underlayment of paint, use the leftover partially dried-up stuff. Practice loading the brush and applying thick paint. Let dry and drag on top of that. See how many layers you can build and the resulting effect. It's a game-changer.

"Remember, if you got it once, you will get it again. The work is not precious, the intent is."

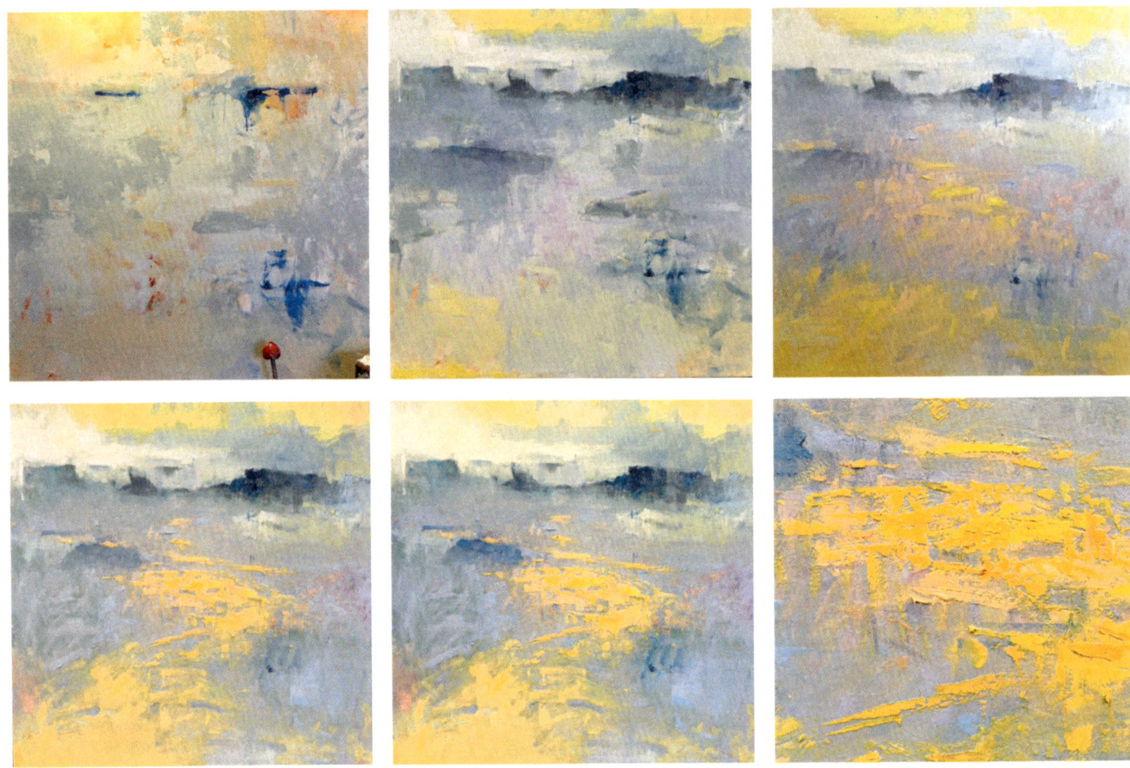

11C Layer builds

The power of a color is in the relationship with its neighbors, the ones it lives next door to and the ones nestled quietly beneath. Build up towards a color in multiple steps.

D) Instant texture. There are countless additives for paints to thicken, infuse texture or alter viscosity, especially for the acrylic medium. They are certainly fun, but can feel gimmicky if overused. I choose my textures to back up the intent of the work, thin in the darks and fat in the lights. For oil painters, there are several different ways to create a textured surface:

1) Create a terrain like under-surface with heavy body gesso.

2) Wick the linseed out of the oil paint to be used by squeezing it onto a piece of cardboard for several hours.

3) Use unusual tools to lay paint on, like rollers, rags, trowel or comb. Be thoughtful about it; remember that variety applies to surface as well.

4) Try cold wax medium for oil paints. It provides great texture variety, use it throughout or on top. Any percentage mix of oil and wax is workable. It also doubles the volume of the paint.

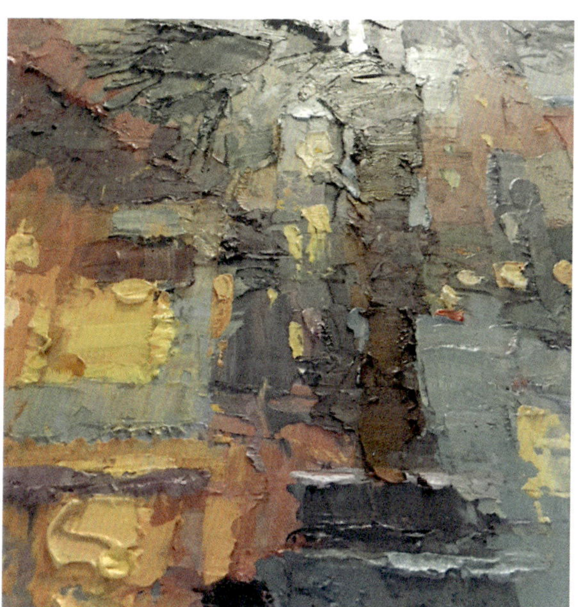

11D Surface

The last bastion of 2-dimensional art is surface and texture. It draws you in in a way that digital art cannot. This detail is a mix of oil and cold wax medium that lends more body to the paint. Applied with a trowel.

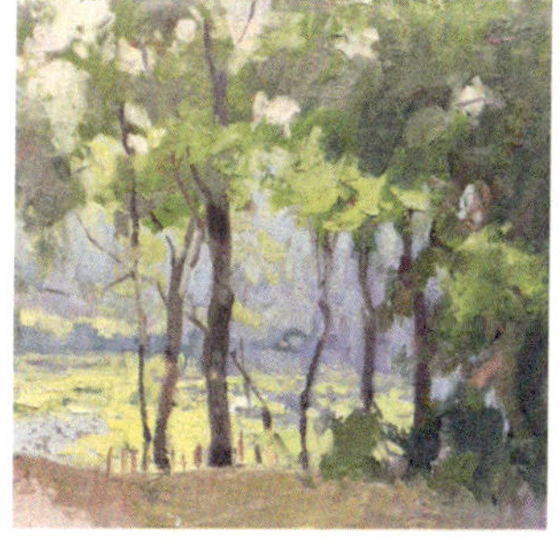

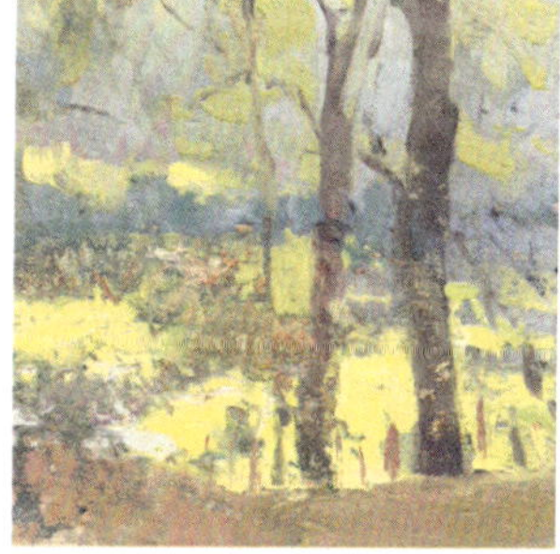

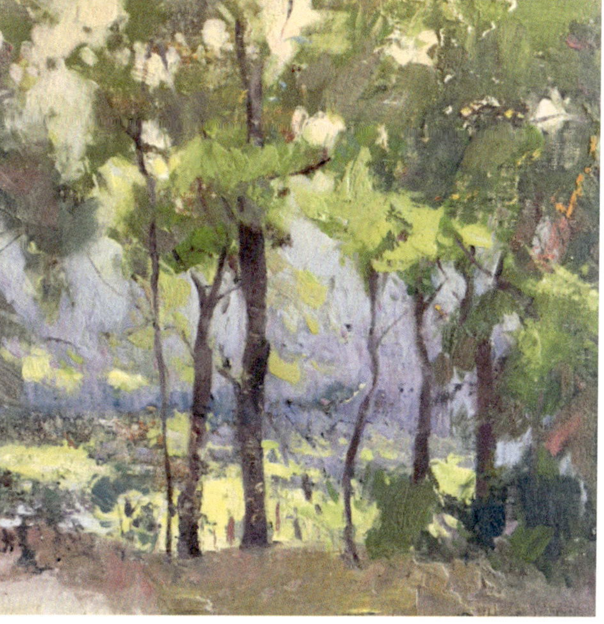

E) The sand-down. Take any of these experiments and sand down a layer. John Henry Twachtman did it, worked for him. It's a way to produce a little more mystery in how the work was done. In some cases, it can become a major player in the repertoire.

11E The sand-down

UL, The original with a few layers. UR, Thoroughly sanded until the canvas almost starts showing. The final involved some reworking of edges in the trunks and leaves but leaving the more bare parts untouched.

12) Division of space.

A canvas is just a rectangular space waiting to be broken up into smaller spaces. Though the confined area is finite, there seem to be an infinite number of ways to divide it up. It's a bit like the variety of songs out there, most using common note structures, but arranged in a vast variety of ways, with periods of fast and slow, busy and quiet. And yet, many have tendencies towards the same configurations. If you are an abstract artist, and especially a realist painter, playing with how you divide up that canvas can bring much more dynamic constructions to your work. Pushing elements to the very perimeter, what is called *activating an edge,* is something that very few do. Who says all the energy must be contained in that center cut portion? Who says a canvas has to be rectangular? Or even canvas?

A) Play with space. A good exercise for DOS is simple ink pen and watercolor thumbnails, trying very hard not to paint something (objective). Simply concentrate on spatial / color relationships. Take a pad of heavy watercolor paper or similar, divide it up into smaller rectangles and just move shape, line and color arrangements. Whatever your standard M.O. is, do something else. Practice seeing unusual divisions of space by taking a crop tool and looking around the room, moving off-center from what feels obvious. Draw it, paint it.

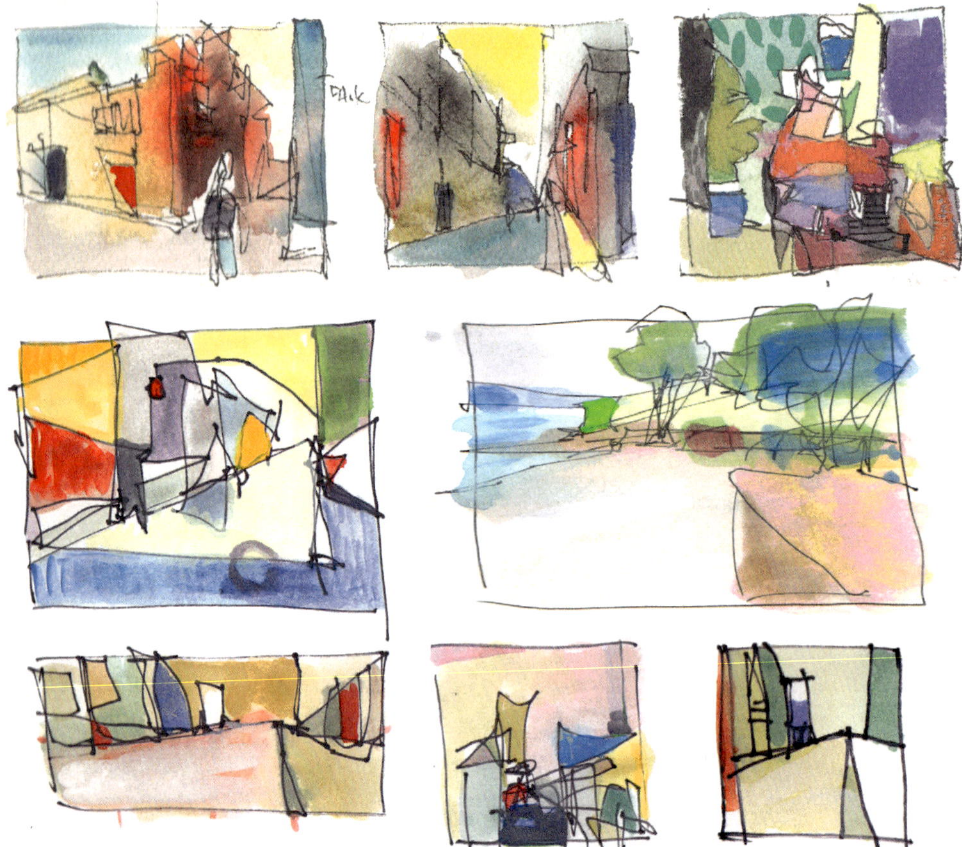

12A Play with space

Concentrate on spatial relationships and breaking up the format in unusual ways. Don't make a drawing, make a design. Once you've finished with the line, remove the reference and add values and color according to your personal aesthetic.

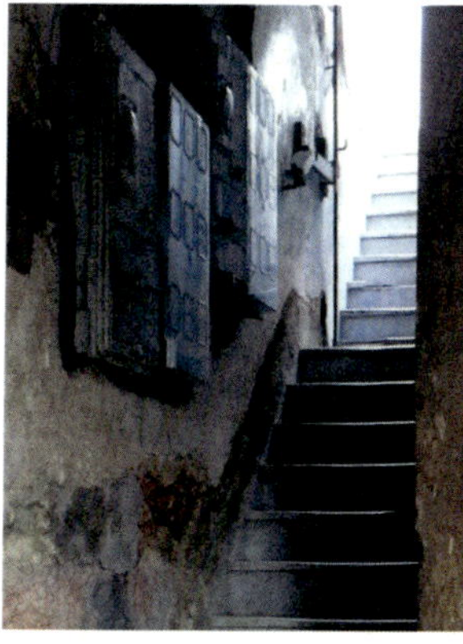
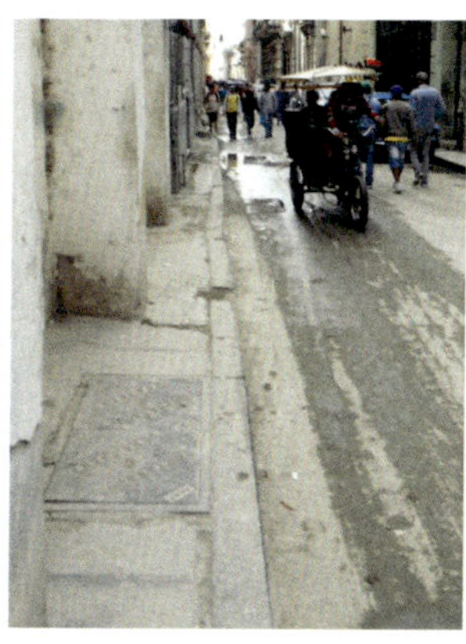
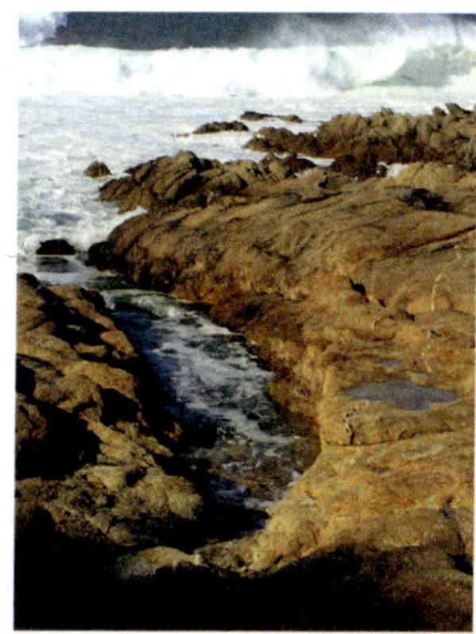
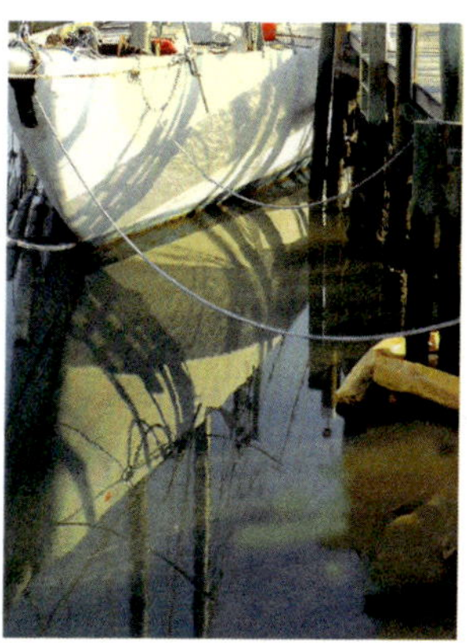

B) Unusual crops. Use your phone or camera to capture and focus on unusual crops, move off-center from a framed shot and see what you end up with. The pano function on a smart phone works wonders for this, crop as needed.

C) The beauty of random. Take shots with camera or phone without looking. Put your photo-making apparatus on burst and move the arm, sift through to find the interesting ones. Ask what it is that you find interesting in them and apply it to your next work.

D) Random pics. Go on a visual walkabout and record the things you don't usually pay attention to, like sidewalks, construction sites and heavily-used billboards.

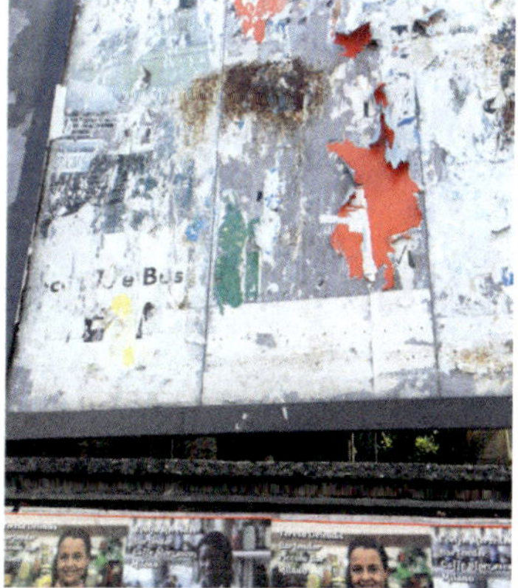

12C and D Random pics

Random events in photos are different from the dramatically cropped. Especially with apps like Slowshutter and Pano on the smart phones that can give tremendous results. The trick is to look for the beautiful in the happenstance, find the lovely mistakes and figure out ways to incorporate the ideas into your own efforts.

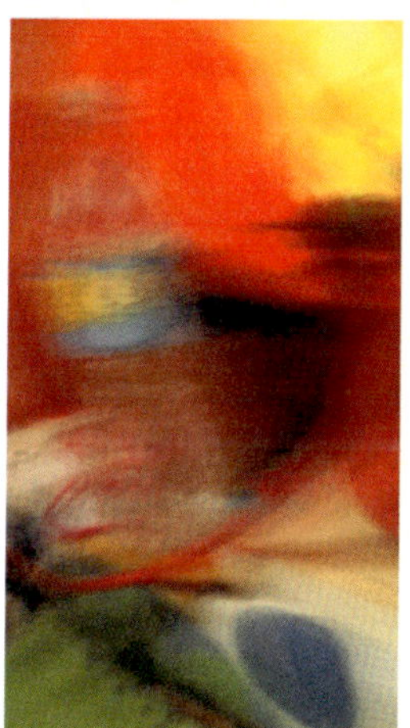
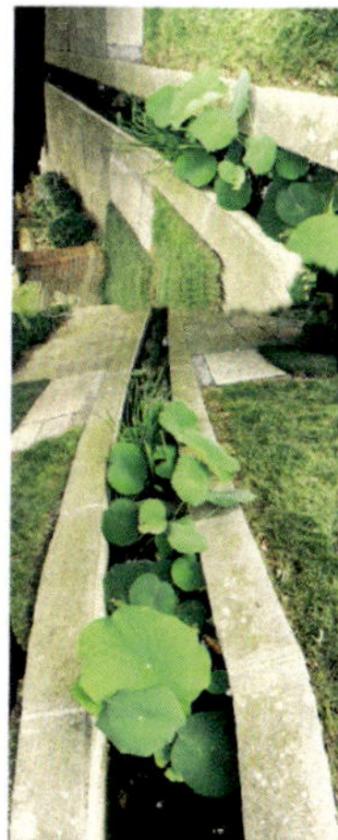
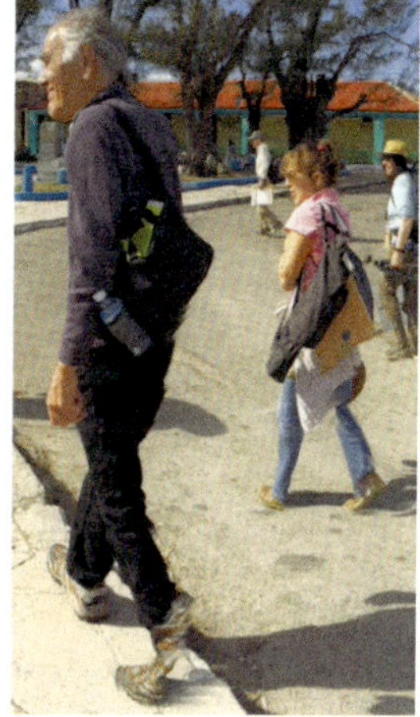

13) Juxtaposition.

This is a rather open component in that it can refer to a direct visual tension created by pitting one shape against another, or the energy that is produced by contrasting two different colors, or the more conceptual placement of two or more out-of-context elements together to make a new reality. It is the stuff of many, many great paintings. Juxtaposition creates energy through the close proximity of two opposing forces and it can show up in all of the components: value, color, division of space, surface, shape.

A) Color vs color. You could learn a thing or two from Josef Albers, who wrote *The Interaction of Color.* Repeat the same basic design of three or four squares and create variants by altering the colors in each. Play with color over color, transparency and, of course, juxtaposition of color relationships. Assign mood keywords to each if that helps. Any medium.

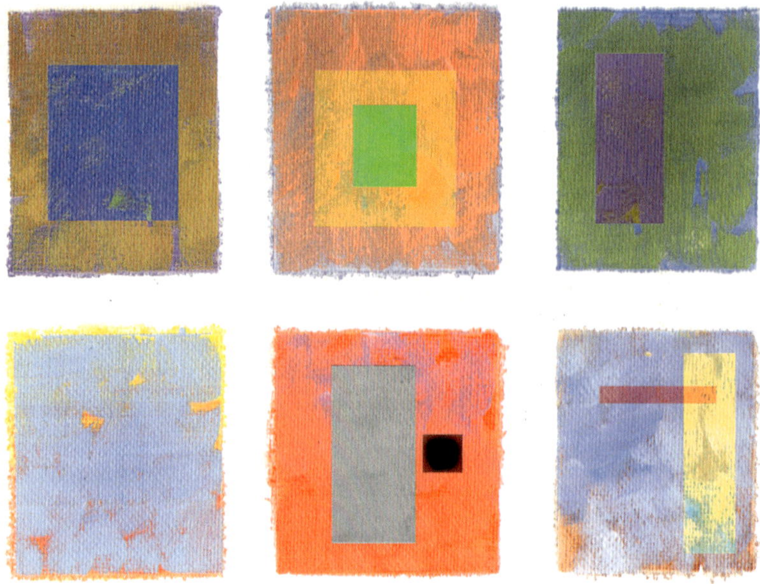

13A Color v. color

A color's power is dependent on the color it's next to and the only way to learn this is to do it. Color needs to be layered in order for it to "vibrate" or create visual energy. Tape off several boards into small squares and have at it.

B) Shape vs Pattern. Explore the effects of pitting these two components together. As you create these, think in keywords, like tension, somber, snow storm, peaceful, excited, anger, Mozart... anything that you can imply or suggest by contrasting one against the other. Work in simple flat colors at first and let components like edge come into play where needed. Watercolor or gouache is best.

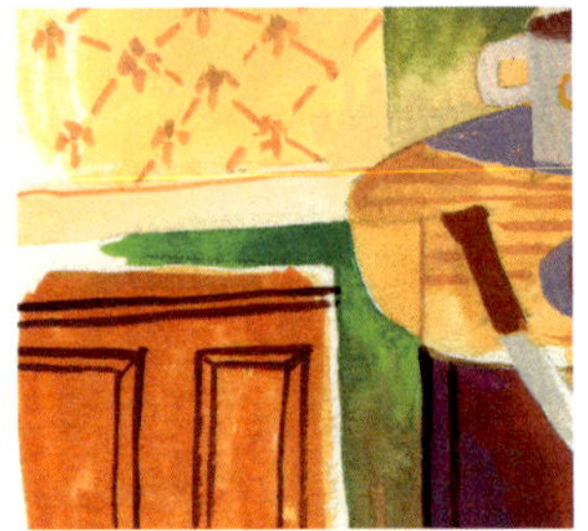
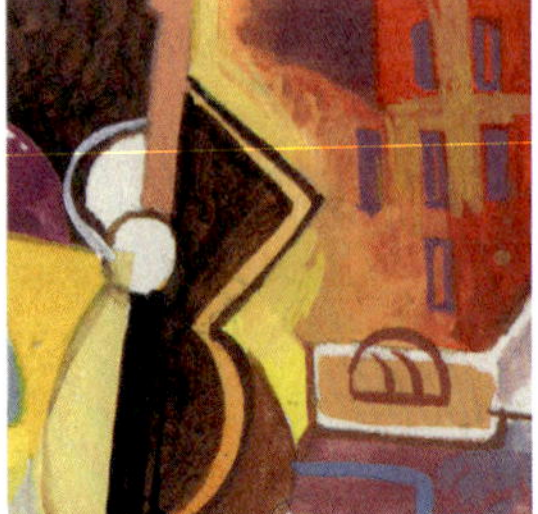
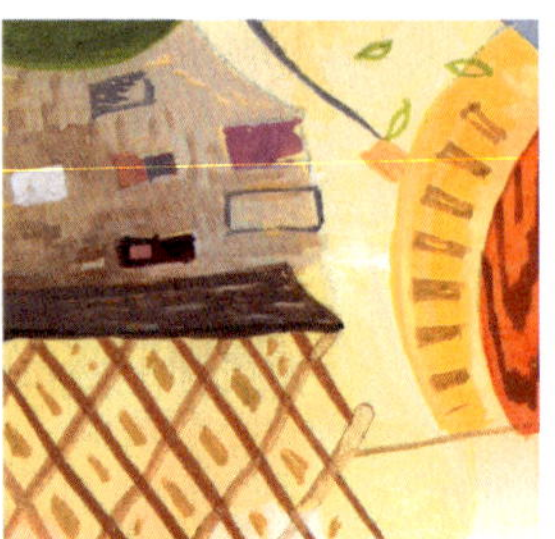
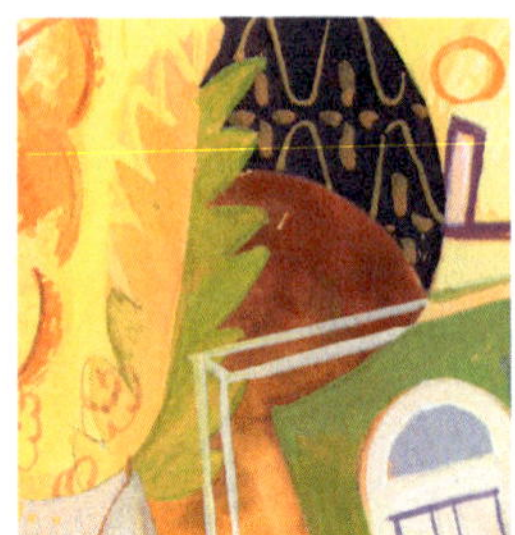

13B Shape and pattern

These panels are sections of various wallpaper designs for a national restaurant chain and were created in gouache. The premise of most wallpapers is this very theme. Tension is created in the relationship between the two components.

C) Geometric vs Organic. Round against flat, oval versus pointed, building structures vs clouds, soft versus hard, curvilinear shapes overlapping rectangular, Venus and Mars on canvas. Vary the emphasis of one over the other and use color and edge to enhance the differences.

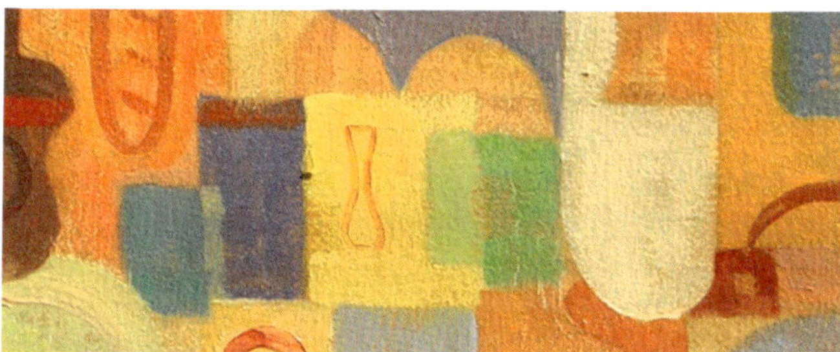

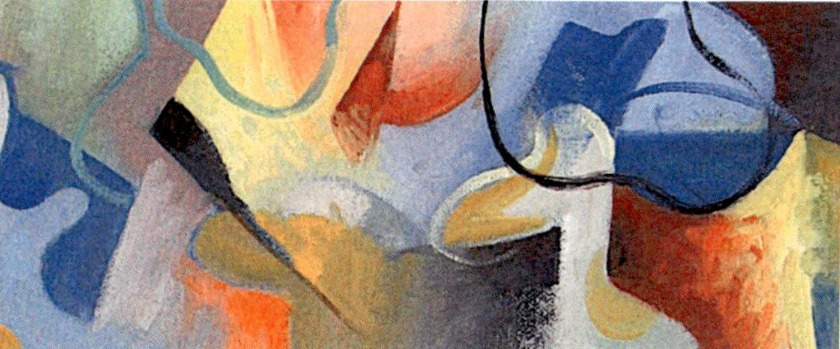

13C Organic / geometric

Pitting round shapes against hard mechanical ones creates energy, as does the contrast between clean edges vs soft color transitions. Exploring these components shows us how such contrasts move the eye.

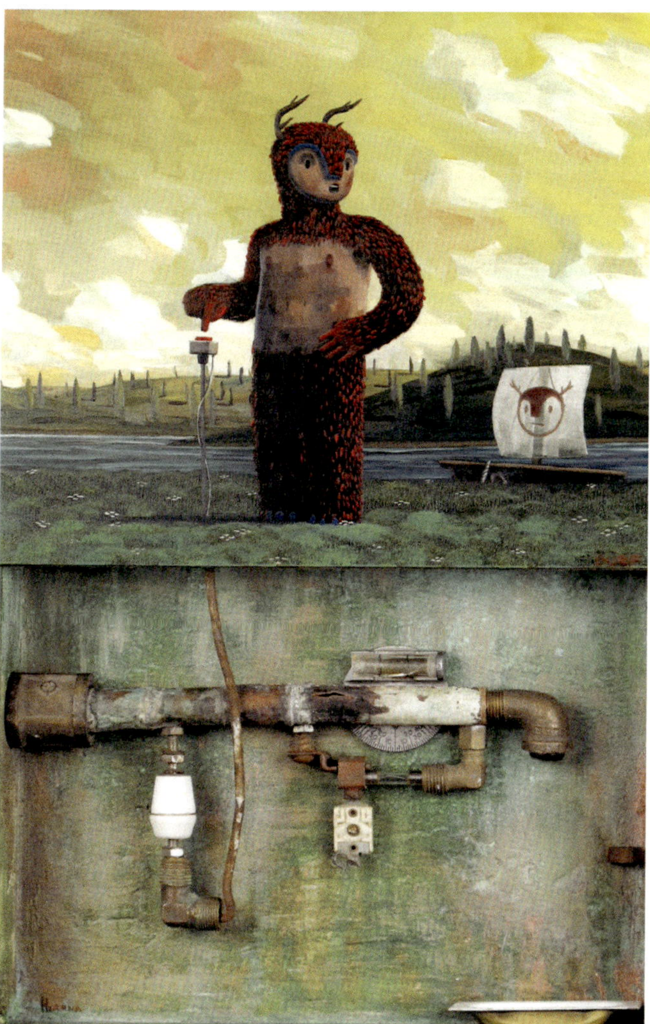

D) NaCl. Sodium chloride. Salt... Two things combine to make the third thing, it's a simple notion with complex results. What happens when you place unlike elements – childhood toy, desiccated flower, dog tags, found object, barbed wire -- next to one another? A new compound emerges, a story or implied event that is sometimes humorous, thought-provoking or volatile. It's often the unadorned idea behind an evocative or controversial piece of art.

13D Compound

The combination of two unlike elements to make a new amalgam: Nathan Durfee (top) and Hirona Matsuda (bottom) collaborated to create a piece rife with juxtaposition. Two very different styles, 3D and 2D, whimsical and industrial, new and old with a subtle connector that makes a story the viewer can begin and finish. Brilliant.

Curiosity got the best of Hector, 12"x 28" mixed media

E) Make your own. (I'll leave this one up to you, I'm going to bed.)

14) Pattern and rest.

A form of juxtaposition... for pattern to work, it usually needs its opposite, rest, and vice versa. Pattern can be represented in a variety of ways, as broken color, foliage in trees, literal patterning, like on a dress or wallpaper, application of paint, ducks in a row, light sparkles on water and so forth. I use the billboard analogy when teaching the concept of too much pattern -- also works for hierarchy -- as in type, photos, phone numbers. But you don't see any of it if there's a consistent pattern. In fact, it's annoying. However, in the right proportion, you see exactly what you are meant to see in the order it is intended to be seen. As it should be in art.

Pattern recognition is also an important aspect of the visual language. Everything has a uniquely identifying pattern, from a fish to wood floors to feathers, that make it recognizable, whether implied or directly stated. In conjunction with the concept of pattern recognition is the *odd man out reflex.* An example would be a photo of 100 white chickens with one pink one. Where would your eye go? The pink one. The one thing that is not like the others becomes dominant. This can show up, even in a sea of visual chaos. The one odd thing registers unconsciously until you identify it as the unusual suspect. Like the one guy in an airport with no shoes.

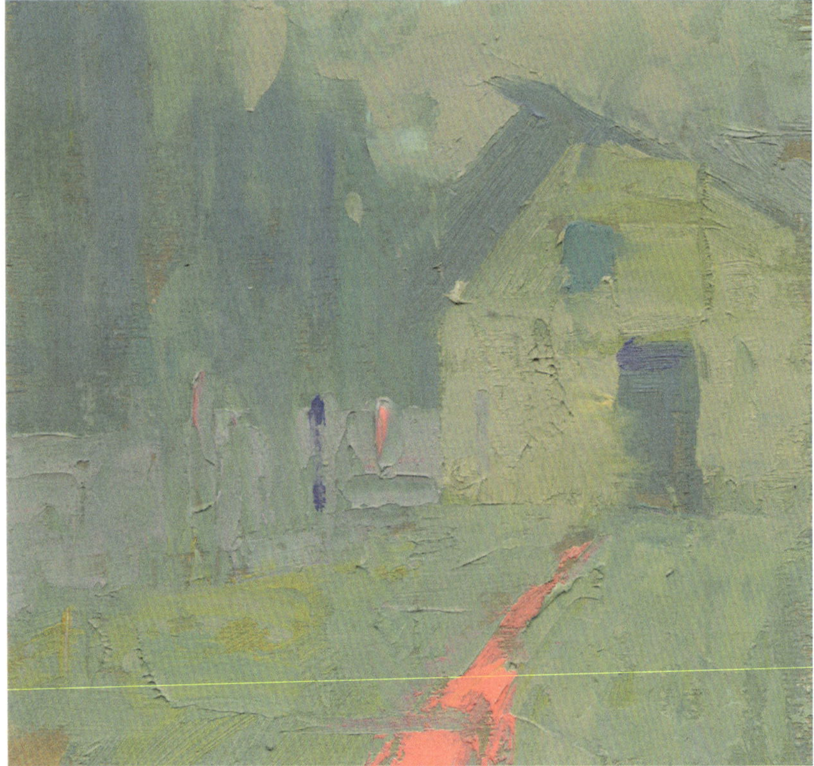

14A Color punctuation
Place a note or two of what is called "alien color" into a sea of counter or complimentary colors and pay attention to the weight that single color has.

A) Color punctuation. The power of just one note. Take an existing work that you are okay with altering and drop one intense color note that is out of place with the rest of the work. Pure bright red is always good. There's an old saying, "If you can't make it good, make it big or make it red".

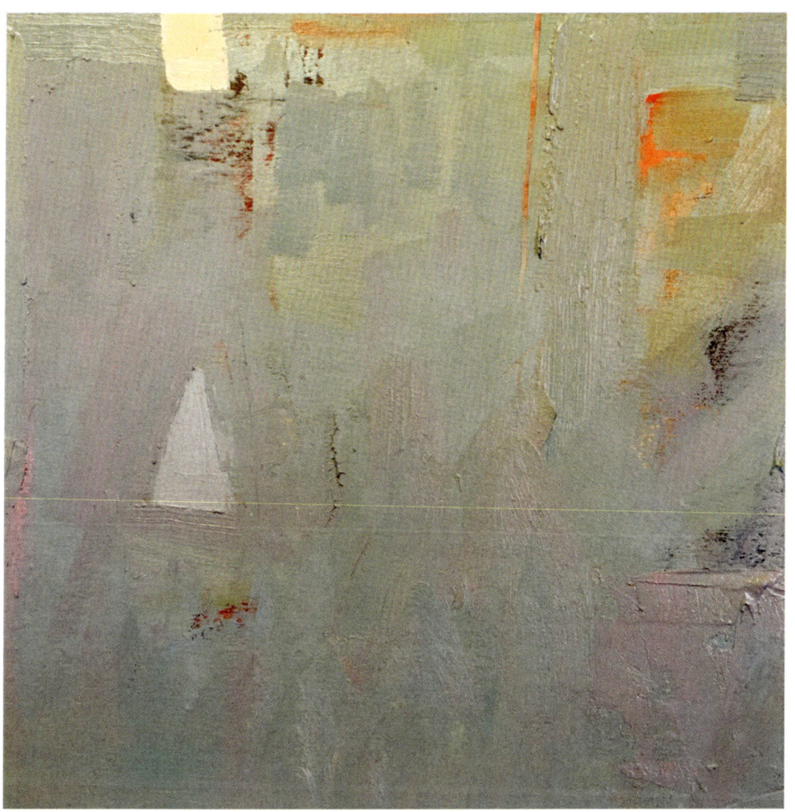

B) Sea of notes. Large canvas, a sea of movement in three closely-related colors like blue green, teal and gray green. Somewhere in there drop in a few off-color notes, like pink or lilac, and see what happens.

14B Sea of notes

Without content to dominate the canvas, color can do all of the heavy lifting. These simple experiments can inform your work with a better understanding of color vibration, edge, value, layers and the power of one decisive note.

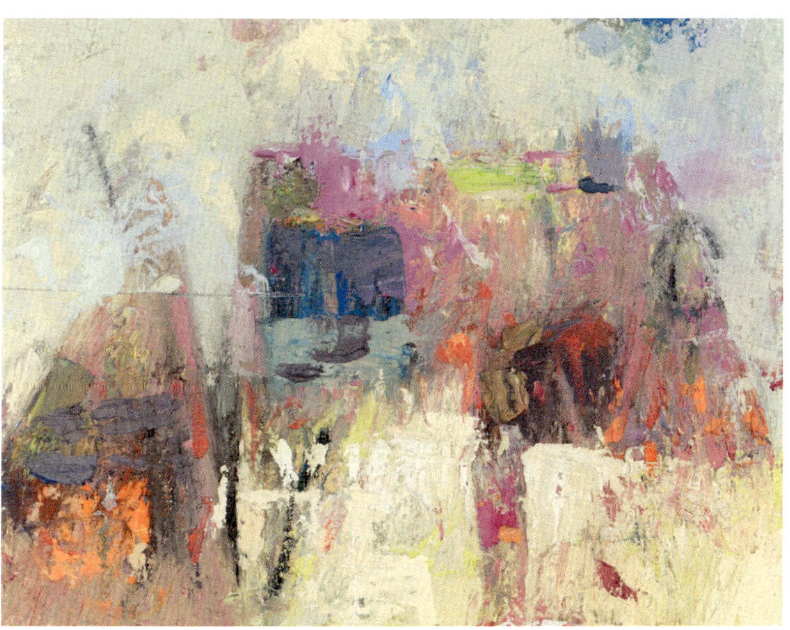

C) Music pages. A canvas filled with notes, a visual symphony of color. Large canvas, an array of brushes, put your fave concerto on the boom box and transcribe the music. Little notes = little marks, quiet = soft, big notes = big notes. Go.

14C Music pages

You can't know the power of a mark unless you just play with paint and tools. Any painting, whether abstract or realist, is enhanced by this kind of variety. Turn on some music and respond with marks and color. Experience synesthesia, hear music and see color.

D) Pattern challenge. Do a web search on wallpaper patterns, click on images in the nav-bar and look at the vast variety. Wow! That's a lot of pattern variety. Save the ones you like, could be Art Deco, Hawaiian chic, Tartan, Rococo, birds and flowers or Laura Ashley paisley bombs. Try recreating the idea of these with your normal method of doing. Don't copy, adapt. Alter one of the pattern pieces with color or scale or value, just to see what shows up.

©New York Public Library

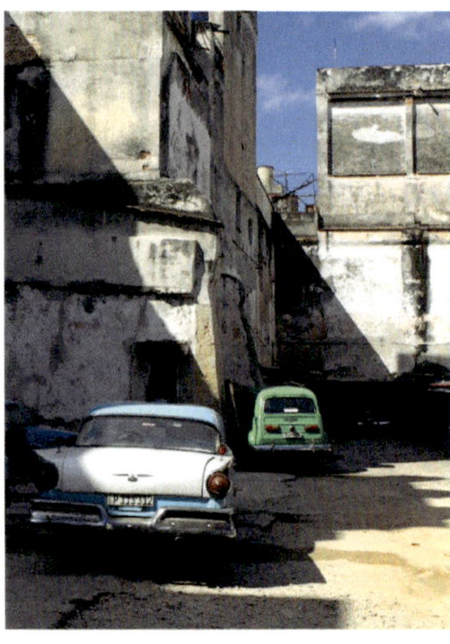

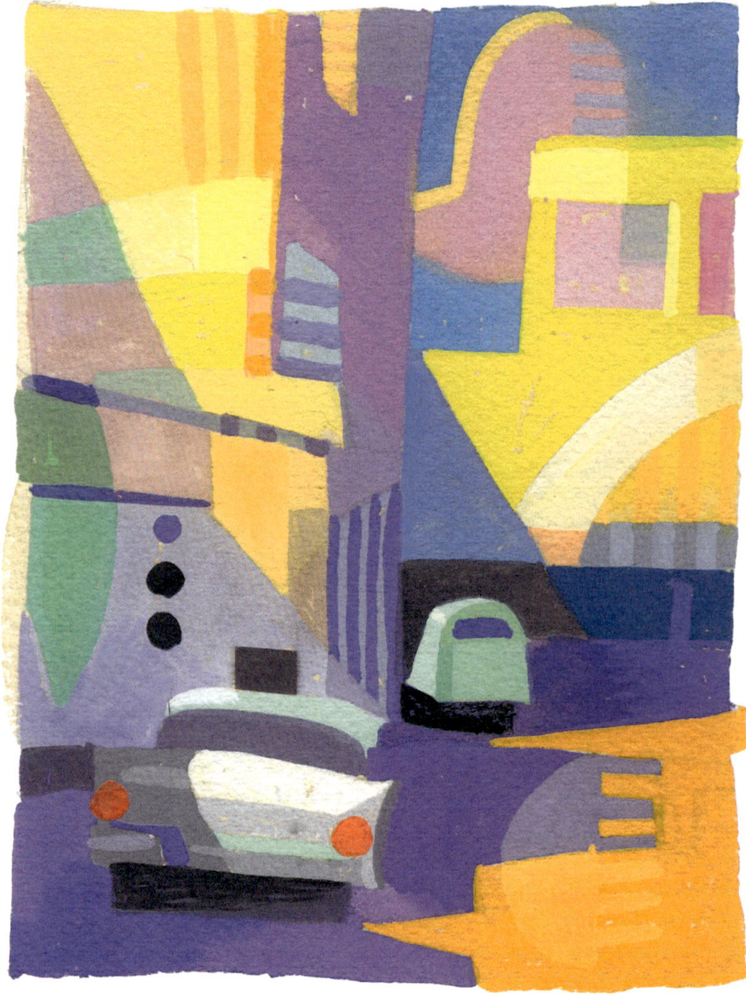

14D Pattern challenge

Apply thing A, a Deco pattern, to thing B, a photo from the streets of Havana, Cuba, and a style is born. Gouache, 5 x 7 in.

15) Layers.

Always -- no wait -- never go straight for the top color notes. Good art needs patina, history, surface, something way beneath the top stuff to be captivating to the eye and pull us in closer. It's what compels a viewer to stare intently at a good painting. Mystery, it worked for Agatha Christie and it can work for you. To make this happen, learn to think in layers by practicing in layers. Build up to color and to light. Each layer adds that much more to the depth of the work.

"A color's power is dependent on the color it is next to."

A) Wet over wet and wet over dry. Wet paint on a dry, textured surface is going to look and feel different from wet into wet paint. There are effects that you can get with one that you can't get with the other. The combination of both can give you more nuance, and nuance is the thing that separates the great from the pretty good. Set up several different surfaces, some more textured and absorbent and some less. Experiment with different ways to build color in layers.

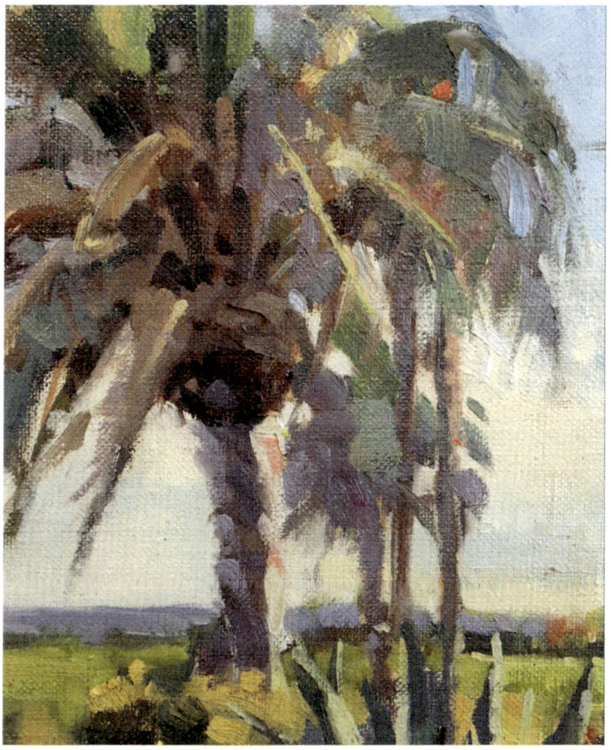

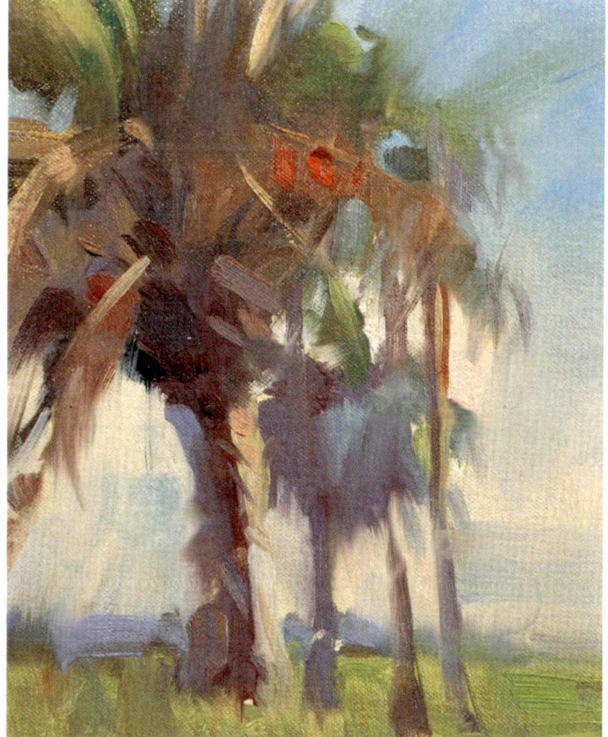

15A wet/dry, wet/wet

There are many ways to present this, but a side-by-side comparison shows the textural differences between wet paint over dry and wet over wet. The version on the left, an oil plein air painting, got another pass of color notes on the crispy, dry surface and the version on the right was done all at once with a little linseed oil in the oil paint mix. Softer transitions, looser blends and a little less control on the right. Pick the process that works with your sensibilities.

B) Glaze. Or magic sauce, as I call it. A glaze is simply a transparent mix of a medium and a color tint, with about a 25 to one ratio, respectively. Linseed oil or Galkyd for oils or glazing liquids by Liquitex or Golden for acrylics. It adds luminosity and depth to the color in the way that stained glass adds color to light. Mix a batch of yellow-orange to warm a painting or a sky, brush it on and wipe it off until you are satisfied with the amount. Multiple layers add more and more intensity because light passes through and bounces back to meet the eye with glee. Experiment on old work.

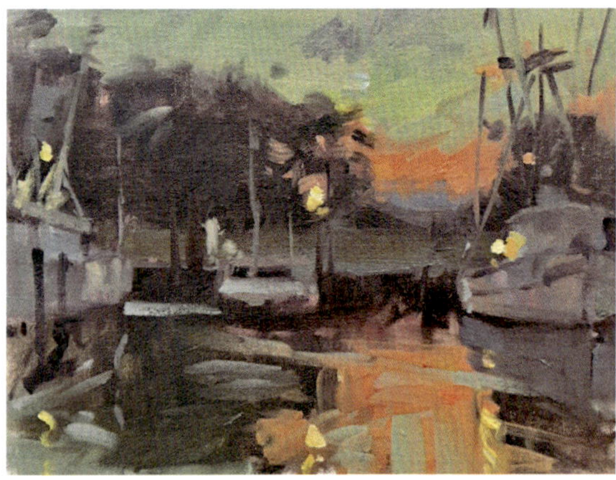

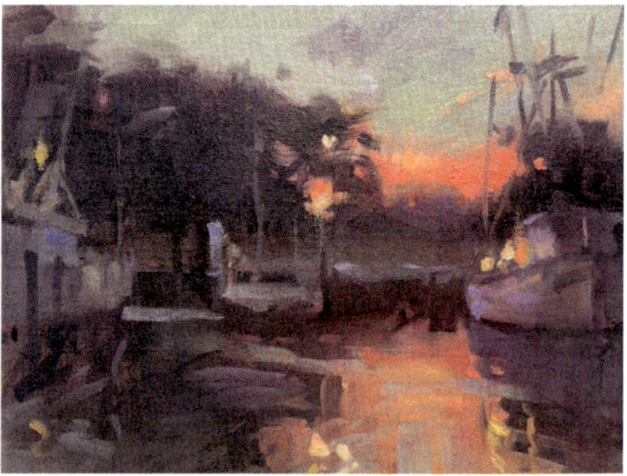

15B Glaze magic

The 8x10 oil (right) was painted in the dark. Needs a little glaze love. The "after" version has 3 glazes, the first pass was just alizarin crimson and medium to warm it overall. The 2nd was alizarin and Prussian blue, a more neutral glaze for the darks, once dry, another pass in the darks. The trick is to wipe out the lights as you go and restate a few areas (pink in the sky and boat lights). Pick your glaze colors based on the need to warm, cool or darken.

C) Half-paste. A semi-opaque glaze made with medium, a little white and a tint. It's a little like having a light fog roll in on your painting. You control the weather by controlling the amount of white and tint. A great way to obscure sections or the entire event. Mix up about a 20 to one ratio, brush it on and wipe off to taste. The tint color depends on whether you want a warm or cool fog. Experiment on old work, or even some of the experiments here when you are done with them.

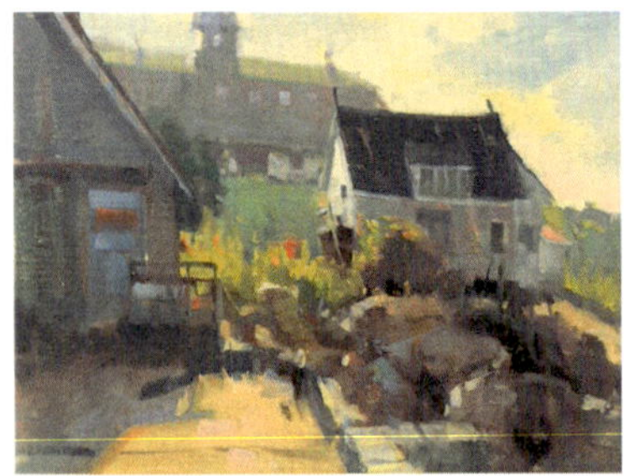

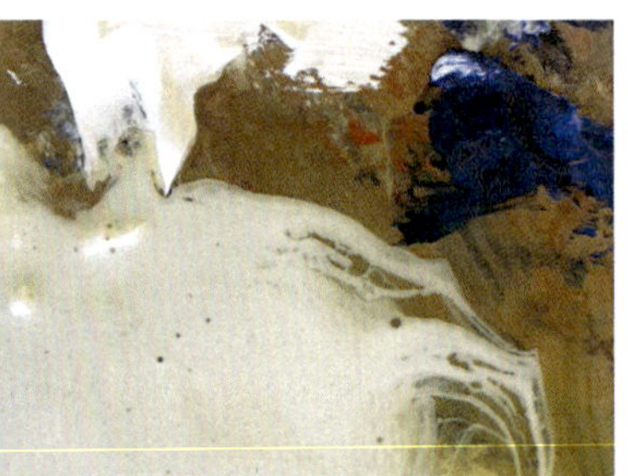

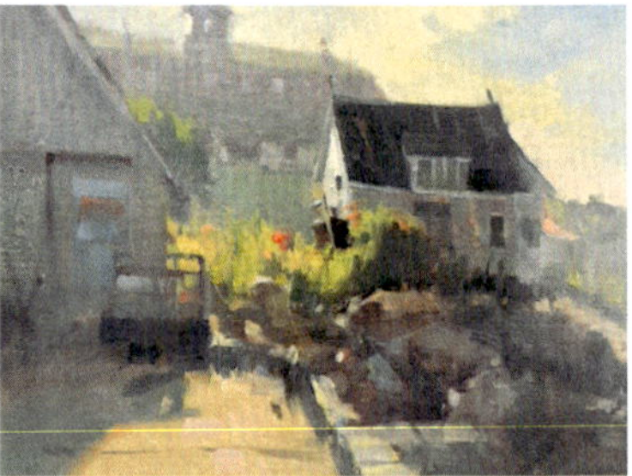

15C Half-paste

This method of using a "fogging" agent is for both realist and abstract artists. Like any such trick, the key is not to overuse it. The mixture was applied thinly in 3 layers after each had dried. After the last coat was applied, I restated some of the darks and added color back in to the fogged areas to bring up the intensity and hide the method.

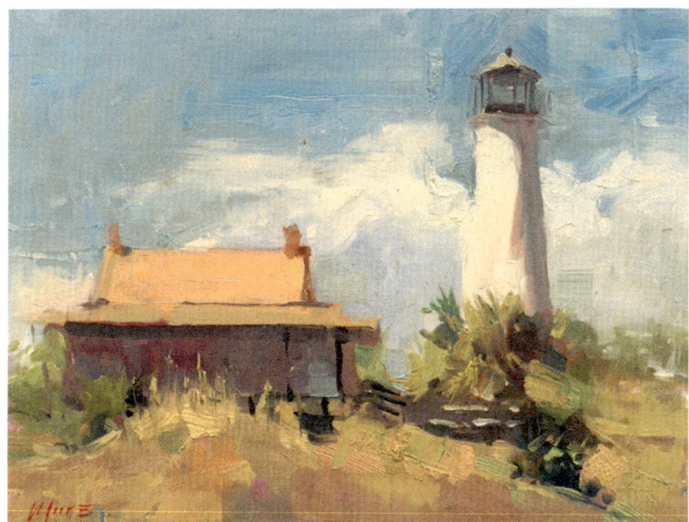

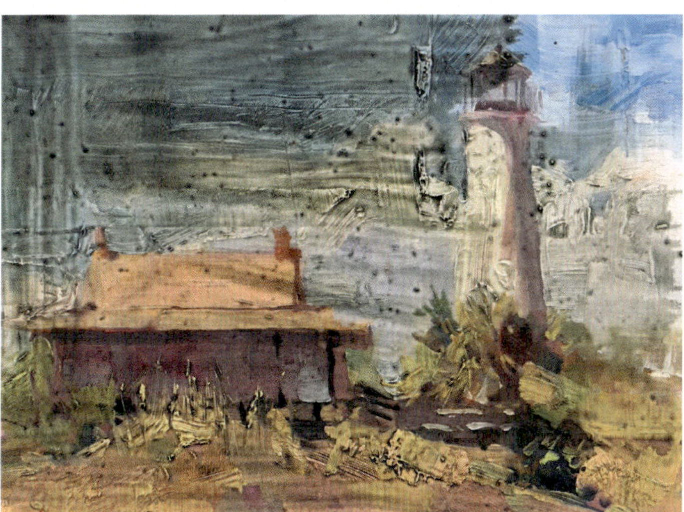

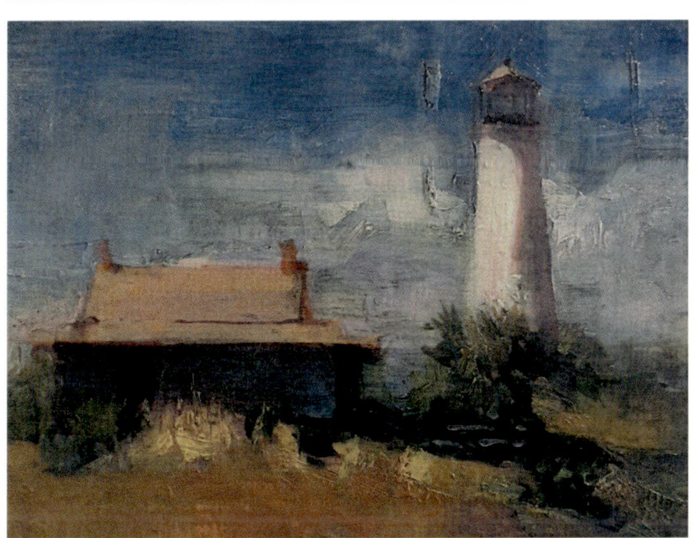

D) The Mocturne. Remember the old western movies where the night scenes looked a little off? It's because they filtered the daylight and stopped-down the lens to fake a night scene. This is the same idea. Take an old painting and rub a glaze of Prussian blue with Burnt Umber on it, wipe off to taste with a little extra wipe where you want it warmer. Rework while wet so it's not so obvious.

15D Mocturne

Take an old painting, mix a little Prussian blue and a touch of brown to taste into a puddle of painting medium, brush it on, smooth it with a soft brush and wipe out the lighter areas. I reworked and warmed the foreground so that the glazing technique was not obvious. A wonderful lesson in transparent layers and tonalism. Make sure the glazes are in the same medium as the original. 10"x12" oil on wood.

E) Color field. This is exercise #5E plus... using the idea of color vibration and taking it further by going bigger and layering more, 20"x30" and up. Just start layering with successive coats of color marks, glazes, more marks, half pastes and more marks over those layers with glazes on top. All that color at the end of the day that you were going to toss? Loosely mix it up and start brushing, let dry and next time you have extra color, add another layer. Give it a month or two to see what real depth looks like.

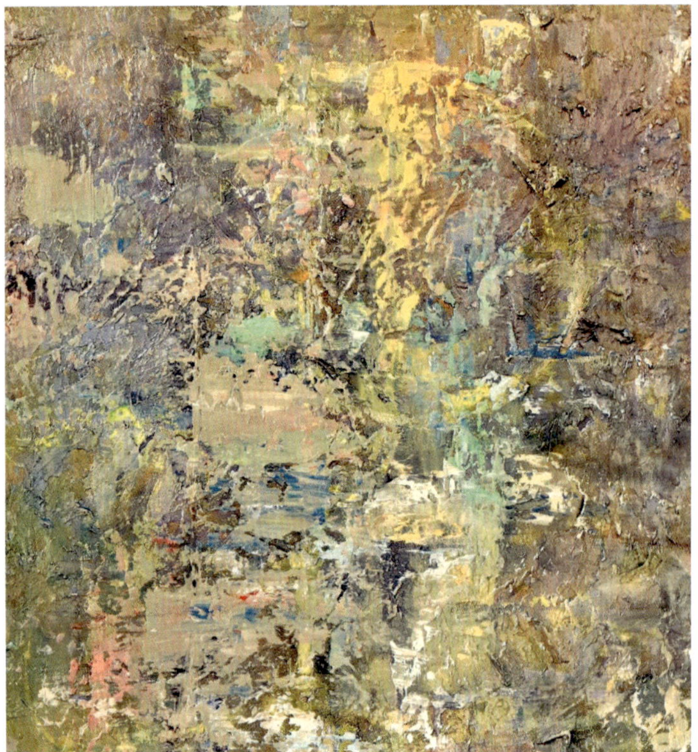

15E Color fields

More layers equal more interesting. Build up toward a color rather than just first layer stuff. This beautiful paint experiment by Scott Christensen could be an abstract or a section of a rock wall. How you apply this technique is dependent upon your intent.

16) Methods / materials.

If you want to change something about your work or discover something new, change the materials you use. A simple modification of surface, if you are a painter, can give you a whole new take on your process. Materials are to art as instruments are to music. Any variant can influence the tenor or effect. If you like guitar, get a lute or a psaltry with a completely different sound, or in the case of some guitar enthusiasts, eight guitars and a really good Lyre. Whatever the instrument or surface, how it is manipulated is everything. These painting methods can add volumes to the mystery of a piece. The general notion is to take the "What if" principle and apply it to any of these suggestions. There is no right or wrong way.

Thinking through the stages of your painting is a critical step toward figuring out which surfaces, tools and mediums will be best suited. The suggestions here are by no means a magic trick. Using an odd tool to paint with does not a good painting make. Overusing any device can become obvious unwanted noise; too much of a good thing is rarely a good thing.

A) Hardware. What constitutes a brush? It doesn't have to be made with Snow Leopard hair and a two-foot Harry Potter handle. A painting tool can be anything that can be used to apply the medium and, as I've discovered, a variety of unusual tools make for a vast variety of marks and applications. Many of my favorite tools don't come from an art store. They come from Home depot or the MaPa hardware stores. Odd tools -- like a squeegee, foam brush, roller brush, tooth brush, $1 brush, knockdown knife, putty knife, Swiss Army knife, airless paint sprayer, printer's brayer and trowel -- all have different properties and do unique things. I recommend the Home Depot challenge. I could do a DVD on this one topic. Go and try for yourself, look at the tools and get your DIY on.

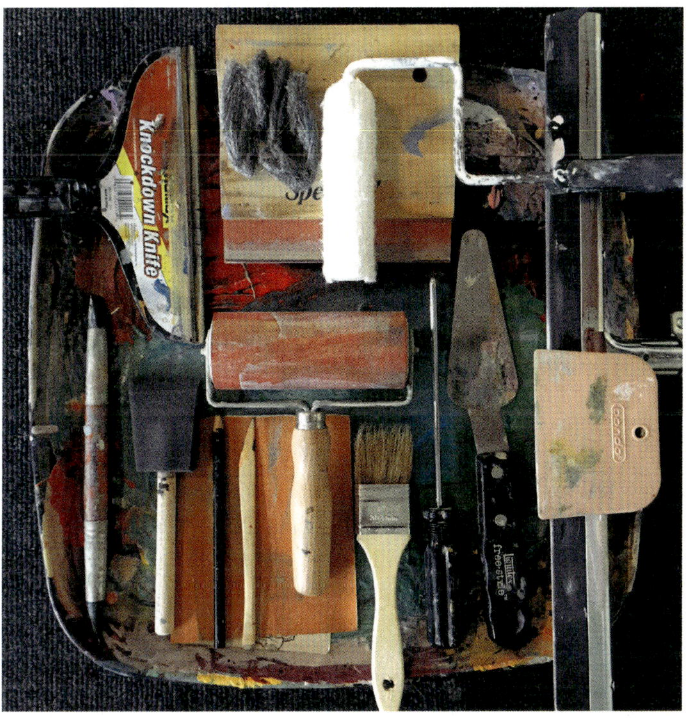

16A Hardware

An assortment of tools can be used in place of expensive high-end brushes to achieve effects that you could never get with traditional tools. Most of these came from hardware stores or silkscreen supply places. Next time you look at any tool at the store, ask yourself, "What if?"

B) Viscosity. Water has many states; solid, liquid, gas, and many powerful effects like rain, fog, snow, dew, steam, glaciers, and ice cream. Why should paint be any different. We buy our pigments in the tube or jar and they come in generally-accepted viscosities -- oils especially -- but they don't have to be used as intended. The paints can be thinned, poured, used like watercolor on a flat surface, ragged on and off, applied wet into wet, spattered, slathered, dripped, and blown with compressed air. Or, conversely, thickened with additives like cold wax for oil and heavy gel for acrylic and spread like peanut butter. Don't assume that it has to be used the way everyone else does. *Consider your intent* and then figure out how the paint should behave within that frame. Yet another DVD to be made.

C) Pour. Liquify, mix, drip, manipulate with gravity or a spreader. An entire movement of The Abstract Expressionist branch of art bloomed out of this one simple premise. Helen Frankenthaler and Morris Lewis, to name two, made large-scale works this way because the paint allowed for that. This is an expressive and quick way to cover a canvas, to be manipulated, subtracted from or added to as needed. A realist artist can use this as a device just as well as a non-objective artist. Check the back lower left corner of your Artistic License, it states this clearly.

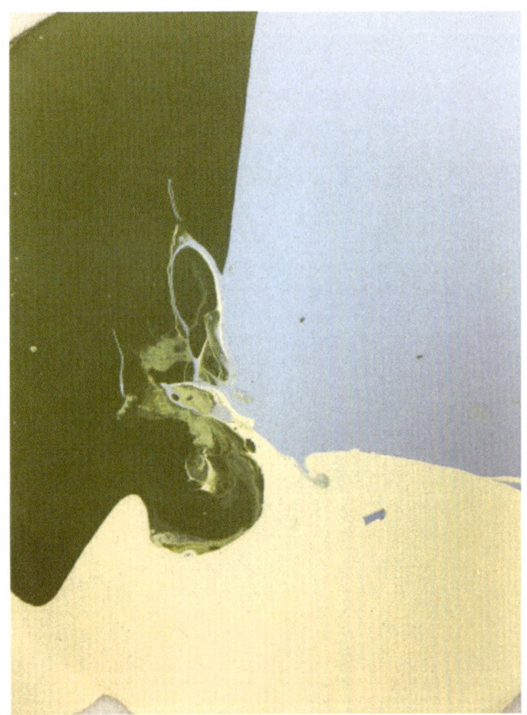

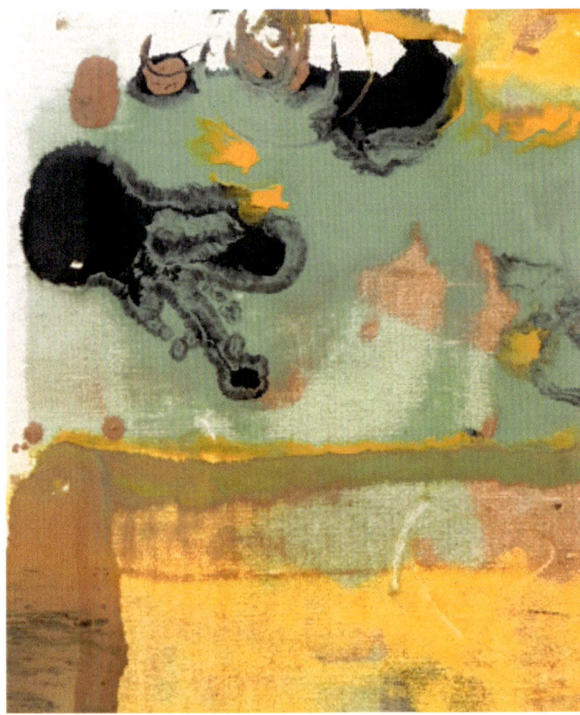

16C Pour

Acrylic to the left (house paint) and oil to the right. Each medium reacts differently and each surface will influence the paint in different ways. The tube oils were mixed with a medium like Galkyd or Linseed oil and a little turpentine. Drip, splatter, manipulate with a squeegee, draw into it. Expect the unexpected.

D) House paints. This utilitarian medium is the most versatile, freeing, fun, expressive way to explore building surface, layers and mystery in a painting. The use of hardware-store latex acrylics paint also makes working larger that much easier. House paints you say? Store-bought gesso is made of pigment, chalk, and acrylic polymer as a binder. Water-based house paints are made of pigment and an acrylic latex binder. Start with the color testers on a gessoed hard ground like spruce ply panel or similar. The flat- or eggshell-finish latex paint can be brushed, spread, poured, scooped and manipulated easily, and it dries fast. You can go over it with acrylics because they are cousins. Give it a coat of clear gesso and you can over-paint with oil. It's also amazingly easy to make a painting that matches your couch. And it's cheap. I rest my case.

One caveat: I am not a paint rocket scientist. These ideas are for play and exploration only. You can take the lessons learned and work them back into your usual pigments. However, the artist Lee Krasner, just one example of many mid-century contemporary artists, used oil, paper and canvas collage using God knows what kind of glue, and she's hanging in the major museums. It's their problem.

One other thing, no acrylic anything on top of oil anything. It don't work.

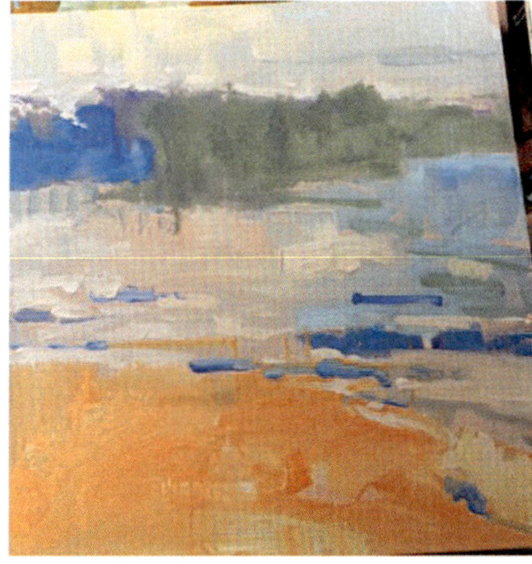

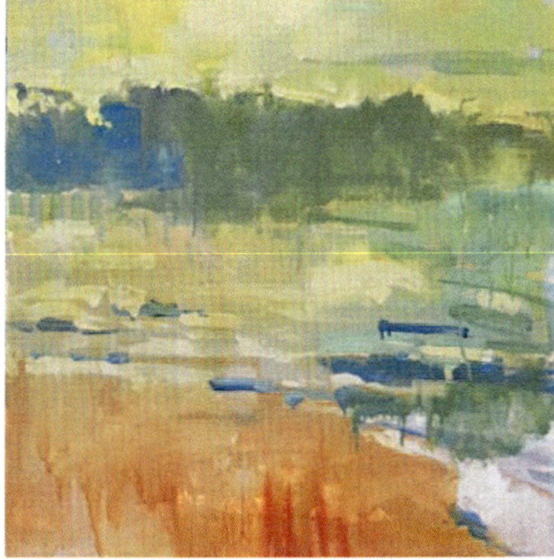

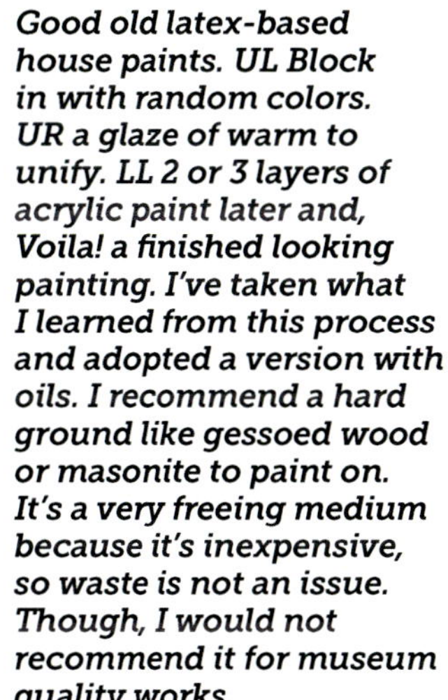

16D House paints
Good old latex-based house paints. UL Block in with random colors. UR a glaze of warm to unify. LL 2 or 3 layers of acrylic paint later and, Voila! a finished looking painting. I've taken what I learned from this process and adopted a version with oils. I recommend a hard ground like gessoed wood or masonite to paint on. It's a very freeing medium because it's inexpensive, so waste is not an issue. Though, I would not recommend it for museum quality works.

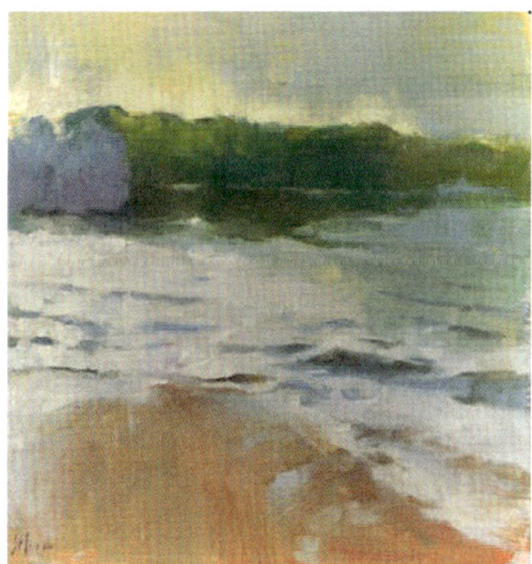

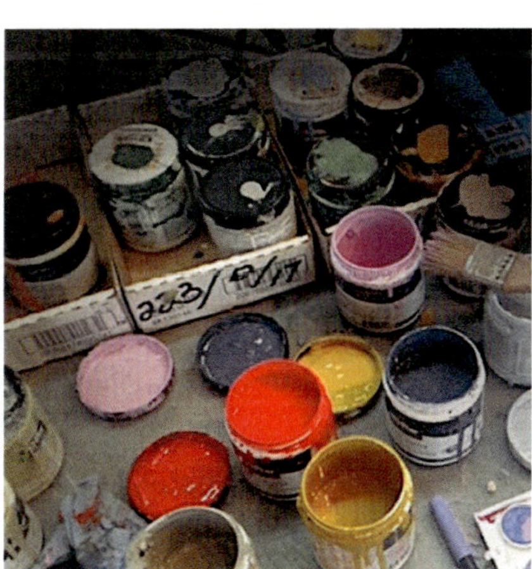

E) Flat and gloss. Another variant in approach to surface to consider is shiny versus matte finishes. Often, we varnish to unify a surface. If you are an oil painter, Gamblin paints has a highly informative post on how to attain anything from glossy varnishes to eggshell using three components, varnish, thinner and cold wax. The final finish coat not only integrates all the shifts in surface, it protects the paint as well. Gamblincolors.com is where you can find that info. In addition, **if it falls within the intent of the work,** one can employ a variety of finishes in one piece, either through using mixed media for surface juxtaposition or the application of mixed surface paints. With acrylics, there are additives to enhance this property --gloss medium, matte medium and a host of others. Same is true with house paints. They come in the can, either flat or high gloss, and all steps in between. (Yet another thing to mess with your brain.)

F) Obscure. In exercise #15C, I talk about half-paste. It's a wonderful way to create mystery and history in a work, obscuring the under-layers just enough to make it feel as if they were under water. Cold wax is another way to achieve this, with oil mediums only. Gamblin and other sources make this easy-to-use product. The smallest amount of pigment folded into the wax adds a tint to this translucent medium. Heavier proportions of paint to wax make for a thick, spreadable mixture that can be applied with a spreader, brush or squeegee. Alone, it's a wonderful finish that can be buffed to a gloss or left matte. In heavier layers, it will diminish what is under it. And, a huge plus, it can be (carefully) melted with an iron using a sheet of parchment paper in between... on a very low setting. But, don't leave your cold wax paintings in the car during the summer for very long.

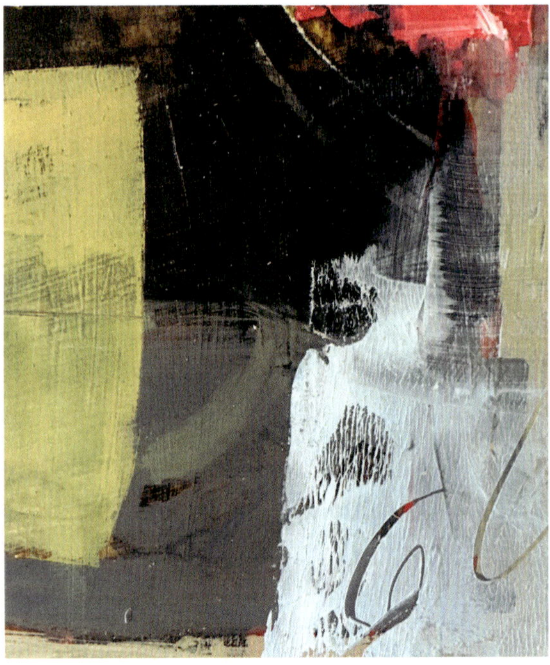

16F Cold wax

Magic butter. This stuff has 101 uses. Shown here, the wax is simply spread like butter over dried paint, in this case, acrylic, to ghost back what is underneath. It can be tinted and carved into, with a thin application it creates an eggshell finish. Once dry it can be buffed to a gloss. There's no right or wrong way to use this stuff. Only thing you can't do is mix it with a water based pigment. Oil and water... you know.

G) Squeegee and knock-down knife. Mentioned previously, in addition to their actual intended use for home stuff, these tools can be used in ways other than adding paint to canvas. They are great for removing as well. After I've applied a few wet notes over a dry surface, I'll run one tool or the other across the top to "knock down" the note, minimizing it. Occasionally, I'll apply a coat of glaze or half-paste with either, even in realism-based work. I like a painting that makes it hard to discern how it was developed.

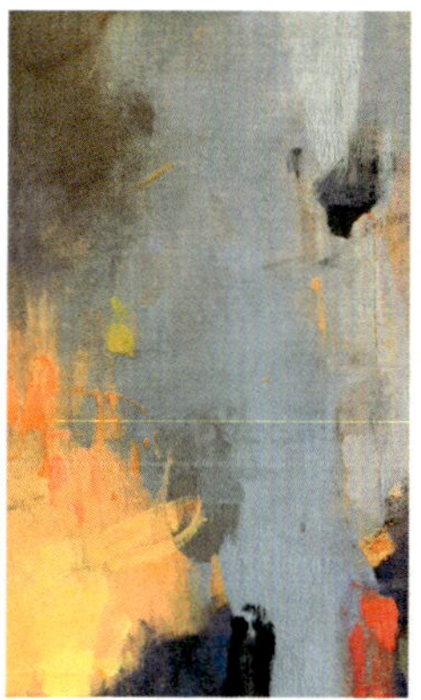
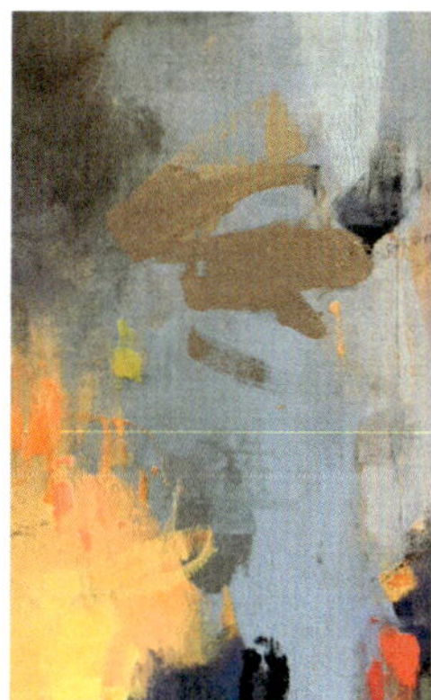
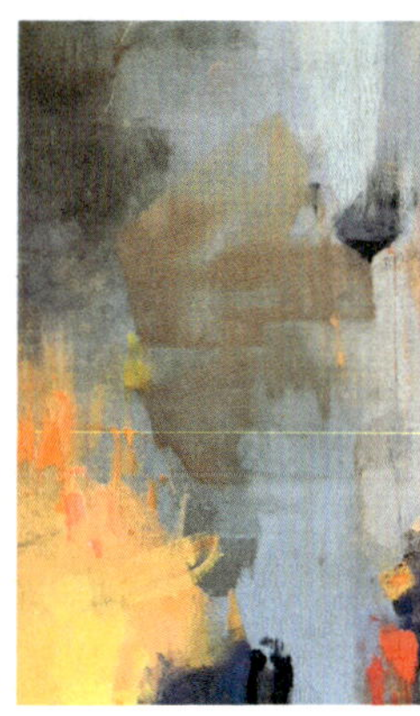
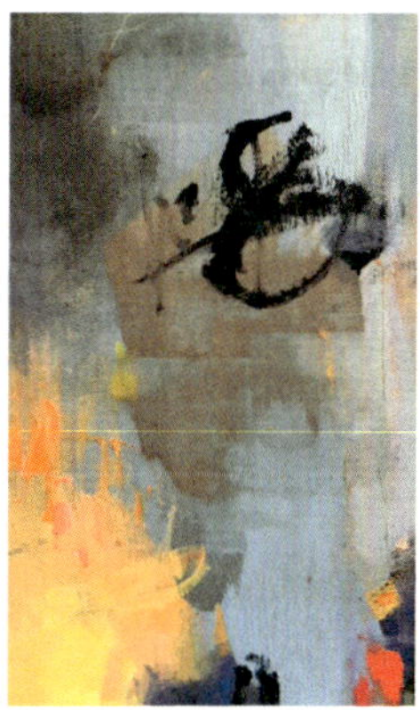
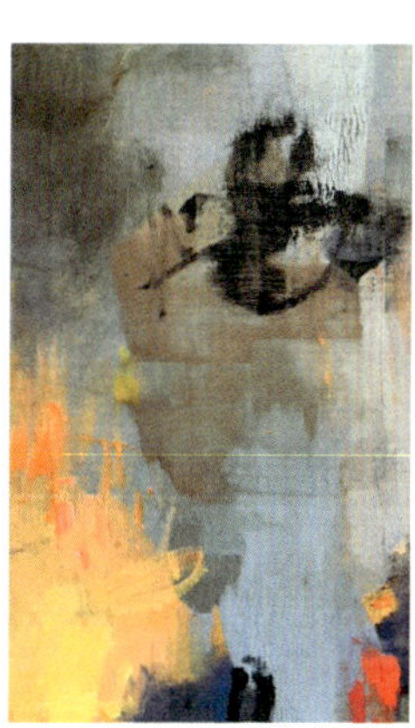

16G Knockdown

From left to right; a dry canvas, a note of wet color, a pull down with the knockdown knife to diminish the mark, another wet note of black on top and another pull with the knockdown knife. The important lesson is how, by adding or diminishing the mark, the composition shifts and the eye-flow changes. This can be used in realist work as well as abstract.

H) Slow dry. Mediums and pigments do different things. Oils stay wet longer than acrylics, which means they stay workable and don't shift in color until dry. Wet into wet means more merged colors and edges and less hard separations. Additives like Safflower oil or clove oil (in baby doses) slow the process even more, if it's an important aspect of the expression to be kept malleable till the end. Only problem is they take a really, really long time to dry, so avoid if your show deadline is in a month.

I) Fast dry. If more texture, broken marks and color are desired, there are ways to speed that up. For oils, working on a highly absorbent ground like gessoed wood with alkyds or alkyd dryer additives will speed it up so fast you will go back in time. Acrylics are designed to dry quickly, so that's never a problem. It has been said by people who care that one should never apply oil over acrylic because of a surface cohesion issue. But if you give the underpainting a coat of clear gesso, it shouldn't explode. Or, better yet, just stay with the acrylics. To make these decisions in support of your work, it's good to think through the process to see if there are areas or stages that will require blendability. One thing for sure, there is an end-around for every problem with current mediums and additives. Just ask the Great Google.

J) Mixed media. This topic --which deserves its own book, and there are many out there -- is the embodiment of visual play. Because drawing is out of the equation, each element -- from cut and torn note papers to nature's leavings to vintage toys -- is considered on its own merit as a component of texture, color and story. A hard-wood ground (like an old box), house paints, clear gel medium or Elmer's as glue for papers and silicon glues for 3-D objects, combined with a treasure trove of found stuff that you probably have in your garage, make for rich playgrounds indeed.

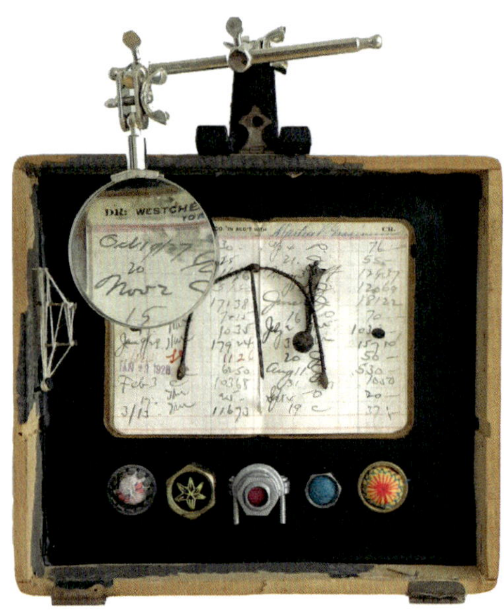

16J Mixed Media

This elegant assemblage piece by Robin Howard exhibits the beauty of vintage ephemera when it is combined in unusual ways. While the parts have meaning only to the maker, the viewer is invited to make up a story to go along with the collection. Found objects take on new meaning when placed in synergetic relationship with other bits and parts. One trick to this process is to think of each piece as an actor in a play. Too many actors and the plot becomes confused, too few and it is incomplete.

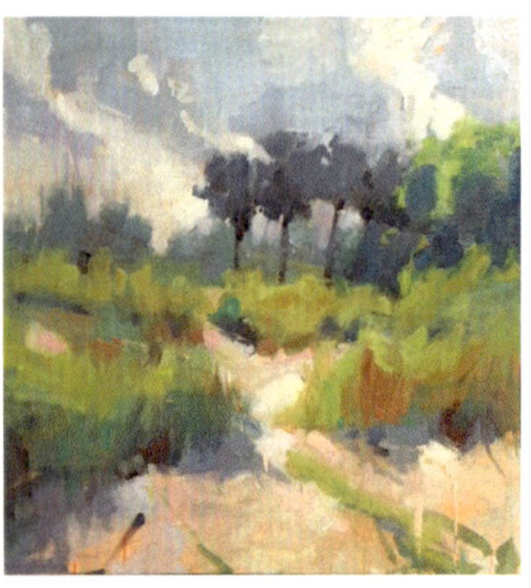
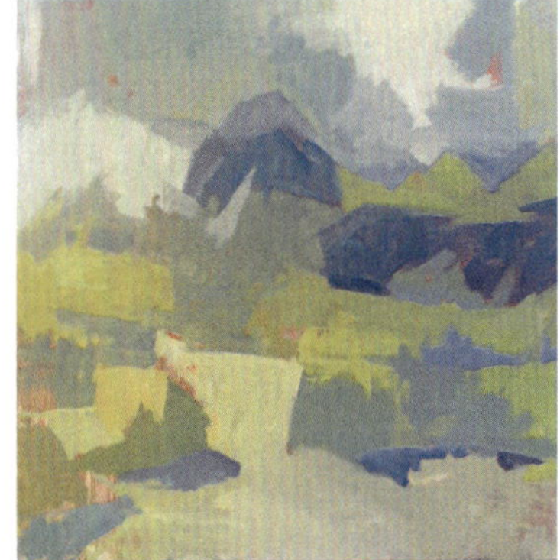
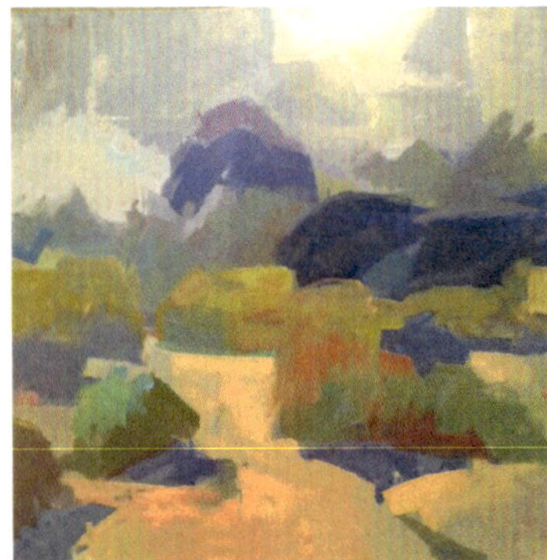
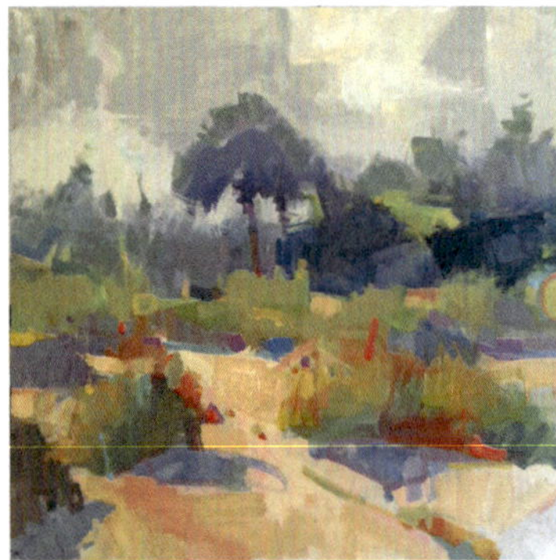

K) Shape-driven painting. The way a painting is started or blocked-in informs the finish, which is why I suggest doing exercises K though M. A shape-based start is one where the most dominant and important elements are defined as large simplified color shapes, as if they were cut-out paper, filling up the surface with the color arrangements as swiftly as possible. Start thin and move quickly to build color relationships without too much of the canvas showing through, because the canvas holes become extraneous and disruptive shapes. Then proceed to subdivide shapes, add detail and finesse edges.

16K Shape driven

UL, small oil study. UR, limited palette block in, then color variations in the big shapes and then final tweaks. 48"x48" oil

L) Line-driven painting. Similar to exercise K, the dominant shapes are indicated as light pencil outlines. This allows for a little more freedom in color choices and under-color decisions for what will be placed on top. It also gives an opportunity to think like a graphic designer and not a renderer. The outcome will be more mechanical unless you give yourself permission to break up the edges.

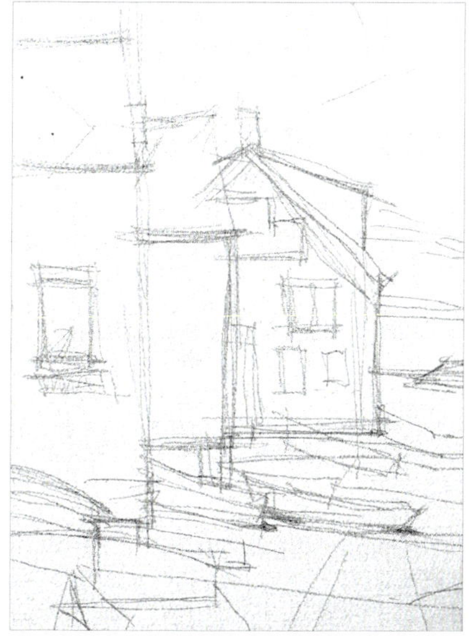

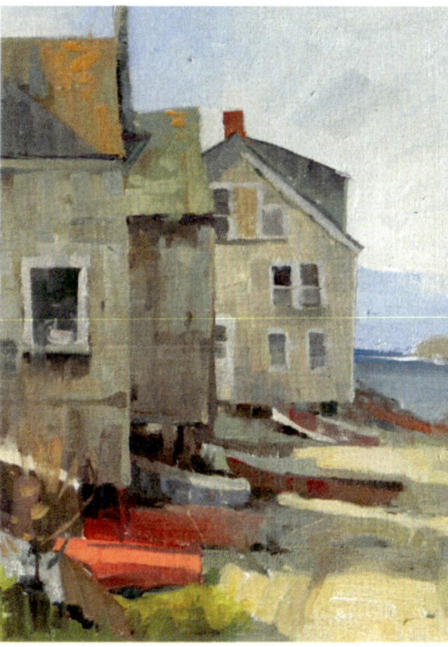

16L Line driven
This 11x14 plein air oil incorporates the line-based start, which allowed for a more graphic assignment of shapes and division of space. The under-color was varied for each section, knowing that the final color choices would be more neutral. How you start informs how you finish.

M) Out of focus, to in. Big, soft, loose, wet-into-wet descriptions of the most basic components. Don't see the objects. See the shapes. Work without hard edges, build in successive soft layers and placing sharp notes only where you need them, so you aren't chasing every edge. Put successively thicker (fat) notes of paint on top. If you wish to paint loose, this is how you do it. A tight drawing makes for a tight painting. Loose description keeps it loose and keeps it real, yo.

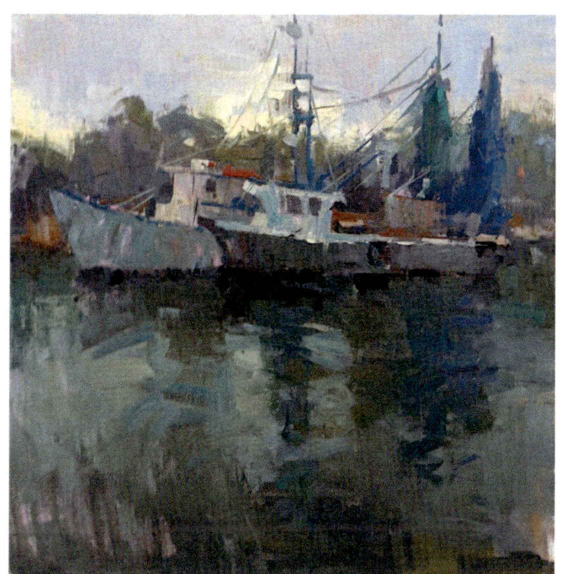

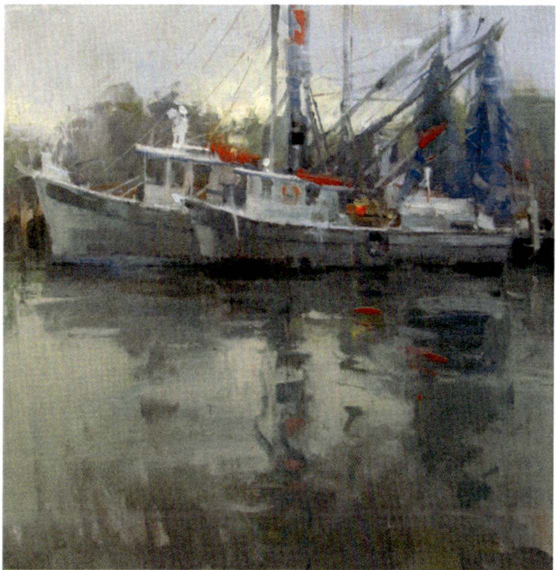

16M Loose block-in to tight
Big, loose color / value shapes to small / tight info but only where detail is really needed. 30"x30" plein air oil.

17) Composition / hierarchy.

This concept runs through all forms of creative expression, from music to paint, and is the toughest to explain because it relies or depends on the selected components, including intent, to function. It is why I teach the Abstraction from Nature classes. Usually, most of the energy in a realism-based painting class goes toward making the painting look like the thing the painting is based on. Less focus is given to the other components, including interpretation and hierarchy. Hidden behind any notable realism-based painting are powerful abstract concepts, with focus on specific components, all in service to the intent of the work. In viewing thousands of paintings over the years, I've noticed that the two precepts that underlie most good painting compositions are:

1) Something needs be the boss (dominant). From this come the secondary and tertiary elements (subordinate) and so forth, that are either in support of or counter to the main event, usually culminating in some form of asymmetrical balance, also known as dynamic symmetry.

2) The use of repeating or reinforcing patterns of the chosen components, much like the main melody in a symphonic concerto, a theme that resonates throughout the work.

The analogy I use in presentations is the billboard. Perhaps a little crass, but we've all seen the ones that have so much stuff on them you don't know what to look at. Paintings work in the same way. Something needs to be the president and the other components should follow in order of rank, even in a sketch of a few flowers. It's the one, two, three of importance.

The dominance of one thing over another is not always defined by the size of an element. It can be achieved with color, value, edge, placement or the psychological weight of the element (as in a small figure in a grand landscape). But the visual weight or energy of an element is never repeated. A good painting moves the viewers' eyes throughout, giving information as it's required. Look for the competing parts of the puzzle and seek ways to make one thing dominant and the other parts subordinate in the food chain.

The ultimate goal is eye flow and asymmetrical balance. You know this has been achieved when the weight of each part falls into an order of being seen, or the hierarchy of elements. American artist Edward Hopper knew this better than anyone. His paintings weren't as much about objects as they were about the relationship of one thing to another. His sense of asymmetrical balance is mastery. Remove one piece of the composition and the painting feels off-kilter. If a painting feels flat or off, it's usually the result of a lack of dynamic balance. Always reevaluate the parts and their relationship to one another.

When you do any of these exercises, you are in some way exploring not just the component but composition as well -- division of space, edge, color -- all are ways of moving or pulling the eye through space. It is an inherent part of any of these practice runs. Even the placement of a simple line on a page should be a conscious choice. I can show you what makes a good composition, according to me. But it's more important that you figure out what works for you. However, since it is the number one question I'm asked in my classes, I'll present a few favorites and explain the thought behind the work.

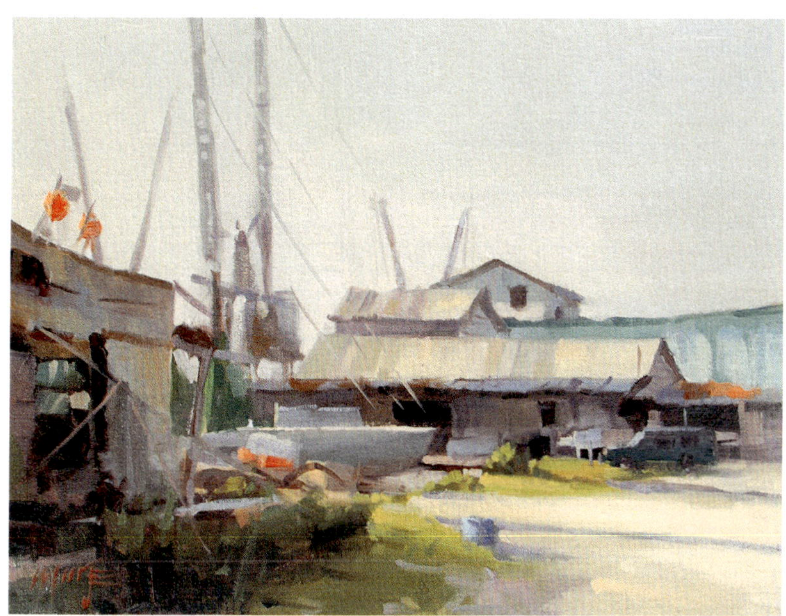

17.1 Composition

This older plein air painting just works for me. It has a solid, light dominant value plan, a seemingly split down the middle (but isn't) division of space and good positive and negative shapes with variety in each. And just enough uprights to break up the dominant sky shape. A predominantly warm palette is countered with the cool blue-green of the roof-line and color resonance in the use of the orange notes. There is no single focal point, only a well-constructed hierarchy.

Snead's day off, 12 x 16 in.
oil on canvas

Note: You will not find the term 'focal point' here. It's too limiting. Often, when I am painting, I let the work evolve and grow around a basic premise and tell me which element should carry more weight and which should have less. Identifying a focal point from the start presupposes the end result. In some cases, it is helpful, but it's more of a suggestion than a rule.

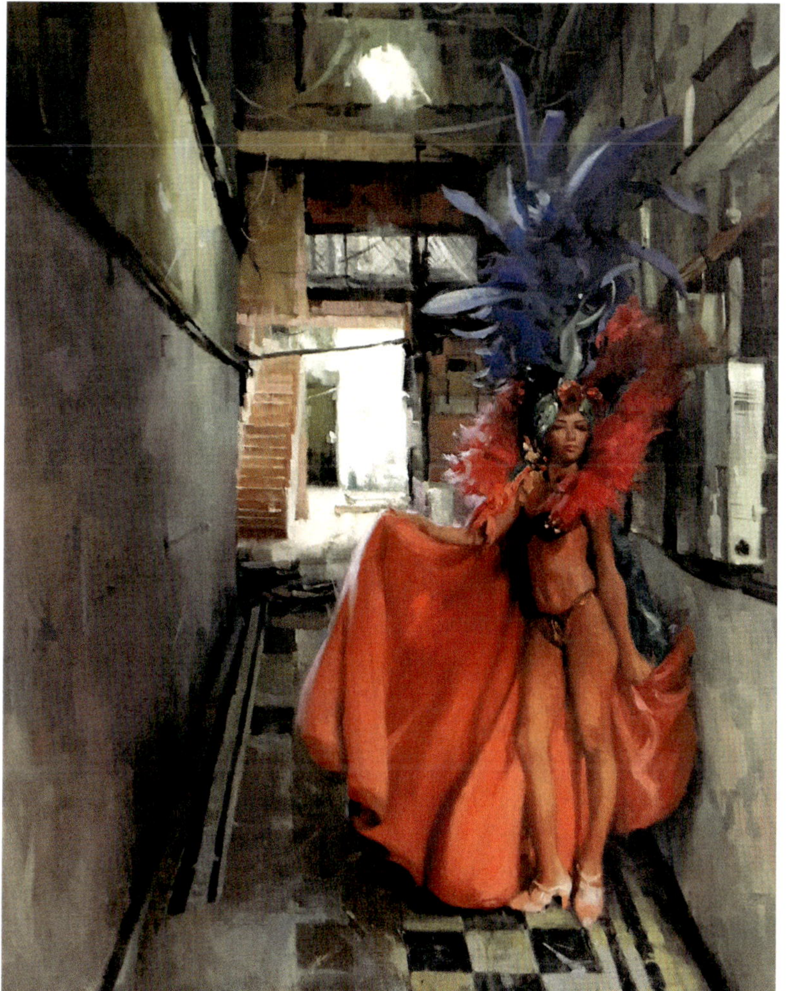

17.2 Composition with a message

While the figure is certainly a center of interest, aided by the use of "alien" color, there are also counter-points in the light at the end of the hallway and the dark mechanical lines of the architecture. The use of juxtaposition occurs not only in color but content with the contrast of the fantasy show girl and the reality of the gritty living conditions.

No place like home, 24 x30 in.
oil on canvac

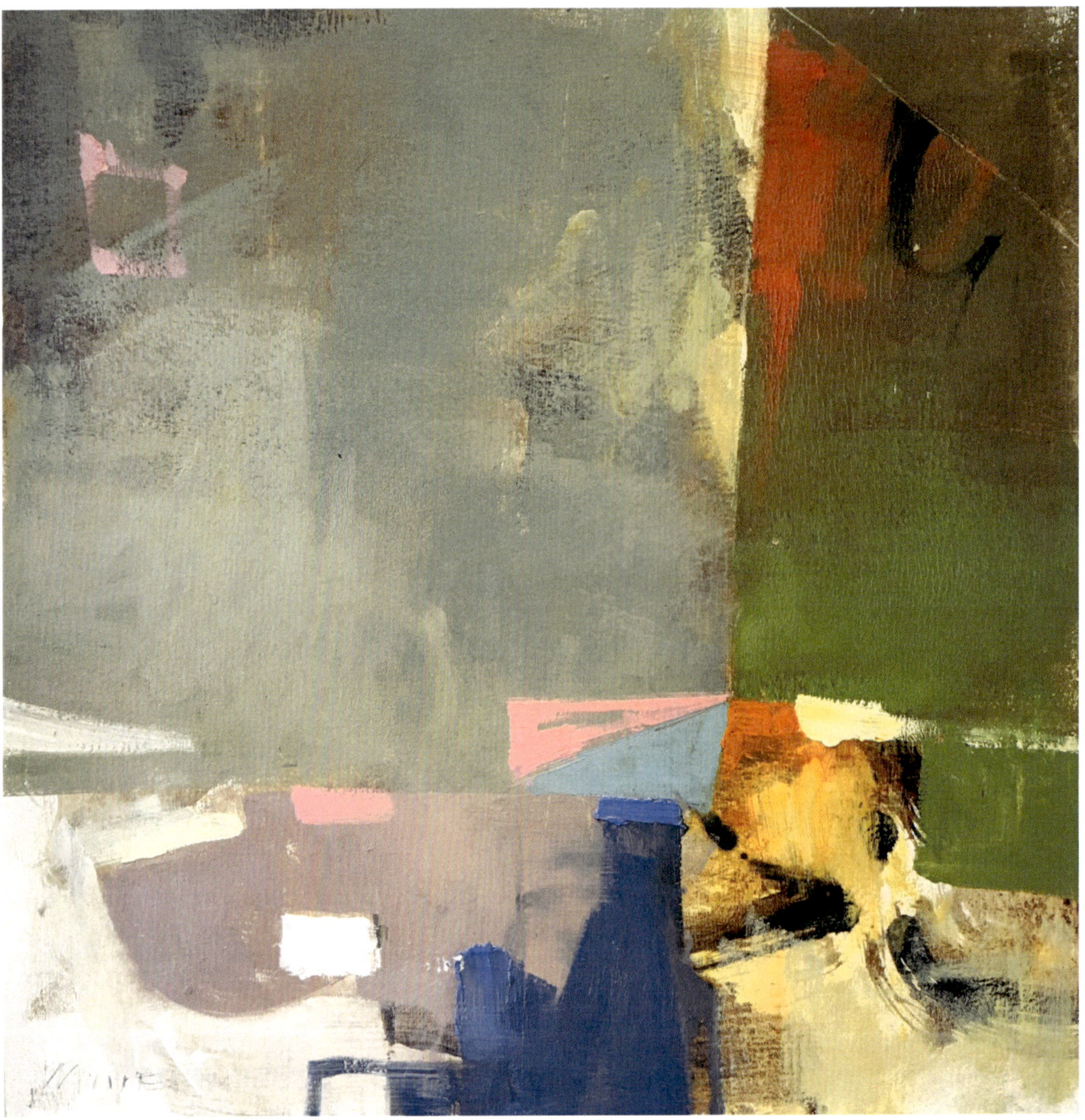

17.3 Abstract

A good way to think about any painting is that each element of the composition has energy. Every piece of the puzzle, from the pink triangle to the large textural gray shape and the out-of-context cobalt mark, carries a specific amount of visual weight. Abstract art is a balancing act to achieve dynamic symmetry, the energy or weight of each piece must be considered against the whole.

Aftermath 16 x 16 in. oil and cold wax on wood

Dynamic symmetry is both an intellectual challenge and a battle of tendencies. It is inherent in our nature to move toward the symmetrical... flattened, centered expressions of form and subject. We must be ever-vigilant to challenge our basic patterns. One way to do this is to imagine the arrangement of the elements as a balancing structure, like a fulcrum or a mobile. Each component and element carries weight, and each weight generally requires a counter-weight to maintain the energy of balance. Mass, contrast, pattern, value, color, brushwork, edge and the rest pull the eye with their own gravitational force. Getting them to work in unison is quite the trick.

A) The Compositron. It's a pretty simple notion. Take just a few elements and a limited range of values in a limited palette and explore ways to combine them in a rectangle -- enlarge, overlap, positive / negative, large vs small, reverse, rearrange, repeat. See how many variations you can get compositionally with just these elements. What looks at first to be an elementary school game can yield some impressive results. I invited a few friends to create some of these just to see what they would come up with.

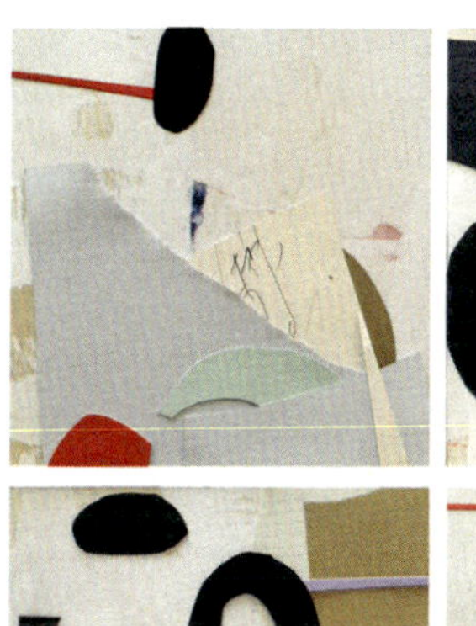
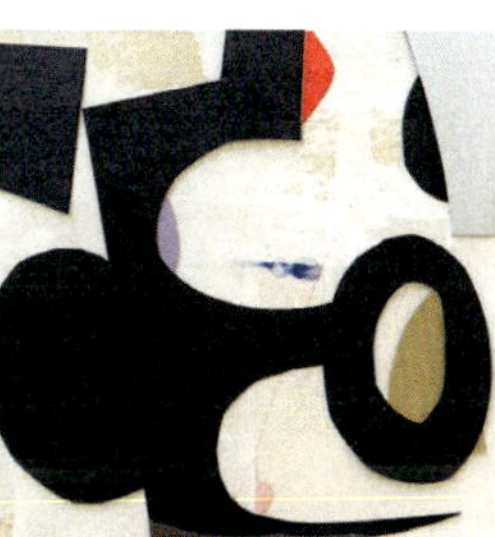
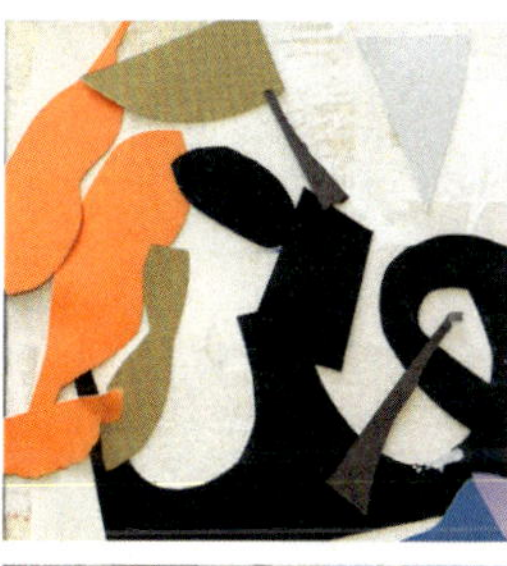
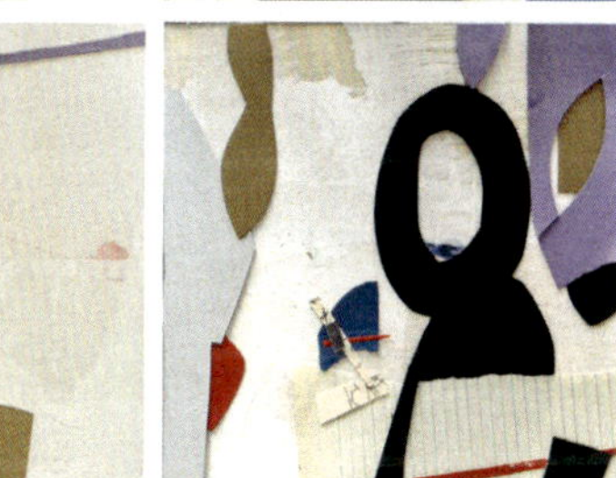

17A The Compositron

A more controlled version of 6A. Make a rectangular format (I just taped off a piece of wood and gessoed it), cut and tear a limited number of pieces of paper, fabric, leaves, whatever you find interesting and start composing. It's not that different from composition in outdoor painting. You have a set number of elements and the ones you choose and how you arrange them on a canvas make all the difference. See how many variations you can get.

B) Motif variations. Exploring multiple compositional motifs on one subject is the quickest way to learn to push the boundaries of what you are familiar or comfortable with. This can be done simply and quickly. I can never say this enough -- the more the better, not just two or three, 20 or 30. Just as in free-association responses to a word, the first ideas to pop up are the most obvious and these are what we tend to go to. Only after the obvious solutions have been explored will the good stuff come to the surface.

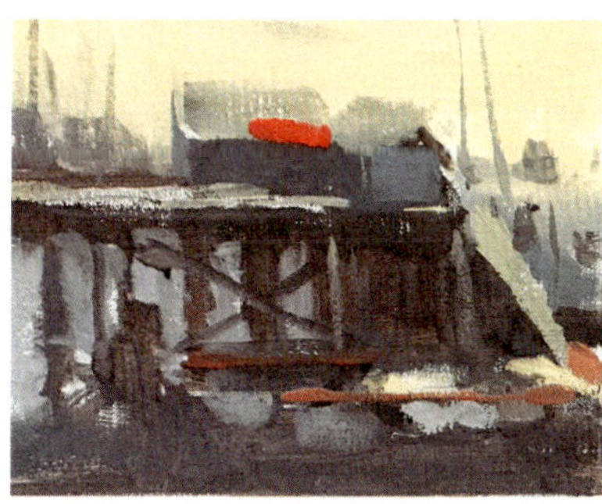
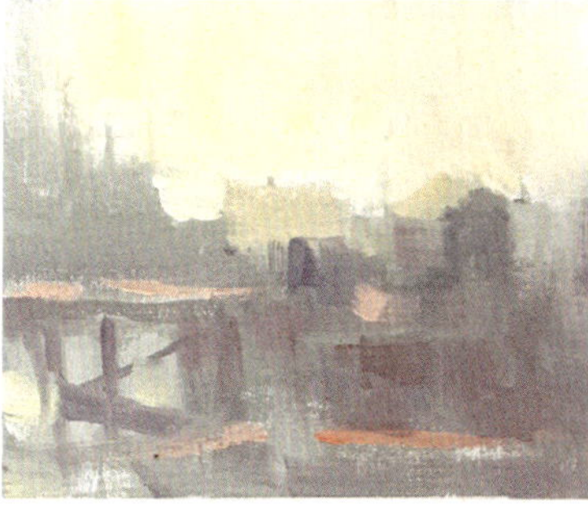
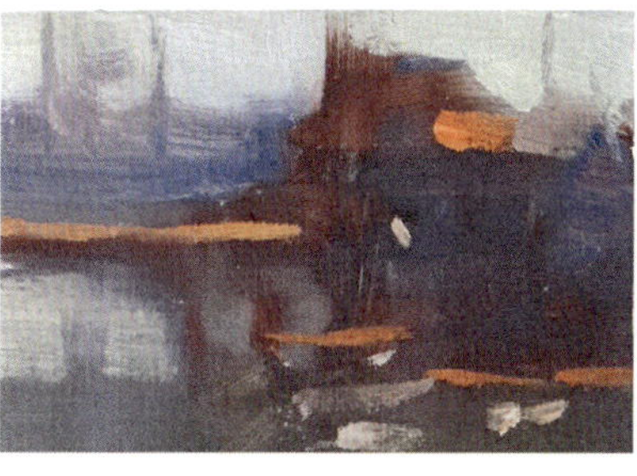
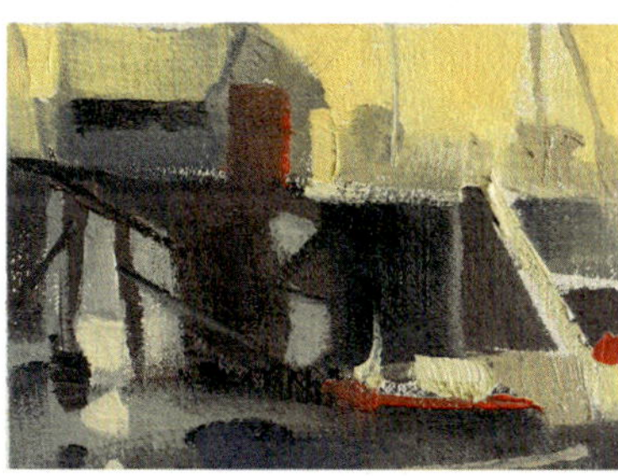
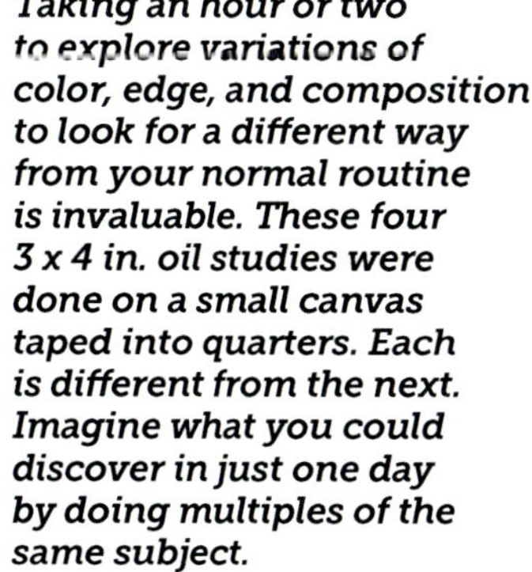

17B Motif variations

Taking an hour or two to explore variations of color, edge, and composition to look for a different way from your normal routine is invaluable. These four 3 x 4 in. oil studies were done on a small canvas taped into quarters. Each is different from the next. Imagine what you could discover in just one day by doing multiples of the same subject.

C) Decomposing. One of the best ways to show how a composition works is to take a good one and remove the balancing elements, just like when someone uses their thumb to cover an unnecessary part of a painting. It's helpful, but then there's a big thumb there. Look at a side-by-side of a painting I did a few years back that I've always considered as a fulcrum, with weight on one side and counter-weights on the other. By changing just a few components of color, value or edge, the painting feels unbalanced.

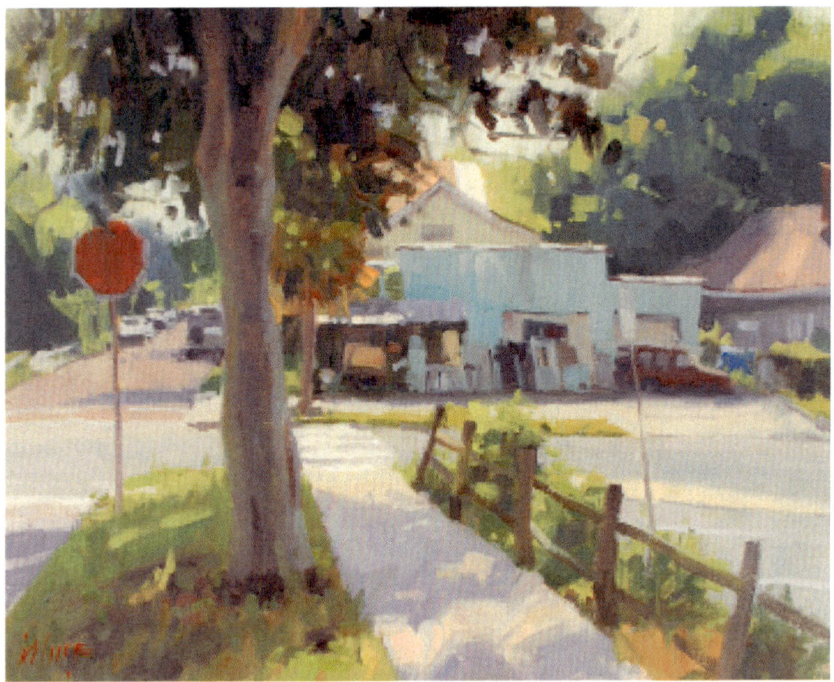

3C Decomposing

Every element carries weight, has mass and energy. By altering the balancing pieces, the dynamic symmetry is thrown off and the weight is on the trees shoulders. Note that by moving the fence to the right, the negative spaces become equal and a little more boring.

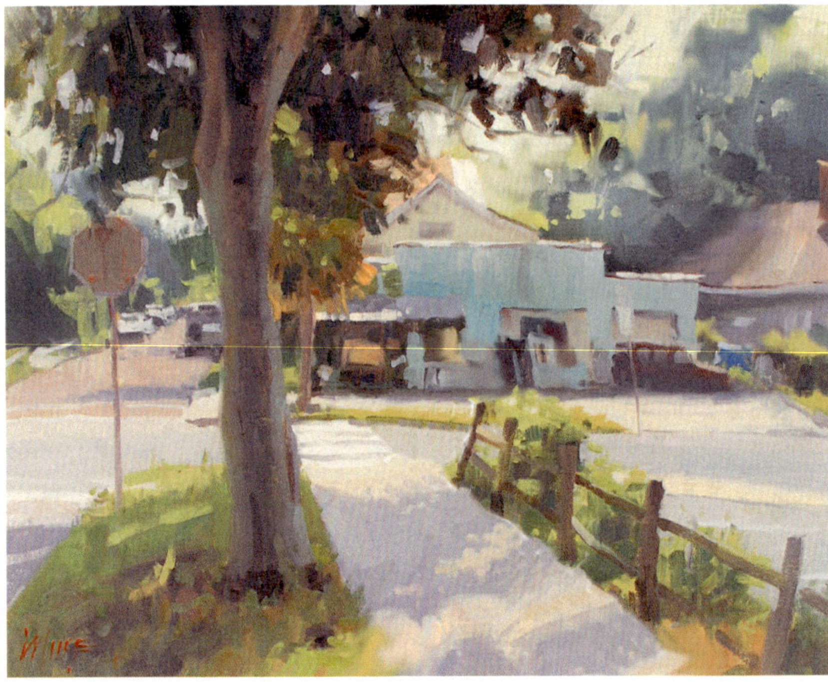

D) Hierarchy. Controlling the order in which elements are received takes years to master. If you can learn to see it in others' work, you can make it happen in your own. A painting is a lot like a good book; the information comes to you on a need to know basis. Manipulating the order is the ultimate task of the visual communicator. It is utilized in every form of expression from graphic design to interior design. The master creator alters the parts in service to the whole, sometimes disregarding the literal "truth" of a scene by restructuring the visual weight of each part. The next time you experience anything with good design -- a book cover, a painting, a great living room -- be aware of how you are pulled through it. A great painting is like a good toupee; you don't notice how it works, it just does.

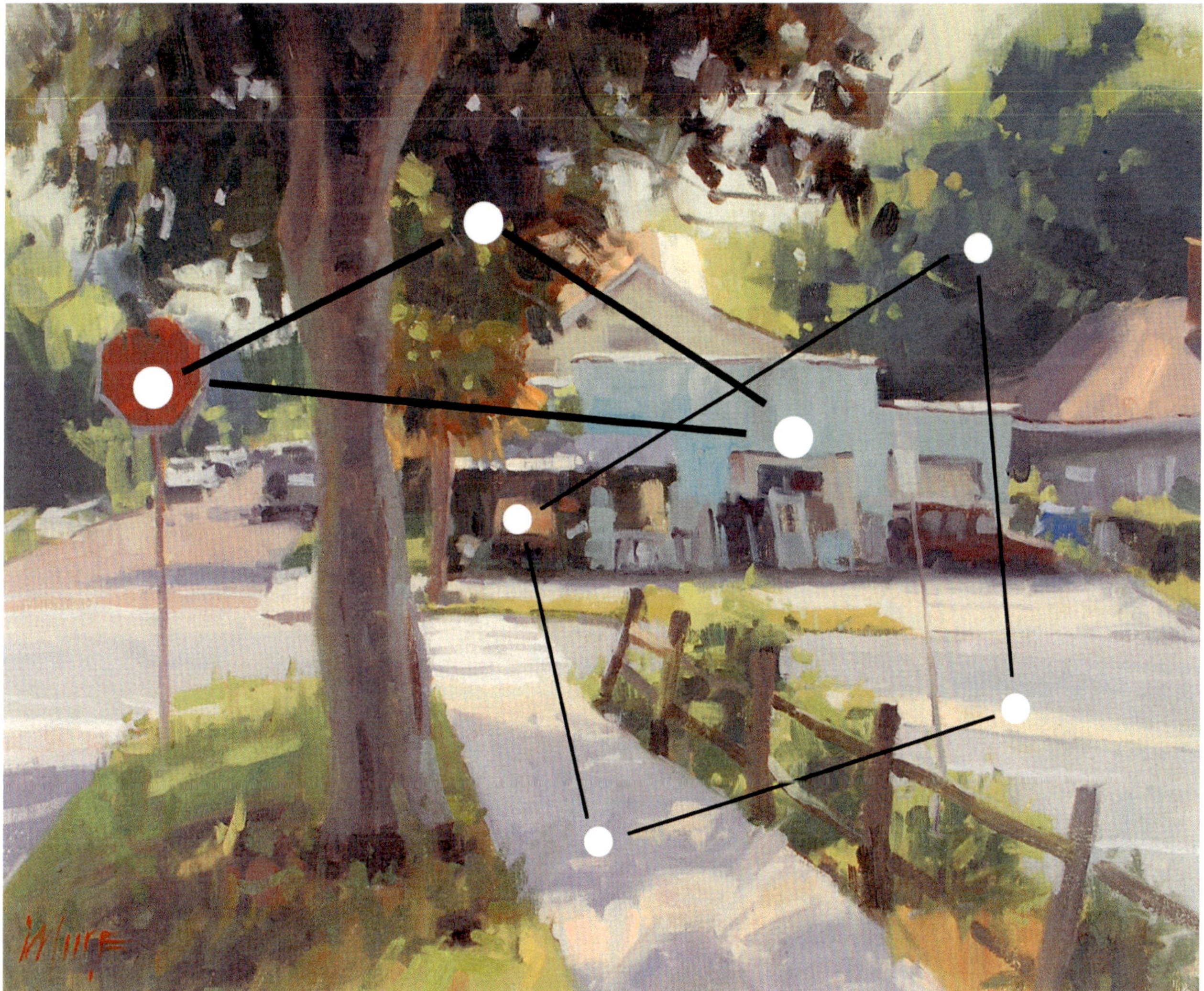

17D Dominant/subordinate

All elements align in order of visual hierarchy by utilizing all the tools of size, color, edge, etc. If everything has the same weight, the eye doesn't know where to go. Strive for the 1, 2, 3 order in levels of import.

E) Abstruction. I love a good neologism, it is synergy to my ears. This exercise is a bit like taking all the pieces from two jigsaw puzzles, pouring them out on a table and making something happen. This is a design exercise in spatial relationships, it doesn't have to look like anything. Cut up a few paintings on canvas that are on the chopping block into random shapes. Rectangular shapes are a little easier to snap together. See how many variations you can get out of a few pieces. Take a pic of your favorites before you go on to the next.

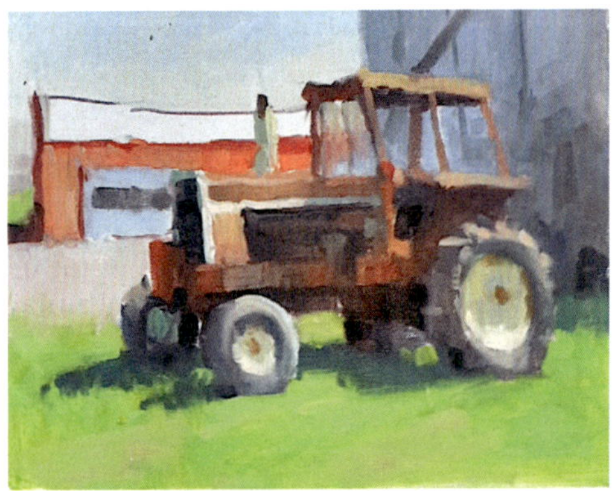

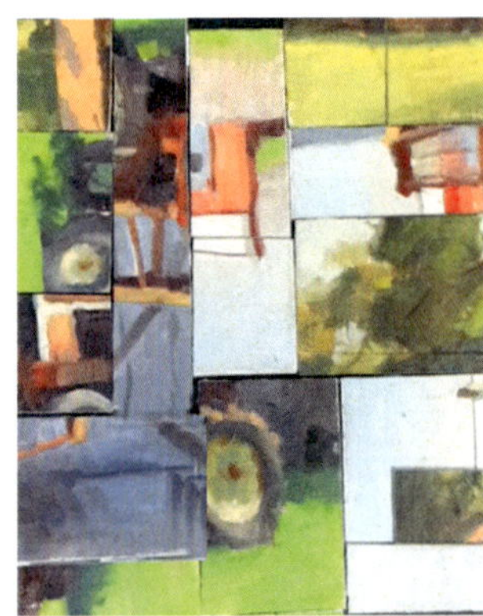

17E Abstruction

Cut two canvases up into a variety of sizes and move the parts around. Strive for division of space, pattern and rest and hierarchy. You were going to throw those canvases away anyway...

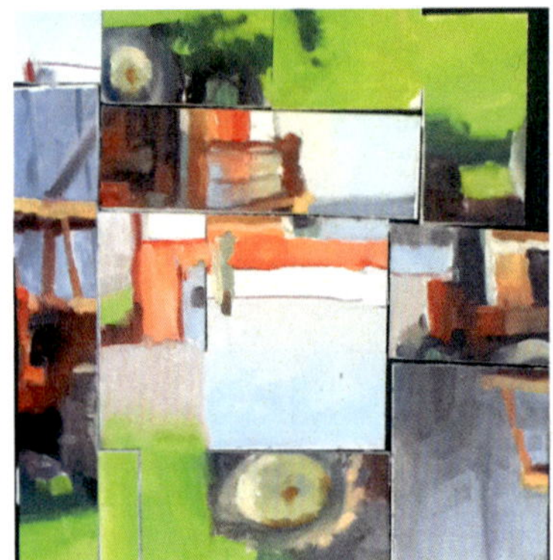

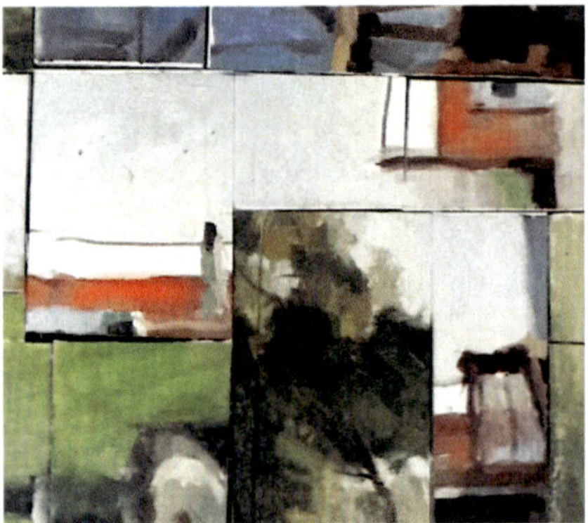

18) Intent.

There's been enough said about intent that, by now, you should have some ideas of what to try. As an example of coming at an intent problem from multiple directions, I was approached by a woman after a talk about the voice of the artist. She asked, "I love painting outside. But I also love being a weaver. Do you have any ideas on how I can combine the two?" What a marvelous question that was. I was really excited to sit down with her and go over how the two could be merged. Here is some of what we came up with:

1) As for materials, why can't a piece of woven cloth or fabric be adhered to a portion of a painting, or painted on like a canvas?

2) As for methods, a painted canvas can be cut into thin strips and rewoven.

3) As for paint methodology, a painting could be done with long thin interwoven lines of paint, much like a fabric is made.

4) As for connectivity, a painting on canvas can be cut into pieces and sewn together like a quilt or clothing.

5) Dryer lint is fabric that has been culled from the herd. Can it be assembled, as in a depiction of a scene or abstract?

6) Free association: paint = pattern and color + woven = clothing + fashion = wearable art.

7) Two words... Art quilt.

A) Reframe your intent. Sometimes, taking a new look at what you do, and restating it more specifically, is all you need to regain excitement or move to a refined path. Alex Kanevsky spoke about his series of figures in a bathroom saying, "I wanted access to the places where no one is allowed". Rather than saying that a particular series of paintings was simply figurative, he assigned a more personal, if not a little voyeuristic, intent, which narrows and focuses the body of work. Look at your existing work from a different direction and restate the intent. Figure out what you are really after and write it down.

B) Movie log line. Just like they do in presenting a movie concept... take your idea and distill your intent down to its simplest expression. Apollo 13: Problems going to the moon. Fishing for Elephants: Creativity for artists and other humans. Into the Wild: man vs nature, nature wins. Maynard Dixon: Distillation of the Southwest into form and color. Frankenstein, Terminator, I Robot, Space Odyssey 2001, The Bible: The creation turns on the creator. This reduction becomes your mantra as you make your choices and decisions.

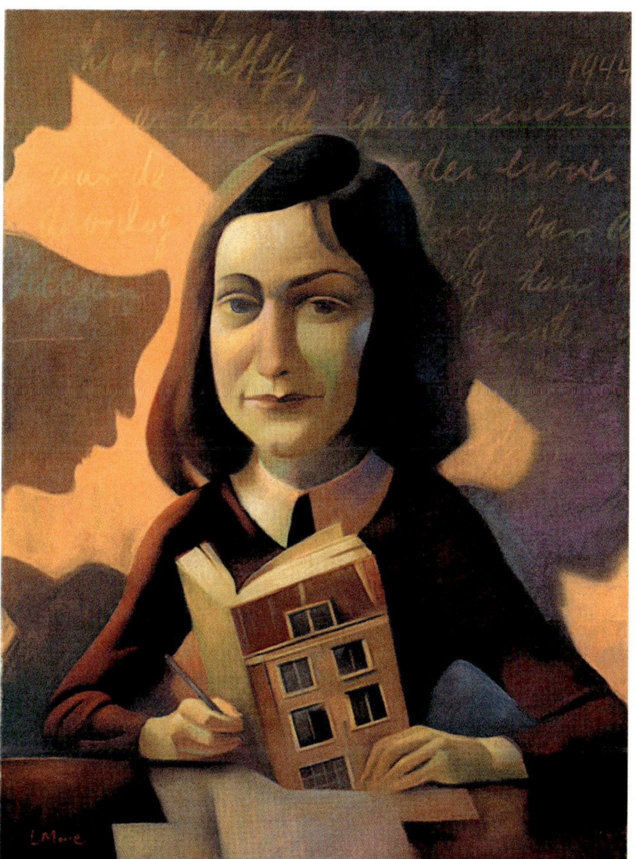

18B Movie log line

This is one story that everyone knows. But how to tell it in such a limited space? A young girl's real life experiences, hidden away in a house while trying to evade the Gestapo. 5 elements of this tragic account are carefully combined to get the story across to the viewer.

The Diary of Anne Frank, 18x24 pastel on paper.

C) Reframe your point of view. When you have an idea, but your usual way of presenting a solution won't get you there, it's time to look at the idea from a different angle. Coming up with a unique solution usually requires unique handling of the pieces-parts. Idea first and then we figure out how to make it happen. Example:

Creative person: War is such a downer... let's make a live TV war-time musical! I'm thinking Disney meets Apocalypse now.

Pragmatic person: That's never been done... for good reason.

Creative person: We have sponsors and a two-hour time slot. Figure it out.

Pragmatic person: Sure. I'll just go give the Secretary of Defense a call.

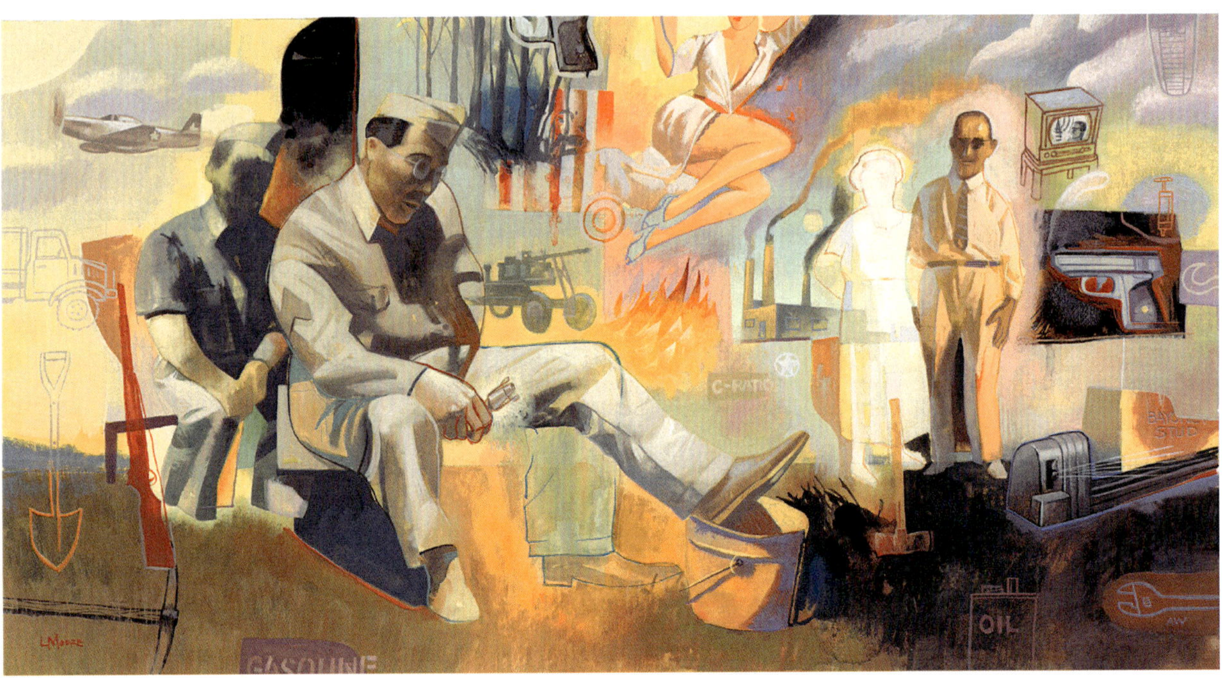

18C Reframed P.O.V.

Granted, it's not a musical, but it is a war-time piece. In order to resolve the intent of depicting this complicated statement of the effects and affects of war I had to find a different way to solve it visually. I adapted the reportage method (exercise 3H) to get all the disparate pieces to fit into one puzzle.

Dialogue, 14 x 30 in. gouache.

Think how many ways the tools here can help you move forward using your own story, your intent, in combination with a little brain power and play. This can be applied to any creative approach, any methodology, any medium or cross-platform expression forms, like music and art. One powerful method to change what you love doing is to alter how you think about your process. Rather than just painting another still life, think of it as a family portrait. Instead of a figure study, think of yourself as a visual psychologist trying to transcribe the essence of a person's temperament into two dimensions.

Combo platter

A final exercise in this VoiceFinding course is to do these buffet-style. "I'll have the 3E with the 13A please. Just put them on one plate, thank you." Pick your two favorite exercises, the ones that really ring your chimes, and put them together. You like them by themselves; you'll love them together. Just like Simon and Garfunkel and Lewis and Martin. This may seem like a little thing, but it's not. The whole idea of addressing the components individually is not only to learn how they operate individually, but also to find which ones you most respond to. These are your authentic components and, if you can find the right combo, there's no telling where you can go with it. Once you have a handle on the double combo, add a third component and stand back.

Doodles with color juxtaposition (13A) = Paul Klee

Colortan (7B) and Shape variations (7C) = Maynard Dixon

Narrative (1D) and Shape variations (7C) = Thomas Hart Benton

Mark-making (9B) and Division of space (12A) = Franz Kline

All of them combined = Joaquin Sorolla or John Singer Sargent

Convergent thinking and the inner critic

Creating the perfect bite. I sat across the table from a friend, who poked her fork through a mixture of quinoa, green things and spices laid beautifully beside an herbed filet of baked river trout, saying, "I did not get the cherries and almonds that are supposed to be in here. It was on the menu."

I may have eye-rolled a bit. She explained that she wanted the "perfect bite" with each forkful. She was paying for a nice meal and wanted to experience it to its fullest, applying her personal aesthetic with determination. I understood. It's what we do when we have highly developed individual tastes. We make decisions on how to correct or improve the fruit of the effort, whether for personal enjoyment or personal gain.

The number one question in workshops is "How do you know when the painting is done?" It should be: "How do you know when it is good?"

It's a three-part answer that incorporates a strong personal aesthetic (subjective) and the general set of factual tenets (objective) the work is founded on, along with a mindful and decisive intent. If you are operating within a known frame, as in following a traditional methodology or meeting an external need, like that of a client, then that is where the bar gets set.

If you are marching to your own drum and there is no identifiable bar, you damn well better have a powerful intent and a strong personal aesthetic in play. In other words, are you designing your own house or an office building for others to use?

The inquiry process

As the last section, **Discernment,** deals more in depth in the judgment arena, with criteria for deeming an idea worthy, the focus here will be on what makes a painting operate and how to develop the personal inquiry system, your inner critic.

No single form of critical questioning works for everything. The assessment should be based on the intent of the artist. In a mixed-media creation, drawing may not play a big part of the equation. And that's also true in pure abstraction, so traditional drawing is left to the side and the other components are of more concern.

You have to know who you are, your skill level, what you are after, and the height of the bar you are jumping over; these things should comprise your guiding beacon. If you're in a growth phase, these analytical questions may change, because what you are after has changed.

Note: Sometimes the only way to know what works best is to find out what doesn't. It's often the process of elimination that facilitates growth.

I (obviously) don't shill for a specific way of doing things when I teach. My goal is to give the students a tool set to explore and judge for themselves whether the outcome is worthy. The following list is designed for most, but not all, forms of the painted expression. By now, you understand which components are important to you, so insert them or edit them accordingly. The intrepid creatives will take this idea and mold it to their needs.

What's the big idea?
What is my motive?
What is the intent of the piece?
Verbalize the concept
Did I stick with the original idea?

How are my fundamental components?
Drawing
Value
Form
Color
Other
Are the things I've created reading as intended?

Is the reality I created consistent throughout?
Light. Is it consistent? Harmonious?
Color palette, form, interpretation
Continuity in tone or tenor of the work

Composition:
- Hierarchy. Are there dominant / subordinate relationships?
- Asymmetrical balance or dynamic symmetry
- Anything need to be diminished or strengthened in service to the whole?
- What can I edit?
- Anything in conflict, fighting for attention?
- How are my shapes?
- Any repeating or duplicates?
- Pos / neg shapes, is there variety in each?
- How does my eye flow through the piece?

Division of space:
- Is there variety of space?

Is there variety of:
- Brushwork?
- Shape / mass?
- Edge?
- Rhythm and rest?

What aspects of my existing method do I not want reinserting themselves?
- Too tight / too loose
- Over worked / overly vague
- Poorly drawn / over-explained
- Loss of form
- Overthinking / Underthinking
- Too literal / not literal enough

Which assumptions that I am basing my work on should be reconsidered?
- Have I exceeded my expectations?
- Which lessons can I take into the next painting?
- Authenticity?
- Is this true to my voice?

Here's a shocker. This is complicated because we are complicated. The reason it takes a lifetime to achieve some level of self-actualization and authenticity is because we just keep getting in our own way. Even when we know we are doing it. If we got it right every time then we'd be on to the next thing.

What I believe keeps us in the game is the search for self.

VoiceFinding: Seeking authenticity

The preceding statement is the perfect segue for this, the ultimate purpose of this book. So, without further ado, here's the big one ladies and gents, the Big Top of Progress, the Way, the Jeep CJ of learning tools, the intent locater... insert your analogy here.

This process reveals your authentic aesthetic faster than anything else I've done or taught. I've used it in every aspect of my life as a visual communicator, in my studio and in all my abstraction classes with amazing results. The students often don't even know where their creation came from, *it just showed up*. It is the creative spirit at work and you are your own muse.

The proviso -- you let go of what you know to be open to the new information and ideas that you will generate. Play as a child, without assumptions, shoulds, inner adults and old habits. Play like the wind.

Key: Finding out who you are not is a big part of discovering who you are. It involves a lot of small efforts, or multiples, to weed out that which does not fit your aesthetic and your intent. The play at first is divergent, working out toward multiple ideas and then convergent, narrowing down to a solution.

This process works for all levels. The premise is to start with the familiar and slowly venture into the unknown, concentrating more and more on the components of art-making rather than the content. If you are a staunch realist, this process may hurt a little. If you are more expressive in nature, the beginning stages may feel somewhat constraining. It should be a little uncomfortable at certain stages, if it's not you may be doing your usual process.

Everyone, from beginners to established artists, needs a comfortable starting point. Turn off the desire to solve each step to completion and concentrate on quantity. Once you've landed in piles of new directions, you can start narrowing them down, and then repeat and refine the process.

It's a little like a family tree. You start with the parent ideas. They have lots of offspring. Those offspring spawn off more. You pick the one family you like and live with them for a while, at least until they grow up and go to college.

This is an act of personal discovery. You are looking for the real you by experimenting without influence and judgment, the work you don't love is put to the side. The work you do, even if it's just a part of one of the multiples, goes into the "Like" or "Love" pile. And these pieces become the next level of offspring to inspire new lines of thought.

"Creativity is allowing yourself to make mistakes. Art is knowing which ones to keep."

- Scott Adams

At the very least, you will learn more about your process in a few days than you would in a few years. The efforts from one workshop have spawned enough studies to inspire a year's worth of work, or a new life path. This, in effect, is condensing down a few years of explorative progress into a few days, what any committed artist does over an extended course of time.

The idea isn't to turn you into an abstract artist, per se. It's to help you think more abstractly and concentrate more on what paint, shape, composition and color can do, rather than how to make a boat in water look like a boat in water. All these components are at play, no matter what kind of artist you are. For the record, you will only take these lessons back to fold into your regular way because, for change to be authentic, it should be gradual. But, you will have a better idea of who you truly are, not who you want to be like.

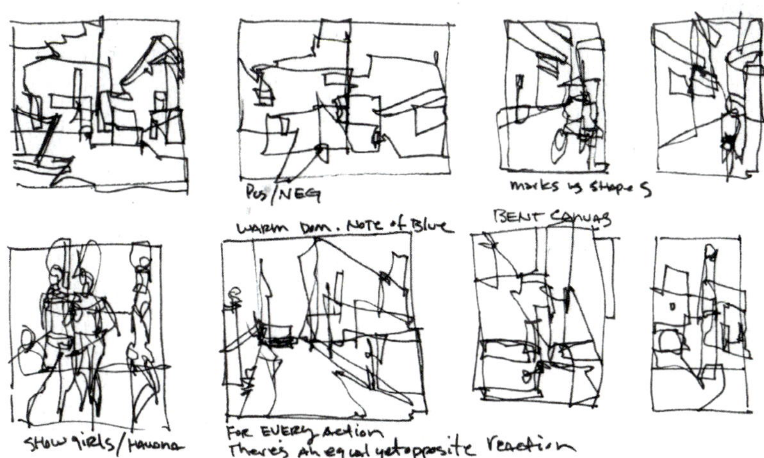

The start

Working from photos of Havana, Cuba, I used this etch-a-sketch method to break me out of my usual way of starting, which is the entire point. This is about discovery. Once you get the nature of this exercise you can play with other drawing vocabularies; thin and thick, brushy, gestural.

The start

Tools: Reference, heavy paper, pencil or fine ink pen, round watercolor brushes, black watercolor pigment and water.

1) Set up. Draw a series of boxes in which to sketch on a 9x12-ish pad. Fill the page up with six to 10 biz-card-sized rectangles of varying proportions. Don't stop until you have about 40 to 50 little boxes.

2) Working from life or reference, grab your drawing utensil, preferably a fine permanent felt-tipped pen or pencil, and start the drawing, BUT you can't lift the instrument off the paper (as in exercise #3C). It's a continuous line. Let it cross over and overlap other lines as you draw. Draw through the lines. Use whatever floats your boat to draw from... still life, photo of your favorite place, an existing painting or study, any inspiration source that speaks to you.

Be free and fast, as in gesture drawing. Concentrate on line variety. Use round and straight lines, angles and curves. Try watercolor brushes for line variety in a thin wash of black. Work on shape variety and division of space. One to three minutes per. It helps to assign key words as you work, like shape, division of space, overlap, mechanical... sensation terms like joy, lost, dream, energy, conflict.

Don't go to the next step until you have all the boxes filled. Make notes to the side about what you were doing or thinking. They will come in handy later.

Color time

Tools: Watercolor set (cheap) 10-20 colors. Get the kiddie version. A variety of watercolor brushes and water. Gouache is a great add here for its opacity.

1) Put the reference away. Use your notes to the side and memory only.

2) Begin coloring using memory and intuition. Try not to turn them into little renderings and resist the urge to look at the reference. Just **play with colors you like** and don't always color in the lines (exercise #12A), but do stay within the boxes. The first page will be the hardest, but it gets easier and more fun as you go. Experiment with layering colors and dropping wet notes into less wet passages. Work patterns of color with the lines. Make quick color ideas. Trust in your gut. Do not judge them as good or bad. That just gets in the way. Fill all the boxes up.

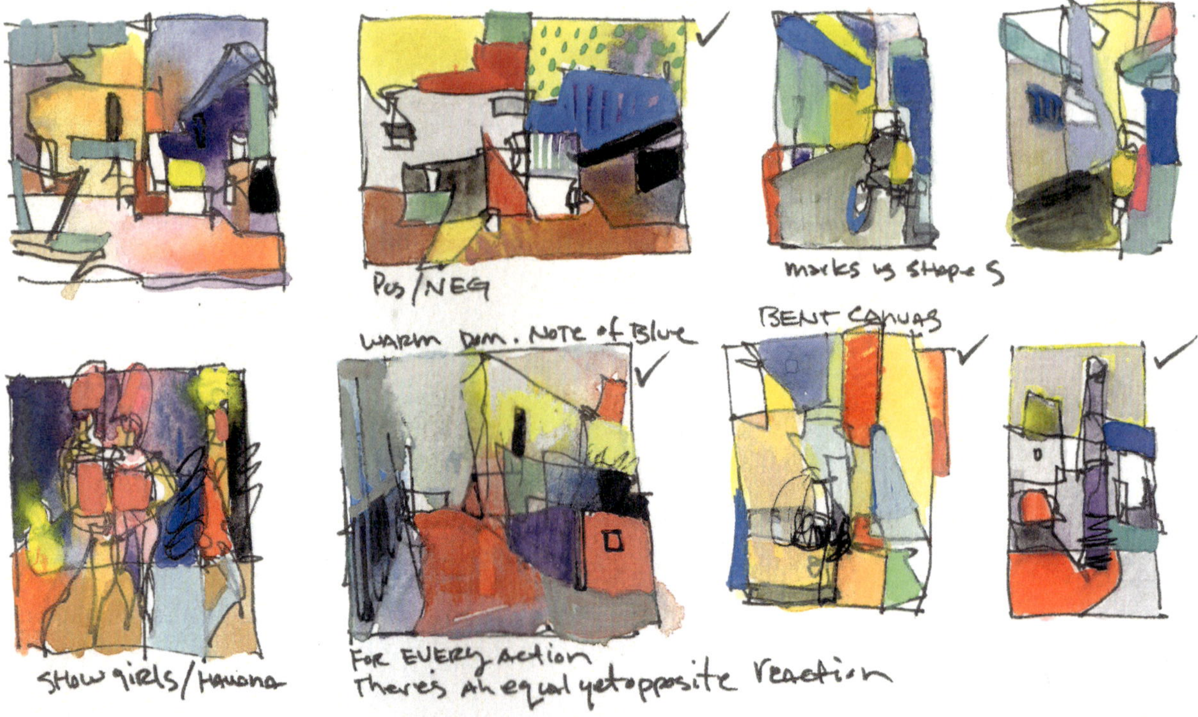

Color

Using watercolor and/or gouache, begin the color process with a random approach. We are looking for new ideas and that takes a little digging, hence the 40 or 50 small drawings. As you progress through these, your color and design ideas will evolve, take the ones that you like and apply that aesthetic to the next round. Work from your gut, these can go either toward abstraction or be modified to more realistic depictions in later rounds.

3) Review your collection of smalls. Go through, check off the ones you like the most. Don't think about why. Just go on intuition. Shoot for about 10 good ones. Go back through the 10 and pick your top three to five. You will be working from these studies. If you need to cut them out to cull them from the herd, do it. Or cover up the rejects with white copy paper.

Phase 2, multiples from your top picks.

1) What do you like about the three or so you've culled out? Palette, brushwork, raw energy, shape, pattern...any of the components. And whatever key words pop into your mind, write them down next to the small studies.

2) Take a stack of primed canvases, panels, Masonite, watercolor paper, or whatever you want to work on, all the same size, 12" x 16" or so. Tape them off into four smaller sections so your brain knows that these are just studies. Lay out your initial choices, no other reference. Using your medium of choice, work from each of your chosen phase 1 color studies, doing four versions on each canvas.

Explore your inherent color, edge, shape, brushes. Alter one component in each of the quadrants. **Focus on what feels right.** Remember the free-association exercises? This is that, only with paint, it's variations on a theme. Don't stop at four. Do as many versions as you can muster until you end up with 30 or more.

This doesn't have to be done all at once, do it over a span of two or three days, if need be. Take your time (but not too much).

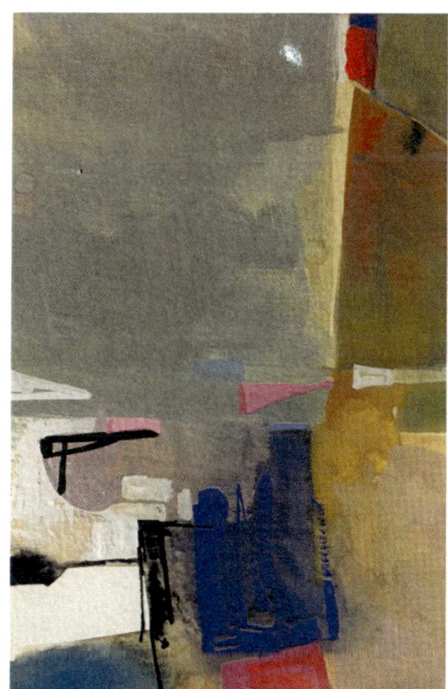

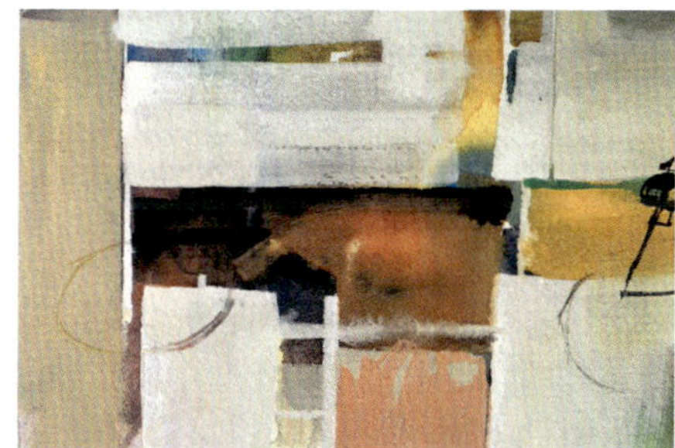

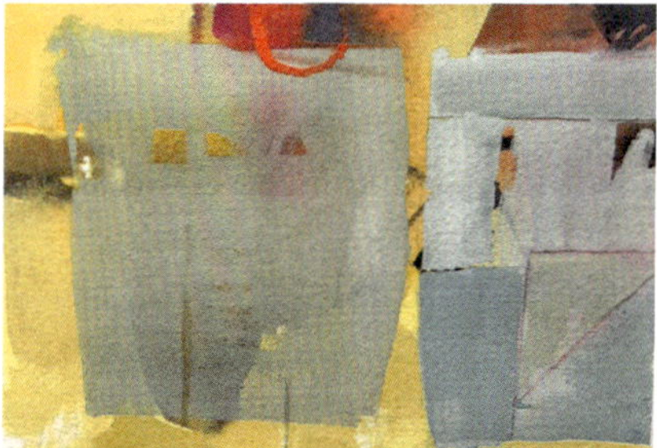

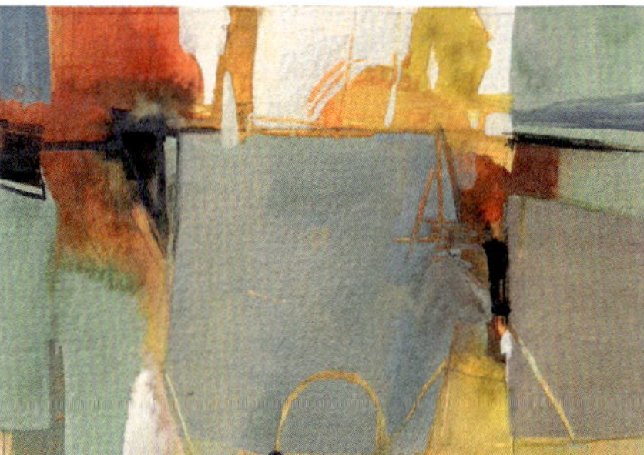

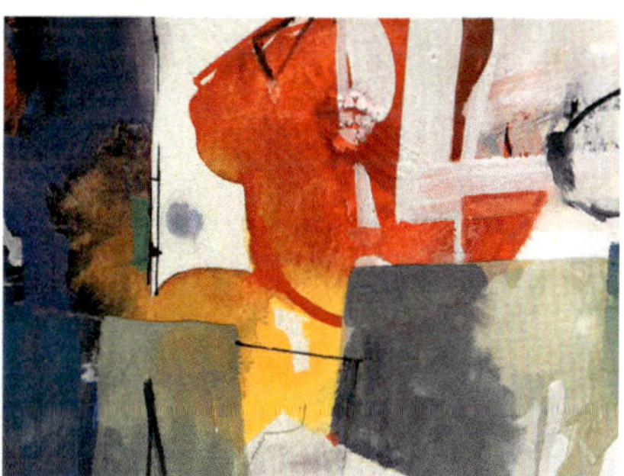

Studies from studies

Working from the first-round picks, the intent begins to unfold. Your choices should be made from the gut and this next level will be a refinement of those aesthetic decisions. More exploration and more decisions about which way to push the ideas. These 5 x 6 in. gouache studies were created with a clear movement towards abstract expression. Certain elements started showing themselves and a theme started to come to the surface.

3) From your stacks of 30 to 50 quadrants. Pick your three to five favorites, based on your gut, your personal aesthetic. These will be the foundation for the next level, the mid-sized models in your preferred medium.

Prepare 10 canvases in the 12"x16" range (not taped off), you can vary the proportions on some; square, horizontal, vertical.

Now is the time to really start finessing and focusing on the components that interest you the most. If there is narrative involved at this stage, it's okay to bring in some reference of figure, visuals, animals, ice cream cones, whatever. Small pencil sketches can assist in thinking through each idea. This is the time to play with materials, get a feel for how to layer, scrape, overlap and edit.

Get through your 10 and revisit in a day or three. If dry, rework as needed.

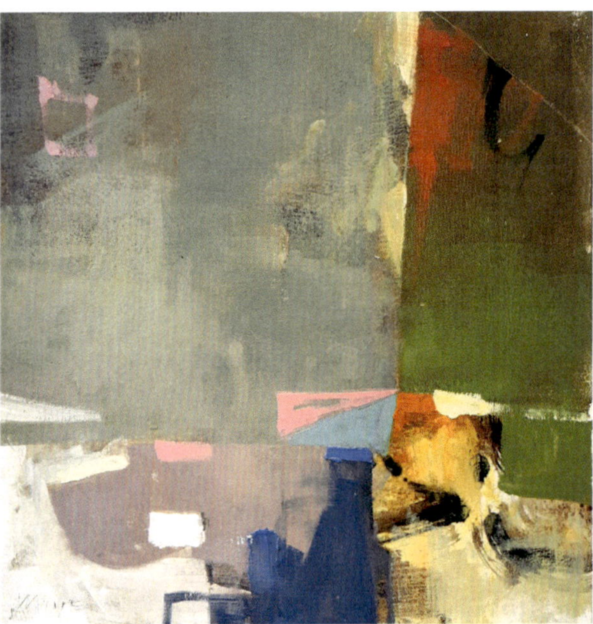

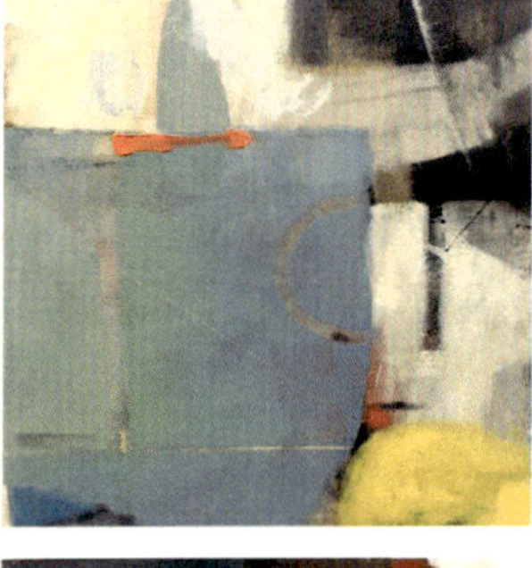

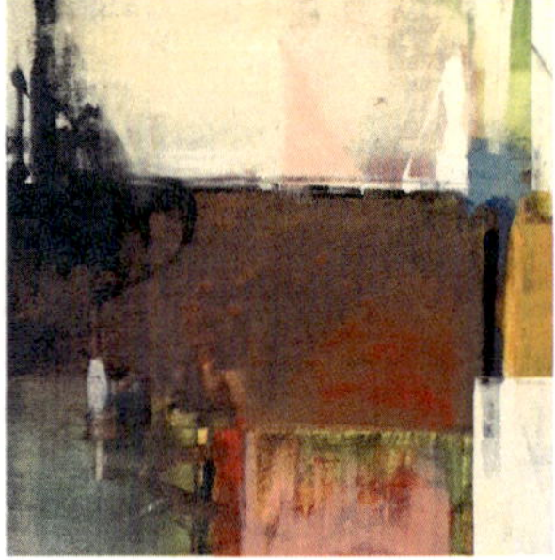

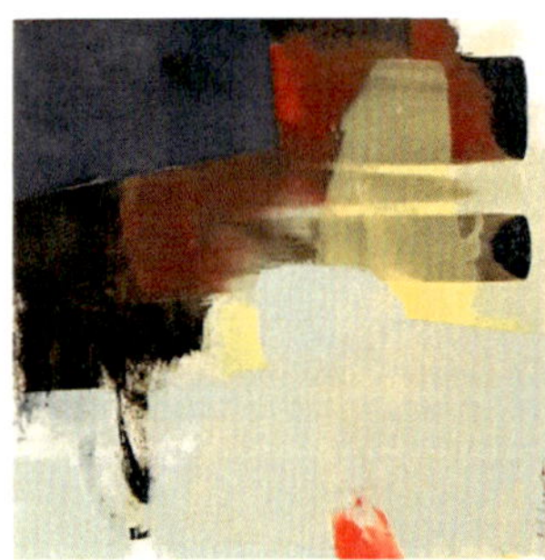

Mid-sized studies

With the ideas developed in phases one and two, it's time to apply the medium of choice in a larger format. Changing mediums changes everything. These 16 x 16 in. pieces are finished works in their own right, the ones that worked were presented along with the larger works and the ones that didn't became under layers for another effort. Acrylic, oil, cold wax, oil bar, graphite and odd tools on wood.

4) Now it's time to go big. You have completed your homework, done the hard work and really burned this process of VoiceFinding into your mind. Take some time, but again, not too much, and allow your subconscious to quietly work on these. Wait awhile for the "what if" connections to start. Take the time to think through what steps you will be using, how it will be layered, the medium and method that will best support your ideas.

Know which components you will feature and which you will not need. Know your Intent. Visualize the finished pieces, just like they do in the Olympics. Picture the gold-winning long jump in your mind. Gather your tools and paints.

Pick a size that is a little past your comfort zone, so you'll have to think a little harder and stretch the art muscles even more. This is the time for full concentration, approaching it like the final putt at the US Open. Use both sides of the brain, the logic, the objective, the mechanical and the emotional / subjective. Prepare your work space. Prepare your surface. Mix large piles of the colors you will need on a large palette, so that there is no need to waste time remixing or finding space.

From block-in to final strokes, remember that nothing is precious. Everything is just a layer and that this is only the beginning. Imagine that you will be burning the whole pile of work at the day's end, just to remove the burden of preciousness. There is no one else. There is only you and the creative effort before you, and the two of you are having a dialogue. And it IS a two-way conversation.

If you start to feel hesitant, you always have your maps to go by. The first one is always the hardest and, though they are rarely easy, they do flow more freely the more time you spend at the canvas. Funny how that works.

Don't just copy from the study, use your gut, use the force. Think of it as a jazz rendition rather than a recital. Don't just reproduce the studies, riff off of them.

Apply all the tools now at your disposal from the sections of *Connectivity, Intent, Discernment and Inner Critic* to assess, evaluate and revise. If you don't get there at the first go, fret not. We rarely do. There is always an improvement to be made, a different path to take, another thing to try.

This is what keeps us in the game, the search for the perfect solution. The realization of our greatest potential. Any master would say the true joy is in knowing that we are even in the game at all.

This, as we all are, is a work in progress. Willem de Kooning sometimes worked for years on his paintings, spending as much or more time thinking as performing the physical act of creating. And that meant ample amounts of editing, reworking, rethinking and scraping off entirely down to the bones (never underestimate the power of a good wiping out) to each work's final stage, if there is such a thing.

A painting is done when it's time to ship it.

Once you've run through this process of discovery, distillation and assessment, give yourself time to absorb what you've learned. Look through the body of work, the studies, the middle stages and the final efforts and make note of what components, materials and application processes are speaking to you.

Resist the urge to look to others for solutions or make sure you are "right."

Now, how should you fold these lessons back into your existing way? Or should you? Or is it time to move down new paths forged by your efforts. Change should be gradual, but it doesn't have to be. It's a series of decisions that only you can make.

"The reason it takes a lifetime to achieve some level of self-actualization and authenticity is because we just keep getting in our own way."

This is just the beginning. If you do end up with something worthy of exploration, stay with it for the long haul. The most notable artists have found their voice, their combination of components, and stayed with them like a long marriage. The work grows by inches, by nuance and subtleties. Methods are modified and edges polished down. As the partnership ages, the battles become less frequent and the efforts grow more graceful. You will know that you need to see it through because there is still the next hill to climb, one more package to open on Christmas to see what it holds, another story to be told. The beauty of this relationship is in its subtleties and in the dialogue of the parts

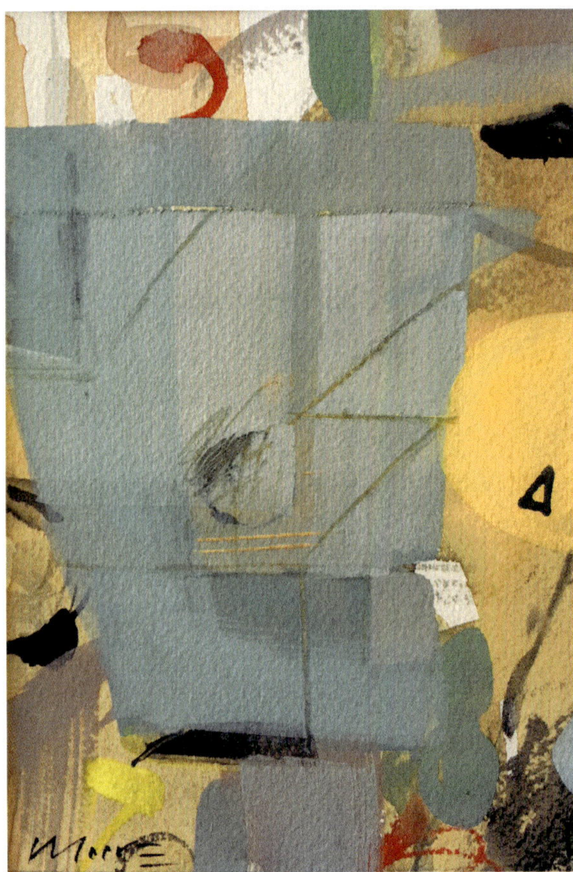

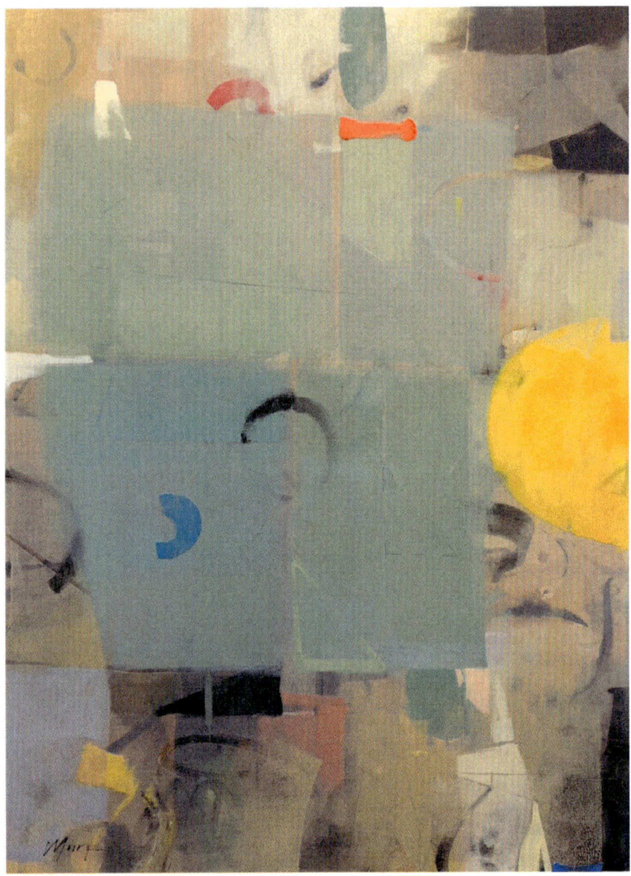

The final

Using all of the tools presented in this book of concept development, intent building, play, openness, and the creative spirit, an idea emerged. A series of 30 paintings under the umbrella theme of Newton's Third Law (a gift from my subconscious), for every action there is an equal and opposite reaction. A principle of painting that I had not yet considered.

The 3 x 4 in. study on left grew up into a 36 x 48 in. painting and an ongoing body of work.

Step #98: Repeat

This method of tiered intent and discovery can work for any mode of expression, with some adaptations. This process is never a one-and-done kind of deal. It's a way of ever-evolving growth and exploration. It's not for everyone. Many are content with the basic act of creating and making, playing the well-worn tunes, knitting the sweaters, throwing a coffee mug on the potter's wheel for the 500th time. It is a most Zen act.

There is nothing wrong with time-honored traditions or repetitive motifs, laying the artist's hand to another beautiful sunset. Often, the ones who are remembered aren't those who invented an entirely new tea pot. They simply made it their own.

Whatever your path and whatever you do, it is my fervent hope that this effort makes your efforts even a little richer, and unique to you. If you are brave, allow yourself to be open and put in the hard work, you may be lucky enough to find your authentic self, an endeavor that is about as easy as fishing for elephants.

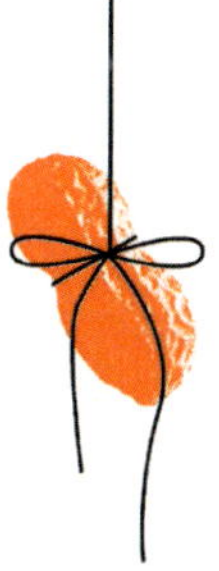

11. Case studies:

Authenticity and intent. Two very important characteristics of the unique creative voice. We know it when we see it, usually by some subtle (or not so subtle) break from the norm, a deliberate shift in one or more of the components that distinguishes the end product from the herd. So, how do these qualities present themselves in a specific work of art? More to the point, what were the creators thinking when developing these following examples of exemplary 2-dimensional visual communication?

The pieces presented here are chosen either for the artist's consistently compelling oeuvre, for the intent evident in the work or for the thought behind a piece that is seemingly unclear to the viewer, or for the conscious choices that comprise the distinctive style and voice of the art. This is more of a problem / solution discussion than an abstract philosophical one. Certainly, how the artist achieved the final outcome is important, being part of the intent, but let's look at why the choices were made.

The lessons from each are universal.

Jody Hewgill

Illustrators are just like regular artists, only they have to visually communicate someone else's content in a compelling way, work in tandem with an art director or committee, make something that the readers will understand, and do it all in a hurry. If painting were a house cat, illustration would be a room filled with tigers. Canadian artist Jody Hewgill is one of the best in the business. She's worked for magazines like Time, Rolling Stone and Playboy. She's received the highest levels of recognition internationally with the pinnacle being The New York Society of Illustrators' Gold medal, which is akin to winning gold at the Olympics. And she's won several.

Intent is foundational for any good illustrator. Having a clear, unique voice is the only way to sustain a quarter-century career. Jody's work has both. Her passion for commenting on the human condition shows in every piece, from a portrait of Johnny Depp to a rendition of Harper Lee's "To Kill a Mockingbird", telling a story is the heart of her work.

This illustration was commissioned for Entertainment Weekly's Top 10 issue to depict the movie *Before Midnight,* one part of a trilogy about a tumultuous relationship that spanned (and was filmed) over 18 years. Not only did she have to meet her own exacting standards of research, concept and execution, she had very little time to get it done and it had to be approved by the client.

An illustration of this nature has to capture the essence of the thing it represents at a glance. In order to accomplish this single-frame story, a different language is required, one that says a whole lot in a little tiny space. The use of many knives to suggest relational turmoil is not a literal device but a figurative one. The knives and wounds are shown in stark contrast with the casual posture of the two figures as they reach for each other which creates a compelling and painfully familiar story. A powerful example of juxtaposition of two unlike things that create a third idea.

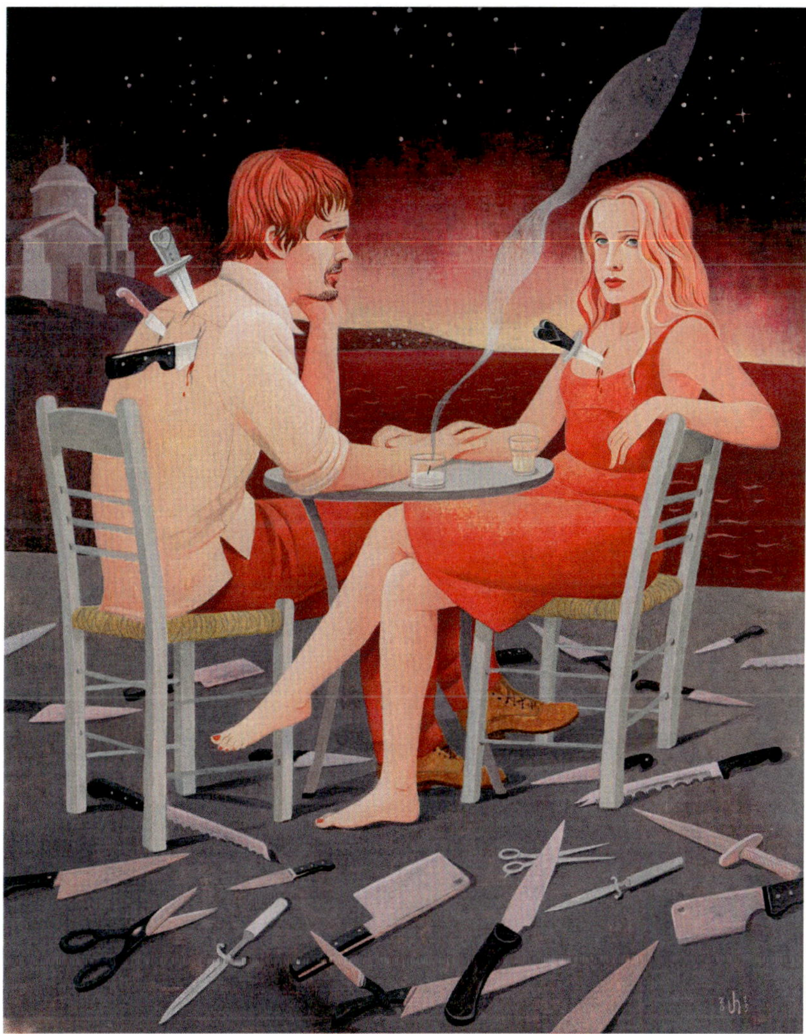

Jody Hewgill
Before Midnight
16 x 20 in. acrylic on canvas
Entertainment Weekly

I know you like to research a project thoroughly, did you watch the movie? The trilogy?

JH: I had seen the first in the series "Before Sunrise" many years ago, so I was familiar with the narrative and the relationship of the characters. When I was given the assignment, I watched "Before Midnight" and then felt compelled to watch "Before Sunset". I'm an "all in" type of person.

The message is clear in this piece, the trauma of relationship has passed and yet they're still connected. How do you know when the concept can be interpreted by the viewers correctly?

JH: I strive to make the concept evident to the art direction team, and hopefully their reaction reflects how viewers will interpret the image. Trying to maintain objectivity is difficult when you are an image maker, so I think it's important to avoid becoming attached to the preciousness of the work. My process involves doing several preliminary drawings in a sketch book to visually work out a variety of directions. These are very loose drawings to flesh out the ideas. Then I step away and look at them again with a fresh eye, and ask myself the question: Does this image serve the project, or is this self-serving? I usually run my sketches past my husband, Balvis Rubess, prior to making my final selection to develop into tighter linears to present to the client. I find it extremely valuable to receive honest feedback, even if the answer means my going back to the drawing board at midnight.

The color palette is unusual for you, was there a conscious choice behind it or was it more of a feeling?

JH: The color palette of my work is dictated by the mood I want to project. There is a process to how I select color: I begin by highlighting what are the key elements and parameters of the project. In this case, art director Kory Kennedy didn't have any specific parameters for this assignment, which was wonderful. The essential factors in conveying this narrative was the midnight seaside in Greece and passion. I don't recall painting a figure in pink tones prior to this piece, it felt like an unconventional approach for a commissioned portrait (double portrait in this case), but I boldly decided to follow my intuition. A bit of serendipity occurred when creating the colour comps for myself; the placement of Céline and Jesse's figures create a heart shape. Balvis pointed this out to me after I had completed the sketch, so I purposely kept the figures in a red palette to emphasize their union.

You can see more on the development of this piece and Jody's amazing body of work at jodyhewgill.com

Chip Kidd

A prolific and versatile book jacket designer, his work appears on covers from Alfred A. Knopf, Scribner, HarperCollins and Penguin Random House, for writers like Michael Crichton, John Updike and David Sedaris. He has consistently been the most recognizable name of his craft for decades. If you are a graphic designer, Chip Kidd is a rock star.

His passion for the comic arts is well known. In addition to designing countless covers for books on the subject, he also oversees comic book covers at Pantheon.

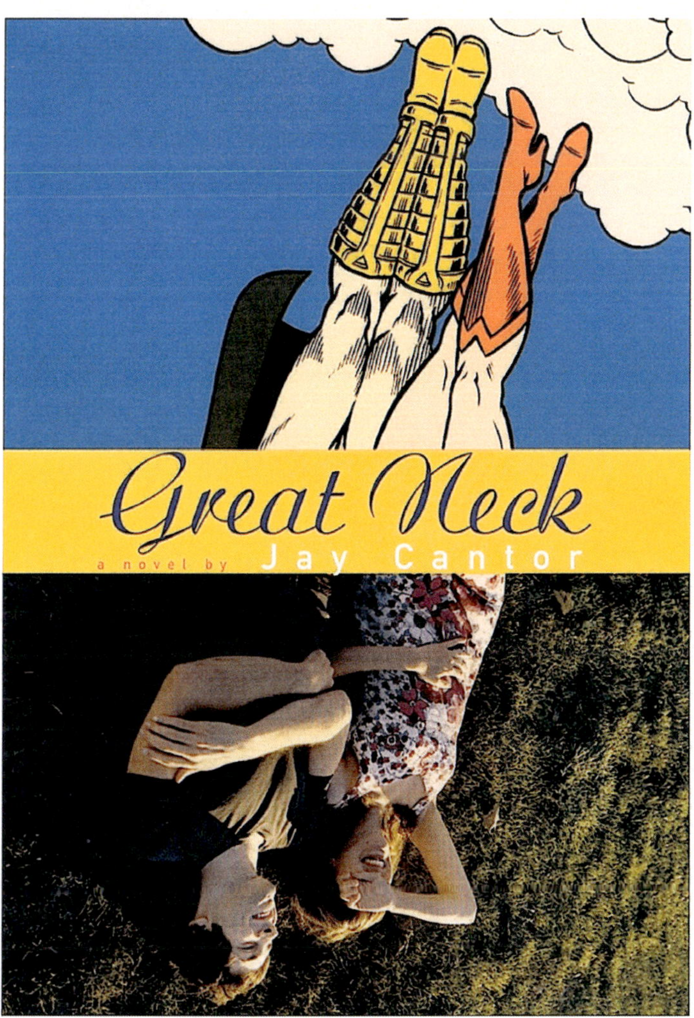

Chip Kidd
***Great Neck* by Jay Cantor**
published by Alfred A. Knopf 2003

Mr. Kidd is not a follower of trends. If anything, he intentionally moves away from them (the definition of authenticity), employing the words of a college instructor who told him, "Look around at what the other students are doing and do something different."

While his work is thoughtful and provocative, he does not consider himself an artist, but a designer. The work he creates is not for personal expression, but to tell an author's story quickly, and get a potential reader to crack open the book and read it.

A book jacket has to communicate with great brevity the nature of what it's covering; sardonic wit, dark forces, dinosaur thriller, poetry or Batman compendium. Mr. Kidd's work has to satisfy his own aesthetic, art directors, editors, marketing people, the author and, ultimately, the readers.
It ain't for the faint of heart.

The complicated epic novel by Jay Cantor, based around growing up Jewish in the 60's and 70's, has a lot of sub-plots; the Civil rights movement, friends turned into comic book superheroes, the loss of a loved one, a murder mystery, even a hint at the paranormal... how does one choose to encapsulate all of this visually? A book cover has less than a handful of elements to communicate as much as possible: the title, the font, the main image and the color palette. Oh, and it's 6"x9." These limitations mean that every choice is critical. A bad solution is like a bad toupee, you know it when you see it, the good ones are seamless and compelling.

This cover gets its power from the duality presented in a happily-resting-in-the-grass couple whose inverted torsos mysteriously transform behind the title banner into comic book superheroes. Real life meets fantasy. So, I asked Mr. Kidd why these particular choices were made.

The simplest ideas are sometimes the hardest to pull off, were there a lot of variations considered in fonts, color, and placement?

CK: Not that I remember. The basic concept was as you see it, the logistical issues were about commissioning an illustration that lined up with the photo (the photo came first).

There are a lot of plot lines in the book, why this direction over, say, the civil rights/activist angle?

CK: Because this approach was visually more interesting? We're talking 14 years ago (!!). Obviously, the comic book angle struck a chord with me.

Your cover references a plot line of Great Neck "characters turned comic-book heroes". Was this a "solves itself" solution or did you go through multiple iterations?

CK: The trick with something like this is to create images of what are obviously comic book characters (or the lower halves of them) that do not violate the copyrights of any existing characters. So, it's not like we could show the legs of Batman and Wonder Woman. We had to come up with something unique, which is not easy.

To view Chip Kidd's amazing and diverse portfolio, visit chipkidd.com

Jon Redmond

Jon Redmond is a painter's painter. Receiving a 4-year certificate from the Pennsylvania Academy of Fine Arts and an MFA from the University of Delaware, Jon has spent his career seeking out the beauty in the everyday. Jon says, "My main goal is to make an interesting object." Another way of saying that is what you paint is not as important as how you paint it, a conviction that is true in cases where there is no preconceived message in the work.

Jon prefers not to work from sketches, because, as he states, "I feel it saps the energy from my paintings." Working alla prima on site, he starts by laying large masses down, preferring to do the searching and struggling while he paints. The struggle, the search is what makes the painting become interesting. He goes on to suggest that, the process of searching lines would restrict his painting in a negative way by dictating where things are going to happen in the beginning of the process.

Lines, he feels, tend to make you pay attention to the wrong visual relationships. It's a lazy solution to a visual question, creating a barrier between color relationships.

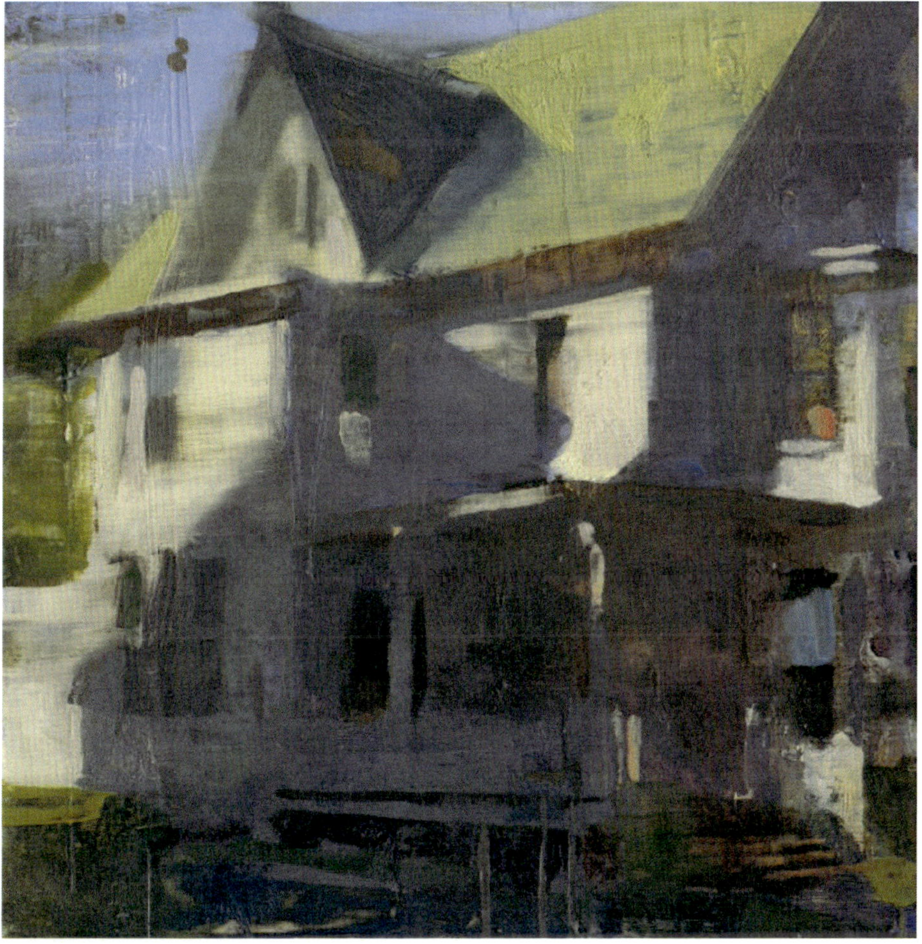

Jon Redmond
Evening in Westchester
10 x 10 in. oil on board, 2013

When I spoke with Jon, he had this to say about his process, "even after 30 years of painting, I'm never quite sure of what it is that I am doing. I start putting paint down and building the image and, in most cases, that is unsatisfactory. So, I then start breaking the image down in an attempt to figure out what doesn't need to be said or what needs to be subtle. I keep going back and forth with this building/destroying process until it starts to feel right.

Our eyes have the ability to see a lot of information; too much, I think, for a good painting.

The key is to make sure I talk about the similarities as well as the contrasts. The contrasts are much easier. Our brains are wired to notice them, but seeing how various elements can be very similar, or even made the same, is a much harder problem. Our brains want to compartmentalize everything, in an effort to try to make sense of it all. As an artist, I need to fight that need.

It is like writing a poem. You need to figure out how to get a lot of information across with just a few perfect words."

When viewing this piece, as in all of his work, there is a dreamy familiarity to it. The places and objects he paints somehow resonate with the same frequency as hazy memories of the past. One way he achieves this is through picking random edges to focus on, allowing the rest to fall into the soft distance. His work, while representational, breaks from the physics of the scene. Another compelling characteristic in his painting is his use of color, how he builds it in broken layers, and the off-kilter warm to cool, flat nature of it. His focus is more on value and color relationships than getting a true-to-life depiction.

Jon Redmond's work can be viewd at jonredmond.com

Alex Kanevsky

Russian-born graduate of, and now instructor at the Philadelphia Academy of Fine Arts, recipient of a Pew Fellowship, Mr. Kanevsky strives to create in the uncomfortable liminal space of uncertainty. His belief -- that the act of creativity is to venture into the unknown. It's what happens when you make something new. Though his work is realist-based, his narratives are born from a merging of figure, feelings and memories. He works in multiple layers, often completely obliterating the start or the middle, sometimes weeks of effort, chasing after only a feeling of what the painting should become. His intent is to have no preconceived intent. The painting finds him, ultimately creating what he views as a kind of Rorschach blot, rather than a painting, to trigger an emotional response.

In an Art and culture lecture in 2012 he said, "Paintings should speak on their own, I'm not a big fan of labels and explanations."

Though he has no clear vision of the outcome in the beginning, he does, at times, have an idea that guides the process. He explains, "(I began a) series of figures in a private environment...the private space means that you are excluded from being there." A much more refined narrative than simply depicting a figure in a bathroom.

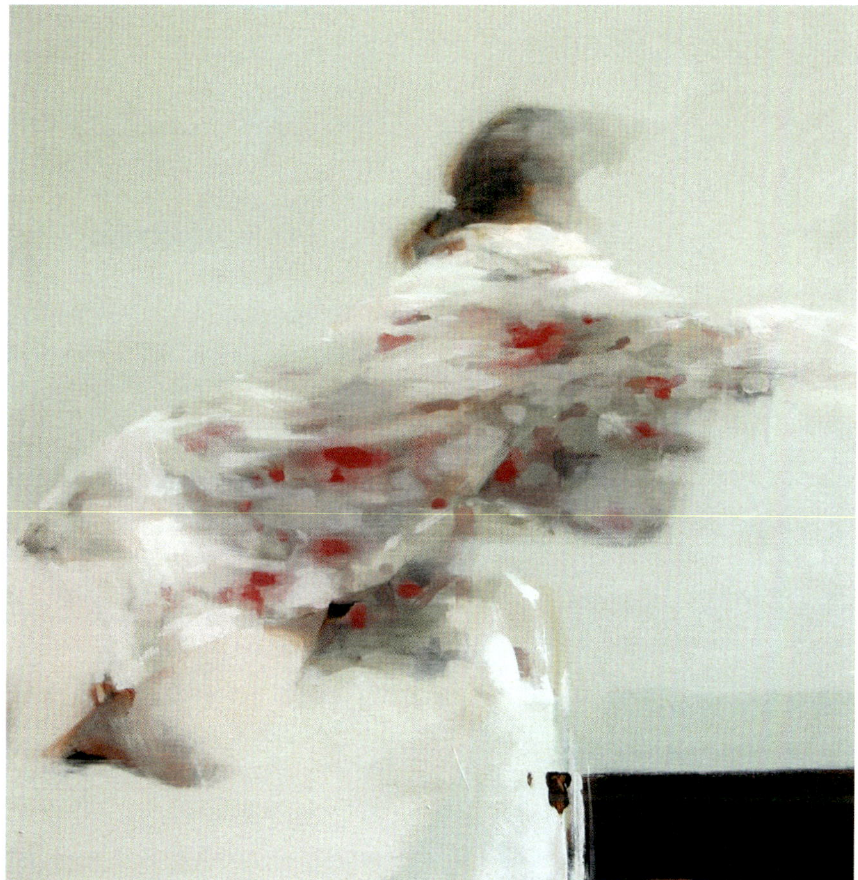

Alex Kanevsky
K.B. with Kimono
24 x 24 in. oil 2005

The featured painting is another unusual take on viewing the figure, "This particular approach came out of observing children, when they talk to adults they tend not to look them in the eye. They are more interested in focusing on... a part of the clothing. So, I tried to do a portrait this way by focusing on the side of her dress." This higher-order system of thought greatly informs the outcome and reframes the way he, and by extension – we -- view the figure.

While many of us prefer the comfort of a known outcome, Mr. Kanevsky believes that "art exists in (the) gray area between your competence and your incompetence ...and that requires openness to experimentation and at the same time a certain ruthlessness with your work."

Please go to somepaintings.net to view Alex Kanevsky's work and make sure you scroll down to the progression series and watch a painting develop.

Scott Christensen

There are only a handful of landscape painters in the last 50 years who are as adept and as influential as Scott Christensen. Through his work and his teaching, he has inspired hundreds of budding artists, giving them a tool set to foster thoughtful evolution. He exemplifies three critical and rare characteristics of the mature artist -- passion, humility and nuance.

His talent has been perfected through determination, with an almost obsessive drive to achieve the elusive consummate solution. He attained *unconscious competency* years ago, but, because of his constant search, he is perpetually honing the blade. Much like the 7th- degree black belt in martial arts who is working towards that 8th-degree, his study is now on a micro-level of finessing an already impressive ability.

This recent work, titled *Raining light,* presents a compelling example of two components of creating powerful imagery -- surface and metaphor as a thematic trigger. In his experiments with surface building through layers and layers of pigment and color relationships reinforced with the paint thickener cold wax, the painting gradually emerged. As the work progressed, as Scott puts it, "the textural marks in the surface prompted the notion of raining light." Once the intent formed up, his final steps maintained this clear direction. I would call that the creative spirit in action.

The result is a surface topography that is juxtaposed against the extremely sensitive transitions of color temperature and value. A push and pull between the illusion of distance and the dimensionality of surface. The viewer is both drawn in and pulled back by the vibration of the two devices.

A big shift can show up on a small level, giving even the most experienced creator new inspiration and insight into the existing process.

Scott's beautiful work can be found at christensenstudio.com

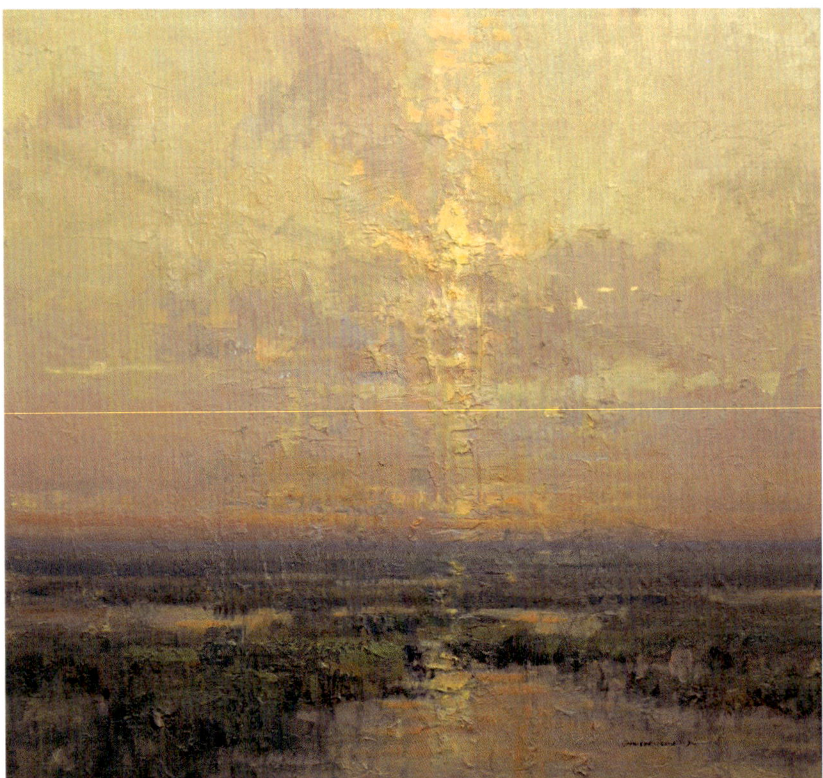

Scott Christensen
Raining light
32 x 30 in. oil and cold wax on linen, 2017

Peggi Kroll Roberts

There is no one better at distillation than Peggi Kroll Roberts. Her small works in gouache and oil harken back to the genre paintings of Edward Pothast and John Singer Sargent, but with a much more contemporary edge. Beneath her seemingly simple constructions of beach-goers under rainbow umbrellas, or white clad figures playing bocci ball on a green field, is a highly-refined understanding of color and form.

While other artists may present perfectly proportioned and rendered, soft brushy-edged depictions of the human figure, hers are interpreted in a graphic manor, pitting a stark cut-out feel against delicate color variations within each structure. This is her superpower. Not only does this unique approach not look like everyone else's, it puts the work in the penumbra zone between realist and abstract. Her art epitomizes authenticity.

I asked Peggi a few questions about her work:

What excites you in a subject?

PKR: The figure. I love painting the figure and fabric, the way the clothes press against the flesh to suggest what lies underneath. The tension poles of light and shadow. I spent a few years as a fashion illustrator and I'm enthralled by the movement, color, and plane shifts of a figure in strong light. I haven't been able to get excited about the landscape unless there is something in it like a chair.

You've been at this a while and it seems you continue to simplify more and more, how do you know when you've gotten there?

PKR: I hope I never "arrive" because there is so much more to explore. There is so much to learn and in order to get to the intuitive response, you have to put in the time.

Which components of painting interest you most?

PKR: Line, shape, hard cut-out edges, and color. I like hard edges and I don't intentionally soften them because that can become a crutch and a way to cover poor drawing.

Ever thought about going large-scale with these?

PKR: Oh yes, though, I haven't quite figured out how to keep the freshness of the small sketches. I'm working on that.

For a look of Peggi's work and that of her husband, Ray Roberts, go to Krollroberts.com

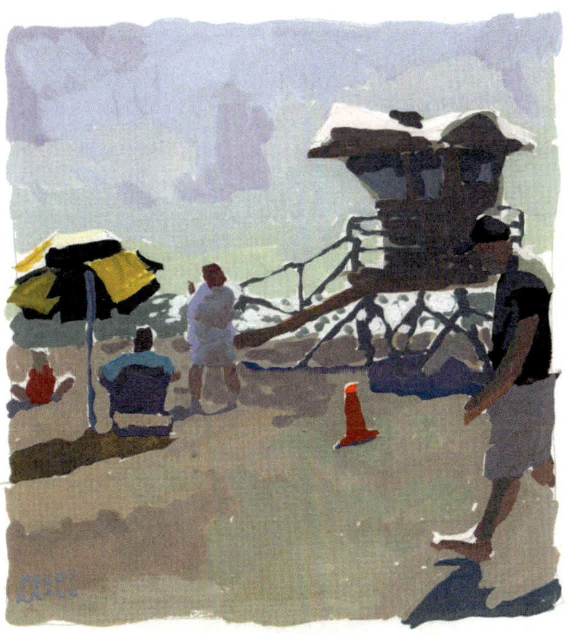

Peggi Kroll Roberts
Late afternoon, Huntington Beach
9"x10" gouache on paper

John Singer Sargent

Arguably one of the most gifted and facile painters of the last several centuries, there is not a realist on the planet who doesn't revere his skill. Not only could he draw lights-out; his technical orchestration of paint appears effortless, the result of a philosophy of scraping or blurring out whatever he didn't get right and starting over from scratch... until he did.

But his real superpower is in composition, whether a figure in a landscape or a portrait of the well-to-do, he pushed the envelope of painting anatomy, placing key parts of the story in the outer boundaries of the frame or moving important figures back into the shadows instead of front and center. Inspired by the work of the Spanish artist, Diego Velazquez, he worked tirelessly through study and sketches (multiples) to imbue the work with the subtle psychology of relationship and stature. The end results contradicted the traditional way these things were done at the time.

In addition, he intentionally did not use every pigment available to him. In contrast to his contemporary Claude Monet, who would be considered more of a colorist by comparison, Sargent regularly used a more limited earthy palette of cadmium yellow, vermilion and Mars red; both alone and mixed, madder, viridian and emerald green, ultramarine or cobalt blue, ivory black, sienna, and Mars brown.

I say intentional, because he clearly was not interested in chasing color, his work in every case was more an expression of value and warm / cool relationships than getting the exact coloration. This same approach to color also shows up in his watercolors. It's an intent decision that allowed more focus on the things that were important to him in a painting.

If I were stranded alone on a desert island and could pick only one companion to live out my years with it would be this painting. It is a masterpiece of psychological dynamics. Through Sargent's unconventional placement of the siblings, we know all we need to know about them. We know who the darling is, the insolent child, the pleaser and the loner. We know they are privileged and dysfunctional. The odd contradiction of spartan space and oversized Japanese vases suggests a rift between being taken care of and being cared for. Sargent really knew these people and it shows. It is a full novel in two dimensions. Interestingly, none of the girls in this painting ever married and the two oldest suffered emotional problems in later years.

An important consideration in viewing these more developed ideas is that every single measure -- space, object and mark -- is thoughtfully applied. Every decision, like the way the rug separates the youngest child from the rest, is made with clear and unfailing intent.

If you really want to be depressed and put in your place, go to johnsingersargent.org

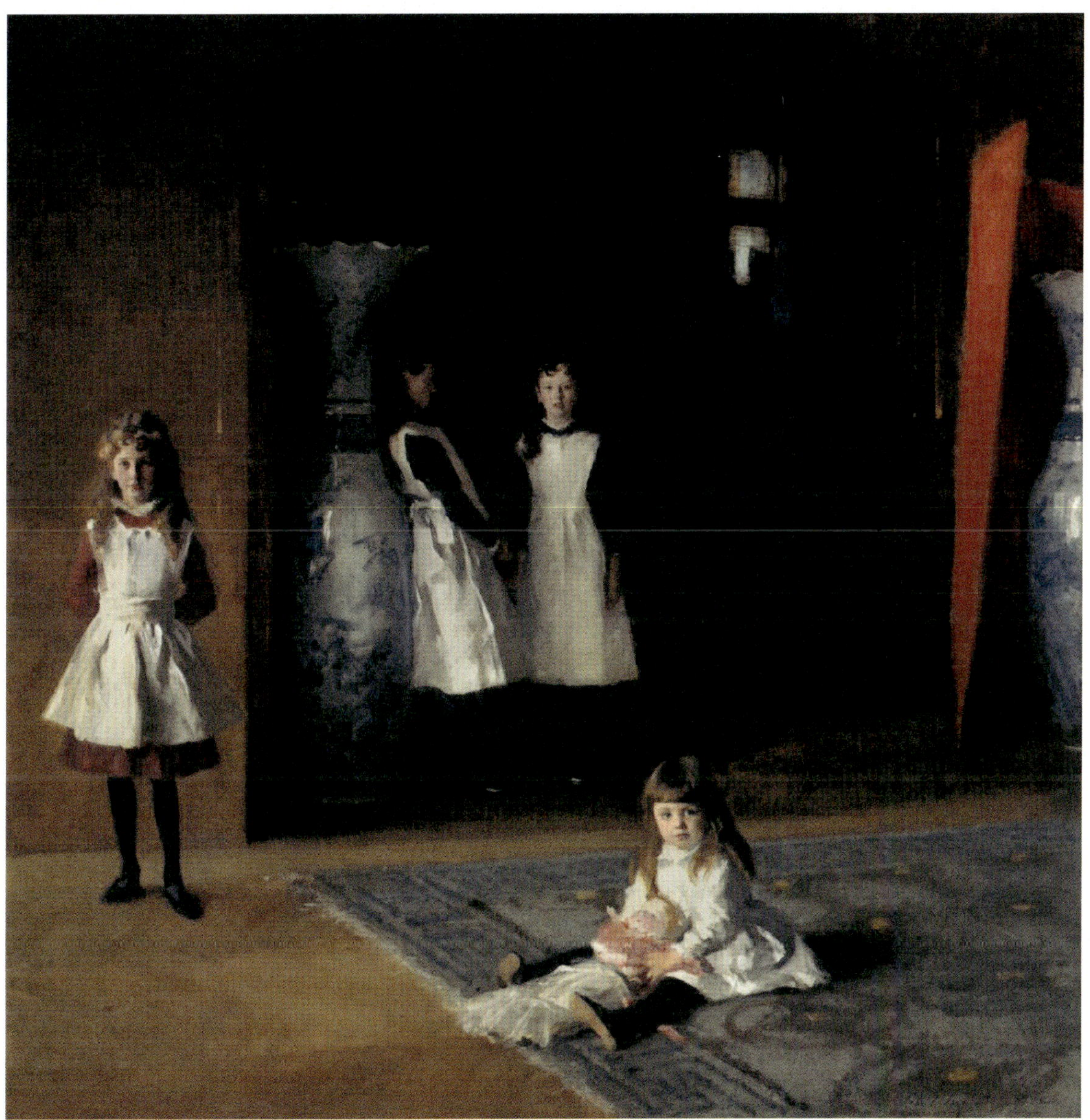

John Singer Sargent
The daughters of Edward Darley Boit
87.6 x 87.6 in. oil on canvas, 1882
Museum of Fine Arts, Boston

Ann Gale

A highly regarded figurative painter (a Guggenheim Fellowship recipient), Ann Gale is one of those artists' artists whom you hear people speak of with quiet reverence. Ask a couple of painters worth their salt who they dream of having on their walls and her name will come up. Though she deals primarily with the head and torso as content, a portrait artist she is not. Rather than developing a likeness, she is after a personal and intimate read of the subject, as she puts it, "every person is shockingly complex, both visually and psychologically."

She arrives at this through the quietly-woven energy of her brushwork, which is both unnerving and soothing at the same time, a contradiction of dramatic movement and soft near-neutral color transitions that conjure up a raw, yet mixed emotional response in the viewer. There is more left unsaid than is clearly stated, as one might find in the more conventional figurative or portrait paintings. Her message seems to exist between the marks, like the white of the page poking through a halftone photo in a magazine. Her paintings are just like the subjects, they are complicated.

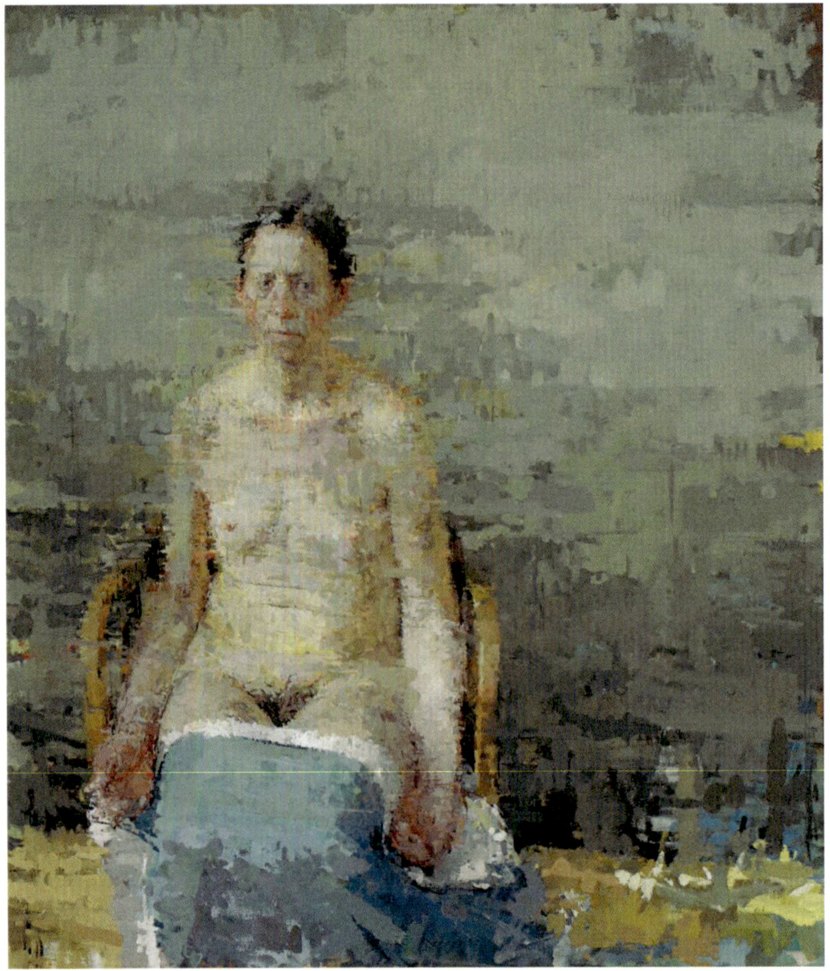

Ann Gale
Rachel with blue
48 x 42 in. oil on canvas 2012

Her process involves assessing what the painting is doing and reacting to its latest iteration. The search is as much about the life of the painting as the life of the subject. Her work is a dialogue between creator and creation; she moves, it speaks, she listens and reacts accordingly.

An interesting thing to note is the lack of defined edges in the work, the only ones visible being found in the hard notes themselves. This duality creates a bit of visual irony, the artist's hand comes to the fore while the actual subject moves vaguely in and out of focus. And if you know the painting process at all, you can tell these aren't done in one sitting. She spends a lot of time trying to pry out the psychology of the individual.

You can more of see Ann's work at dolbychadwickgallery.com

Gregory Manchess

Every craft has its gods and legends. And in the middle-earth realm of illustration, Gregory Manchess is one. A contemporary painter whose skill, work ethic, process and narrative ability are about as close to the Golden Age of illustration (think N.C. Wyeth, Howard Pyle, Dean Cornwell) as anyone has come in the last 50 years. Having lived in that world for a long time, I was always in awe of his work. A master storyteller, he has created compelling images for National Geographic, Omni magazine, Playboy, Tor Books and the US Postal Service, not to mention a handful of gold and silver medals from the prestigious Society of Illustrators in New York.

This is as much a story of faith, commitment and implementation as it is about intent. *Above the Timberline* is a science fiction storybook written and illustrated by the artist with 123 paintings across 240 pages. The original length of 300 pages of story had to be whittled down to 30. It took seven years. The last person I know to put that much effort into a single project was a pharaoh.

The thing about illustration is this: It has to communicate. This is the primary intent of the majority of illustration work. It must be clear, it must be compelling and it must be well-crafted. Not only are the standards of the artist involved, there are clients and clients' clients and, not to forget, the target audience for the work. While the publisher (Simon & Schuster) was the client for this project, they want what the artist wants, a captivating visual essay.

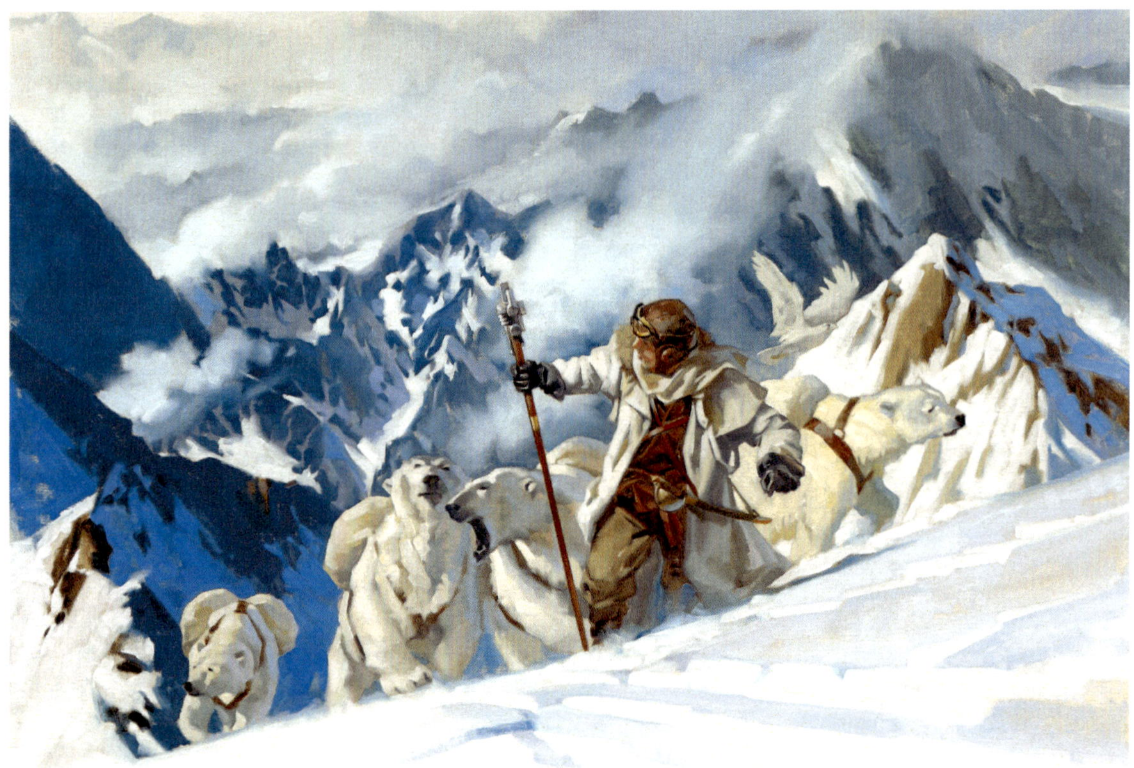

Gregory Manchess
Above the timberline
44 x 18 in. oil on linen, 2017

This example of creativity in action is the opposite of some of the others. Both the visuals and written story involved a lengthy series of edits and revisions, perfecting and simplifying each thumbnail, sketch, and final until they meshed in the most intriguing way possible.

The storyline is set in a future Earth, which has shifted axis, and the snows have fallen for 1500 years. A courageous son sets out to find his lost father and a lost city. Where do these images come from? The mind of the artist. Greg employed extensive research on the arctic, polar bears, lead zeppelins and hybrid-vintage diver snow suits for the bad guys.

Once the publisher bought in, there became yet another hurdle: the deadline. Fortunately, Mr. Manchess is no stranger to these things. And, as they say in the biz, nothing inspires like a deadline.

You can read the story of how this project progressed at muddycolors.com, or you can purchase a hard copy or an e-copy from amazon.com and immerse yourself in the kind of courage it takes to set out on such a journey. Most people break out in a cold sweat just tackling one painting. Could you imagine facing a project of this scope?

To see Greg's full portfolio, go to manchess.com

Richard Diebenkorn

Richard Diebenkorn is widely considered one of the dominant forces of 20th-century Abstract Expressionism and the Bay Area Figurative movement. His seminal *Ocean Park* series, created from 1967 to 1988, spans 20 years and 145 paintings. At first glance, these large-scale abstracts seem to be based on nothing other than geometric arrangements, but nothing could be further from the truth.

Each work was based on interpretations of the hills, streets, and architecture of the area surrounding his studio in Santa Monica, California. More specifically, like the French Impressionist Claude Monet, he was interested in light and its effect on the subjects he worked from. He just put a more geometric spin on it. Once you know the intent behind the work, you can almost see the thing he was basing each painting on; bending streets, arching hills, the mid-day Pacific waters, hints of aerial perspective.

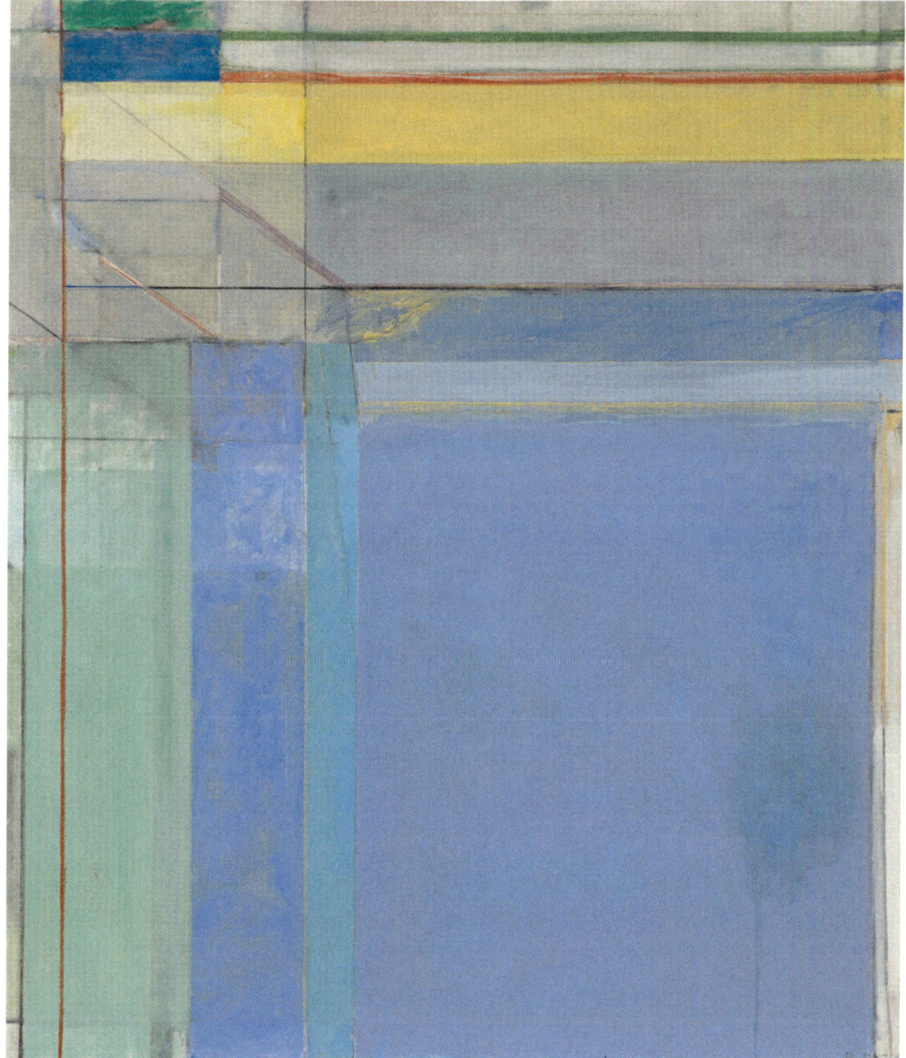

Richard Diebenkorn
Ocean Park #79
93 x 81 in. oil and charcoal on canvas 1975

Philadelphia Museum of Art, Purchased with a grant from the National Endowment for the Arts and with funds contributed by private donors, 1977 © Richard Deibenkorn Foundation

His open, airy compositions offer the history of the work, the decisions, and revisions made over the extended period spent on each canvas, lines and drips left in and only partially scumbled-over, inviting the viewer into his process. The slightly pastel primary-secondary palette almost emits the light he worked to capture. His use of large flat shapes filled with the hum of vibrating color, countered by thin lines of black and bright tones feels as much like music as paint. In fact, he frequently listened to classical music while he worked.

Diebenkorn's two great skills of hierarchy and division of space are at play in this painting. If you think of each piece as having weight or energy, there is a careful balance between all of the parts in the structure. The larger segments carry less visual weight and the smaller more.

The deep cobalt and green rectangles in the upper left corner present the dominant energy, especially when pitted against the strong yellow panel and the red zip. The balance is created between these components in juxtaposition to the larger pastel blue and teal forms. The eye travels like a bee, landing on one colorful square, staying awhile and then on to the next.

Removing one piece of the puzzle would cause an imbalance in this carefully-crafted composition.

The entire oeuvre of Richard Diebenkorn can be found at diebenkorn.org

Jeff Matz, Lure Design Inc.

The world of visual communication is vast and varied. There are a lot of messages and a lot of people to get the messages to. Graphic design was my method of choice for many years and the most intriguing part of being a designer was how malleable we needed to be. One moment it was a Victorian print package for a hotel restaurant, then a Swiss grid annual report and on to a packaging project for Mexican salsa. In order to be good at it, we needed to have a diverse library of visual languages and be able to speak them all fluently. Intent was the driver for every single project.

Jeff Matz, a partner at the graphic design firm Lure Design Inc. in Orlando, has been at the top of my watch list as long as I've known him. The thoughtfully crafted simplicity of his work, compelling imagery and amazing type skills (now a lost art) is as much art as it is design. Where it really shines is in his creation of gig posters for bands like Wilco, Nine Inch Nails and Dave Matthews.

A gig poster not only announces upcoming music events, but it's also a memento for avid concert-goers. Because of the nature of the poster and its limited use, the production numbers are low. The easy way out would be to make a few ink-jet prints on heavy paper, but Jeff chooses to use silkscreen as his medium. Much like painting, you have to know the inks, understand how they operate when layered, and have a good idea how they will look before the hard work of pulling screens begins. Within this process is a lot of room for mistakes, which is what Jeff looks for.

"Screen printing is a pretty arcane process, but I love that it's so hands-on. The final product is so tactile... I love the accidents that happen."

This is an intensely personal form of visual communication. How do you transmit the nature of a band? What do you say? Jeff's primary intent is to create an image that fans can use to relate to a specific song or album title of the band. This is usually his starting point.

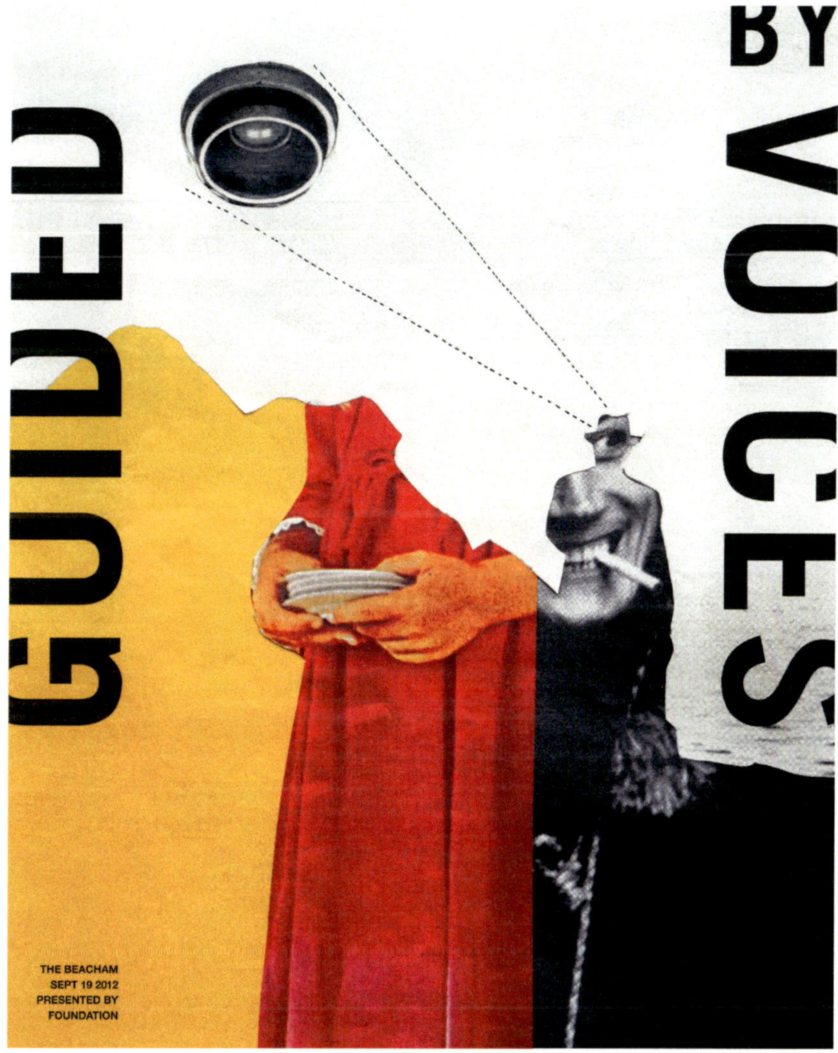

Jeff Matz
Guided by voices
Collage and digital, 2012

A musician in his own right, it was an extra pleasure to create for one of his favorite bands, Guided by Voices. Jeff said, "Thinking it would resonate with the band's fans, I decided to try my hand at collage as an homage to Robert Pollard's work (the band's singer/songwriter). Pollard does collage for many Guided By Voices projects. This may not be so much problem solving, but my intent with gig posters is to be pretty direct... The album they were touring on at the time (2012) was "Class Clown Spots a UFO."

As this is a more self-expressive form of mass communication, there are scant parameters for this kind of project. Jeff goes on to say, "I usually have some nugget of an idea. But often I just start designing, find bits and pieces, put them on the page, and let it happen organically. Usually, there's a moment when you discover a twist that brings the piece alive. I just try to work it till that happens."

Sounds like art to me.

His choice to place the band name at the periphery of the poster, what is called *activating the edge* is not just unconventional. It allows more space for the stark visual to operate. The proportions and weight of the type keep it plenty readable, and the eye gets to float around in the collage. The concept of pattern / rest is seen in the tension between image and white space. The lens like UFO is dominant in the hierarchy and the eye bounces back and forth between it and the sneering face tucked into the silhouette of the figure. All elements of the album title communicated brilliantly at a glance.

Looks like art to me.

To view the portflio of Jeff and his partners at Lure Design, go to luredesigninc.com

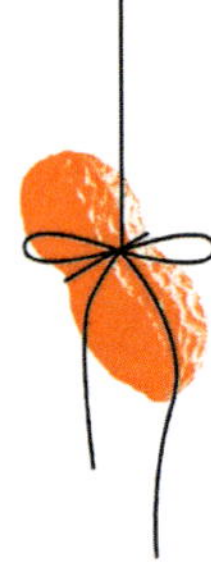

Through my years as a graphic designer, an advertising art director, an illustrator, a fine artist, instructor and a writer, it has become clear that the one common trait that connects all of the greats in the broad field of visual communication is a strong intent. The why behind the work, it is the driver of confidence, ability and authenticity. So much attention these days is given to technique, the icing on the cake, but the beating heart of the voice of the artist is intent.

To find authentic intent, the writer, the painter, the musician, all must walk the long road, logging the miles of experience required to find what message they each have to offer. There are no magic tricks for this.

References

The following is a list of the artists and movements mentioned in this book. If you are curious about the artist's work, or if you just want to know more, Google image and Wikipedia are great places to start. Wherever possible, a dedicated website for the individual artist or movement is listed alongside the name.

Artists mentioned / **case studies:**
Josef Albers — albersfoundation.org
Thomas Hart Benton — artnet.com/artists/thomas-hart-benton/
Sandro Botticelli — www.sandrobotticelli.net
Alexander Calder — www.calder.org
Mary Cassatt — marycassatt.org
Paul Cézanne — paul-cezanne.org
Scott Christensen — christensenstudio.com
Dean Cornwell americanartarchives.com/cornwell.htm
Richard Deibenkorn — diebenkorn.org
Maynard Dixon — maynarddixon.org
Helen Frankenthaller — frankenthalerfoundation.org
Quilts of Gee's Bend — soulsgrowndeep.org/gees-bend-quiltmakers
Antoni Gaudi — Wikipedia.org
Ann Gale — dolbychadwickgallery.com
Andy Goldsworthy — goldsworthy.cc.gla.ac.uk
Jody Hewgill — jodyhewgill.com
Edward Hopper — edwardhopper.net
Alex Kanevsky — somepaintings.net
Chip Kidd — chipkidd.com
Paul Klee — paulklee.net
Gustav Klimt — klimtgallery.org
Franz Kline — moma.org/artists/3148
Willem de Kooning — dekooning.org
Lee Krasner — pkf.org
Peggi Kroll Roberts — krollroberts.com
Gregory Manchess — manchess.com

Michelangelo Buonarroti — michelangelo-gallery.org
Jeff Matz — luredesigninc.com
Joan Mitchell — joanmitchellfoundation.org
Piet Mondrian — piet-mondrian.org
Claude Monet — claudemonetgallery.org
Grandma Moses — Wikipedia.org
Alphonse Mucha — alphonsmucha.org
Georgia O'keeffe — okeeffemuseum.org
Jon Redmond — jonredmond.com
Robert Rauschenberg — rauschenbergfoundation.org
Pablo Picasso — pablopicasso.org
Jackson Pollock — pkf.org
Norman Rockwell — nrm.org
John Singer Sargent — johnsingersargent.org
Joaquin Sorolla — sorollapaintings.com
Nikolai Timkov — leningradschool.com
Henri de Toulouse-Lautrec — Toulouse-lautrec-foundation.org
John Henry Twachtman — johnhenrytwachtman.org
Vincent Van Gogh — vangoghgallery.com
James McNeill Whistler — jamesabbottmcneillwhistler.org
N.C, Jamie, & Andrew Wyeth — brandywine.org

Movements mentioned:

Art Deco — Wikipedia.org
Byzantine — Wikipedia.org
The Ashcan School — Wikipedia.org
Golden Age of Illustration — artcyclopedia.com/history/golden-age.html
Post-Impressionism — Wikipedia.org
Tonalism — artcyclopedia.com/history/tonalism.html

Additional reading on creativity:

A whack on the side of the head — Roger van Oech
Lateral thinking — Edward De Bono
The war of art — Steven Pressfield
Big magic — Elizabeth Gilbert
The courage to create — Rollo May
Multiple intelligences — Howard E. Gardner
The untethered soul — Michael Singer
Abraham Maslow — wikipedia.org
Hierarchy of need
Levels of comprehension

Acknowledgements

One can't take on a project like this without the love and encouragement of family, friends and professionals for guidance. A most special thank you to my Mom, Joan Moore, who has always been an inspiration and my champion encourager. And to my siblings; Anne, Randy and Dave who have been my rock(s) and supported me throughout.

Thank you also to Psychotherapist Dr. Connie Porter-Richard for her expansive understanding of what makes people tick, and her guidance and advice to me along the way.

Thank you to my friends for their support and contributions, and in particular the phenomenal artist Scott Christensen, who inspired me to get into this art mess in the 90's and has been a trusted friend and sounding board since.

A huge thank you to Michael Ludden, bad-ass writer and editor, without whom this book would be discombobulated and riddled with commas. His knowledge and his enthusiasm for this project, quite frankly, gave me the confidence to get it done.

Index

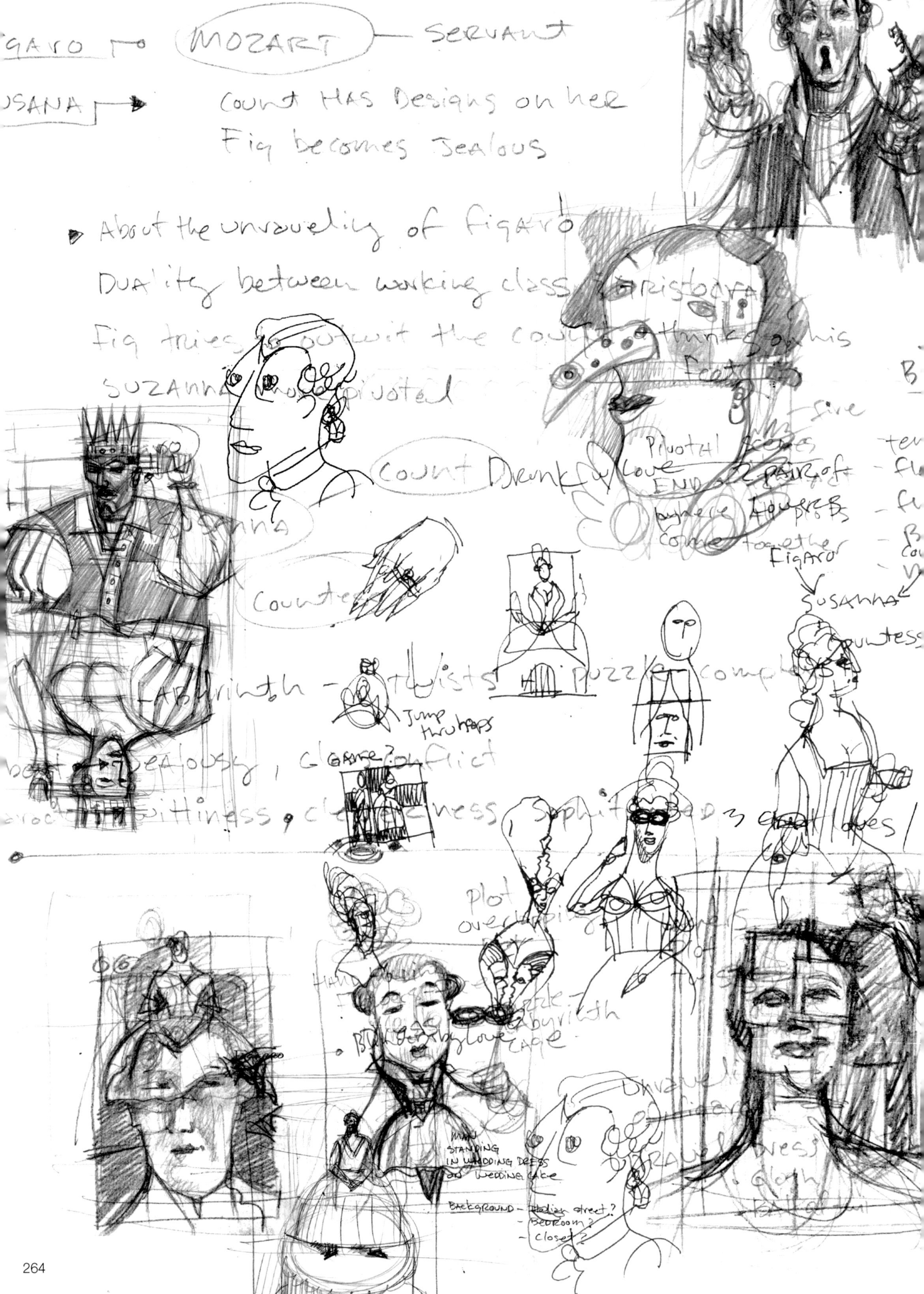
MOZART
SERVANT
Count HAS Designs on her
Fig becomes Jealous
About the unraveling of figaro
DUAlity between working class
Count Drunk
Countess
Pivotal
Figaro
Susana
Countess
Jump thru hoops
Plot
MAN STANDING IN WEDDING DRESS ON WEDDING CAKE
BACKGROUND - Italian street?
- BEDROOM?
- Closet?

Made in the USA
Lexington, KY
19 May 2018